THE IRISH PRESIDENCY

THE IRISH PRESIDENCY
POWER, CEREMONY AND POLITICS

EDITORS
JOHN COAKLEY
KEVIN RAFTER

FOREWORD BY PRESIDENT MICHAEL D. HIGGINS

IRISH ACADEMIC PRESS

First published in 2014 by Irish Academic Press
8 Chapel Lane
Sallins
Co. Kildare
Ireland

British Library Cataloguing in Publication Data
An entry can be found on request

ISBN: 978-07165-3203-3 (cloth)
ISBN: 978-07165-3206-4 (paper)
ISBN: 978-07165-3222-4 (e-book)

Library of Congress Cataloging in Publication Data
An entry can be found on request

Printed in Ireland by SPRINT-print Ltd

CONTENTS

LIST OF TABLES

LIST OF FIGURES

LIST OF PLATES

Notes on Contributors

JOHN COAKLEY is Professor of Politics in the School of Politics and International Relations at University College Dublin and in the School of Politics, International Studies and Philosophy at Queen's University Belfast. He has published extensively on Irish politics, comparative politics and nationalism, is contributing editor or co-editor of *Politics in the Republic of Ireland* (Routledge, 2010, 5th edn.) and *Pathways from Ethnic Conflict: Institutional Redesign in Divided Societies* (Routledge, 2010), and author of *Nationalism, Ethnicity and the State: Making and Breaking Nations* (Sage, 2012) and *Reforming Political Institutions: Ireland in Comparative Perspective* (IPA, 2013).

ROBERT ELGIE is Paddy Moriarty Professor of Government and International Studies in the School of Law and Government at Dublin City University. He has published extensively on the topic of presidents, prime ministers and semi-presidentialism. He is the author of *Semi-Presidentialism: Sub-Types And Democratic Performance* (Oxford University Press, 2011). He is the editor of the journal *French Politics* published by Palgrave Macmillan. He is also the lead co-editor of the forthcoming *Oxford Handbook of French Politics* published by Oxford University Press. He has just begun a two-volume study of political leadership.

MICHAEL GALLAGHER is Professor of Comparative Politics and Head of the Department of Political Science at Trinity College, University of Dublin. He has been a visiting professor at New York University, City University of Hong Kong, and Sciences Po Lille. He is co-editor or co-author of *Representative Government in Modern Europe* (McGraw Hill, 2011, 5th edn), *How Ireland Voted 2011* (Palgrave Macmillan, 2011), *The Politics of Electoral Systems* (Oxford University Press, 2008), *Politics in the Republic of Ireland* (Routledge, 2010, 5th edn), *Days of Blue Loyalty* (PSAI Press, 2002), and *The Referendum Experience in Europe* (Macmillan, 1996).

YVONNE GALLIGAN is Professor of Comparative Politics at Queen's University Belfast. She has published widely on gender and political representation, institutional reform, and democratic policy and process in a range of journals including *Parliamentary Affairs, Gender & Society* and *European Politics and Society*. Her book publications include *Gender Politics and Democracy in post-socialist Europe* (2007, with Sara Clavero and Marina Calloni) and *Sharing Power: Women, Parliament, Democracy* (2005, contributing editor with Manon Tremblay). She was a Fulbright Scholar at American University, Washington DC during 2004–05. She edited *International Political Science Review*, 2006–12, and was a member of the McKay Independent Commission on the 'English Question', 2012–2013.

CIARA MEEHAN is a Lecturer in History at the University of Hertfordshire. Her research interests include the transformation of the Irish state after independence and the development of Irish social policy. She is the author of *The Cosgrave Party: A History of Cumann na nGaedheal, 1923–33* (Royal Irish Academy, 2010) and a monograph on Declan Costello's Just Society and Garret FitzGerald's Constitutional Crusade, *A Just Society for Ireland? 1964–1987* (Palgrave Macmillan, 2013).

GARY MURPHY is Associate Professor of Politics and Head of the School of Law and Government at Dublin City University. He has written extensively on contemporary Irish politics. Recent book publications include *In Search of the Promised Land: Politics in Postwar Ireland* (Mercier Press, 2009); *Continuity, Change and Crisis in Contemporary Ireland* (Routledge, 2010) co-edited with Brian Girvin; *Regulating Lobbying: A Global Comparison* (Manchester University Press, 2010) co-authored with Raj Chari and John Hogan. He is a regular contributor to debates on Irish politics in the national media. During 2011–12 he was visiting Fulbright Professor of Politics at the University of North Carolina, Chapel Hill. He is currently completing a major work on the politics of modern Ireland.

EOIN O'MALLEY is a Senior Lecturer in Political Science at the School of Law and Government, Dublin City University. His research is mainly on Irish politics, with over 40 journal articles and book chapters published. He is also author of *Contemporary Ireland* (Palgrave, 2011) and co-editor with Muiris MacCarthaigh of *Governing Ireland: From cabinet government to delegated* *governance* (IPA, 2012). He is currently working on a book on taoisigh and political leadership in modern Ireland.

KEVIN RAFTER is a Senior Lecturer in Political Communication and Associate Dean for Research at Dublin City University. He has published widely in the areas of political communication, journalism studies and Irish politics. Prior to 2008 he worked as a political journalist and held senior editorial positions with RTÉ and several Irish national newspapers. He is the author of several political biographies and histories of Democratic Left (Irish Academic Press, 2011), Fine Gael (New Island, 2011) and Sinn Féin (Gill and Macmillan, 2005). He is the editor of *Irish Journalism before Independence: More a Disease than a Profession* (Manchester University Press, 2011) and co-editor of *Independent Newspapers: A History* (Four Courts Press, 2012).

THERESA REIDY is a Lecturer in the Department of Government at University College Cork, where she teaches Irish politics, political economy and public finance. Her research interests lie in the areas of electoral behaviour in Ireland and public finance. Her research on Irish politics has appeared in journals such as *Irish Political Studies, Politics* and *European Political Science*. She is currently co-editor of *Irish Political Studies*. She was a visiting research fellow at Universität Konstanz, Germany, during 2013.

PREFACE

The year 2013 marks the 75th anniversary of the inauguration of the first President of Ireland. Remarkably, though, only one book-length study of the office has appeared since the office was created: a monograph by the first Secretary to the President, Michael McDunphy, published in 1945. The present book is designed to fill this gap.

This volume emerged out of a special issue of *Irish Political Studies* (volume 27, number 4, December 2012). We were fortunate in being able to work with the two editors of the journal, Richard Grayson and Theresa Reidy, in bringing what turned out to be phase one of the publication process to a positive conclusion. Thanks are also due to the various anonymous referees who reviewed the articles and whose helpful suggestions improved the overall quality of the text. In moving the project to book publication stage, we were pleased to receive the approval of Taylor and Francis (publishers of *Irish Political Studies*) and the enthusiastic support of Lisa Hyde and her colleagues at Irish Academic Press.

We are delighted at the honour President Michael D. Higgins has done us in writing the foreword for this volume. We would also like to thank the staff at Áras an Uachtaráin for their assistance with various queries posed during the writing and editing process.

The photographs used in the book chart a pictorial record of the presidency through the nine holders of the office. These photographs were supplied by *The Irish Times*. The newspaper's editor, Kevin O'Sullivan, was very generous in offering assistance, while his colleagues, Frank Miller and Lynda O'Keeffe, kindly facilitated us in locating appropriate images. We are also grateful to Angela Hall, who diligently and efficiently compiled the index, and to Diarmuid Ó Sé for checking our translations of Irish language text.

During the preparation of this work we were fortunate in having the help of the National University of Ireland in hosting a one-day seminar of the contributors at its offices in Dublin, and to the Political Studies Association of Ireland for supporting this seminar. Early versions of several chapters were also presented at the 2011 conference of the Political Studies Association of Ireland. The editors would like to acknowledge the generous support of the Humanities and Social Sciences Publication Fund at Dublin City University, which assisted with the production of this volume.

—*John Coakley and Kevin Rafter*
October 2013

FOREWORD

BY PRESIDENT MICHAEL D. HIGGINS

I am very pleased to welcome this book that focuses on the Presidency. The publication of this volume of essays – addressing various aspects of the office, its history and the process of selection of its incumbents – is very timely since this year marks the 75th anniversary of the election of the first President, Douglas Hyde.

Over those 75 years, the Presidency has not attracted an over-abundance of academic attention. What has been published has tended to be quite diffuse in nature, using material extracted from various discrete essays and biographies. Until now, no single volume has provided a comprehensive overview of the office as an institution and an experience in history. The editors, John Coakley and Kevin Rafter, together with the various contributors, are therefore to be congratulated for addressing this lacuna.

This volume will be welcomed by the political scientists and jurists who are interested in the nature and extent of the office, how it was shaped by the colonial arrangements that preceded it and how it compares with other presidencies across the globe. It will equally provide sustenance to historians who are interested in the political narratives of the eight distinguished incumbents who held the office prior to November 2011. Those who relish electoral analysis and the agonies and ecstasies of campaigning will also find plenty to absorb them – and to debate – in the two chapters dealing with the seven presidential elections that occurred between 1945 and 2011.

To seek to comprehensively address an institution of state and its 75-year history in a single volume is a very ambitious task. Inevitably, some readers may take issue with certain views that have been articulated in the essays. For instance, I would not readily subscribe to Michael Gallagher's statement (in what is a fine essay) that 'the President of Ireland cannot be identified as a significant political actor' – unless of course the latter term is only to be understood in its partisan meaning.

It is precisely these types of dissenting opinions and the ensuing debate that provides the stimulating template for the next chapter of scholarship. What is undeniable, and what will be the lasting achievement of this volume, is that it will provide a robust introduction to the presidency for students and general readers alike. Furthermore, I hope and believe that it will promote further debate and research on the history of the presidency, as well as its role in contemporary Ireland.

At their inauguration, all Presidents of Ireland swear a declaration to maintain the Constitution of Ireland and uphold its laws, to fulfil their duties faithfully and conscientiously and to 'dedicate my abilities to the service and welfare of the people of Ireland'. In reflecting on how the eight previous holders of the office discharged that duty of service, I am very conscious that each of them brought to the office their own individual talents, skills, life experience and sense of idealism. I also fully appreciate that each of them discharged their duties during different periods and circumstances, and that those varying contexts brought with them specific constraints, as well as opportunities.

As Ciara Meehan's chapter makes clear, the great achievement of the first three Presidents was to establish a new office of state and to consolidate its legitimacy and credibility in the eyes of citizens. The 35 years that spanned the presidencies of Hyde, O'Kelly and de Valera were skilfully used to clearly establish the dignity and independence of the office and the protocols relating to an appropriate relationship with government.

The three succeeding Presidents operated in a more challenging environment with the conflict in Northern Ireland impacting at times on the very stability of the state. Despite these difficulties, and as Kevin Rafter acknowledges, the Childers, Ó Dálaigh and Hillery presidencies saw a greater outreach to local communities than had been experienced hitherto and a greater emphasis on the representational role of the office abroad.

I would, however, beg to differ somewhat from the assessment of the Hillery Presidency. It fails, in my view, to take adequate account of the very difficult circumstances in which President Hillery took up office following the traumas of the respective untimely death in office and resignation of his two predecessors. In this context, the understandable imperative was to maintain the stability and dignity of the office which President Hillery, as a former and progressive European Commissioner, did very well indeed.

Yvonne Galligan's account of the Robinson and McAleese presidencies reminds us of how these two women significantly developed and extended the office. Each came into office with a clear vision of what their presidency represented and with exceptional abilities – personal and professional – to articulate their themes and communicate their messages. Both were also adept, as Galligan says, in 'finding the spaces on which the constitution was silent' and using propitious opportunities to articulate more inclusive social values and to promote the cause of peace and friendship on the island.

At the end of their introductory chapter, the editors pose an intriguing question:

> It remains to be seen how far the current President of Ireland and his successors will extend the domains of perceived legitimate presidential involvement, especially in times of rapid socio-economic change and political institutional evolution.

As noted above, all Presidents bring to the office their own unique talents, experience and aspirations and all of them dedicate themselves to the service and welfare of the people of Ireland. In the majority of cases, our Presidents have also secured an electoral mandate based on a programme that has been presented to the people. It would therefore scarcely serve the people or the office if its holder adopted a self-denying ordinance that – in deference to some narrow definition of constitutional propriety – prevented him or her from making a meaningful contribution to the betterment of public life and wider society.

All political institutions evolve to take account of change in wider society. If such institutions are to survive and prosper, they must be capable of reading the signs of the times and adapting themselves accordingly. Otherwise, they atrophy and lose purpose, as well as the ability to serve the people.

The history of the first 75 years of our presidency is that its incumbents have conscientiously maintained the constitution and upheld its laws without compromising their commitment to use their abilities to serve the people of Ireland. My hope is to follow the distinguished path of my eight predecessors and build on their achievements, while maintaining my own contribution based on my inaugural address and my mandate. The words of the declaration on taking office acknowledge both a great responsibility and a great opportunity to serve the Irish people, including as it does the commitment – 'mo lándícheall a dhéanamh ar son leasa is fónaimh mhuintir na hÉireann'.

I commend the editors and contributors on a fine volume of essays. I have no doubt that it will be a valuable tool to inform readers and students about the genesis, history and contemporary nature of the Irish Presidency. Building on that knowledge, I also hope that this volume will inspire others to undertake further research on an institution of state, which, it is generally accepted, has served our citizens well.

1

Introduction: New Perspectives on the President of Ireland

John Coakley and Kevin Rafter

Introduction

The inauguration ceremony that marked the accession of Michael D. Higgins as ninth President of Ireland on 11 November 2011 attracted a wide degree of public interest and a spectrum of political reaction that suggested that this office is now recognised and valued as an important symbol of national unity and identity.[1] It was not always so. When the draft of de Valera's new constitution was first published in 1937, it drew a mixed reaction from commentators. One of the features that proved most controversial was the new office of President of Ireland. As one national newspaper put it at the time:

> The new President will occupy a position in some respects identical with that of the abolished Governor-General, and in other respects similar to that of dictator above the people's Parliament, with a hand-picked Council of State (clearly a revival of the British Privy Council) to advise him (*Irish Independent*, 1 May 1937).

By the time the first President of Ireland, Dr Douglas Hyde, took office on 25 June 1938, it was clear that these fears were unfounded: the elderly, nonpartisan, principled Hyde was an unlikely candidate for the role of dictator. The range of criticisms that the new office attracted while the constitution was being debated in the Dáil, however, suggests that the precise nature of the new office was unclear, and echoed the confusion of the *Irish Independent* editorial as to whether it would be all-powerful or quite powerless. Would the new President be 'an autocrat or dictator', as Fine Gael's Dr T.F. O'Higgins put it, or a 'royal lounger', as his party colleague Professor John Marcus O'Sullivan argued?[2] Would the new office be vested with 'unjustifiably wide powers and uncontrolled discretion', the expressed view of Fine Gael leader William T. Cosgrave, or would its powers be 'exceedingly limited', as independent TD Frank MacDermot saw it?[3]

These diverging judgements are the starting point for this book, the aim of which is to review the office of President of Ireland over its first three-quarters of a century. The debate on the extent to which the President of Ireland may be the occupant of a 'despotic' office now seems far-fetched; but a healthy discussion has been generated over the years about the extent of the powers that are associated with the presidency. The present book tackles this question by setting the Irish presidency in comparative and historical context, by assessing the formal powers of the President, by exploring the manner in which successive incumbents have discharged them, and by examining the routes by which these individuals have won office. A concluding chapter revisits the issues raised in this introduction and seeks to generalise about what we have learned about the presidency and to speculate on its future.

This opening chapter clears the ground for the chapters that follow. We begin with an outline of the constitutional and political framework that defines the operation of the Irish presidency, the circumstances associated with its creation, and the manner in which it has evolved. We continue by exploring the institutional architecture within which the presidency is embedded: those bodies such as the Council of State and the Presidential Commission which normally coexist passively with the President but which are brought to life from time to time, and the permanent support body of the President, the secretariat at Áras an Uachtaráin. We then look more explicitly at three aspects of this office that are discussed later in this book: the role of the President of Ireland in comparative and historical perspective, the manner in which incumbents have shaped the office, and the process by which the President has been selected and elected, from 1938 to 2011.

THE OFFICE OF PRESIDENT

It is conceivable that Ireland could have ended up without a president as its head of state; introducing this office was a significant innovation of the 1937 constitution. Prior to that, the term 'President' was used to refer to the President of the Executive Council, an office that was repackaged in 1937 and relabelled *Taoiseach*. The 1922 constitution had in effect imposed the King as head of state, and created the office of Governor-General as the King's representative in the Irish Free State. The history of the 1920s and early 1930s was, however, one in which the role of the Governor-General was progressively reduced, to the point where the office was finally removed from the constitution in 1936 (Sexton, 1989).

The political system could have continued to function without a separate head of state. With the disappearance of the Governor-General, his duties had been either eliminated or, as in the case of formally summoning and dissolving the Oireachtas and signing bills, transferred to the Ceann Comhairle. This resembled the practice that was later adopted in several communist states, by which the president of the (collective) presidium of parliament discharged these honorary functions, becoming the figure that most closely resembled a head of state. But other models from the interwar period were available to de Valera and to those responsible for drafting the new constitution. Most of the functions of the head of state could instead have been vested in the Taoiseach, as in Estonia and Switzerland, where the head of government also served as head of state.

As early as 1935, though, de Valera had indicated his preference for a new constitution that would include a directly elected President alongside the prime minister, and provision was made for this in successive drafts of the constitution (see Keogh, 1987; Keogh and McCarthy, 2007; Hogan, 2012). The final draft presented to the Dáil in 1937 proposed the creation of an office of President with strictly limited areas of responsibility. Notwithstanding this, the opposition expressed fears that a future President could usurp enormous powers, by having additional functions conferred on him by ordinary law. Just how groundless this fear was emerges from the chapters included in this book, and it is useful to begin by considering two aspects of the new office: the selection mechanism, and the functions that the incumbent was expected to discharge.

The 1937 constitution provided a unique method of choosing Ireland's new President: according to article 12, the President would be 'elected by direct vote of the people … by secret ballot and on the system of proportional representation by means of the single transferable vote'. This seemed initially to stand in stark contrast to the earlier system, by which the Governor-General had been formally appointed by the King, but where the substantive decision on who would be appointed was made by the government. It certainly contrasted with the hereditary principle in accordance with which monarchs succeeded to office by virtue of descent (though it should be recalled that leading republicans in 1916 had been sympathetic to the idea of offering the throne of an independent Irish state to Prince Joachim, son of the German Kaiser).[4] The choice of popular vote seems to have been designed to highlight a break with the British tradition; and the new office holder would no longer be beholden in any way to the British monarch (Duffy, 1993: 177).

In practice, though, the restricted nomination process, which required candidates to have the endorsement of either 20 members of the Oireachtas or four county or county borough councils, had the effect of conferring decisive power on the leaders of the main parties. Thus, in filling the vacancy on the very first occasion, in 1938, the parties collaborated in nominating Douglas Hyde as candidate without opposition, and he took office following a selection process that was certainly more open and more consensual than that associated with the nomination of Timothy Healy as Governor-General in 1922, but one that still lacked the legitimacy of direct election. This set the pattern for relatively 'closed' presidential contests; while there were elections in 1945, 1959, 1966 and 1973 (all but the first two-horse races), there was only one candidate in 1952, 1974, 1976 and 1983. The fact that there was no presidential election between 1973 and 1990 undoubtedly weakened the moral authority of the President (Duffy, 1993: 136–137). This restricted public involvement in the process was predictable in the 1930s; with the Dáil dominated by three parties and with local authorities controlled by the two largest of these, fears of an outside challenge could be discounted, and a long line of would-be candidates failed to secure nomination from local councils or otherwise from 1945 to 1990.[5] Against this background, the opening up of the nomination process from 1997 onwards described by Murphy and Reidy in Chapter 8, as local councillors began to express their independence of the national leadership, was novel and unexpected.

As to the actual electoral system, the adoption of the single transferable vote system was unsurprising. This system had been taken for granted as the 'normal' system in Dáil and local elections since 1922, and it had been used to fill single vacancies in by-elections (in that context, it is usually known as the alternative vote). In Chapter 2, Robert Elgie indicates just how unusual this system has been: direct election of a ceremonial president was already unusual enough in the 1930s, and the system adopted in Ireland was unique. Most other countries where the president is elected by popular vote use the two-ballot system; only Sri Lanka uses a system that bears some resemblance to the Irish one (there, voters are allowed to rank

their top three candidates; if no candidate wins a majority of first preference votes, all candidates except the two leading ones are eliminated and
their further preferences are distributed to determine the winner).[6]

It is possible to track changes in thinking about the powers that would be
associated with the new office of President of Ireland by examining successive drafts of the constitution over the period 1935–37. Drawn up initially
by a committee of civil servants on the basis of guidelines provided by de
Valera, the text of the constitution was influenced by representations solic-
ited from government departments and others (notably the Jesuit order),
and it was debated clause by clause in the Dáil. This process draws attention to three respects in which the final document was different from what
it might have been as regards the office of President. First, an early draft
in 1935 provided that the President would have the characteristic powers
of a head of state in all areas, including that of international affairs. The
President would accredit Ireland's diplomatic representatives, receive the
credentials of incoming diplomats from other states, and represent the state
in assenting to treaties, for instance. This disappeared quickly: de Valera's
intention always was to leave space for the King, and later drafts eliminated
any role for the President in the area of international relations (it was only
in 1949, when the Republic of Ireland Act, 1948, came into effect, that
responsibility in this area passed from the King to the President). Second,
early drafts envisaged an important role for the President during a period
of 'national crisis or emergency whether internal or international', when, at
the request of the government and with the agreement of the Dáil, he could
head a national government. But this, too, had been removed by the time
the draft constitution made its way into the Dáil for substantive discussion. Third, while the presidential profile was reduced in the two respects
already discussed, the President would not be altogether devoid of power.
Although an early draft gave him functions similar to those exercised by
the Governor-General (with no discretion on any matter), two important
discretionary powers were later introduced: to withhold a dissolution of the
Dáil when requested by a prime minister who had lost the confidence of the
Dáil, and to refer a bill to the Supreme Court to test its constitutionality.

THE INSTITUTIONAL ENVIRONMENT

As well as considering the constitutional and legal framework that defines
the role of the President, it is important to note the significance of three other

institutions that help to oil the machinery of the Irish presidency – each corresponding to a similar body in other states, but each given a distinctive character by Ireland's historical experience. First, all heads of state have an advisory body, and we review the Irish counterpart to this, the Council of State. Second, there is always provision for a mechanism to replace the President during short or extended periods of unavoidable absence or unavailability; the Presidential Commission is the mechanism used in Ireland for this purpose. Third, and most importantly of all, the President cannot function without a sizeable staff, a body of people who do not merely seek to discharge the President's wishes but also offer advice and explore options that may be available to the President in particular circumstances.

The term 'Council of State' is potentially misleading from a comparative perspective. In other countries this expression (or its equivalent in the local language) may refer to a quite different type of institution: to the cabinet itself, as in Norway and Finland, to the upper house of parliament, as in India, or to a high judicial body, as in France and Belgium. Prior to 1922, members of the Irish government in Dublin Castle, together with other persons, made up the Irish Privy Council, theoretically an advisory body to the crown and its representative, the Lord Lieutenant; in 1922 it had 104 members (calculated from *Thom's Directory*, 1922: 748). Under the Government of Ireland Act of 1920, the Irish Privy Council would have been an all-Ireland body, and its members would have included the Northern Irish and Southern Irish cabinets (it would have coexisted with the Council of Ireland, which would have included members of the Northern and Southern parliaments). But the creation of the Irish Free State brought this institution to an end; and the Lord Lieutenant was replaced by a Governor-General in the South and by a Governor in the North. The Irish Free State nevertheless followed the British Commonwealth norm in having an 'Executive Council' to 'aid and advise' the Governor-General, in whom formal executive power was vested. Unlike other dominions, though, the distinction between executive council and cabinet was never fully developed in Ireland. In other dominions, the executive council (in Canada known as the Privy Council) is formally chaired by the Governor-General, but performs only a rubber-stamping role; the cabinet is chaired by the prime minister, and makes substantive decisions. In the Irish Free State the two bodies were virtually indistinguishable, with the executive council constituting the notional core of the full government rather than, as in the other dominions, forming a broader body of which the cabinet was in effect a subcommittee.

Under the 1937 constitution, the Executive Council was replaced by the Government, a new body from which the President is excluded (this represented another departure from the Commonwealth norm, under which the Queen or Governor-General is formal head of the executive). With a small number of exceptions, the President acts only on the 'advice' of the Government. But a second 'advisory' body was introduced in 1937 – the Council of State. This bears a slight resemblance to the Privy Council, in that certain leading office holders become life members, if willing and able: the President, the Taoiseach and the Chief Justice. In addition, it includes the current Taoiseach and Tánaiste, the presiding officers of the two houses of the Oireachtas (the Ceann Comhairle of the Dáil and the Cathaoirleach of the Seanad), the two most senior judges (the Chief Justice and the President of the High Court), and the Attorney General. The President may also appoint up to seven members at his or her discretion for the duration of the presidential term of office. Presidents commonly use this device to ensure symbolic representation of otherwise marginalised groups, or to maintain political balance.

The Council of State has few functions and meets rarely. Its sole power has never been used: it is required to make provision for the exercise of the President's powers in any area not covered by the constitution, an eventuality that has never arisen. While its members have sometimes assembled for ceremonial or social reasons, it has met formally on only 29 occasions since it first came into existence in 1938. These meetings, all of which are convened by the President, are intended to match the President's discretionary functions. On 25 occasions, the Council met to advise the President as to whether a particular bill should be referred to the Supreme Court to test its constitutionality (on two of these occasions, it discussed two bills; see Chapter 3). On a further four occasions (1969–99), the Council has met to advise the President on addressing the Houses of the Oireachtas. There are two other contexts in which the President might summon the Council at his or her own discretion: to advise the President on an address to the nation, or on convening a meeting of either or both houses of the Oireachtas. No President has ever chosen to exercise these functions, however.

There are three other circumstances where the President might convene a meeting if this is triggered by some other body. First, on the request of a majority of the Seanad and one third of the members of the Dáil, the President may, after consulting the Council of State, refer a bill to the people, though this need not entail the holding of a referendum; the government may decide instead to call a general election. Second, on the request of the Seanad, the President may appoint a committee of privilege to adjudicate as to whether a particular bill is a finance bill, again following consultation with the Council. Third, on the request of the Taoiseach, he or she may summon the Council to advise as to whether he or she should agree to abridge the amount of time available to the Seanad for considering emergency legislation. In any event, in no case is the President required to follow the advice of the Council; he or she is required only to listen. In fact, there is one (and only one) discretionary power where the President is not required to consult the Council of State at all: whether to grant or withhold a request for a dissolution of the Dáil in circumstances where the Taoiseach has lost the confidence of the Dáil.

The mechanism for deputising for the President also bears some similarity to the position in the pre-1922 period. In some countries the constitution provides for a separate office of Vice-President, as in India and the USA. In others, succession passes temporarily to another designated office holder, such as the Prime Minister in Finland, or the President of Parliament in Portugal. In pre-1922 Ireland, the formula was one by which 'Lords Justices' deputised for the Lord Lieutenant. There were normally three Lords Justices. In the eighteenth century, these typically included the Lord Primate (the Protestant Archbishop of Armagh, representing the religious establishment), the Lord Chancellor (head of the judicial establishment) and, until the Union, the Speaker of the Irish House of Commons (representing the political world). After the Union the Commander-in-chief of the army usually replaced the Speaker (Wood, 1935: 5). When the Irish Free State was established as a dominion and the Governor-General replaced the Lord Lieutenant, there was some change in this formula. As in other dominions, the default mechanism was that the Chief Justice would stand in for the Governor-General (some dominions made alternative provision). This system was tested in 1932, when the new de Valera government in effect forced the Governor-General to resign. But the Chief Justice, no ally of de Valera's, refused to act in the place of the Governor-General, as this would have required him to take the oath of allegiance, which he declared he would not do. Following exploration of a number of other options, the speedy appointment of a new Governor-General appeared to offer the best solution, and got de Valera off the hook. When the office of Governor-General was abolished in 1936, its most significant function, giving assent to legislation, was transferred to the Ceann Comhairle.

The 1937 constitution reverted to the old formula in providing for temporary replacement of the President. When the President is unavailable, responsibility passes to a three-person Presidential Commission, made up of the Ceann Comhairle, the Cathaoirleach of the Seanad and the Chief Justice, a set of office holders not unlike the three Lords Justices of the earlier period. On occasion, the Presidential Commission has had a relatively long period of activity, when there was simply no President – for six months from the date the constitution came into effect on 29 December 1937 to the date on which President Hyde took office on 25 June 1938, for instance, and for shorter periods during the gaps caused by the death of President Childers (1974) and by the resignation of Presidents Ó Dálaigh (1976) and Robinson (1997). The Commission also acts when the President is abroad; thus, it was the Presidential Commission that granted a dissolution to Albert Reynolds in 1992 when the Fianna Fáil – Progressive Democrats coalition broke up.

Undoubtedly the most important of the bodies on which the President relies on a day-to-day basis is the secretariat at Áras an Uachtaráin. By comparative standards, this is modest. It includes about 30 administrative staff, headed by a Secretary General, and about a dozen full-time household staff, responsible for catering and general upkeep of the house. It is very difficult to make cross-national comparisons due to varying criteria for inclusion, but some tentative generalisations may be made. The office of the President of Ireland is a little bigger than the office of the Governor-General of New Zealand, which in the early twenty-first century consisted of about 15 administrative staff and about a dozen household staff.[7] The secretariat itself is similar in size to that of the President of Croatia (which has at least 29 administrative and advisory staff), and it is a good deal smaller than the office of the Federal President of Austria (with at least 80) and that of the President of Estonia (at least 42).[8] Not surprisingly, it is dwarfed by the royal households in the United Kingdom (about 1,200 in all), the Netherlands (almost 300 people) and Denmark (about 130), with their many ceremonial officers.[9]

It is similarly difficult to make comparisons over time because of inconsistencies in defining where the boundaries of such offices begin and end. Before 1922, the office of the Lord Lieutenant of Ireland was a good deal larger than that of the President today, but that was in part because of the other ceremonial offices which were attached to it. At one time, it had included the State Music (an ensemble of 25 musicians) and the

Battle-Axe Guards (a ceremonial troop with about 55 members), but these were phased out in the 1830s (Brynn, 1978: 72–3; Robins, 2001: 118). It also included the Office of Arms, which, however, became a free-standing office in 1922 and disappeared in 1943, with some of its functions being repatriated to London and others transferred to a new office, that of the Chief Herald, a division of the National Library of Ireland (Hood, 2002: 160–64). Some of the officers who attended the Lord Lieutenant on ceremonial occasions simply vanished with the old regime: the chamberlain, the state steward, the gentleman usher, the gentlemen of the bed chamber, the gentlemen at large, the pages, and the master of the horse. Others, however, survived in the office of the Governor-General: the comptroller, the private secretary, administrative and clerical staff, the aides-de-camp and medical officers, though the aides-de-camp were now drawn from the quite different social and political background of the officers of the new National Army. The downgrading of the office that took place in 1932 resulted in effective disbandment of the Governor-General's office, leaving him with only a personal secretary and a Garda bodyguard.

The office was reconstituted to serve the President under the 1937 constitution. A new government-appointed secretary replaced the comptroller as head of the office, and the other main officers reappeared. The size of the office remained small (with about 10-12 people) until the 1990s; since then it has almost trebled in size, reflecting (and facilitating) a much more active role on the part of Presidents. It is headed by the Secretary General, and includes also a private secretary to the President, four military aides, four appointees of the President who act in advisory and support roles, and about 20 professional civil service staff at varying levels.

One of the provisions of the 1937 constitution is that 'the President shall have an official residence in or near the City of Dublin'. The obvious mechanism for dealing with this was to use the Viceregal Lodge, one of the impressive state buildings in the Phoenix Park, where the chief officials of the Irish government had lived until 1922.[10] The lodge was constructed in 1751 and served as main residence of the Lord Lieutenant from 1782 to 1922 (during the Dublin 'season', each spring, the Lord Lieutenant stayed in Dublin Castle). Enlarged to host royal visits in 1849 and 1911, it became the official residence of the Governor-General after 1922, in part for security reasons. It was abandoned, however, in 1932, when the new Governor-General appointed by the Fianna Fáil government took up residence in a much smaller house in Monkstown, part of de Valera's plan to downgrade the office. Despite the fact that the Viceregal Lodge was seen as symbolising British rule, it eventually became the home of the new President of Ireland, and was renamed Áras an Uachtaráin.

The cost of the Irish presidency is not high by international standards. The President's salary and allowances, which, according to the constitution, may not be reduced during the President's term of office, are set at a level that marks the standing and prestige of the office (the salary is defined as 10 per cent above that of the Chief Justice). In practice, since the onset of the post-2008 economic crisis, presidents have returned a significant proportion of this sum to the exchequer, but the statutory provisions have remained unaltered for legal reasons. Of course, the costs of maintaining the President's office are much greater than this, and, as in the case of comparable offices abroad, it is very difficult to compute them accurately and consistently, since they occur under a number of budgetary lines. In addition to the office itself, other costs are covered by the Department of Foreign Affairs and Trade, the Department of Defence, and the Office of Public Works. Allowing for all of this, there appears to have been a considerable increase in cost over time, from about £20,000 in 1940–41 to about £700,000 in 1990, to about €7.3m in 2010.[11] But these are nominal figures; in reality we need to take account of increases in the cost of living index, which would account for much of the appearance of cost inflation. The big increase between 1990 and 2010 is attributable also to a significant expansion in the office in the 1990s, but it should be borne in mind that the size and cost base of the secretariat had remained static for more than four decades before that. In any case, by 2010 the cost of the President's office accounted for only 0.016 per cent of the cost of total public service appropriations. Though higher than the cost of the New Zealand Governor-General's office (€3.3m), it is much lower than the cost of the presidency in Germany (€31m) and of the monarchy in such relatively small countries as the Netherlands (€35m), Norway (€25m), Belgium and Sweden (€14m each), Denmark (€13m) and Luxembourg (€9m), though direct comparison is extremely difficult due to different criteria for inclusion and uneven transparency in the data themselves (Matthijs, 2012).

EXPLORING THE IRISH PRESIDENCY

While the office of President of Ireland lacks the powers of other major constitutional office holders such as the Taoiseach, its symbolic and ceremonial

significance raises important and interesting questions about its role in the
Irish political system, questions that, however, have gone largely unaddressed
in the existing literature in this area. There is, for example, no single work on
the President comparable with Brendan Sexton's (1989) definitive study of the
office of Governor-General. The Governor-General's predecessor, the Lord
Lieutenant, has attracted rather more analytical attention; aside from many
studies of individual lords lieutenant and older surveys of the office such as
O'Mahony (1912), there is an important recent collection that looks at major
aspects of this office (Gray and Purdue, 2012b).

The existing writing in the area of the Irish presidency is, then, sparse.
It includes an early study by the first secretary to the President, Michael
McDunphy (1945), a chapter by Basil Chubb (1978: 24–31), articles by
Michael Gallagher (1977; 1988; 1999) and a chapter by John Coakley
(2013: 44–89). Jim Duffy (1990) has produced a series of useful newspaper
articles on the topic, and is also author of an important, detailed study
of the office and its incumbents (Duffy, 1993). The contributions of individual office holders are covered in many of the biographies of particular
presidents that are cited in Chapters 5-7, and there are several overviews
of the incumbents, including Kenna, 2010. The office has received more
extensive treatment by lawyers, with chapters on the presidency in well-
known texts on constitutional law by such authors as Brian Doolan (1984:
36–46), Michael Forde (1987: 100–111), James Casey (1992: 67–84), David
Gwynn Morgan (1985: 46–53) and Fergus Ryan (2008: 55–62), as well
as in Gerard Hogan and Gerry Whyte's edition of John Kelly's influential text (2003: 193–228). An interesting comparative study of the office
of President of Ireland and Governor-General of New Zealand (Harris,
2009), though designed to draw lessons for New Zealand, also casts useful
comparative light on the position of President of Ireland. The present
collection is, however, the first that attempts systematically to assess the
President's powers and to explore the manner in which successive presidents have used them.

The chapters that follow each tackle a specific aspect of the office
of President of Ireland, and are collectively designed to address three
questions:

- To what extent does the role of the President of Ireland resemble that of
  other heads of state and, in particular, that of other elected ceremonial
  presidents?

- What functions are allocated to the President by the constitution, and how has the exercise of these functions been influenced by the character of individual presidents, and by the nature of the political context within which each has operated?
- What impact has the nature of the process by which the President of Ireland has been selected or elected had on the discharge of the President's role?

The first question, the comparative one, is tackled directly by Robert Elgie in Chapter 2, which sets the Irish presidency in the context of its counterparts in other countries, and offers a challenge to the often-repeated orthodoxy that the office of President of Ireland is a unique one. Noting that the Irish presidency may well be unusual (and its electoral system is certainly unique), the chapter explores the extent to which there are shared features with other countries which have a directly elected but weak presidency.

The second question is addressed in a cluster of articles that explore the evolution of the office of President. In Chapter 3, Michael Gallagher considers the range of powers and functions that are vested in the President by the constitution, and provides an overview of the exercise of these powers by successive presidents. But occupants of the office of President of Ireland did not start with a blank sheet. The manner in which they conducted the office was conditioned by public perceptions of the manner in which the President's predecessors – representatives of the King, whether as Lord Lieutenant or as Governor-General – discharged their duties. This historical legacy is considered by John Coakley in Chapter 4, which sets the office of President in the context of earlier constitutional arrangements which marked Ireland's relationship with the United Kingdom, and which also examines the role of the British monarchy after 1922, and even after 1937.

Three core chapters then turn to the contribution of the eight presidents who have so far completed their terms of office, following a common framework: the President's prior political or other career, the process by which he or she emerged as President, his or her vision of the office (as articulated, for example, in the inauguration speech), and the manner in which the President's functions were discharged. In Chapter 5, Ciara Meehan addresses this question for the first three presidents, Douglas Hyde, Sean T. O'Kelly and Eamon de Valera. Kevin Rafter takes the issue up in Chapter 6 in respect of Erskine Childers, Cearbhall Ó Dálaigh and Patrick Hillery. Yvonne Galligan concludes this review in Chapter 7 by examining the contribution of two women presidents, Mary Robinson and Mary McAleese.

The third question concerns the route to Áras an Uachtaráin, which also has much to tell us about the nature of the presidential office. Gary Murphy and Theresa Reidy analyse the nature of this process in Chapter 8, addressing not just the important topic of presidential elections but also the vital question of how candidates for this office are filtered: the nomination procedure. In Chapter 9, Eoin O'Malley presents a detailed case study of the 2011 presidential election, one in which issues of candidate selection, electoral campaigning and patterns of voter response are analysed.

We conclude the book in Chapter 10 by focusing on two perspectives. The first is the track record of the Irish President: to what extent has the experience of the Irish presidency over the past three quarters of a century conditioned the freedom of action of the current President of Ireland? In this, we return to the three questions raised above: about the comparative status of the President, about the manner in which presidents have shaped the office over the decades in such a way as to give life to the framework defined in the constitution, and in the significance of the selection and election process for the nature of the office. The second perspective is the future. In this, we speculate about the extent to which the process of development of the presidential office that was initiated by Mary Robinson in the 1990s has exhausted the range of changes that may be achieved within constitutional limits; must any further change depend on constitutional amendment?

With a view to offering further documentation on the office of President, we include three appendices in this book for reference purposes. These cover the results of all elections to the presidency; inauguration speeches of each president on taking office; and a listing of all meetings of the Council of State, indicating the nature of the business transacted.

CONCLUSION

At least some answers to the questions we have posed about the nature of the Irish presidency emerge from this analysis of presidential elections, presidential powers and presidential personalities. Opinion poll findings that show extremely high levels of satisfaction with the way in which presidents are doing their jobs suggest that the Irish electorate is relatively happy with the manner in which the functions of the office are discharged. Perhaps reflecting this, the terms of reference of the Constitutional Convention launched by the Fine

Gael and Labour coalition partners 'to consider comprehensive constitutional reform' barely touch on the presidency, confining themselves to examination of the President's term of office (whether this should be reduced from seven to five years). In the event, the convention voted 57-43 in favour of retaining the current seven-year term (Convention on the Constitution, 2013).[12]

The vision of recent Irish presidents for their terms of office – and, indeed, of their predecessors also, in large measure – is summarised in the inaugural speech of the current President, Michael D. Higgins:

> My Presidency will be a Presidency of transformation, recognising and building on the many positive initiatives already under way in communities, in the economy, and in individual and collective efforts throughout our land. It will be a Presidency that celebrates all of our possibilities. It will seek to be of assistance and encouragement to investment and job creation, to innovation and original thinking – a Presidency of ideas – recognising and open to new paradigms of thought and action (see Appendix 2).

These sentiments are undoubtedly non-political in the narrow sense of the word, but they point to a vision of the presidency that has at its core a concept of social leadership. This may well help to provide a functional definition of the presidential role that isolates it from the political world, thus minimising the risk of a clash with the government. But politics may be understood more widely than this, and the boundary between political and non-political matters is a porous one. It remains to be seen how far the current President of Ireland and his successors will extend the domains of perceived legitimate presidential involvement, especially in times of rapid socio-economic change and political institutional evolution. The remaining chapters in this book are designed to contribute towards our understanding of the office and of its role in the Ireland of the twenty-first century.

NOTES

1. This chapter develops themes first outlined in Coakley and Rafter, 2012. The remaining chapters in this book, apart from the conclusion, appeared in earlier form as a special issue of *Irish Political Studies*: Elgie, 2012; Gallagher, 2012; Coakley, 2012b; Meehan, 2012; Rafter, 2012; Galligan, 2012; Murphy and Reidy, 2012; and O'Malley, 2012.

2. *Dáil Debates*, 12 May 1937, vol. 67, cols 269-70 and 209–304.
3. *Dáil Debates*, 14 June 1937, vol. 68, cols 349 and 359.
4. Desmond FitzGerald reported that this was conveyed to him by Patrick Pearse and Joseph Plunkett in the General Post Office at the beginning of the 1916 rising; see FitzGerald, 1968: 140–41. Inviting a German prince to become King of a newly independent state was a common formula before the principle of monarchy became widely discredited at the end of the first world war; German princes succeeded, in different ways, as kings of the newly independent states of Belgium (1831), Greece (1833), Romania (1878) and Bulgaria (1908). Some nationalist leaders in Finland and Lithuania proposed offering the crown of their new states to German princes as late as 1918 (Coakley, 1986: 191–2).
5. Examples include Patrick McCartan (1945, though he eventually did secure nomination from members of the Oireachtas), Alfie Byrne (1952), Patrick McCartan again (1959), Eoin O'Mahony (1966), and Carmencita Hederman (1990); see Duffy 1993: 145, and Murphy and Reidy in Chapter 8.
6. A similar system operates in elections to the post of Mayor of London, but there voters may rank only two candidates.
7. Derived from gg.govt.nz/sites/all/files/u2/GH_Org_Chart.pdf and information from Mr Antony Paltridge, Public Affairs Manager, Government House, Wellington, New Zealand. For a comparison of the two offices, see Harris, 2009.
8. These figures are based on staff lists available at www.predsjednik.hr/OFFICEOFTHE, www.bundespraesident.at/aufgaben/praesidentschaftskanzlei/mitarbeiterinnen/#c11, and www.president.ee/en/5381-staff/.
9. See royal.gov.uk/theroyalhousehold/overview.aspx; www.koninklijkhuis.nl/globale-paginas/taalrubrieken/english/organisation/; kongehuset.dk/english/Organisation-and-Contact/Employees.
10. The other important buildings were the residence of the Chief Secretary (political head of the Irish government to 1922), now the home of the American Ambassador; the residence of the Under-Secretary (permanent head of the Irish civil service), which became the Papal Nunciature but was demolished in the 1970s, though one portion, Ashtown Castle, remains; and the residence of the Private Secretary to the Lord Lieutenant, now known as Ratra House. On the history of Áras an Uachtaráin, see Casey, 2005.
11. These calculations are based on the annual reports of the Comptroller and Auditor General on the appropriation accounts.
12. Though required only to make a recommendation on the duration of the presidential term of office, the Convention also considered certain supplementary issues; it voted 94–6 in favour of giving citizens a say in the candidate nomination process (Convention on the Constitution, 2013); on 29 September 2013 it recommended that Irish citizens resident outside the state be made eligible to vote in presidential elections.

2

THE PRESIDENT IN COMPARATIVE PERSPECTIVE

ROBERT ELGIE

INTRODUCTION

This chapter places the institution of the Irish presidency in comparative perspective. Is the presidency *sui generis* when compared with equivalent institutions elsewhere, or does it exhibit a set of characteristics that are common to other contexts? Certainly, there is a long-standing belief that the Irish presidency is a unique or at least a very unusual institution. In 1945, an *Irish Times* editorial referred to the uniqueness of the Irish case (*The Irish Times*, 7 June 1945). Almost 30 years later, Brendan Halligan (1974) argued that in a European context the Irish presidency was unique. Later still, Garret FitzGerald (2007) identified a number of unusual features of the presidency. To what extent are such observations justified? To answer this question, we compare the Irish presidency with other presidencies in five key ways: the system of election, its status in relation to the government, its constitutional powers, the cycle of renewal and the debate over reform. We conclude that the Irish President is not unique. In all significant respects, the presidency exhibits and has always exhibited commonalities with equivalent institutions. However, in a number of regards the presidency has always been and remains relatively unusual. Thus, while the Irish presidency is not one-of-a-kind, it is not an entirely generic institution either.

THE SPREAD OF DIRECT PRESIDENTIAL ELECTIONS

The Irish constitution of 1937 created a new office – a directly elected President. To what extent was direct election an unusual constitutional feature at that time? How common is direct election currently?

There are three standard ways of selecting a head of state: there can be some process of hereditary succession; there can be the indirect election of a president by some type of electoral college, such as the members of the legislature and/or local authorities; or there can be the direct or direct-like election of a president either by a direct popular vote or by the popular election of an electoral college with de facto binding mandates, as in the USA, or non-binding mandates, as in Finland, up to and including the 1988 presidential election. In Europe since the end of the nineteenth century there has been a shift from monarchs to indirectly elected presidents and, in the post-war period and particularly since 1990, from indirectly elected to directly elected presidents. This shift is captured in Table 2.1, which takes a snapshot of all sovereign European states in 1911, 1936, 1986 and 2011 and identifies the percentage of monarchies, indirectly elected presidents and directly elected presidents.[1]

Across the world, the popularity of direct presidential elections has increased over time. In the USA the direct-like election of the President was well established by the 1840s (Blais et al. 1997). In Liberia, the first direct presidential election was held in 1847. In Latin America direct presidential elections have taken place since the second half of the nineteenth century and became relatively common by the early twentieth century. In Europe, the direct election of the president was very slow to take hold. Here, the first direct

TABLE 2.1   Distribution of monarchs, indirectly elected presidents and directly elected presidents in Europe, 1911, 1936, 1986 and 2011

Year	Monarchs	Indirectly elected presidents	Directly elected presidents	Total
1911	90.0 (18)	10.0 (2)	0.0 (0)	100.0 (20)
1936	50.0 (13)	42.3 (11)	7.7 (2)	100.0 (26)
1986	38.1 (8)	28.6 (6)	33.3 (7)	100.0 (21)
2011	19.5 (8)	29.3 (12)	51.2 (21)	100.0 (31)

Note: in each column, the first figure refers to a percentage and the second to the number of cases.

presidential election took place in France in December 1848. However, the next such election in Europe was not held until 1918. In Portugal a direct presidential election was held in April of that year. However, this election was contrary to the constitution, which stated that the president would be elected by parliament. In January 1925 the President of Finland was popularly elected and in March of the same year there was the first direct election for the President of Germany. There were regular elections in Finland thereafter. The second and last direct election in Germany was held in 1932. In 1933 Portugal adopted a new constitution and direct presidential elections were held intermittently between 1935 and 1958, although in a number of cases there was only a single candidate and they were not held democratically. The next European country to hold a competitive presidential election was Ireland in 1945. Austria held its first competitive presidential election in 1951, with Iceland following suit the next year. In Cyprus the first direct presidential election was held in 1960. In France, the first direct presidential election since 1848 took place in 1965. In Portugal, direct presidential elections were reintroduced following the restoration of democracy and the first election was held in 1976. Thus, in Europe there were only seven countries with directly elected presidents by the end of the 1980s.

Elsewhere, the popularity of direct presidential elections also increased only gradually. In Asia, direct presidential elections were adopted relatively early. In the Philippines there were regular elections from 1935. In South Korea the first direct presidential election was held in 1952 and in South Vietnam three presidential elections were held from 1961 to 1971. In Sri Lanka the first direct presidential election was held in 1982. In Africa, the wave of decolonisation in the 1960s led a number of countries to adopt direct presidential elections. Leaving aside Liberia, presidential elections with more than one candidate or one de facto candidate were held in Burkina Faso in 1978, Dahomey (Benin) in 1968 and 1970, Equatorial Guinea in 1968, the Gambia in 1982 and 1987, Ghana in 1979, Nigeria in 1979 and 1983, and Senegal after 1978. That said, even if these elections were competitive, they were not always free and fair.

The explosion of direct presidential elections came with the wave of democratisation and the creation of newly independent states in the 1990s. Monarchy is now no longer a common constitutional choice. Cambodia is the only country to have restored its monarchy in this period.[2] Monarchies now tend to be confined to the British Commonwealth and a handful of established realms in Western Europe, as well as a small number of countries in Asia, the

Middle East, North Africa and the Persian Gulf region. The indirect election of the president has also become a less popular constitutional choice than it was previously. In Europe, Albania, the Czech Republic, Estonia, Hungary, Latvia and Moldova all underwent regime change and chose indirectly elected presidents. Elsewhere, while countries such as Bangladesh, Pakistan and South Africa have democratised to a greater or lesser degree and maintained their indirectly elected presidents, Iraq is the only country to have undergone a profound regime change and chosen to select its head of state in this way. By contrast, most countries have chosen a directly elected president. This method of selection was chosen by most of the countries of the former Soviet Union and the former Yugoslavia, much of Africa, and parts of Asia, including Indonesia, Singapore, Taiwan and Timor-Leste. Indeed, a recent inventory has shown that 101 of 186 countries in the world currently have a directly elected president.[3]

Overall, we can conclude that the adoption of the direct election of the President in Ireland was consistent with a general historical trend. That said, while Ireland was never unique in having a directly elected president, it was a relatively unusual choice to make in 1937, particularly in the European context at that time. Thus, Ireland was a relatively early adopter.

THE SPREAD OF AN UNUSUAL CONSTITUTIONAL MIX

In Ireland the direct election of the President is combined with the collective responsibility of the head of government and the cabinet to the lower house of the legislature. To what extent is this an unusual constitutional combination?

Taxonomically, it can be argued that there are four basic forms of democratic government. There are parliamentary monarchies and parliamentary republics, in both of which the government is responsible to the legislature, but in the former the head of state is a monarch while in the latter the head of state is an indirectly elected president. There are also presidential systems and semi-presidential systems, in both of which the president is directly elected, but where the government is responsible to the legislature only in the latter.[4] According to such a taxonomy, from a constitutional perspective Ireland can be identified as having a semi-presidential system.[5]

Whereas direct presidential elections were pioneered in the Americas, the combination of a directly elected president and collective cabinet responsibility was a European invention. The first countries to adopt this combination, Finland and Germany,[6] did so in July and August 1919 respectively. In

December 1929 Austria passed a constitutional amendment that bolted the direct election of its President onto its existing parliamentary system. In 1937 Ireland became only the fourth country in the world to have ever adopted this constitutional mix. By this time, though, the situation in Austria and Germany had already changed. In Austria, no direct election was held prior to the introduction of an authoritarian constitution with an indirectly elected president in 1934. In Germany the constitution of the Weimar Republic was suspended in the same year. Thus, in 1937 only two countries in the world, Finland and Ireland, had a semi-presidential constitution.

Given that semi-presidentialism has never been adopted extensively in Latin America, the spread of this form of government was even more gradual than the spread of direct presidential elections themselves. In 1944 Iceland adopted a constitution with this mix. In 1945 the pre-1934 Austrian constitution was reinstated. In 1962 an amendment to the 1958 French constitution combined the direct election of the President with collective cabinet responsibility. In 1976 Portugal adopted the same constitutional mix. Elsewhere, Senegal and Upper Volta (Burkina Faso) experimented with semi-presidentialism in the 1970s, but the system was not maintained. In Sri Lanka this system was introduced in 1978. In South Korea it was in place from 1980 to 1987. In 1987, Haiti adopted semi-presidentialism. By 1988, therefore, only nine countries in the world had both a directly elected president and collective cabinet responsibility, and six were in Western Europe.

Again, the upheaval of the early 1990s transformed this situation. What had previously been an unusual constitutional combination became commonplace. There are now more than 50 countries with a semi-presidential constitution.[7] Whereas prior to this time the adoption of direct presidential elections usually meant the introduction of a purely presidential system, since the early 1990s around 70 per cent of the countries that have decided to select their head of state in this way have also chosen to combine this feature with collective cabinet responsibility. The result is that Ireland is now one of many countries with a semi-presidential constitution.

As before, even though Ireland was never unique in having a constitution that combined the direct election of the President and collective cabinet responsibility, for a long time Ireland was highly unusual in this regard, belonging to a very restricted set of mainly West European countries with this constitutional mix. Now, Ireland is one of the majority of countries in the world with a directly elected president and one of a large number of countries with a constitution that makes provision for both a directly elected president and collective cabinet responsibility to the legislature.

PRESIDENTIAL POWERS IN COMPARATIVE PERSPECTIVE

The unusual nature of the Irish presidency is most usually expressed in terms of the powers of the office, or lack of them. There is a tendency to think of the presidency as being one of the weakest in the world and perhaps the weakest of all countries with a directly elected president. To what extent is this the case? In this section and the next we restrict the comparison to the set of democracies, defined as countries that have recorded a score of at least +6 for at least the last five consecutive years on the Polity 2 scale.[8] On this basis, we compare 43 democracies.[9] In all of them the prime minister and cabinet are collectively responsible to the legislature. In 29 there is a directly elected president and in 14 the president is indirectly elected.

There have been various attempts to measure presidential power comparatively. To place the power of the Irish presidency in comparative perspective, Table 2.2 reports the scores for three measures of presidential power. The first is based on the Siaroff (2003) index, which identifies nine powers and gives a score of 1 if the president enjoys that power or 0 otherwise, thus generating a 10-point scale from 0 to 9. However, one of the powers that Siaroff identifies is direct election. For the purposes of this chapter, we subtract one point from each of the countries with a directly elected president. This alteration facilitates the comparison of the Irish presidency with the president in countries where the head of state is indirectly elected. The second measure reports the scores based on the methodology set out by Shugart and Carey (1992). They identify 10 powers, all of which range from 4 (unrestricted power) to 0 (no provision). Thus, there is a maximum score of 40. The scores reported here are from various sources (Elgie, 2009; Elgie and Moestrup, 2008; Moestrup, 2010; Wu and Tsai, 2010), but they all use the original Shugart and Carey coding criteria. The third measure is based on a revised version of the Shugart and Carey methodology that was devised by Metcalf (2000), who identifies 11 powers, each of which again ranges from a score of 4 to 0. We report the scores recorded by Tavits (2009), who used the Metcalf-revised Shugart and Carey criteria. Table 2.3 reports the mean standardised presidential power scores for all three measures.[10]

The results confirm that Ireland has a weak presidency relative to many other countries with a directly elected president. While the scores in Table

TABLE 2.2   Presidential powers in 43 countries

Country	Siaroff	Shugart & Carey	Tavits
Directly elected			
Austria	0	4	5
Bulgaria	2	2	2
Cape Verde	5	12	–
Croatia	3	7	–
Finland	1	1	8
France	6	5	9
Georgia	6	19.5	–
Guinea-Bissau	5	13	–
Iceland	0	11	13
Ireland	2	0	7
Lithuania	3	6	8
Macedonia	3	2	3
Mali	6	6	–
Mongolia	3	5	–
Montenegro	–	1	–
Namibia	6	12	–
Peru	6	9	–
Poland	2	6	9
Portugal	2	7.5	10.5
Romania	4	7	9
São Tomé e Príncipe	7	10	–
Senegal	–	20	–
Serbia	–	2	–
Slovakia	1	3	5
Slovenia	0	4	3
Taiwan	4	13	–
Timor-Leste	–	5.5	–
Turkey	2	–	7.5
Ukraine	6	13	–
Indirectly elected			
Albania	2	–	7
Czech Republic	1	–	5
Estonia	2	–	6
Germany	0	–	3
Greece	0	–	3
Hungary	1	–	10
India	2	–	–
Israel	1	–	–
Italy	2	–	6
Latvia	1	–	3
Malta	0	–	8
Mauritius	2	–	–
Moldova	2	–	–
Trinidad and Tobago	1	–	–

Note: the potential range for Siaroff is 0–9, Shugart and Carey 0–40, and Tavits 0–44.

2.3 should be handled with some care, they suggest that the Irish President has fewer powers than his or her counterpart in countries such as Mongolia, Poland and Portugal, where the presidency is still only a moderately powerful institution. Table 2.3 also indicates that a number of indirectly elected presidents have more powers than the directly elected Irish President. These countries include Albania, Hungary and Estonia. However, we should also note that the Irish President has more powers than the equivalent office in a number of countries with a directly elected president. These countries are Austria, Bulgaria, Finland, Montenegro, Serbia, Slovakia and Slovenia. Unsurprisingly, there are also countries with an indirectly elected president where the presidency has fewer powers than the Irish case. These countries include Germany, Greece and Latvia. Overall, while Tables 2.2 and 2.3 show that the Irish President has relatively few powers in comparative perspective, they also indicate that any perception that Ireland has the weakest directly elected president in the world, never mind the weakest presidency, is quite mistaken.

There is the possibility, though, that Tables 2.2 and 2.3 do not capture the real situation. Both the original Shugart and Carey scores and the Metcalf-revised Shugart and Carey scores are based on the constitutional powers of presidents.[11] The Irish President may have equivalent constitutional powers to other institutions, but perhaps those powers are exercised much more rarely than in other countries. If so, then it may be the case that even if in theory Ireland belongs to a set of countries with weak but directly elected presidents, Ireland may still be unusual because the president's powers may be used less frequently than elsewhere. Gallagher (1977: 376) hints at this argument when he refers to the 'disinclination of Presidents to assert their full power'. The Siaroff index provides us with the means to explore whether or not this is the case. This measure of presidential power is based on constitutional prerogatives but also 'on actual political practice' (Siaroff, 2003: 303). Siaroff gives a score of 1 to Ireland in two categories labelled by Siaroff as 'VT', the power of the president to veto legislation, or more accurately the right to return legislation for further consideration, and 'AP', the discretionary appointment by the president of some key individuals such as the prime minister, other cabinet ministers, high court judges, senior military figures and/or central bankers (Siaroff, 2003: 304). The VT power clearly refers to Article 26.1.1 of the Irish constitution: 'The President may, after consultation with the Council of State, refer any bill to which this Article applies to the Supreme Court for a decision on the question as to whether such bill or any specified provision or

TABLE 2.3   Mean standardised presidential power scores in 43 countries

Country	Score
Senegal	0.79
Georgia	0.78
São Tomé e Príncipe	0.65
Ukraine	0.65
Namibia	0.63
Guinea-Bissau	0.58
Cape Verde	0.56
Peru	0.56
Taiwan	0.52
Mali	0.50
France	0.44
Romania	0.39
Croatia	0.33
Iceland	0.33
Portugal	0.33
Lithuania	0.32
Timor-Leste	0.30
Mongolia	0.29
Poland	0.29
Turkey	0.28
Albania	0.27
Hungary	0.27
Estonia	0.25
India	0.25
Italy	0.25
Mauritius	0.25
Moldova	0.25
Macedonia	0.19
Ireland	0.18
Czech Republic	0.17
Finland	0.17
Malta	0.17
Slovakia	0.15
Bulgaria	0.14
Austria	0.13
Israel	0.13
Latvia	0.13
Trinidad and Tobago	0.13
Serbia	0.10
Slovenia	0.10
Montenegro	0.08
Germany	0.06
Greece	0.06

Source: Author's calculations.

provisions of such bill is or are repugnant to this Constitution or to any provision thereof'. To what extent has the Irish President used the power of referral/veto relative to other presidents elsewhere?[12]

The Irish President has referred 15 bills to the Supreme Court since June 1938, or one nearly every five years (see Chapter 3). However, there have been seven referrals since 1990, or one every three years on average. This is a period during which most of the presidents in this study have been active and constitutes a more appropriate period for comparison. While there is no dataset that records presidential vetoes cross-nationally, it is clear that even compared only with those countries with weak but directly elected presidents, the Irish President is particularly disinclined to assert this power. For example, in Bulgaria President Parvanov vetoed four bills in 2010 and two in 2011. In Slovakia President Gašparovič vetoed three bills in June 2011 alone. Poland provides another good comparison. Here, Wyrzykowski and Cieleń (2006: 260) show that from 2000 to 2005 President Kwaśniewski referred 12 bills to the Constitutional Tribunal for review. This is perhaps the closest equivalent to the power of the Irish President under Art. 26.1.1 of the 1937 Constitution. In addition, Wyrzykowski and Cieleń (2006: 260) show that President Kwaśniewski also vetoed 24 bills during the same period. Therefore, even though the Polish President under the 1997 Constitution is recorded by Siaroff as having both the same amount of power as the Irish President and the same constitutional powers (AP and VT), it is clear that in Poland the presidency is a much more active institution. In fact, even indirectly elected presidents are often more active than the Irish President. Tavits (2009: 60) shows that the President of Estonia vetoed 41 bills from 1992 to 2001 and seven bills from 2001 to 2005. That said, we have to acknowledge that there are some directly elected presidents who are also very inactive. For example, in Finland the President has not vetoed a single piece of legislation since the introduction of the new Finnish Constitution in 2000.[13] Equally, in Iceland even though President Grímsson has vetoed three bills and, thus, provoked three referendums since 2004, these remain the only vetoes that have been exercised since 1944 and, indeed, almost the only examples of the Icelandic President exercising any sort of power since that time. So, while it is reasonable to conclude that in practice the Irish President is one of the least interventionist presidents from a comparative perspective, Ireland is not unique in this regard.

Overall, we can conclude that from the late 1930s to the late 1980s the Irish President had the fewest constitutional powers of all countries with a directly elected president and that this was certainly the case for countries with both a directly elected president, a prime minister and collective cabinet responsibility.[14] However, since the increase in the number of countries with directly elected presidents in the early 1990s Ireland is no longer unusual in this regard. There are now directly elected presidents with as few if not fewer constitutional powers than the Irish President. For example, the Presidents of Croatia, Montenegro, Serbia, and Slovenia do not even have the power to refer bills to their respective constitutional courts. We can also conclude that even if there are other countries with presidents that have as few powers as the Irish President, in Ireland these powers have been used very sparingly. Again, though, Ireland has not been the only country to have a hyper-inactive president. Arguably, even though they have more constitutional powers, the Presidents of Austria and Iceland have always been less active than their Irish counterpart. Currently, Ireland is a member of a small set of countries whose presidents scarcely ever intervene in the political process. The other countries in this set are Austria, Croatia, post-reform Finland, Iceland, Montenegro, Serbia and Slovenia. There is always the possibility that particular incumbents of these institutions may push the boundaries of the office. President Grímsson in Iceland is a case in point. Generally, though, these presidents are figurehead leaders and in the exercise of their office they resemble equivalent leaders in pure parliamentary systems. Indeed, certain indirectly elected presidents have been more interventionist than the Irish President and other equivalent cases.

THE PRESIDENTIAL TERM AND THE PROCESS OF ELECTION

Another element of the Irish presidency that might be seen as unusual concerns the presidential term of office and the electoral process generally. The length of the president's term, the system used to elect the president, the process by which presidential candidates are nominated, the low number of candidates at elections, and the high number of uncontested elections all have the potential to make Ireland stand out from other countries. Is it so exceptional in reality?

In 1937, de Valera justified the President's proposed seven-year term on the basis that 'the period set down is a very common term for a Presidency. … It is the term in the case of a number of Presidents in other countries, and consequently it seems to be a reasonable term' (*Dáil Debates*, 67: 1071, 25 May 1937). At the time, he was correct. If we take a snapshot of the constitutions of

European countries with directly or indirectly elected presidents in 1937, the presidential term was seven years in six countries (Austria, Czechoslovakia, France, Lithuania, Poland, and Portugal),[15] six years in two countries (Finland and Spain), five or four years in just one country each (Greece and Turkey respectively), and three years in two countries (Estonia and Latvia). Therefore, in 1937 a seven-year presidential term was easily the modal category. As Table 2.4 demonstrates, though, Ireland and Senegal are now the only democracies with a directly elected president and a seven-year term, though Israel and Italy, both of which have indirectly elected presidents, also have a seven-year term. For directly elected presidents, the modal category is now five years. In France the President's mandate was reduced from seven to five years in 2000. A five-year term is also the modal category for indirectly elected presidents. Among the 14 pure parliamentary democracies identified previously, 10 have a five-year presidential term (Albania, Czech Republic, Estonia, Germany, Greece, Hungary, India, Malta, Mauritius, and Trinidad and Tobago), two have a seven-year term (Israel and Italy), and two have a four-year term (Moldova and Latvia). Thus, within the set of countries with a directly elected president and collective cabinet responsibility Ireland certainly stands out. When countries with an indirectly elected president are included as well, then Ireland belongs to a very small set of countries with what is now a relatively long presidential term.

In cross-national terms, Table 2.4 shows that Ireland is unequivocally exceptional in terms of the method by which the president is elected. Easily the modal category is a two-ballot runoff system. In this system, there is a second ballot if no candidate wins a majority of the vote at the first ballot. At the second ballot, usually only the top two candidates at the first ballot are allowed to stand. Only four countries, including Ireland, deviate from this system. In Iceland and Taiwan there is a single-ballot plurality system. So, for example, in Taiwan Chen Shui-bian won the 2000 presidential election with just 39.3 per cent of the votes cast. In Namibia, Article 28 (2) (b) of the 1990 Constitution states that 'no person shall be elected as President unless he or she has received more than fifty (50) per cent of the votes cast and the necessary number of ballots shall be conducted until such result is reached'. The SWAPO party has, however, been so dominant since independence in Namibia that a majority has been forthcoming at the first ballot. Thus, Ireland is unique in using the alternative vote system (or the single transferable vote system with a district magnitude of one) to elect the presidency.[16] Indeed, Ireland has been exceptional in this regard since 1937.

TABLE 2.4 Presidential elections in 29 countries

Country	Term	Electoral system	Mean no. of candidates	Total elections	Mean effective no. of candidates
Austria	6	2-round runoff	3.0	11	2.13
Bulgaria	5	2-round runoff	13.0	5	3.11
Cape Verde	5	2-round runoff	2.6	5	2.01
Croatia	5	2-round runoff	9.0	5	3.47
Finland	6	2-round runoff	5.3	13	3.80
France	5	2-round runoff	10.1	8	4.80
Georgia	5	2-round runoff	6.5	2	1.92
Guinea-Bissau	5	2-round runoff	11.0	4	3.78
Iceland	4	plurality	1.7	15	1.48
Ireland	7	alternative vote	2.5	13	1.86
Lithuania	5	2-round runoff	7.6	5	3.42
Macedonia	5	2-round runoff	4.5	4	3.24
Mali	5	2-round runoff	12.8	5	3.18
Mongolia	4	2-round runoff	2.8	5	2.16
Montenegro	5	2-round runoff	4.0	1	2.86
Namibia	5	absolute majority	6.3	4	1.64
Peru	5	2-round runoff	11.6	8	3.43
Poland	5	2-round runoff	10.6	5	3.48
Portugal	5	2-round runoff	4.6	8	2.44
Romania	5	2-round runoff	11.6	5	3.75
São Tomé e P.	5	2-round runoff	4.8	5	2.51
Senegal	7	2-round runoff	11.5	2	3.06
Serbia	5	2-round runoff	9.0	1	3.36
Slovakia	5	2-round runoff	9.7	3	3.32
Slovenia	5	2-round runoff	8.0	4	3.11
Taiwan	4	plurality	3.3	4	2.39
Timor-Leste	5	2-round runoff	5.0	2	3.29
Ukraine	5	2-round runoff	13.6	5	3.68

Another potentially unusual feature of the Irish system is the restricted process for nominating presidential candidates. The system is criticised for being dominated by established political parties and for making it difficult for independent candidates and candidates from minor parties to stand. Table 2.5 shows that Ireland is certainly exceptional in the specific restrictions that it places on potential presidential candidates, though it could be said – as the 2011 contest showed – that more recently no serious candidate has been denied a nomination. However, Mongolia and Turkey also have very restrictive constitutional procedures that resemble the Irish case.[17] In all other countries, the process of nomination is more open. In many countries, the regulations are set out in law rather than in the constitution. While such laws can usually be amended much more easily than a constitutional provision, sometimes the legal measures are extremely restrictive. This is particularly the case in Taiwan. Therefore, in terms of formal procedures for nominating candidates, the Irish case is restrictive, but again Ireland is not entirely unusual in this regard.

How do the formal procedures correspond to political practice? If we record an uncontested election as a single-candidate contest, then the figures in Table 2.4 show that presidential elections in Ireland have indeed been contested by a relatively small number of candidates.[18] For example, if we take the average number of candidates across the whole set of presidential elections in any given country, then only in Iceland has there been on average fewer candidates than in Ireland. If we take the average effective number of candidates, then there have been fewer candidates in both Iceland and Namibia.[19] Therefore, Ireland has not had a uniquely small number of presidential candidates on average. If we count only elections since 1990, then this conclusion is reinforced (see Table 2.6). This is a period when the majority of direct elections have occurred. Therefore, a better comparison can perhaps be made. During this period, there was an uncontested election in Ireland (in 2004), but still the average number of candidates in Irish presidential elections was higher than in Austria, Cape Verde, Iceland, Mongolia and Taiwan. If we take the average effective number of candidates, then there were also fewer candidates in Portugal and São Tomé e Príncipe. There are some clearly identifiable reasons why some of these countries have had fewer candidates. In Mongolia the restrictive rules have helped to keep the number of candidates even lower than the figure for Ireland. A similar point applies to Taiwan. In Cape Verde the two-party system has meant that other candidates have tended not to emerge even though the rules are not particularly restrictive.

In Iceland, the weakness of the presidency has discouraged elections and has also restricted the number of candidates when elections have taken place. A similar point applies to Austria. Here, in 1998 the Social Democrats and the Freedom Party both declined to stand a candidate against the incumbent President from the People's Party, while in 2010 the People's Party made the same decision when faced with a popular Social Democratic President. Thus, the Austrian case bears some similarities to the situation in Ireland. In Austria, the nominating procedures are not particularly restrictive, but the presidency is very weak and occasionally one or more of the main political parties has decided not to contest the election, thus reducing the mean number of candidates over time.[20] So, whether we count all presidential elections or only a more recent subset, we can conclude that Ireland is not unique. There are countries that typically have fewer presidential candidates

TABLE 2.5   Rules for the nomination of presidential candidates in 29 countries

Country	Nomination process
Austria	Art. 60: process regulated by law (signatures of 6,000 voters)
Bulgaria	Art. 93: process regulated by law (signatures of 15,000 voters)
Cape Verde	Art. 11: signatures from a minimum of 1,000 and a maximum of 4,000 voters
Croatia	Art. 94: process regulated by law (signatures of 10,000 voters)
Finland	Art. 54: each party with at least 1 deputy in parliament, or signatures of 20,000 voters
France	Art. 6: process regulated by law (signatures of at least 500 deputies/MEPs/local councillors from at least 30 departments and with no more than 50 from any one department)
Georgia	Art. 70: signatures of 50,000 voters
Guinea-Bissau	Art. 60: process regulated by law (nomination by a political party or signatures of 5,000 voters including at least 50 from at least 5 regions)
Iceland	Art. 5: signatures from a minimum of 1,500 and a maximum of 3,000 voters
Ireland	Art. 12: 20 members of the Oireachtas, or four councils, or former/retiring presidents
Lithuania	Art. 79: signatures of 20,000 voters
Macedonia	Art. 81: signatures of 10,000 voters, or 30 representatives

TABLE 2.5   Rules for the nomination of presidential candidates in 29 countries

Country	Nomination process
Mali	Art. 33: process regulated by law (10 deputies or 5 local councillors in each region)
Mongolia	Art. 31: nomination by parties represented in the legislature
Montenegro	App. Art. 8: process regulated by law (signatures of 1.5% of the total electorate)
Namibia	Art. 28: process regulated by law (nominated by a political party, or signatures of 300 voters from at least 10 regions)
Peru	Art. 106: process regulated by law (political party or independent group registered with the National Election Board)
Poland	Art. 127: signatures of 100,000 voters
Portugal	Art. 124: signatures from a minimum of 7,500 and a maximum of 15,000 voters
Romania	Art. 73: process regulated by law (signatures of 200,000 voters)
São Tomé e P.	Art. 98: process regulated by law (no information)
Senegal	Art. 29: nomination by a political party plus signatures of at least 10,000 voters across 6 regions with at least 500 in each region
Serbia	Art. 114: process regulated by law (signatures of 10,000 voters)
Slovakia	Art. 101: 15 representatives, or signatures of 15,000 voters
Slovenia	Art. 87: process regulated by law (10 members of the National Assembly, or a party nomination plus either 3 members of the National Assembly or the signatures of 3,000 voters, or the signatures of 5,000 voters)
Taiwan	Art. 46: process regulated by law (nomination by a political party that received at least 5% of the valid vote in the most recent presidential or legislative election, or signatures of at least 1.5% of the total number of voters registered in the most recent legislative election)
Timor-Leste	Art. 75: signatures of 5,000 voters
Turkey	Art. 101: 20 members of the Grand National Assembly, or nomination by parties that won 10% at the previous legislative election
Ukraine	Art. 103: process regulated by law (signatures of 500,000 voters with 20,000 in various regions)

Source: Constitutions and electoral laws.

TABLE 2.6   Mean number of presidential candidates in seven countries, 1990–2011

Country	Mean no. of candidates	Total elections	Mean effective no. of candidates
Austria	3.3	4	2.20
Finland	8.7	3	4.00
France	12.3	3	6.43
Iceland	2.0	5	1.48
Ireland	4.0	4	2.65
Peru	11.5	6	3.54
Portugal	4.6	5	2.42

and fewer effective candidates. That said, Ireland is still among the set of countries where the number of presidential candidates has been relatively low in comparative perspective.

The final aspect in which the Irish electoral process might be considered unusual is the high number of uncontested elections. There have been 13 presidential elections since 1937, of which six have been uncontested. This is a very high figure, but it is surpassed by the Icelandic case, where there have been 15 presidential elections since 1944 and nine have been uncontested. Ireland and Iceland clearly stand out in this regard. However, there have been uncontested elections elsewhere. In Cape Verde President Monteiro was re-elected unopposed in 1996 as 'a token of the high esteem that he had acquired while in office' (Meyns, 2002: 162). In São Tomé e Príncipe Miguel Trovoada was the sole candidate at the 1991 presidential election. This was the first election following democratisation and the absence of competition was at least partly due to the fact that the former ruling party declined to stand a candidate on this occasion. In both cases, voting still took place. In Finland, there have been occasions when elections have not been held. In 1940 President Kallio resigned. Rather than having a new election during wartime, the 1937 electoral college reconvened and President Ryti was elected for the remainder of the term. In 1943 President Ryti was re-elected but also by the 1937 electoral college. In 1944 President Ryti resigned and parliament appointed a new President, Marshal Mannerheim, changing the law to permit him to serve for a full term without an election. When he resigned in 1946, parliament elected President Paasikivi to serve out the remainder of the term. Thus, there were no presidential elections from 1937 to 1950, even though there were four occasions when one might have been held. Clearly, wartime circumstances account for this situation.[21] Generally, the situation in Ireland and Iceland is very unusual, even if uncontested elections are not unheard of elsewhere.

Overall, we can conclude that in all regards the general context in which presidential elections are held in Ireland is very unusual. Even so, only in relation to the electoral system is Ireland unique. As regards the term of office, the procedure for nominating candidates, the number of candidates contesting elections, and the presence of uncontested elections, Ireland is one of a very small set of countries with the same or equivalent features. However, the set of countries varies according to each aspect of the electoral process.

PRESIDENTIAL INSTITUTIONS AND POLITICAL REFORM

To what extent are presidential institutions likely to converge? Will the Irish presidency be reformed in a way that makes it more or less like other presidencies? Will other presidencies be reformed in a way that makes them more like the Irish presidency?

The issue of reforming the presidency is periodically on the Irish political agenda. In this regard, the direct election of the President is generally accepted. The Committee on the Constitution (1967: 9–10) presented arguments for and against direct election, but, as in so many other respects, failed to make a recommendation. The Constitution Review Group (1996: 29) acknowledged that its members were divided on the issue, but made no recommendation for change at least partly because there was no public demand for it. The All-Party Oireachtas Committee on the Constitution (1998: 5) came to the same conclusion. Therefore, to the extent that there has been a general move towards the creation of directly elected presidents, there is little likelihood of Ireland going against this trend. With regard to presidential powers, the Constitution Review Group (1996: 31) wished to reduce the President's powers, particularly with regard to Article 13.2 and the right to refuse a dissolution of the Dáil in certain circumstances. However, the All-Party Oireachtas Committee on the Constitution (1998: 5) was by and large happy for the President's few existing powers to be maintained. Whereas there is some disagreement in this regard, we can safely conclude that there is a general consensus that the President's powers should not be increased. Thus, Ireland is likely to remain in the subset of countries with a weak directly elected president. In this context, what are the prospects for presidential reform in other countries?

There is little evidence that the worldwide trend towards the direct election of presidents is likely to be reversed. Cuba, Germany and Moldova are the only countries that currently have an indirectly elected president that previously had a directly elected president. In Estonia the first round of the 1992 presidential election was a direct election, even though the second and decisive ballot was indirect, by members of the legislature. Estonia has since abandoned this system in favour of pure indirect election. With these few exceptions, when countries adopt the direct election of the president, they tend to maintain it. In Finland there is a debate as to whether the President should continue to be directly elected, but, as in Ireland, there seems to be public support for the idea (Arter and Widfeldt, 2010). In Iceland, a debate about constitutional change dating from 2009 culminated in the formation of a constitutional assembly, which presented a series of wide-ranging constitutional reforms in 2011; but the issue of abandoning the direct election of the president was not among them. In other countries with a weak directly elected president, such as Montenegro, Serbia, Slovakia, and Slovenia, there is currently no debate about abolishing direct presidential elections. So, as things stand, we can safely assume that direct election is likely to remain the modal way of selecting the head of state for some time to come. Indeed, in the Czech Republic the first direct election took place in January 2013. More than that, various countries are actively considering introducing the direct election of the president. In Italy, the issue of direct election has been on the political agenda for years. In Nepal there is a transitional system, with certain decision-makers lobbying strongly for the introduction of direct presidential elections. In Moldova there was a referendum to reinstate the direct election of the President in September 2010. There was a large majority in favour of the proposal, but it failed to receive the support of a sufficient number of voters to be implemented. Overall, Ireland is likely to remain a member of the club of countries with a directly elected president and, if anything, more countries are likely to join that club in the coming years.

There is some evidence that countries are increasingly inclined to reduce the powers of their presidents. In 1997 the new Polish constitution weakened the powers of the President relative to the so-called 'Little Constitution' that had preceded it. In 2001 Croatia drastically reduced the powers of its President such that the country now has one of the weakest directly elected presidents in the world. In Finland, the power of the President was progressively diminished in the 1990s with the new 2000 constitution creating a very weak institution and with further reforms in October 2011 rendering the presidency weaker still.[22] In France constitutional reforms in 2008 placed new albeit limited restrictions on presidential power. In 2010 Georgia passed a wide-ranging set of constitutional amendments that decreased the power of the President and increased those of the Prime Minister. That said, the movement towards reducing presidential power is not a one-way process. In Portugal a 1997 constitutional amendment increased the president's power to call a referendum. In Mali, constitutional amendments that would have considerably increased the power of the President were planned prior to the coup in 2012.

Generally, whereas previously it would be commonplace to hear the argument that there is little point in creating a directly elected president if the institution did not have considerable power, now this argument seems to have lost its force. In 1999 Slovakia introduced the direct election of the President without increasing presidential powers, thus creating a weak but directly elected president. The same was true in Turkey in 2007, though a new constitution is likely to be introduced in the next period. The introduction of direct presidential elections in the Czech Republic in 2013 was not accompanied by any increase in the President's powers, leading to the creation of yet another country with a very weak but directly elected president. Overall, while countries have not been explicitly copying the Irish model, the idea of establishing a weak but directly elected president is no longer unusual.

CONCLUSION

It is very tempting to see the Irish presidency as unique. Directly elected presidents are usually considered to be strong, so one would expect only indirectly elected presidents to be as weak as the Irish President. This line of reasoning is false. As we have shown, Ireland was certainly an early adopter when it came to the introduction of the direct election of the president, particularly in a European context. Similarly, for a long time Ireland was one of only a handful of countries anywhere with both a directly elected president and collective cabinet responsibility. In the contemporary context, though, Ireland is part of the mainstream in both regards. Moreover, even though the Irish President undoubtedly has relatively few powers, there is nothing unique about the Irish case in this regard. Ireland is now one of a small group of countries that have a directly elected but weak president. The same story can be told in relation to the process of election. The Irish presidency may be unusual in almost all aspects of the electoral process, but in each aspect, with the exception of the electoral system, the Irish case has equivalents elsewhere. Indeed, in terms of future reforms it is likely that more countries may join the set of countries with a weak but directly elected president. Overall, it would be an exaggeration to say that the design of the Irish presidency is now commonplace, but it is certainly not as unusual as commentators have often seemed to imply.

NOTES

1. The table includes Russia and Turkey, but excludes micro-states and communist regimes. The early constitutions are available in Wright (1919). In 1936 Bulgaria, Estonia and Germany are excluded because their constitutions were suspended at this point. There is a similar table in Strøm and Amorim Neto (2006: 622).

2. In a 1999 referendum Australia chose to maintain its parliamentary monarchy.

3. See www.semipresidentialism.com/?cat=56 (accessed 23 October 2012). This inventory excludes eight countries where the constitution was suspended or where there was an explicitly transitional constitution.

4. By their nature, absolute monarchies, where there is no government responsibility, are not democratic. There are no countries where the president is indirectly elected and where the government is not responsible to the legislature.

5. For students of Irish politics, the standard way of identifying the Irish system is to refer to it as a parliamentary democracy. However, students of comparative politics often refer to it as semi-presidential.

6. There is a highly contentious argument that the 1937 Constitution borrowed directly from the 1919 German Constitution in relation to the presidency. The two institutions 'exhibit so many secondary resemblances ... that a direct importation must be suspected' (Hogan and Whyte 2003, 4.1.61). There is no doubt that de Valera and others did consult other constitutions, but there are so many differences between the presidency in the 1937 Irish and 1919 German Constitutions that if there was any 'direct importation' then it was strictly limited.

7. See the list in Elgie, 2011: 24-25.

8. The Polity 2 scale runs from -10 (absolute autocracy) to +10 (absolute democracy). Information about Polity IV can be found at: http://www.systemicpeace.org/polity/polity4.htm.

9. We include Iceland and São Tomé e Príncipe in the list of countries with a directly elected president and collective cabinet responsibility, even though they are too small to be included in the Polity dataset. We also include Malta in the

list of countries with an indirectly elected president, even though it is too small to be included there. We exclude Pacific micro-states. We also exclude Botswana and South Africa where there is an indirectly elected president, but where there is no prime minister.

10. Even though, as noted in Table 2.2, the potential range of the Siaroff (2003) and Shugart and Carey (1992) scales is 0–9 and 0–40 respectively, the actual scores range from 0-8 and 0-24 respectively (note that not all countries scored by these authors are included in Table 2.2). We standardise these two scales on the basis of the range of actual scores, i.e. 0–8 and 0–24, rather than the potential range. The actual scores on Tavits's (2009) version of the Metcalf's (2000) revised version of the Shugart and Carey scale range only from 2–13. This is because Tavits is engaged in an exercise that measures only presidents with relatively few powers. Accordingly, we standardise the scores on the basis of the 0–24 range in order to ensure that the standardised scores on Tavits's scale are not artificially high. Where a country records a standardised score on more than one of the three scales, the mean of the standardised scores is reported in Table 2.3.

11. Clearly, constitutional powers are an imperfect guide to presidential power in practice. This is particularly the case in countries with uncodified constitutions, such as the UK, but also in other monarchies, including Belgium, Denmark and Sweden.

12. It is certainly true that the threat of a veto, such as happens in the USA, may be enough for a bill to be amended or even withdrawn. Even so, the veto example helps to illustrate some of the issues regarding the actual use of constitutional powers.

13. I am grateful to Tapio Raunio for confirming this point.

14. Both Shugart and Carey (1992) and Metcalf (2000) record a score of 8 for Finland prior to the reforms in the 1990s.

15. Prior to the suspension of the constitution in 1934 the German president also served for a seven-year term. The fact that a seven-year term was the modal category at the time is one of the reasons why the extent of any 'direct importation' from the 1919 German Constitution can be questioned.

16. Sri Lanka uses a form of preferential voting for presidential elections, but it is not included in the comparison here because it does not meet the requirements for a democracy that were identified previously.

17. In Turkey there has been no direct presidential election yet and the constitutional situation is currently under review.

18. In two-ballot runoff systems, the number of candidates at the first ballot is counted.

19. The effective number of candidates is a notional figure. However, it helps to control for the relative permissiveness of the nominating procedures and the relative fragmentation of the party system.

20. In Austria in 1980 the People's Party also declined to run a candidate against the incumbent Social Democratic president. In Portugal in 1991 the main

opposition party declined to stand a candidate against the incumbent, again artificially reducing the number of candidates and leading to the easy re-election of the incumbent.

21. In 1973 parliament passed a law extending President Kekkonen's term for four years. This meant that the election that was due in 1974 took place in 1978.
22. See www.semipresidentialism.com/?p=196 (accessed 23 October 2012).

3

THE POLITICAL ROLE OF THE PRESIDENT

MICHAEL GALLAGHER

INTRODUCTION

The 2011 presidential election witnessed some discussion as to whether the Irish presidency should be seen as a political role or as one that is 'above politics'. For some, it was clear that the office has to be seen as political – the President, after all, is constitutionally defined as part of the Oireachtas (parliament), so those candidates whose interpretation of the presidency excluded a political dimension could be portrayed as lacking the basic knowledge needed to discharge the responsibilities of the office adequately. For others, 'politics' conveys an image of party politics, of argument, insincere promises, self-promotion and criticism of opponents, and party strategists were convinced that candidates who were perceived as one-dimensional 'politicians' would fare poorly in the election (see Chapter 9).

We can see these somewhat different expectations in operation when we examine the powers and role of the President. Most of what presidents do is not political in the conventional sense, yet the Irish President has certain prescribed powers, two at least of them potentially very significant, and the occupant of the office has the capacity to be an important political actor in particular circumstances, even if these circumstances very rarely arise.

CONSTITUTIONAL CONTEXT

Simply reading the constitution does not convey a clear sense of what kind of political actor the President is and of whether the role is essentially active or passive, politically engaged or 'above politics'. Partly for this reason, the articles dealing with the presidency generated considerable debate when the draft constitution was being debated in Dáil Éireann in 1937 (see Chapters 4 and 5), with the opposition Fine Gael party expressing unease and suspicion about the office. There was no real equivalent position in the 1922 Irish Free State constitution – the Governor-General clearly occupied a 'dignified' rather than a politically active office and was not elected by the people, and indeed the position was abolished in 1936 (see Chapter 4). Consequently, the presidency was an entirely abstract institution to observers in 1937. Opposition TDs were unable to work out whether the President might be an embryonic dictator – not a completely outlandish fear in 1930s Europe – or the facilitator of a government bent on domination, or, just possibly, a figure who, although elected, was otherwise not too different from a constitutional monarch. The first possibility was given credence by some of de Valera's 'explanations' of just what the role of the President would be. He declared that the role of the President was 'to guard the people's rights and mainly to guard the constitution', maintaining the 'mastery' of the people between elections, and added that 'nobody would propose getting the whole people to elect a person unless it was proposed to give him substantial powers' (*Dáil Debates,* 67: 40, 51, 38, 11 May 1937).

In reality, the presidency does not live up to the expectations, or fears, that might be raised by such statements. The rights of the people and the constitution itself, are protected by the judiciary, rather than by the President, while the President, despite being directly elected, simply does not have significant power.

The Constitution of Ireland outlines the powers and role of the President in Articles 12, 13, 14, 26 and 27. These articles need to be read together since an apparently unequivocal statement in one place may be qualified by another in quite a different place (such as Article 13.3.2 by 26.1, or 13.6 by 13.9).

Article 12 is mainly concerned with the nomination process (see Chapter 8) and the means of removing a president (discussed later in this chapter). It declares, in broad terms, the primacy of the office, stating in Article 12.1 that the President 'shall take precedence over all other persons in the State'. The specific powers of the office are, so to speak, scattered through the other four articles, and we may draw up the following list of the five most important powers:

1. The timing of elections is ordinarily at the discretion of the Taoiseach of the day, who gives 'advice' to the President as to the dissolution of the

Dáil (Article 13.2.1). Under normal circumstances, the President has no discretion in the matter. However, if this advice comes from a Taoiseach 'who has ceased to retain the support of a majority in Dáil Éireann', the President may refuse to grant a dissolution of the Dáil (Article 13.2.2).

2. Once bills have been passed by the Houses of the Oireachtas, they go to the President for promulgation by signature (Article 13.3). In the case of most bills (the exceptions are bills containing a proposal to amend the constitution, money bills, or bills deemed urgent), the President has the right not to sign the bill but instead to refer it to the Supreme Court for a decision on whether, in part or in whole, it is constitutional (Article 26). The court hears argument by or on behalf of the Attorney General as to why the bill should be considered constitutional, and from counsel whom it appoints to argue the other side of the case. On one occasion, in April 1995, when considering the constitutionality of a bill concerning the provision of information about abortion facilities available outside the state, the court appointed two legal teams to argue against the bill: one representing the interests of the mother and one the interests of the unborn. The constitution specifies (Article 26.2.1) that the Supreme Court must give its decision in open court, implying that it may if it chooses hear the arguments behind closed doors, though this has never happened. Once the Supreme Court has made its decision, the President has no further discretion; in other words, he or she must sign a bill that the court pronounces constitutional, and may not sign a bill declared unconstitutional.

3. The President has the final say on whether certain bills are put to the people. A majority of senators, along with a third of TDs, may request the President not to sign a particular bill but instead to ascertain the will of the people on the matter (Article 27). If the President accedes to this request, he or she refuses to sign the bill unless either (i) the people approve of the bill at a referendum held within eighteen months (and the threshold for approval is set at quite a low level, as we discuss later), or (ii) following a general election, the new Dáil passes a resolution approving the bill. The President does not, then have the power to call an immediate referendum on a bill if petitioned, as a government determined to have its proposal passed urgently may instead dissolve the Dáil and call a general election – at which, it can be assumed, the measure is likely to be a major issue.

4. The President may convene a meeting of either House, or both Houses, of the Oireachtas (Article 13.2.3).

5.　The President may communicate by message or address with the Houses of the Oireachtas, or the nation, at any time, though every such message or address must have received the approval of the government (Article 13.7).

The President also has a role in certain disputes between the Dáil and the Seanad. If the Seanad challenges the Dáil's characterisation of a particular bill as a money bill, the President decides whether to accede to the Seanad's request to establish a joint committee to decide the matter (Article 22); and if the government decides that the passage of a bill is urgent and that accordingly the Seanad must complete its consideration of the bill by a certain time, the President's agreement as well as that of the Dáil is needed to give effect to this (Article 24.1). Neither situation has ever arisen, so we will not discuss these further.

Before we examine each of these powers in detail, there are three general points to make. First, all the President's powers, other than the first (to withhold the granting of a dissolution in certain circumstances), require prior consultation with the Council of State. This body, defined in Article 31, consists of the great and the good from the political and judicial worlds: the Taoiseach, the chief justice (and all former holders of those two positions), former presidents, the Tánaiste, the Ceann Comhairle of the Dáil, the Cathaoirleach of the Seanad, and the Attorney General, as well as up to seven other individuals chosen by the President. The President must listen to the advice of each member of the Council (which, though it meets collectively, does not need to offer a collective view) but is not bound by the advice or opinions expressed. We will say more about the Council later in this chapter. Second, these five powers have very rarely been used. In fact, only the second has ever been employed in any real sense (it is true that the fifth has been used, though never by a president acting against the wishes of parliament or government). However, the existence of the first has sometimes been politically salient. Third, the list of powers is notable not just for what it contains but also for what it does not contain. The President is not given any role in the government formation process, can neither initiate nor veto legislation, has no power over the budget, does not select or have veto power over the appointees to any public positions, and has no role in foreign policy.

Considering first the President's power to refuse to grant a dissolution of the Dáil (and hence an election) to a Taoiseach in certain circumstances, it is clear that the exercise of this prerogative, or indeed a decision not to exercise it, would have major political consequences. This power is unique in the sense identified by Michael McDunphy, who served as secretary to the first President, Douglas Hyde, and then wrote a short book about the office:

> It is the only case in which the President has an absolute and unquestionable right to act in direct opposition to a constitutional request from the Head of the Government, to reject an advice which in other matters is equivalent to a direction, which must be complied with as a matter of course (McDunphy, 1945: 52).

There has been much discussion of the question of when a president could or should use this power. Evidently, if a Taoiseach has lost a confidence vote in the Dáil the President is entitled to reject a request for a dissolution. There are other situations in which a Taoiseach might be thought to have de facto lost the confidence of the Dáil: for example, if a central plank of a government's programme such as a budget has been defeated in the Dáil, if a coalition government has broken up or is about to do so, or if the Taoiseach's party has ousted – or is about to oust – the Taoiseach as party leader. It is no oversight that the constitution is laconic on this point rather than attempting to provide an exhaustive list of contexts in which the President may or may not withhold consent to a dissolution. The effect is to give the President considerable discretion as to when this power may be employed. Indeed, in practical terms, if a president refuses a dissolution under any circumstances where such a step could be justified, there is little that a Taoiseach could do even if he or she felt that the President was acting ultra vires.

As well as refraining from purporting to supply an exhaustive list of the circumstances in which a president would be entitled to use this power, the constitution is silent as to the kind of considerations a president might weigh up when deciding whether or not to exercise it. Presumably there are situations in which the President should, and others in which he or she should not, refuse a Taoiseach's request for a dissolution, but the constitution supplies no guidance as to how we or the President might tell one from the other. It seems that the President might most reasonably request such a request if either of two conditions holds. The first would arise if the President believes that even though the existing government has in effect lost the support of the Dáil, there is an alternative government that could command such support. This could occur if, for example, a coalition government breaks up and one of its components declares its willingness to join with a different set of parties to form a new government, which appears to have reasonable prospects of stability and durability. The second would be if the President believes that while the current Taoiseach has lost the support of the Dáil, this does not betoken a rejection of the government as a whole, and that this government is likely to continue once the party holding the position of Taoiseach selects a new leader. As we shall see later, no president has ever refused a Taoiseach's request for a dissolution, though there have been a number of cases where the words of the constitution would have provided justification for such a refusal.

Turning to the second of these five powers, the President's right to refer to the Supreme Court any bill presented to him or her for signature, once again the constitution offers no guidelines as to when a President might decide to do this. If presidents were partisan political actors, one might expect their approach to vary according to whether their party is in government or not, characteristically signing into law bills that their party supported and attempting to thwart, by bringing in the Supreme Court as a veto player, bills that their party opposed. In France, for example, any 60 deputies may refer a bill to the Constitutional Council, and as a result the opposition of the day uses this tactic against virtually all major pieces of legislation. One interpretation of Irish presidents' use of this power is that it is, or has been in the past, primarily driven by presidents' political preferences, in that presidents are less likely to refer bills when the government contains the party to which they belong, or used to belong, than when it does not (Tavits, 2009: 112–14). Alternatively, if presidents are essentially non-partisan actors, they may refer bills only if they harbour serious concerns about their constitutionality, regardless of whether they are supportive of the bills' substance. The President is given strong discouragement to refer bills to the Supreme Court in that Article 34.3.3 declares that if a referred bill is upheld as constitutional by the Supreme Court, its constitutionality can never again be challenged, so a referral is by no means a cost-free option for a president who harbours reservations about a bill.[1]

The third power, the Article 27 referendum provision, includes the President only as one link in a long and rather complicated chain, as a result of which it is something of a damp squib. It applies only to bills passed by the Dáil but opposed by a majority of senators – a rare situation in itself, given the Taoiseach's power to nominate 11 of the 60 senators, and one that would, of course, have no relevance at all were the Seanad to be abolished, as proposed by the incoming Fine Gael–Labour coalition in its March 2011 programme for government. Should this situation arise, however, the constitution once again offers no guidelines or constraints regarding the President's decision.

The significance of this power is diminished not only by the unlikelihood of the situation arising in the first place but also by the small print setting out the terms and conditions of any resulting referendum. To start with, as we have seen, the Taoiseach might choose to avoid a referendum by opting instead for a general election. But if a referendum were to go ahead, the bill that has been challenged by a third of TDs and a majority of senators is not deemed to have been vetoed by the people (in other words, it is deemed to have been approved) unless a majority of votes are cast against it, and this majority amounts to at least a third of registered voters (Article 47.2.1). This requirement is quite demanding given the record of turnout at referendums. The average turnout at the 37 referendums held in the period 1937–2013 was 50 per cent, and were the turnout at an Article 47 referendum to achieve this average level of turnout it would require a No vote of around 67 per cent to result in the defeat of the bill. This may be compared with the provision in the Danish constitution (Article 42) that gives a third of deputies the power to demand that any bill passed by the Folketing be put to a referendum, in which the votes in favour of vetoing it must amount to a majority of those cast and to at least 30 per cent of the electorate (Svensson, 1996: 34–5).

The fourth power, entitling the President to convene a meeting of one or both of the Houses of the Oireachtas, would, if used without the agreement of the government, presumably be reserved only for exceptional situations in which for some reason the Taoiseach was unable or unwilling to convene the houses himself or herself. The fifth, allowing the President to communicate a message to the Houses or to the nation (provided this message has received the prior approval of the government), gives something of a platform to the President while not amounting to hard power.

Putting these five powers together, and trying to place ourselves in the position of an observer who has no information about how the office has been interpreted since Douglas Hyde entered office in 1938, we could sketch a maximalist and a minimalist version of how significant a president operating under these constitutional provisions might be. A maximalist president could be either a partisan political actor or non-partisan. In the latter case, he or she would do everything possible to advance his or her own political goals, attempting to thwart actions of governments of any political persuasion that did not meet with his or her liking. In the former case, a partisan maximalist president would be keen to support measures passed by a parliament controlled by the party to which he or she belongs and to delay or block measures emanating from governments of the opposite political persuasion. Such a president would routinely refer major bills to the Supreme Court either in the hope of having them struck down (if they came from a government controlled by the President's opponents) or with the aim of having them upheld and hence protected for all time against further constitutional challenge (if the promoting government was of the President's affiliation). If a situation arose in which Article 13.2.2 could be invoked, he or she would accept or reject a request for a dissolution depending on where the political advantage to his or her party seemed to lie.

A maximalist president would make frequent speeches and addresses in support of the government at times when his or her own party was in office and would test to the limit the power to address the nation by attempting to communicate messages critical of the government at other times, as well as frequently convening parliament so that it could hear his or her views on current events. Such a president might feel secure in office in that the process of removing a president, which we discuss later, is not straightforward and in practice requires the support of the opposition as well as the government. Presidential elections would be intensely partisan affairs, with party allegiance being a strong predictor of voting behaviour, and the political affiliations and preferences of the candidates would be closely scrutinised. It might well matter, in policy terms, who became president.

In contrast, a minimalist president would operate much like a ceremonial monarch, discharging the formal duties of the office (greeting foreign dignitaries, making state visits, signing bills into law, visiting groups in civil society and praising their contribution, and so on) but without seeking any involvement in day-to-day politics. Presidential elections would not be dominated by partisan considerations. While some candidates would be more credible than others in promising to bring dignity and sound judgement to the office, it would not really matter, in policy terms, who became president. Presidential elections would be candidate-dominated, with party allegiance having only a minor impact on voting behaviour.

In practice, presidents since 1938 have borne considerably more resemblance to the minimalist model but, as we shall see, they have on occasion made choices that have had political overtones.

POLITICAL CONTEXT

In the previous section we outlined five powers conferred upon the President, and in this section we examine the use that presidents have made of these. We will concentrate upon the first two, concerning the dissolution of the Dáil and the referral of bills to the Supreme Court.

DISSOLUTION OF THE DÁIL

As we said in the previous section, the President ordinarily has no discretion as to whether to accede to a request from a Taoiseach that he or she dissolve the Dáil and hence bring about a general election, but when the Taoiseach 'has ceased to retain the support of a majority in Dáil Éireann' the President may decline the request. To date there have been at least five occasions when this power might have been exercised (Gallagher, 1999: 116–17). In 1944 and January 1982 a Taoiseach who had seen a legislative proposal defeated in the Dáil – a minor one in 1944, a major one in 1982 – sought a dissolution, and while it was accepted that the President of the day was entitled to withhold consent to the dissolution, he did not do so (see Chapters 5 and 6 for fuller details of these incidents). Characteristically, McDunphy, though closely involved in the 1944 discussions as secretary to the President, and privy to Hyde's reasons for acceding to de Valera's request for a dissolution, simply states that the President granted the dissolution, without drawing any inferences from his action (McDunphy, 1945: 53). Similarly, in November 1982 President Hillery granted Charles J. Haughey a dissolution after Haughey had lost a vote of confidence in the Dáil, and in November 1992 Albert Reynolds was accorded a dissolution after losing a confidence motion. On each occasion, the President (or, in 1992, the presidential commission – see below) may well have reasoned that there was no likelihood that the existing Dáil would be able to elect a stable government and hence no alternative to an election.

The fifth occurred in 1994, when, it is stated by Hogan (1997), President Robinson 'has let it be known' that if the Taoiseach, Albert Reynolds, had sought a dissolution, this request would have been refused. The signals that she sent out at the time, including a high-profile consultation with the chair of the Bar Council, may well have been a factor in his deciding not to do so (see Chapter 7 for fuller discussion of this incident). Reynolds had not sustained any defeat in the Dáil, but given that his coalition with Labour had broken up and that Labour was declaring that it would join with the other opposition parties to bring down the rump Fianna Fáil government at the first opportunity, the President understandably saw no reason why she should be compelled to act as if she was the only person in the country unaware that Reynolds no longer retained the support of a majority in the Dáil.

In the past it was unclear under what circumstances a president might validly exercise this power, but it seems clear now that the President has considerable discretion in deciding when this power may validly be exercised. We might speculate on the consequences had Reynolds sought and been granted a dissolution. According to opinion polls at the time, the preferred government, far more popular than any alternative, was a renewed coalition between Fianna Fáil and Labour (Marsh and Wilford, 1995: 288–9). Thus, had the President, or a different president, behaved differently at this critical moment, then, other things being equal, it is possible that a new Fianna Fáil–Labour government might have come into being following an election late in 1994 (almost certainly under a leader other than Reynolds), and the Fine Gael–Labour–Democratic Left 'Rainbow' government would never have come into being. Moreover, had an election taken place in 1994 it is unlikely that there would have been an election in 1997, so the Progressive Democrats would not have entered government in 1997 or perhaps at any time after 1992, and the economic record of the country might have been quite different.

REFERRAL OF BILLS TO SUPREME COURT

This has been the only substantive power expressly exercised by presidents. As we mentioned earlier, the President can exercise this power only after consulting the Council of State. Between 1938 and 2013 this body was convened on 29 occasions: four times in advance of an address by the President to the Houses of the Oireachtas, and on the other 25 occasions to advise the President about the possible referral of a bill to the Supreme Court (on two occasions, two bills were under consideration). It can be seen from Table 3.1 that the frequency of meetings has increased markedly since Mary Robinson's entry to office. Between 1990 and 2011 it met more times (admittedly, still less than once a year on average) than it had between 1938 and 1990. One interpretation of the figures is that both Mary Robinson and, even more, Mary McAleese, were more inclined than their predecessors to summon the Council when they entertained any doubts about whether a bill should be referred, as shown by the number of times they convened a meeting of the Council but ultimately decided against referring a bill: five times in the case of Mary McAleese, compared with just four times for the first six presidents put together. Moreover, on one of the latter occasions the convening of the Council had an immediate effect: when President de Valera summoned it in March 1967 to advise him as to whether to refer a taxation bill to the Supreme Court, the government

TABLE 3.1   Meetings of the Council of State 1938–2013

President	Number of times summoned	Summoned in connection with a bill (no. of bills)	Referred the bill
Hyde	2	2	2
O'Kelly	1	1	0
de Valera	3	2	1
Childers	0	-	-
Ó Dálaigh	3	3	2
Hillery	4	4	3
Robinson	8	6	4
McAleese	7	8	3
Higgins	1	1	0
Total 1938–2013	29	27	15

Note: on two occasions, President McAleese convened the Council of State to advise her on two bills simultaneously. In June 2000 she decided to refer both bills to the Supreme Court, and in July 2009 she decided to refer neither bill. President de Valera once (December 1968), President Robinson twice (June 1992 and January 1995) and President McAleese once (October 1999), convened the Council of State in advance of an address to the Houses of the Oireachtas.

Source: see Appendix 3.

promptly introduced a new bill to repeal the most contentious provisions (Hogan and Whyte, 2003: 219).

Not much is known about how the Council of State functions, as, by convention rather than by legal requirement, it operates in a spirit of confidentiality. No information on this is supplied by the secretary to the first president, Michael McDunphy, whose book on the office is no doubt prescribed reading for incoming presidents but who for the most part confines himself to reiterating the formal constitutional and legal position with little attempt at exegesis (on the Council, see McDunphy, 1945: 32–40). It appears that members give their opinions on the issue of referral specifically – even though most of them have no particular expertise in constitutional law – rather than ranging more widely to supply their views on the political merits or demerits of the bill. This was reported in a newspaper account of a 1984 meeting of the Council, which named particular Council members said to have advised for or against referral (*The Irish Times,* 6 December 1984). It appears that presidents open the question for general discussion, with members free to contribute as they wish or to remain silent if they choose, rather than the President going round the table to elicit a contribution from everyone. Former Labour Party minister Barry Desmond, who was first appointed to the Council by President Erskine Childers, apparently under the mistaken impression that Desmond was the son of a former Labour TD whom Childers admired, and in all attended seven meetings over a 17-year period, indicates that the Taoiseach and the Attorney General were 'invariably the first to respond to the President's invitation to advise him on the constitutionality of the Bill' (Desmond, 2000: 188–90). He indicates that members are circulated in advance with copies of the Dáil and Seanad debates on the bill, so they are aware of the arguments around both the substance of the bill and the question of its constitutionality. Meetings, he says, 'were very formal'. We might imagine that the opinions of the Chief Justice and the President of the High Court, should they express any, are listened to with particular interest, given that as members of the Supreme Court they might well be involved in deciding the constitutionality of the bill should a referral take place. We do not know whether the President interrogates some members of the Council, or expresses his or her own views, or simply listens as members deliver monologues seriatim. We do not know whether minutes of meetings are kept. Nor do we know how often presidents do not follow the majority recommendation, if there is one; Desmond reports that presidents did not give the meetings any indication of what their ultimate decision would be.

By August 2013, presidents, after consulting the Council of State, had made 15 referrals of bills to the Supreme Court (see Table 3.2). On eight occasions the court pronounced the bill constitutional, on three it struck down a section of the bill, and in the other four cases it declared the entire bill to be repugnant to the constitution. There is no indication that presidents are using this power to try to advance a personal political agenda or to thwart a government of a different complexion from their own. The only time this has been seriously alleged was when President Ó Dálaigh referred the Emergency Powers Bill to the Supreme Court in 1976. While there were indeed doubts as to the bill's constitutionality, and in this sense Ó Dálaigh's action could be seen as perfectly justified, the government was incensed not only because of the perceived urgency of the legislation but also because it believed that legislation introduced under the formula spelt out in the 'emergency' article of the constitution (28.3.3) was by definition immune from constitutional challenge and scrutiny by the courts. It is clear that Ó Dálaigh was very much opposed to the legislation, which he believed jeopardised the fundamental rights of citizens, and he reacted with outrage to the Supreme Court's decision that the legislation was constitutional. He was on the verge of resigning from the presidency in order to make manifest his displeasure with the decision but stayed his hand (Fanning, 2006), only to resign a week later in protest at the Taoiseach's failure to dismiss the Minister for Defence for remarks branding the President 'a thundering disgrace' for referring the legislation to the Supreme Court in the first place (see Chapter 6 for a full account). It is clear that Ó Dálaigh held strong personal feelings about the legislation rather than acting out of partisan motivations, although it is true that his relations with the Fine Gael–Labour government (he was a former Fianna Fáil Attorney General and Dáil election candidate) were poor long before this incident.

This case apart, it would be impossible to characterise presidential referrals as having had partisan motivations or indeed as having been prompted by anything other than concerns as to the constitutionality of the proposed

TABLE 3.2   Referrals of bills by President of Ireland, 1938–2012

	Bill	Outcome
1	Offences against the State Bill 1940	Upheld
2	School Attendance Bill 1942	Struck down
3	Electoral Amendment Bill 1961	Upheld
4	Criminal Law (Jurisdiction) Bill 1975	Upheld
5	Emergency Powers Bill 1976	Upheld
6	Housing (Private Rented Dwellings) Bill 1981	Struck down
7	Electoral Amendment Bill 1983	Struck down
8	Adoption No 2 Bill 1987	Upheld
9	Matrimonial Home Bill 1993	Struck down
10	Abortion Information Bill 1995	Upheld
11	Employment Equality Bill 1997	Struck down
12	Equal Status Bill 1997	Struck down
13	Illegal Immigrants Trafficking Bill 2000	Upheld
14	Planning and Developing Bill 2000	Upheld
15	Health Amendment No 2 Bill 2004	Struck down

legislation. Were a president to think in partisan terms then the provisions of Article 34.3.3, copper-fastening the constitutionality of the legislation for all time, would amount to a significant disincentive to refer legislation unless there are genuine doubts as to its constitutionality – and, of course, unless the President was making the referral with the precise aim of having it upheld and thus protecting it for ever against future constitutional challenge.

OTHER POWERS

The other three powers that we listed in the previous section have, in effect, lain more or less latent. No president has ever been petitioned under Article 27 to refer a bill to the people. The rarity of government defeats in the Seanad helps to explain why this situation has never arisen, and it may be that most presidents have been grateful for this, as when faced with such a petition a president might find himself or herself in an unenviable position, perhaps under pressure from the media, interest groups and large sections of public opinion to allow the people to deliver their verdict on the bill in question, while under strong implicit or explicit pressure from the government not to do so. Article 27 generally languishes in obscurity as far as practical politics is concerned, though it was brought into the light of day in February 2012 when a group of independent TDs floated the idea of attempting to use this route to force a referendum on the EU's fiscal compact. Their chances of gaining the support of a majority of senators would have been very slim but, clearly, had they somehow succeeded in meeting the requirements for an Article 27 petition, President Higgins's decision would have caused anger either to a significant section of the public (if he had decided to sign it notwithstanding the petition) or to the government (if he had decided not to sign it until the will of the people could be ascertained). In the event the situation did not arise, as the government's legal adviser decided that the government could not sign the fiscal compact under the constitution as it stood and hence a constitutional referendum was needed.

Only three presidents, Éamon de Valera (in 1969), Mary Robinson (in 1992 and 1995), and Mary McAleese (1999) have addressed a meeting of the Houses of the Oireachtas, and on each occasion this was a step taken with the full concurrence of the government. This apart, no president has issued a message or address to the nation, other than their inaugural address. There is no tradition of Irish presidents making their views on the state of the nation known, in the hope of influencing public opinion, in the same manner as, say,

Italian presidents are prone to do, so there is little sign of presidents being able to compensate by means of 'soft power' for their evident lack of 'hard power'.

The constitution does not make explicit just how openly a president can convey his or her views on issues short of delivering a 'message to the nation'. De Valera's intention seems to have been that because of Articles 13.9 and 13.11 (stating that presidential powers, apart from those where the constitution gives the president discretion, 'are exercisable and performable by him only on the advice of the Government'), the president could not convey his or her views to a third party or to the media without government approval (see his exchange with Deputy Patrick McGilligan, *Dáil Debates*, 67: 1281, 28 May 1937). The tone of exasperation in his insistence to McGilligan that the situation needed no clarification, and his reference to 'all sorts of nonsensical points' being raised, was unwarranted, because McGilligan was highlighting a zone of uncertainty as to how far the constitution permits presidents to allow their views to become known. Evidently, not all presidents share de Valera's interpretation. Seemingly Charles Haughey, while Taoiseach, took the same view as de Valera, but found himself powerless to prevent Mary Robinson giving media interviews (O'Leary and Burke 1998: 153). As noted by Galligan (see Chapter 7), when Haughey made clear on behalf of the government in 1991 that he did not want Robinson to meet the Dalai Lama but she refused to change her plans, he realised that he simply had neither any means to prevent this nor any credible sanctions to threaten to employ against her, so he had little option but to back down. Haughey's ultimate decision may have been influenced by the high approval ratings that Robinson enjoyed in opinion polls, but even without this factor his government would have been powerless to prevent Robinson going ahead with the meeting given her determination to do so. It seems, then, that in practice, whatever de Valera's intentions, the constitution does not prevent a president expressing his or her views on matters of government policy, whether by words or by actions.

While the conventions now surrounding the office strongly militate against any partisan behaviour by a president, such as speaking out against a government proposal of which he or she disapproves, there are obviously more subtle but equally effective ways in which a president can signal approval or disapproval of a particular policy measure, something that might be thought of as contravening the spirit, but does not flout the letter, of the constitution. Perhaps the most notable example came in 1993, when President Robinson visited Northern Ireland and, against the clear wishes of the Minister for Foreign Affairs, Labour leader Dick Spring, though not those of the Taoiseach, met and shook hands with Gerry Adams, the leader of Sinn Féin, at a time when the IRA was still engaged in violence; Spring was privately 'livid' at her action (Duignan, 1995: 107–8; O'Leary and Burke, 1998: 209–12; Reynolds, 2009: 293). The uncertainty, or disputed nature, of the precise bounds was illustrated soon after President Higgins took office, when government ministers were said to be 'alarmed' by his comments that he might summon the Council of State if the government were to decide there was no need to hold a referendum on the EU fiscal compact, and 'there were also some raised eyebrows in the Labour Party at the President expressing opposition to privatisation in the week that the government decided to sell off stakes in state companies worth €3 billion' (Collins, 2012). As we will now see, raising its eyebrows is about all a government can do in these circumstances.

INSTITUTIONAL CHALLENGES

The first president, Douglas Hyde, set a tone for the office that was dignified, non-partisan, and 'above politics', and each of his successors has operated according to much the same set of conventions. To characterise the evolution of the office as one of path dependency might be to overstate the matter, but in many ways Hyde's presidency left a lasting imprint on the interpretation of the office. It is clear that, in terms of the way in which we outlined these approaches earlier, presidents have interpreted the office more in the minimalist way than the maximalist way. If, instead, when the first president was to be elected, all the main parties had nominated heavyweight political candidates and the President had been elected on a partisan platform, the subsequent development of the office might conceivably have been quite different, with presidents inclining more towards the maximalist end of the spectrum. In November 2012 President Higgins, responding to questions as to whether some earlier comments by him on a matter of public concern had stepped over the boundaries of the office, said 'I can assure you as a political scientist for nearly 40 years, I'm very well aware of not only the constitutional limits on the president but what the people might correctly expect from their president' (*Irish Independent*, 22 November 2012). Such expectations, it may well be argued, derive largely from the way the role of the office has been discharged by its incumbents, with Hyde having established a set of norms that acquired legitimacy and against which a maximalist interpretation of the role would now appear transgressive.

It is still possible that at some point in the future a president might come to office with the intention of expanding the scope of the office as far as the constitution allows, or even further. A president might, for example, refer a budget to the Supreme Court for a decision on its constitutionality (even though money bills are expressly excluded from the scope of Article 26), pardon a convicted criminal or commute a prison sentence (Article 13.6) without having been 'advised' by the government to do so (Article 13.9), simply refuse to sign into law a bill that he or she disliked, and/or make a habit of expressing negative opinions about various aspects of government policy. According to the conventions surrounding presidential behaviour, this would amount to a president 'going rogue' – but, if it were to happen, how could such a president be reined in or ousted?

Any attempt to refer a budget to the Supreme Court would create a complicated situation. It would raise the question of whether the Supreme Court is obliged to consider the constitutionality of every bill referred to it by the President, or whether it is entitled, perhaps at the prompting of the government, to 'look behind' a referral and decline jurisdiction on the ground that the referral itself was invalid. Only the Supreme Court itself could provide the answer to this question.[2]

If that were sorted out, there would still be the difficulty of a president who simply refused to sign a bill into law. According to both the letter of the constitution and established practice, this could not happen, and both the government and constitutional commentators would immediately point this out. In this situation, the hypothetical president might, say, declare himself or herself to be answerable to the Irish people by whom they had been elected, and not to the letter of a constitution written in 1937 by the proverbial dead white males who could not have envisaged, for example, the economic crisis of the period from 2008 onwards. The President might justify his or her stance by claiming to be guided by the 'directive principles' listed in Article 45 of the constitution, such as Article 45.4.1°:

> The State pledges itself to safeguard with especial care the economic interests of the weaker sections of the community, and, where necessary, to contribute to the support of the infirm, the widow, the orphan, and the aged.

The preamble to Article 45 says that these principles 'are intended for the general guidance of the Oireachtas', and, after all, the President is part of the Oireachtas (Article 15.1.2). The President, then, might defend his or her behaviour by denying that he or she is in any way disrespecting the constitution but might claim, rather, to be acting in accordance with its spirit in refusing to sign into law a budget imposing severe spending cuts and in demanding that parliament produce what he or she regards as a less harsh or simply a fairer budget.

The constitution has three means of dealing with a president who goes rogue. These are securing a declaration from the Supreme Court that the President is 'incapacitated' (Article 12.3.1), the stepping forward of a presidential commission to fill the void created by the president's 'failure to exercise and perform the powers and functions of the office or any of them' (Article 14.1), or impeachment (Article 12.10).

The presidential commission acts when the President is not in a position to exercise his or her functions – through absence from the country, for example, as well as for reasons such as incapacity. In November 1992 it was the presidential commission that granted a dissolution to the Taoiseach, Albert Reynolds, as President Robinson was out of the country. Its composition and role are defined in Article 14. It consists of the Chief Justice and the chairpersons of the two Houses of the Oireachtas (the Ceann Comhairle of the Dáil and the Cathaoirleach of the Seanad), and can act by any two of its members. It also takes over the presidential functions if the President dies or resigns.[3] As McDunphy observes, no action is needed on anyone's part to 'set up' the commission, each of its members acting ex officio, so in a sense it is 'always in being' (McDunphy, 1945: 30). The commission could, therefore, step into the breach if the President's misdemeanour was one of omission, such as failing to sign a bill into law within the specified period (McDunphy, 1945: 59).

This apart, none of these steps would be a straightforward process. The first, securing a declaration of incapacity, would hardly be applicable, as we are hypothesising a president in full control of his or her capacities. The second, attempting to sideline the President in favour of the presidential commission, would be a fraught process. While the commission might be able to fulfil tasks neglected by an inert or deliberately inactive president, it would be much more difficult for it to try to block or undo disputed actions by a rogue president. In addition, the President would be likely to resist his or her attempted displacement. It is unclear who could resolve this, and indeed the constitution seems to contain something approaching a contradiction, conferring on the Supreme Court the decision as to whether a president is 'incapacitated' (12.3.1) while at the same time asserting that the President is not answerable to any court for any of his or her actions (13.8.1). Matters are complicated by the fact that the Chief Justice would be a member of the presidential commission that sought to take over the President's powers.

The impeachment process is at least more clearcut and has the advantage that the matter is resolved entirely by political actors without involvement by the courts. The bar to securing an impeachment, though, is very high, and indeed in comparative terms impeachment in Ireland is an unusually demanding method of removing a president. Essentially, it entails two-thirds of the members of one House preferring a charge of 'misbehaviour' against the President, and two-thirds of the members of the other House declaring that the charge has been sustained (Article 12.10). This is not, it should be noted, a requirement just for a two-thirds majority among those voting but that two-thirds of the total membership must vote for the motions: that is, with a Dáil of 166 members and a Seanad of 60 (the situation from 1981 to 2012), 111 TDs and 40 senators. As it happens, the government elected in March 2011 had, uniquely in the history of the state, two-thirds of TDs in the ranks of its supporters, but the large number of independents among the Taoiseach's 11 nominees to the Seanad meant that the support of 40 senators could certainly not be taken for granted even in that situation.

The Constitution Review Group, when discussing the question of being more precise and detailed in specifying the powers of and constraints upon the President, declared in its 1996 report that such a step was unnecessary and undesirable, as 'Matters of this kind are best left to the wisdom and sense of propriety of those entrusted with high public office' (Constitution Review Group, 1996: 27). What happens when a president's conception of wisdom and propriety comes into conflict with that of the government may yet, depending on the result of some forthcoming election, be tested.

CONCLUSION

Quite evidently, the President of Ireland cannot be identified as a significant political actor. If we imagine that past presidential elections had turned out differently – if MacEoin had defeated O'Kelly in 1945 or de Valera in 1959, if O'Higgins had defeated de Valera in 1966 or Childers in 1973, if Lenihan had defeated Robinson in 1990, if Banotti had defeated McAleese in 1997, or if Gallagher had defeated Higgins in 2011 – there are no obvious grounds for supposing that any aspects of public policy would have been different. The main exception, as we discussed earlier, was Mary Robinson's 1994 indication that she would not have granted a dissolution to Albert Reynolds. If a different president – Brian Lenihan, for example, the runner-up in the 1990 contest – had granted Reynolds a dissolution, subsequent events might have taken quite a different turn, both politically and economically. However, this would not have been foreseeable by the President of the day, and it simply emphasises that actions can have unpredictable and perhaps unintended consequences rather than indicating any presidential capacity to determine the country's course.

It might be argued that Robinson's election in 1990, given her close identification with the 'liberal agenda', signalled a change in the country's attitudes towards moral issues and paved the way for the removal by referendum in 1995 of the constitutional ban on the legalisation of divorce. But even if this were the case it would be the election result itself, rather than anything that Robinson did as President, that had this effect. With the possible exceptions of Cearbhall Ó Dálaigh's dramatic resignation in 1976 and Mary Robinson's handshake with Sinn Féin leader Gerry Adams in 1993, a presidential action has rarely had a direct impact upon political life. While the office has an important symbolic role, it is not surprising that, in a comparative context, the presidency of Ireland is generally perceived as lacking significant political powers (see Chapter 2). Ireland has a 'centi-presidential' rather than a 'semi-presidential' system of government.

NOTES

1. The 1967 Oireachtas committee on the constitution recommended that such laws be open to challenge after seven years, and the 1996 Constitution Review Group report advocated deleting Article 34.3.3 in its entirety. In July 2012 the Minister for Justice announced that 'consideration' would be given to amendment of this Article, perhaps allowing challenges after a period of five years; see press release at http://www.inis.gov.ie/en/JELR/Pages/PR12000214, accessed 17 July 2012.

2. In July 2012 the Minister for Justice announced that 'consideration' would be given to conferring upon the Supreme Court a power to determine whether a presidential referral of a bill could be rejected 'due to the absence of a proper factual or evidential basis on which to conduct such adjudication' (see http://www.inis.gov.ie/en/JELR/Pages/PR12000214, accessed 17 July 2012). The wording of the statement is obscure and no timeframe was specified, but it may be that such a change would clarify this question.

3. It may be worth noting that the constitution does not prescribe the procedure governing the resignation of a president; in 1976, President Ó Dálaigh simply sent messages to the members of the presidential commission who would take over from him, along with courtesy copies to the Taoiseach, the Tánaiste and the leader of the opposition (Hogan and Whyte, 2003: 84).

4

THE PREHISTORY OF
THE PRESIDENCY

JOHN COAKLEY

INTRODUCTION

Like most other European constitutions, the constitution of Ireland appears to grant the country's head of state an impressive array of powers in the legislative, executive and judicial domains. As in most other cases, though, these are subject to a disabling clause that comprehensively negates almost all presidential discretion: Article 13.9 provides that all constitutional powers and functions are to be discharged by the President 'only on the advice of the Government', except where the constitution explicitly provides otherwise. This draconian device is commonly to be found in constitutions; it reflects a medieval image of an all-powerful head of state modified by a modern perspective on the appropriate distribution of political power (Coakley, 1998). The presidential role is a function, of course, not just of constitutional provisions, but also of the expectations that have shaped it and that determine the manner in which it is interpreted. In the Irish case, a peculiar combination of constitutional, legal and political cultural factors has produced a presidency that is almost entirely devoid of a political role. This is a peculiar outcome, since the President is directly elected, and direct election implies a mandate to exercise power, though several other countries have found themselves in this position in recent years (see Chapter 2). This mode of selection of the President has led one distinguished analyst of heads of state to misleadingly classify the Irish case as 'semi-presidential' – a system where the President is popularly elected and shares power with a prime minister who is dependent on parliamentary support (Duverger, 1980).[1]

This chapter explores this apparently anomalous combination of direct election with powerless office. It argues that the unusual form assumed by the Irish presidency has been shaped by the distinctive character of the Irish nationalist struggle, and, more specifically, by the legacy of monarchy, whether represented by the monarch in person or by his or her representative at the nominal apex of the Irish constitutional system. The chapter is divided into four main sections. The first looks from a comparative perspective at the head of state as symbol of the nation and explores the particular relationship between monarchy and people in Ireland. The three subsequent sections look at distinctive phases in the evolution of the role of head of state in Ireland: the office of Lord Lieutenant up to 1922, the position of Governor-General from 1922 to 1936 and the residual role of the crown from 1936 to 1949. A short conclusion assesses the impact of this legacy on the contemporary presidency.

HEADS OF STATE AND LEADERS OF NATIONS

Much of the standing of the contemporary head of state, whether elected, nominated or hereditary, may best be understood in the context of the ancient origins of the office. The traditional link between monarch and state was reputedly summarised in 1655 by King Louis XIV of France in the words '*l'État, c'est moi*', and his counterparts elsewhere shared much of this world-view. But while there were cases, such as France in 1789 and Russia in 1917, where monarchical rule was overthrown by violent revolution, there were others, such as Britain and the Benelux countries, and most Scandinavian countries, where the monarchy became entwined in the fabric of modern national life. In these cases, the head of state was not just a powerless survivor from an earlier era; the monarch and the royal family were at the centre of the self-image of the nation, with royal inaugurations, birthdays, weddings and funerals featuring as great national occasions and focal points of popular unity (Coakley, 2011: 272).

In a world of emerging multinational states, however, the link between democratic legitimacy and the rule of dominant national groups was a double-edged sword. In the early twentieth century, the Austrian Kaiser represented the unity of his realms; but some of those over whom he reigned, such as the Poles, were more reserved in their allegiance than were the dominant group, the Germans. The Russian Tsar was a central link in a vast empire; but he had greater difficulty in securing the loyalty of his Finnish subjects than of those with whom he shared faith and language, the Russians. The British King reigned over a powerful west European state and over a vast empire; but the crown was challenged by such groups as the Irish within the United Kingdom and the South African Boers outside it, just as it was warmly embraced by the dominant group, the English.

With imperial disintegration in the early years of the twentieth century came challenging issues of political succession. In much of Europe after the First World War this took the form of competition between radical and conservative models of democracy, but with bolshevism and right-wing authoritarianism also thrown into the mix (Coakley, 1987). By the time the constitutional dust had settled in the early 1920s, it appeared that Europe's crowned heads of state had been largely replaced by very different figures presiding over much smaller successor states. Contrasting principles seem to have lain behind this transition: a *reactive* one, as regards the legitimacy of the office, and either a *reactive* or an *imitative* one, in the definition of the functions of the new office.

The pursuit of a clean break with the image of external rule was responsible for new procedures for the selection of a head of state. Thus, the collapse of the Ottoman Empire in the late nineteenth and early twentieth centuries was associated with a complete departure from the heritage of the traditional dynasty, with indigenous ruling families taking over in Serbia, Montenegro and Albania, and German princes becoming Kings of Bulgaria and Romania. When Norway established its independence from Sweden in 1905, a Danish prince, Carl, took over as King Haakon VII (as the regnal numbering implies, this could be seen as the re-establishment of a Norwegian kingdom rather than a radically new gesture). In the new states that appeared in Europe later, after the First World War, the republican formula was the dominant one: Finland, Latvia, Lithuania, Poland and Czechoslovakia installed elected presidents to replace deposed monarchs.

When it came to defining the powers of the head of state, the new regimes were faced with a choice. In certain cases, while models from some of Europe's longer-established states were important, the legacy of the local old regime left its imprint. Thus, the powers of the President of Finland were modelled on those of the Grand Duke (the Tsar), giving that office an effective political role, especially in foreign affairs (Kastari, 1969; Faloon, 1983: 89–90; Jyränki, 2007: 287). The powers of the President of Czechoslovakia, similarly, were very extensive, inheriting those of the King of Bohemia, the Kaiser (Čapek, 1934: 291–2; Graham, 1949: 112–13, 125–7). When Iceland broke its ties to Denmark in 1944, similarly, it adopted an entirely new system for selecting its President, but this new office was modelled on that of the formally powerful Danish monarch, modified by an expectation that the President would not exercise these constitutional powers (Kristjánsson, 2003: 399–400). Elsewhere, by contrast, suspicion of strong executive power associated with the old regime prevailed. In the new Baltic republics, the Presidents of Latvia and Lithuania were given relatively modest powers, no doubt a reaction against the concentration of power in the hands of the Tsar, while Estonia dispensed altogether with the position of head of state. A parallel pattern was to be seen in the course of decolonisation outside Europe, as in India, where the modest powers of the President reflected 'a distrust of executive power nurtured by the colonial experience', and were based on the relationship between King and government in the United Kingdom (Hardgrave, 1980: 56).

These two principles (reaction against external rule, and a simultaneous disposition, in several cases, to defer to political models associated with the external ruling power) are relevant also in the Irish case. Irish nationalism in the nineteenth century, overtly expressed in the manner of moderate nationalist movements elsewhere in Europe that pursued territorial autonomy, was given added edge by the co-existence of a militant nationalist, separatist, 'republican' strain, a tendency that displaced the mainstream constitutional nationalist movement in the years after the Easter 1916 Rising. While this perspective has been labelled 'republicanism', it was characterised more obviously by militant opposition to British rule than by principled objection to the institution of monarchy (Honohan, 2008; Coakley and McKenna, 2011: 291–2). For this movement, the crown was not just a symbol of monarchy; it was also the instrument through which British rule in Ireland was given effect. Significantly, when the Sinn Féin movement that definitively sidelined the constitutional nationalist tradition in 1918 had redefined its programme in 1917, its uncompromising opposition to British rule had been matched by a decided ambiguity on the form of government, with the possibility of monarchy being left open (Laffan, 1999: 116–21).

Had the United Kingdom simply disintegrated in the manner of Austria-Hungary, the constitutional evolution of Ireland, and the character of its head of state, would no doubt have been different. The United Kingdom indeed suffered a devastating blow when forced to yield to militant Irish nationalist demands, but the blow was not fatal: the United Kingdom survived, as did its vast empire. The Irish experience may have spurred nationalist movements elsewhere within the empire, as in India; but the success of Ulster opposition to Irish nationalism also became 'a beacon for many white settlers', and important lessons in imperial management were learned (McMahon, 1999: 155). As is well known, the British administration was also able to impose a harsh compromise on Irish separatists in 1922. First, though permitted to leave the United Kingdom, the new Irish Free State was given dominion status; it was required to acknowledge membership of the British Empire and to recognise the King as head of state. Second, the jurisdiction of the new state extended over only 26 of Ireland's 32 counties, leaving nationalists on both sides of the new border with an enduring sense of grievance. Together, these issues not only soured the Irish–British relationship but helped to shape Irish perceptions of the British monarchy, and of its representation in Ireland.

Quite apart from the role of the crown as the constitutional and legal centrepiece of British rule in Ireland, the personality and political record of successive kings and queens is likely to have influenced Irish attitudes (see Murphy, 2001; Loughlin, 2007; Kenny, 2009). In reality, the monarch's powers in Ireland were limited. It is true that George III (1760–1820) took an active interest in Irish politics, making decisions on major aspects of policy and on appointments in church and state (Bogdanor, 1995: 9–23). But the transformation of the British monarchy under his descendants into an office of influence rather than power was sharp. Nevertheless, disaffected nationalists did not hesitate to highlight the opposition of monarchs – even when it was ineffective – to Irish popular demands: to Catholic emancipation, reform of the (Anglican) church tithe system, disestablishment of the Church of Ireland, and home rule, for example. Sympathetic royal attitudes, such as that of George V in the last years of British rule, tended to be overlooked. The infrequency of royal visits to Ireland did not help the image of the monarchy. Only eight monarchs visited their Irish kingdom after King William and King James clashed in Ireland in 1690: George IV (1821), Victoria (1849, 1851, 1861 and 1900), Edward VII (1903 and 1907) and George V (1911). In addition, there were several visits by other members of the royal family, including the Prince of Wales. The verdict of historians (and not only Irish nationalist ones) on Victoria's attitude to Ireland has been unkind. Aside from her hostility to those who represented Irish nationalist values, she resolutely opposed plans to establish a royal residence in Ireland, and in her 63-year reign spent less than five weeks there, compared to seven years in Scotland. In part because of the attitude that this represented, it has been said that she 'lost Ireland for England' (Hardie,1963: 177).

Although royal visits were hailed as successes by the political establishment, it is not clear how far popular expressions of support were manufactured or genuine. Dunleary (now Dún Laoghaire, Co. Dublin) and Cove (now Cóbh, Co. Cork) were renamed Kingstown and Queenstown in 1821 and

1849 respectively to mark the first two royal visits, but the key decision makers on such occasions were local authorities which were overwhelmingly in conservative hands, and the sizeable loyalist community swelled the crowds that greeted visiting monarchs. In any case, nationalist ideologists were able to delve selectively into the legacy of the monarchy, presenting it as the prime instrument of British oppression, and deriding its incumbents as anti-Irish. Thus, Victoria was dubbed the 'famine queen' in reference to her alleged indifference to Irish suffering during the famine years in the mid-nineteenth century. The importance of this demonisation was accentuated among militant nationalists by the perceived risk that the image of monarchy would undermine the 'moral fibre' of the Irish nation. It has been argued perceptively that it was not the British monarchy's negative role but rather its very popularity that made it threatening to nationalists (Murphy, 2001: xii). In any case, the ultimate victory of nationalism was symbolised by further rejection of the royal inheritance: after 1922, Kingstown and Queenstown acquired an even more Gaelic veneer than they had originally had, as Dún Laoghaire and Cóbh respectively, King's County and Queen's County became Offaly and Laoighis, and the process of destroying or removing statues of kings and queens continued (Whelan, 2002).

THE LORD LIEUTENANCY

The sheer geographical gap between Ireland and England, together with Ireland's separate constitutional status, left space for the development of a powerful viceregal position, one with quasi-royal functions. Dating from 1171, this position was variously named, but ultimately officially styled 'Lord Lieutenant General and General Governor of Ireland', usually abbreviated to the first two words. Remarkably, the office of Lord Lieutenant and of the 'Irish government' that he headed survived the Union.[2] Notwithstanding the merger of the British and Irish legislatures in 1800, a large, autonomous Irish administration was permitted to continue in existence, and public policy and legislation for Ireland continued to follow a rather different path from that pursued in England and Scotland. Most agencies affecting people's everyday lives, in such areas as education, health, policing and poor relief, operated separately from their counterparts on the other island, were governed by distinct bodies of specifically 'Irish' legislation enacted at Westminster, and were answerable to the Dublin Castle administration rather than directly to Whitehall (McDowell, 1964). This system had a distinctly colonial appearance

(Maguire, 2008: 2–5), but proposals for the abolition of the lord lieutenancy came to nothing. Ambiguous Irish attitudes towards this office were summarised in the response of Henry Grattan junior to its proposed abolition in 1850: whatever its faults, the Lord Lieutenant's office represented 'the remnants of Irish dignity and nationality'.[3] Indeed, while many opponents of the office derided its quasi-colonial trappings, it attracted support from groups as diverse as Irish Tory traditionalists on one side, and, on the other, hopeful nationalists who perceived its symbolic potential (Gray, 2005: 95–9).

From the late eighteenth century onwards, the Lord Lieutenant was appointed for an indefinite term whenever a new government took over in the United Kingdom, and his political views reflected those of the British government. A change in government thus meant a new Lord Lieutenant, though there were some, such as the Earl of Aberdeen (1905–1915), who survived across governments and had to be induced eventually to resign (McBride, 1991: 183). Of the 37 individuals who held this post under the Act of Union, all were peers, all but one (the last) were Protestants, all but four were English or Scottish, and all but six could have been described as being 'out of sympathy' with the political views of the people over whom they reigned.[4] The distance between the office and the bulk of the Irish population was underscored by the fact that it had been exempted from the provisions of the Catholic Emancipation Act of 1829 and had survived later attempts to open it to Catholics, until the Home Rule Act of 1914 (McDonagh, 1915). It was only in 1921 that a Catholic, Lord FitzAlan, was actually appointed – an appointment made 'too late to be of any political use' (Jeffery, 2012: 227). Although a very considerable change in the personnel of the Irish administration took place in the last three decades of British rule, a process described as 'the greening of Dublin Castle' (McBride, 1991), in reality the political complexion of the most senior officers changed relatively little. The overwhelmingly Protestant affiliation of those who controlled the Irish administration led to public hostility to an institution from the upper reaches of which the Catholic majority was effectively excluded (Campbell, 2009: 60–61). Indeed, it has been suggested that the senior officials in Dublin Castle commonly worked against government policy when it took conciliatory rather than repressive form in respect of Irish nationalism (McColgan, 1983: 2–3).

Technically, the powers of the Lord Lieutenant were considerable, originally resembling those of the medieval monarch: command of the armed forces, control of the civil administration, management of the legislative process, exercise of the right of pardon, and the making of appointments to a wide range of posts in church and state. Although many of these powers were used in a formal, rubber-stamping way, they nevertheless helped to enhance the appearance of the Lord Lieutenancy as an office of great prestige (for important overviews, see Gray and Purdue, 2012a; Hoppen, 2012). In reality, though, the Lord Lieutenant's powers were gradually slipping into the hands of the Chief Secretary (Flanagan, 1984; Hughes, 1952). Once a personal appointee of the Lord Lieutenant, after the 1780s the British prime minister played an increasingly decisive role in appointing the Chief Secretary, who was responsible for the conduct of day-to-day administration (Johnston, 1963: 16–44). In many ways, indeed, the relationship between the Lord Lieutenant and the Chief Secretary followed the same kind of transition as that between the King and the Prime Minister in Great Britain, though the political primacy of the Chief Secretary in Ireland was never nearly as complete as that of the Prime Minister in Great Britain. The fact that the Chief Secretary was the person who defended Irish government policy in the British House of Commons strengthened the case for giving him a cabinet seat, and in the later years of the British administration in Ireland he normally enjoyed this position, though the Lord Lieutenant was also sometimes a member of the cabinet (McDowell, 1964: 56–62).

The Lord Lieutenant, as the King's representative, was always a nobleman, but his court never rivalled that of the King, and Dublin Castle compared unfavourably with the royal palaces in England and Scotland (Loughlin, 2012). The Lord Lieutenant was expected to devote attention to the ceremonial aspects of his office. These commenced in the case of each newly-appointed Lord Lieutenant with a state entry to Dublin, an occasion of some pageantry, and a formal swearing-in. Even in the turbulent year of 1921, the inauguration of the last Lord Lieutenant was an occasion of considerable solemnity and ritual, taking place in the Privy Council chamber of Dublin Castle (McDowell, 1964: 53–4).[5] The social programme continued with a series of levees, drawing rooms, balls and dinners in Dublin Castle; and the Lord Lieutenant was expected also to attend a wide range of social functions, and to engage with a range of philanthropic causes (Maume, 2012). As the focal point of Irish social life, he attracted to his court all of the most prominent members of the upper classes; but as a political office holder he also risked offending certain sections of the population. The nationalist-dominated Dublin Corporation, whose Lord Mayor had traditionally led it to welcome each new Lord Lieutenant on his state entry at Westland Row railway station, discontinued this practice in 1885. On the other hand, when the Lord Lieutenant formed part of a pro-home rule administration, as in 1893 and the early 1910s, many members of the established classes boycotted the social functions of the royal representative (Daly, 1984).

The office of Lord Lieutenant therefore played an important role in anticipating the future office of President of Ireland. The main features of the office were inherited by the post-1922 Governor-General, if in modified form: its role as royal representative, its social function, its administrative arrangements and even its physical accommodation (Áras an Uachtaráin, the President's official residence in the Phoenix Park, was formerly the Viceregal Lodge, residence of the Lord Lieutenant since 1781). The Lord Lieutenant's establishment formed the model on which the Governor-General's and President's establishments were later based. The Lord Lieutenant was personally responsible for expenditure in a range of areas (including housekeeping, maintenance of the Viceregal Lodge, dinners, entertainment, gifts, and wages of domestic staff), and was paid an annual stipend for these expenses. However, this payment was commonly insufficient to cover actual expenses, forcing incumbents to dip deeply into their own pockets (McDowell, 1964: 54; McBride, 1991: 4). This stipend was continued at a more modest level in respect of the Governor-General and President; and responsibility for maintenance of Áras an Uachtaráin was transferred to the Office of Public Works. Provision was also made for a sizeable household. Some of the more exotic offices had disappeared already by the 1830s: the ceremonial Battle-Axe Guards, for instance, the Master of the Revels, and the State Music (a kettle-drummer, trumpeters, violins, oboes, French horns and a dulcimer; Brynn, 1978: 72–3; Robins, 2001: 118). Gentlemen-in-waiting disappeared in the early twentieth century (McDowell, 1964: 53). By the last years of British rule, the Lord Lieutenant's household was modest in size and included the Comptroller, the State Steward, a private secretary and other secretarial staff, a master of the horse, aides-de-camp and medical staff.[6] Other components, such as the Ulster King of Arms (responsible for heraldry and state ceremonial), were given a separate existence with the disappearance of the Lord Lieutenancy in 1922.

THE GOVERNOR-GENERALSHIP

The Government of Ireland Act of 1920 provided for the continuation of the office of Lord Lieutenant; together with the Lord Chancellor and the Council of Ireland, indeed, and such minor posts as that of Ulster King of Arms, this office would symbolise a measure of formal unity, notwithstanding the partition of the island (Hood, 2002). The major provisions of this Act were, however, superseded by the Anglo-Irish treaty of 1921, which brought the office of Lord Lieutenant to an end. The powers of the Lord Lieutenant in Northern Ireland were transferred to a Governor of Northern Ireland, an office that survived until 1972. In the Irish Free State, the treaty provided for a 'representative of the crown' who was to be 'appointed in like manner as the Governor-General of Canada and in accordance with the practice observed in the making of such appointments'. The character of the office of Governor-General established in 1922 was the outcome of an extended tug-of-war between the Irish negotiators and the British government, a contest whose outcome had a profound effect on the character of the presidency established in 1937.[7]

The office established in 1922 clashed with Irish nationalist expectations and preferences. When the Sinn Féin MPs victorious in the December 1918 general election assembled in Dublin as the first Dáil in January 1919 and proclaimed the 'Irish Republic', they adopted a constitution that pointed towards a parliamentary form of government: the chief executive was to be a Prime Minister (*Príomh-Aireach*), elected by and answerable to the Dáil. Pressure of political circumstances (and, in particular, the pursuit of recognition in the United States and elsewhere) encouraged a less cautious attitude towards nomenclature, and the title of the chief executive was later changed to 'President'. Furthermore, in an important nuance that was to foreshadow perceptions of the respective roles of president and prime minister in the mid-twentieth century, the incumbent, Eamon de Valera, emphasised that he was President not merely of the government but of the 'Irish Republic'.

Some supporters of the 1921 treaty were attracted to the notion of a President rather than a Governor-General. An early draft of the new constitution made provision for a President (*Uachdarán*) who would be elected by members of the two houses of parliament, and who would have the characteristic powers of a head of state, but this was weakened to a proposed 'Commissioner of the British Commonwealth' who would be appointed with the assent of the executive council (Farrell, 1970–71). Even this departed too far from the terms of the treaty, however, so that the final version of the constitution specified that the representative of the crown would be known as the Governor-General and would be appointed in the same way as the Governor-General of Canada, where the appointment was made by the King on the advice of the British government which had, in turn, consulted with the Canadian government. As in the other dominions, the invariable practice was to appoint to this position a British nobleman who was acceptable to the King.

The new Free State government almost immediately began to flex its muscles in appointing the first Governor-General, pushing aside British preference for a well-known peer (Keith, 1936: 429). Instead, it secured the appointment of Tim Healy, a controversial and outspoken veteran of the nationalist movement who had switched to Sinn Féin in 1918, and who has been described as 'the only Irish nationalist whom there was any prospect of prevailing on the British government to accept' (Callanan, 1996: 596). On the expiry of his five-year term in 1928, Healy was replaced by James McNeill, Irish High Commissioner in London, a former Indian civil servant and brother of Eoin MacNeill, a well-known political figure (Kennedy, 2009). On this occasion, the British government was not involved in the appointment process (Sexton, 1989: 112–13).

New ground was, predictably, broken when the pro-treaty government lost office and Eamon de Valera became President of the Executive Council on 9 March 1932. Following an incident on 23 April (when two government ministers pointedly left a reception at the French legation on the arrival of the Governor-General) and later slights during the Eucharistic Congress in June 1932, the Governor-General, against the advice of the executive council, released to the newspapers the correspondence between himself and de Valera on these matters. On 9 September de Valera advised the King to dismiss the Governor-General, but following resistance from the King, McNeill was allowed to resign (McMahon, 1984: 94–6).

Having got rid of one representative of the King, de Valera was faced with the dilemma of finding a substitute, with various short-term solutions ruled out because of opposition from the King and on the basis of legal advice (McMahon, 1982; 1984: 96–100; Sexton, 1989: 134–151). Only one option remained available: to appoint a new Governor-General. Speculation that de Valera might nominate a close associate and prominent businessman, Stephen O'Mara, was mentioned in the London *Times*, leading the King's private secretary to rebuke the editor privately: 'Mr de Valera can only advise the King in the selection, and I question whether His Majesty would approve of a Limerick bacon manufacturer as his personal representative in the Irish Free State'.[8] This showed little sense of realism: within weeks, de Valera proposed Daniel Buckley (Domhnall Ua Buachalla), a Maynooth shopkeeper, for the position, and the King had no choice other than to acquiesce.[9] Like his predecessor, Buckley was not given an opportunity of serving his full term: the office of Governor-General was abolished in 1936, as discussed below.

The British government initially clearly saw the Irish Governor-General, like his counterpart in other dominions, as a Trojan horse. In 1922 prime minister Lloyd George, whose government would have brooked no interference from the King in the internal affairs of the United Kingdom, emphasised to the Irish government representatives the importance of the monarchy and of the mystic power of the crown, and stressed 'the impossibility of an exact definition of its position' (Sexton, 1989: 58). The British thus argued that in the Irish Free State, as in Canada, it would have to be a fundamental principle of the constitution 'that the executive authority was vested in the Crown, that the Crown was a constituent part of the legislature and that the Crown was the fountain of justice' (Sexton, 1989: 58–9). The Governor-General, then, was expected to act as agent both for the British government and for the King. In his former capacity, he was responsible for transmitting dispatches between the Irish and British governments, but following two incidents in which he made minor interventions, the Irish government made it clear that he would be required to act on its advice alone. In any case this dual role was ended by the Imperial Conference of 1926, which recommended that in future the Governor-General of each dominion would act exclusively as representative of the King, implying that he would act only on the advice of the dominion government, not that of the British government (Harkness, 1969: 106–9).[10]

As representative of the King, the Governor-General was responsible for certain formal functions. According to article 51 of the constitution, executive authority was to be exercised by the Governor-General, but this would be 'according to the law, practice and constitutional usage governing the exercise of the Executive Authority in the case of the Dominion of Canada'. In reality, this comprehensively circumscribed the Governor-General's discretion, but the Free State constitution was, by comparison with those of the other dominions, unusually explicit in restricting this. It was thus provided that the President of the Executive Council would be nominated by the Dáil and that the other members of the Council would be approved by the Dáil on the nomination of the President; the Governor-General's role in appointing them was entirely and explicitly formal. Indeed, the formally marginal status of the Governor-General was underscored by the practice that began in 1932 of expecting him to attend Leinster House to appoint the new government, rather than having the ministers travel to the Viceregal Lodge, causing annoyance in Buckingham Palace.[11]

While the Governor-General was responsible for a wide range of patronage and appointments, here too he was required to act only on the advice of the government. His freedom of speech was also limited, a restriction that was especially significant in the case of the first Governor-General, Tim Healy, who had always been forthright in expressing himself. Although Healy was relatively restrained in public, on several occasions his speeches and comments were of a controversial political nature and attracted criticism from the government (Sexton, 1989: 101–5). His successor, James McNeill, fatally ignored explicit government advice in 1932 in publishing his correspondence with de Valera, as we have seen.

The Governor-General also had a formal role in the legislative process. Article 12 unambiguously defined the King as one of the three components (with the Dáil and Seanad) of the Oireachtas, while article 41 authorised his representative 'to withhold the King's assent or reserve the Bill for the signification of the King's pleasure', though, once again, this was to be done in accordance with Canadian law, practice and constitutional usage. In the other dominions, the Governor-General performed a state opening of parliament, normally in the upper house, and read a speech from the throne. There were signs that this practice might be adopted in Ireland. At a meeting of the Oireachtas after the constitution came into effect in 1922, and again after the 1923 general election, the Governor-General addressed a joint sitting of the two houses, but the event was not described as a speech from the throne, and in a breach with the British constitutional tradition it was delivered in the Dáil chamber rather than in the upper house. It was not the occasion of a major state ceremonial; and in addition to being boycotted by the anti-treaty opposition, the Labour Party also absented itself on both occasions.

Neither did the Governor-General have any discretion on the dissolution of parliament: he was *required* to dissolve on the advice of a President who retained the confidence of the Dáil and *forbidden* from doing so on the advice of a President who had lost this. It also quickly became clear that the Governor-General was expected to sign all legislation automatically, without question. He delayed his signature to two bills in 1923–4, but was bluntly informed by President Cosgrave that he was required to follow the advice of the government on this matter (Sexton, 1989: 93–4). There were no further controversies about this power, and it was simply abolished after de Valera's accession to office by the Constitution (Amendment No. 21) Act, 1933. Another formal duty of the Governor-General (to indicate the purpose for which money was being appropriated in a money bill) was removed at the same time by the Constitution (Amendment No. 20) Act, 1933.

In the judicial arena, the Governor-General's right of appointment of judges was purely formal, and was exercised only on the advice of the executive council. The Governor-General had no role to play in appeals to the Privy

Council (technically, to the King in Council), but it is interesting to note that this function was becoming a dead letter even under the pro-treaty government. The formal right of appeal was finally ended by the de Valera government by the Constitution (Amendment No. 22) Act, 1933.

As successor to the Lord Lieutenant, the Governor-General also inherited a set of expectations regarding his social role as representative of the King. But ceremonial was much more restrained: there was no state entry to Dublin on the inauguration of the first Governor-General in 1922, nor was the viceregal tradition of balls, levees and drawing rooms continued. Even the inauguration itself was a very simple ceremony. Tim Healy was sworn in in the presence of his family, some politicians and a small group of officials at his home in Chapelizod in 1922. His successor was given a more elaborate ceremony in Leinster House in 1928; the inauguration was attended by leading politicians and officials and was followed by a military display, cavalcade to the Viceregal Lodge and dinner in the Shelbourne Hotel. The swearing-in of Dónal Ó Buachalla in 1932, however, was a small, deliberately low-key ceremony that took place in his brother's house in Booterstown, Co. Dublin (Sexton, 1989: 88, 115, 154). Although the Governor-General visited schools and hospitals and participated in other important events in the social calendar, he was a much less prominent public figure than the Lord Lieutenant. The reason was in part social: Tim Healy of Bantry was not Viscount FitzAlan of Derwent, and this distinction mattered to those who had frequented the viceregal court. But the government was also unsympathetic to such pretensions, and the hostility of the Fianna Fáil government after 1932 was particularly pronounced. In any case, the last Governor-General, Daniel Buckley, accepted a general prohibition from de Valera against playing any kind of social role unless this were to be specifically approved by the government, and confined himself to the minimum requirements of his office (Sexton, 1989: 155).

Given the extent to which the Governor-General inherited the Lord Lieutenant's role, it is not surprising that he also moved into his official residence, the Viceregal Lodge. But as part of de Valera's move to downgrade the office, the Lodge was abandoned in 1932 and the new Governor-General moved to a much more modest rented house in Monkstown, Co. Dublin (Sexton, 1989: 154). The Governor-General's household suffered the same fate: the first Governor-General had inherited a sizeable staff from the Lord Lieutenant, but in 1932 most of this staff was dispensed with; only the private secretary remained, and even he was now an official in the Department of the President of the Executive Council rather than an independent appointee. The two remaining aides-de-camp returned to other duties, and were replaced by two civic guards, who focused on matters of security rather than of ceremony. The two dozen domestic staff that Healy had employed dwindled to a cook, a maid and a gardener under Ó Buachalla (Sexton, 1989: 157).

THE CROWN IN INDEPENDENT IRELAND

Although King George V had taken an active interest in the affairs of the Irish Free State, he was helpless in the face of the declining authority of his Irish Governor-General (Judd, 1973; Nicolson, 1952). The royal role suffered a further blow following his death and the succession of his son, Edward VIII, in 1936. The new King's decision to marry Mrs Simpson on her divorce provoked a constitutional crisis in Great Britain. While consultations between the British and other Commonwealth governments established that there was near-unanimity on the imperative that the King should in these circumstances abdicate, the Irish Free State was an exception: de Valera initially took the view that there was no reason that the King should not marry and remain on the throne (McMahon, 1984: 198-202).

Eventually, however, de Valera resolved the matter along lines that he had already been planning before this occasion arose. Two pieces of legislation were quickly enacted. The first, the Constitution (Amendment no. 27) Bill, passed on 11 December 1936, sought to remove all references to the Governor-General and to the King's role in internal Irish affairs. The second, the Executive Authority (External Relations) Bill, passed the following day, conferred on the Irish government responsibility for the conduct of external affairs, but authorised 'the King recognised by [Australia, Canada, Great Britain, New Zealand and South Africa] as the symbol of their cooperation' to act in external affairs on the advice of the government of the Irish Free State. This in effect made no provision for the royal succession, but determined that Ireland should simply follow the lead of the other dominions.

The creation of the office of President of Ireland in the new constitution in 1937 appeared at first sight to take this process a stage further. Provision for direct election of the President can be seen as an important endorsement of democratic values, especially in the context of the 1930s (Kissane, 2007: 221). Furthermore, much of the public debate on the new office focused on the extent to which the incumbent might be able to exercise significant political power (Kissane, 2011: 77-9). But the reality of the new office was more modest, with the constitution drafting committee constrained to draw a fine line between the few domestic functions of the President and the 'constitutional usages relative to external affairs' (i.e. the role of the King), which would remain unaffected by the new constitution (Hogan, 2012: 256–259). Instead of providing any role for the President in the area of external affairs, article 29.4.2, dealing with 'international relations', reserved responsibility for external affairs to the government, but, in an exceptionally complex clause, provided that the government might 'avail of or adopt any organ, instrument or method of procedure used or adopted for the like purpose by the members of any group or league of nations with which the State is or becomes associated for the purpose of international co-operation in matters of common concern'.

In thus leaving space for the King as an anonymous 'organ, instrument or method of procedure', de Valera no doubt threw a few potential critics off the Commonwealth scent, especially in the context of a reference to any 'league of nations' with which the state might become associated (his own role in the League of Nations was prominent at the time). The Executive Authority (External Relations) Act, 1936, thus continued to define the King's powers: to appoint diplomatic and consular representatives and to conclude international agreements on the advice of the Irish government. Then and later, de Valera made every effort to de-emphasise links to the King. As one of his critics, his own diplomatic representative in Berlin up to 1939, put it,

> De Valera's policy was a twofold one: for consumption in Ireland, we were a Republic, since our Constitution did not contain the name of the King; for the rest of the world, we were still a dominion like Canada or Australia, and George VI was the head of our state. Therefore it was essential to him that nothing should be done which would expose the hollowness of his claim to have eliminated the reality of English rule (Bewley, 1989: 174).

The last act in Ireland's formal relationship with the monarchy occurred in 1949, when the provisions of the Republic of Ireland Act of 1948 came into force. This legislation repealed the 1936 Act and declared that 'the President, on the authority and on the advice of the Government, may exercise the executive power or any executive function of the State in or in connection with its external relations', thus bringing the King's role to an end. The act also sparked a long-running diplomatic bush-fire by declaring the 'description' of the state to be 'Republic of Ireland', while leaving the 'name' of the state as 'Ireland', as defined in the constitution – thus providing material for several significant international disputes (Coakley, 2009).

In practice, then, the role of the King after 1922 was most prominent in external affairs, an area in which the Irish Free State slowly developed an autonomous identity (Coakley, 2012a). The admission of the state as a member of the League of Nations in 1923 was an important international recognition of its independent status – 'a rite of passage into the international community', as it has been described (Kennedy, 1996: 41). As a British dominion, the Irish Free State was originally expected to relate to non-Commonwealth countries through the British Foreign Office; but the dominions were already in the process of challenging this norm, and in 1924 the Irish Free State became the first dominion to establish a diplomatic mission outside the Commonwealth, in Washington. The appointment of Irish legations in France, Germany and the Holy See followed in 1929 (Harkness, 1969: 63–7, 140). The right of the Irish Free State to conclude international agreements was conceded in 1927, when the Minister for External Affairs and the Attorney General received royal authorisation to negotiate a naval treaty on behalf of the Irish Free State.[12]

These developments had been facilitated by the changing character of the Commonwealth, as successive Imperial Conferences conferred increased levels of autonomy on the dominions. The 1926 conference was important in this respect; the Balfour Report, one of its important outcomes, stressed the equality of the dominions and in effect undermined the British government's capacity to exercise influence through Governors-General. The 1930 conference went a good deal further, its most significant contribution being incorporated in the Statute of Westminster of 1931, which confirmed the legislative autonomy of the dominions (Darwin, 1999: 68–9). By allowing dominions to repeal British legislation affecting them, this opened the door to the constitutional reform process initiated by de Valera in 1933.

When the Irish Free State eventually managed to engage in diplomatic relations with other states in the 1920s, it was the King to whom the credentials of diplomatic representatives of foreign states were addressed, and by him that the letters of credence of Irish diplomats were issued. This gave grounds for tension between Irish governments and the King, and these became particularly acute after de Valera took office in 1932. Even before that date, the Irish Free State had been in breach of the Commonwealth custom by which the prime minister also managed the external affairs portfolio; President Cosgrave had always appointed a separate minister to this position. Surprisingly, de Valera reverted to the Commonwealth norm by taking the External Affairs post himself; but he was in other respects disposed to assert Irish independence. This was marked by two changes, each of which irked

Buckingham Palace. First, the practice began of issuing letters appointing Irish consuls for signature by the King in Irish.[13] Second, de Valera began to open letters of credence of incoming diplomats before sending them on to the King, a gesture intended to stress the independence of the Irish Department of External Affairs, but one about which the King's private secretary consistently complained, to no avail.[14] Buckingham Palace was involved in brief flurries arising from the establishment of diplomatic relations with Portugal and Italy in the late 1930s. The most sustained difficulty arose, however, in relation to the appointment of the head of the Irish diplomatic mission in Berlin following the recall of Charles Bewley in 1939. The King would not issue letters of credence to a power with which, as King of Great Britain, he was at war; neutral Ireland was thus represented in Germany only by a *chargé d'affaires* for the duration of the war (Wheeler-Bennett, 1959: 414).

CONCLUSION

The constitutional coexistence of the King of Ireland and the President of Ireland from 1938 to 1949 caused few problems in the Anglo-Irish relationship (Coakley, 2012a). This outcome was partly because the two sides were divided by more weighty matters, especially during the war years; partly because there was a clearly-defined functional differentiation between the two offices, with one confined to domestic and the other to foreign affairs; and partly because the language of the 1937 constitution permitted the British to take refuge in the term 'Eire' to describe the state over which the Irish President presided, while the King reigned over 'Ireland' (all 32 counties; the royal title had been amended in 1927 to reflect this).

Of more significance was the indirect legacy of monarchy, through perceptions of the President as successor to the Governor-General and Lord Lieutenant. The Lord Lieutenant may have constituted a post-Union symbol of a separate Irish constitutional identity, but he and his office in Dublin Castle represented, in the fullest sense, British rule in Ireland. In political matters, the Lord Lieutenant and his Chief Secretary represented whichever party was in power in Westminster, and were thus either Conservatives or Liberals; they were never associated with the party supported by the great bulk of the Irish electorate after 1885, the Nationalists. But the Dublin Castle regime was not just politically alien from the perspective of the Irish majority; its political stance linked it in varying degrees to the traditional ruling class, the Anglo-Irish, and their northern Unionist allies (under Liberal administrations the relationship was of course more distant). In social matters, too, the Lord Lieutenant represented a type of society where the Anglo-Irish were at home. It was a society in which the small but growing Catholic middle class might have liked to be included; but for most of the Irish population contact with the Lord Lieutenant was confined to looking in on the pageantry associated with state and social ceremonials and festivities. In this, Irish society resembled other European countries of the time, but with an important difference: the politically and socially excluded in the Irish case belonged to a community which was also sharply differentiated from the dominant minority in respect of its culture and identity – a feature that gave rise to a perception of the incumbent of the Viceregal Lodge as 'alien'.

Not surprisingly, then, there are respects in which the Dublin Castle regime was adapted more faithfully in Northern Ireland than in the South after 1922. The new office of Governor of Northern Ireland was closely and consciously modelled on that of the Lord Lieutenant as regards procedure and ceremonial: as in Dublin before 1922, the inauguration of the royal representative in Belfast after 1922 was attended by the political and judicial establishments and leading officers from local government, the churches, education and the armed forces.[15] The Northern Ireland government also considered offering to host the office of Ulster King of Arms, before that office was merged with that of Chief Herald of Ireland in 1943.[16] In the South, the Governor-General, perceived as an unwanted symbol of the British connection, attracted little sympathy among nationalists, while his low-key social role and humble background simultaneously disappointed the expectations of avid royalists. Nationalist critics dubbed the Viceregal Lodge 'Uncle Tim's Cabin' as soon as Tim Healy took it over in 1923; the house 'was associated in the minds of the Irish people with the most gross form of tyranny, and instead of rejoicing that one of their own kindred had now taken possession of it, some of them cried: "Renegade"' (O'Flaherty, 1927: 312–13). On the other hand, Daniel Buckley's abandonment of the Viceregal Lodge for a suburban house in Monkstown drew a sarcastic response from conservative critics, one of whom mocked its imitation marble pillars and described it as 'a big comfortable house for a fairly large family. It certainly would not have a Ball Room, but probably a Billiard Room!'.[17] An unloved figure, the Governor-General shrank to insignificance following his virtual disappearance from public life after 1932.

To the extent that there is a public need for ceremonial and spectacle of the kind amply provided by royal ceremonies, this may well have been provided in the early years of independent Ireland by the public rituals of the Catholic church, including such events as the Eucharistic Congress of 1932. But if space still existed for a physical embodiment of the state in a single office, this was perhaps filled, especially after 1932, but to some extent also before that date, by another 'President' – the President of the Executive Council, or prime minister. It was in this office that Irish nationalist affections (modified by political differences) were concentrated, and its holder in the 1930s completely overshadowed, in all areas, the semi-visible or invisible representative of the crown.

Not surprisingly, then, the remoulding of these offices into those of Taoiseach and President in 1937 was not associated with any sudden redirection of the limelight: notwithstanding rhetoric to the contrary, Taoiseach de Valera continued to see himself as authentic representative of the Irish people after 1937 as fully as President de Valera did before that date. Indeed, the new President's powers have been described as 'little more than slightly doctored versions' of the powers of the Governor-General (Duffy, 1993: 129). The factors associated with this succession perhaps help to explain why the Irish Taoiseach, uniquely among contemporary prime ministers, continues to be associated with certain of the trappings of a head of state, having his own aide-de-camp and anthem (the little-known *Amhrán dóchais*). It may also help to explain why the President, even after becoming a fully-fledged head of state in 1949, has had to fight a long battle to assert powers for the office that would match those implied in the principle of direct election.

NOTES

1. In an influential but contested reformulation by Elgie (1999: 13), semi-presidentialism has been defined as 'the situation where a popularly elected fixed-term president exists alongside a prime minister and cabinet who are responsible to parliament', a definition that covers typical popularly elected presidents in parliamentary democracies, regardless of their powers.
2. In addition to the Lord Lieutenant, the Irish government was normally seen as including the Chief Secretary, the Lord Chancellor, the Attorney General and the Solicitor General. On the evolution of the office, see Grey and Purdue, 2012a.
3. *Parliamentary debates*, 17 May 1850, 3rd ser., vol. 111, cols. 184–192.
4. These data are derived from O'Brien, 1912: 12–13, updated by the inclusion of the three last Lords Lieutenant. Of these, it has been assumed that Wimbourne and FitzAlan would have been regarded as 'in sympathy with national feeling', though O'Brien's nationalist contemporaries would no doubt have disputed this.
5. For a record of the ceremonial on this occasion, see *Dublin Gazette*, 3 May 1921, pp. 639–640.

6. Information on the Lord Lieutenant's establishment is contained in successive annual editions of *Thom's Directory*.

7. The office of Governor-General has been the subject of a definitive study, by Brendan Sexton (1989), and this is relied on heavily in this section.

8. Sir Clive Wigram to Geoffrey Dawson, editor, *The Times*, 2 November 1932; Royal Archives, Windsor (RA PS/PSO/GV/L/2138/222). I am indebted to Her Majesty Queen Elizabeth II for permission to use material from the Royal Archives, Windsor Castle, and to Lady Sheila de Bellaigue and Mrs Jill Kelsey for making the material available.

9. The Irish High Commissioner in London, John Dulanty, sought to put a positive spin on the nominee by describing him as owner of 'an emporium in the ecclesiastical capital of Ireland' (McMahon, 1984: 99).

10. With the disappearance of the Governor-General's role as an agent of the British government, British High Commissioners, occupying quasi-ambassadorial functions, were appointed in the dominions – except in Dublin, where such an appointment was made only in 1939. This meant that the British government had an extraordinarily low level of information on political developments in Ireland, and this was exposed at its most deficient in 1932 during the transition to the new de Valera administration (O'Halpin, 2000: 62–3).

11. The King's secretary complained that 'what strikes His Majesty as unusual is, that the President summoned the Governor-General, instead of the Governor-General summoning the President to Viceregal Lodge, but I suppose this is the "Irish way" of doing things unlike the procedure in the other Dominions' (Wigram to Colonial Secretary James Thomas, 11 March 1932, RA PS/PSO/GV/L/2138/70). Neville Chamberlain commented: 'It is amazing that our leading papers took no notice of this "outrage". Fancy H.M.'s representative being treated like this!' (Note, 17 March 1932, Neville Chamberlain to Wigram, RA PS/PSO/GV/L/2484/E/1).

12. Statement by John A. Costello, *Dáil Debates*, 12 December 1936, vol. 64, cols. 1480–1481.

13. The King initially refused to sign the Irish versions, as he 'does not at all like the idea of signing a document in a language with which he is not acquainted' (Wigram to Sir Edward Harding, Dominions Office, 20 October 1932, RA PS/PSO/GV/L/2484/C/7). His private secretary suspected that 'this may be a "try-on" and possibly a trap', adding sarcastically that the letters were 'most beautifully designed and all that is lacking is illustrations of Irish life around the outside' (Wigram to Attorney-General Thomas Inskip, 14 October 1932, RA PS/PSO/GV/L/2484/C/1-7).

14. From de Valera's perspective this was a point of constitutional propriety, but the King's private secretary reported to the King that he had 'explained to Mr Dulanty [Irish High Commissioner in London] that this was a personal matter and not a constitutional one, and that gentlemen did not open letters not

addressed to them' (note from Wigram to the King, 26 March 1936; RA PS/PSO/ GVI/C/18/4). Nine years later, the tactful Dulanty was still on the case, explaining that 'De Valera hates like hell having to break the seals, but he is convinced that it is his constitutional duty to do so' (Sir Alan Lascelles, Private Secretary to the King, to Sir Eric Machtig, Under-Secretary at the Dominions Office, 16 August 1945, RA PS/PSO/GVI/C/18/18).

15. See Northern Ireland cabinet papers, Public Record Office of Northern Ireland (PRONI), 'Ceremonial [Governor]', CAB/9T/3/9.

16. See Northern Ireland cabinet papers, 'Office of Ulster King of Arms, 1922–66', PRONI, CAB/9R/52/1.

17. Denis Gwynn to Sir Clive Wigram, 14 December 1932, RA PS/PSO/ GV/L/2138/318.

5

THE EARLY PRESIDENTS, 1938–1973

CIARA MEEHAN

INTRODUCTION

Eamon de Valera light-heartedly remarked in 1967 that when he was writing his 1937 constitution, he wanted to prepare a nice, quiet job without too much work for his old age (Ferriter, 2007: 203). By 1973, when he left Áras an Uachtaráin, the official residence of the Irish President, the presidency was certainly seen as a place of retirement for elder statesmen, and was viewed as something of a distant office. It was an understandable perception. The first President, Douglas Hyde, was almost 85 on his departure, and when taking office seven years earlier had himself expressed concern about his age. At the end of his two seven-year terms, Seán T. O'Kelly – the youngest of the three presidents examined in this chapter – was 75, while de Valera was 90. Theirs tended to be a quiet office, days filled with correspondence and entertaining. O'Kelly once described the function of his job as 'mainly signing on the dotted line' (*Evening Mail*, 26 April 1950). The only major change in the function of the office during that period was the result of new legislation introduced by the then Taoiseach (Prime Minister) John A. Costello, which gave the office holder an international role for the first time. But despite all of this, the early presidents should not be considered passive. Their willingness, where necessary, to exercise their discretionary powers shows that they utilised the functions of the office in the most important way. The history of the early presidencies lacks the drama of the Cearbhall Ó Dálaigh years and the breadth of activity that defined Mary Robinson's and Mary McAleese's time in office. But the early office holders were important in different ways. It was during those first presidencies that the functions of the office were tested and established, and protocol was decided. The task of defining the presidency was not particularly exciting, but it was essential, especially when viewed in the context of the debate that surrounded its emergence.

The office of President of Ireland was a creation of the 1937 constitution. It proved to be one of the two most talked about aspects of de Valera's new constitution – the other being the place of women.[1] It is worth recalling the manner in which the powers granted to the office were perceived at the time (see Chapter 4). The newly-created office, in conjunction with the re-titling of President of the Executive Council as Taoiseach, caused suspicion among the opposition and elements of the press as to de Valera's intentions. Tom O'Higgins, the Fine Gael TD for Laois-Offaly, claimed that the Fianna Fáil leader was 'building a throne for one individual' (*Dáil Debates*, 67: 269, 12 May 1937). Concerns of a dictatorship were further fuelled by emerging reports from Europe – Hitler's Enabling Act had been passed only four years earlier – and by news such as that conveyed by Fine Gael's John A. Costello that the term 'Taoiseach' had been translated on German radio as *Führer* (*Dáil Debates*, 67: 301, 12 May 1937). De Valera had attempted to counter the charges in the Dáil on 11 May 1937, arguing that the 'powers that are given to the President in which I might call definitely the executive domain are relatively small'. He stressed that the President would always act on the advice of others (*Dáil Debates*, 67: 39, 11 May 1937). Because, as de Valera himself pointed out, some critics had 'fastened particularly on the powers that are given to the President', claiming that they were of a dictatorial nature (*Dáil Debates*, 67: 39, 11 May 1937), it was essential that the first office holder in particular would observe the function of the office as it was designed.

This chapter examines the first three Presidents of Ireland: Douglas Hyde, Seán T. O'Kelly and Eamon de Valera. It considers their personal backgrounds and the extent to which this shaped their period in office, their emergence as candidates for the office, their vision for the presidency, and the manner in which they conducted themselves, both at home, and, in the case of the latter two, abroad.

DOUGLAS HYDE, 1938–1945

Douglas Hyde became President of Ireland in June 1938. His cultural background, combined with an absence of political allegiance, made him an obvious choice to become the first office holder. Born in Roscommon in 1860,

Hyde spent the first seven years of his childhood in Sligo, before returning to his county of birth following the appointment of his father, Rev Arthur Hyde, as rector of the parish of Tibohine. It was these surrounds of the province of Connacht, steeped in Gaelic tradition and folklore, which shaped the development of his consciousness (Ó Lúing, 1973: 123). Through contact with locals, Hyde learnt Irish, and once claimed that he dreamt in the language. Under the penname of *An Craoibhín Aoibhinn*, he contributed nationalist-themed poems to *The Shamrock* and *The Irishman*, quasi-separatist newspapers. Among his many other publications are *Leabhar Sgéulaigheachta* and *Ubhla de'n Chraoibh* (Maume, 2009a). In 1893 he was one of the founders of the Gaelic League, which had the aim of preserving and promoting the Irish language and literature. His inaugural address to the National Literary Society, 'The necessity for de-Anglicising Ireland', had provided the impetus for the League's formation. Hyde saw the language as a 'neutral field upon which all Irishmen might meet' (Nic Congáil, 2009: 94), and was anxious to ensure that the movement did not become politicised, thus alienating certain elements. Despite his efforts, the League was used by the Irish Republican Brotherhood (IRB), a revolutionary organisation that sought to break the connection with Britain, as a vehicle to spread its particular brand of nationalism, and he resigned in protest in 1915.

EMERGENCE AS PRESIDENT

The Irish Times argued vigorously that the first President of Ireland should be non-political to ensure that the office had a smooth emergence and that it would be kept 'above the squalor of Irish party politics'. In order to achieve this, the newspaper suggested that a contested election be avoided and that a candidate beyond reproach be agreed by the political parties. The inaugural office holder was envisaged to be a man to whom the mass of the people could look up (*The Irish Times*, 14 October 1937). Several names, including de Valera's, had been mentioned. Hyde's emerged on 27 May 1937. The previous day he had been presented with the first Gregory Medal by the council of the Irish Academy of Letters in recognition of the prominent role that he played in the Gaelic cultural revival. A later profile in the *New York Times* magazine described Hyde as 'a venerable and nationally-loved patriot, scholar and poet who in all his 78 years has never been drawn into the maelstrom of politics'. He came, it was suggested, 'very near to being the embodied spirit of Ireland' (*New York Times*, 29 May 1938). His profile was such that both Fianna Fáil and

Fine Gael agreed that he was the best-suited candidate for the office, and he was installed without an election in 1938.

Hyde was not affiliated to a political party. He had previously refused a nationalist seat in the House of Commons that had been offered by John Redmond, leader of the Irish Parliamentary Party, in 1904 (Maume, 2009a), and although twice a senator (1925, 1938), he primarily represented cultural interests. His only electoral performance was dismal. The 1925 Senate election was the only one to be conducted among a Free State-wide electorate of voters over 30 years old, using proportional representation by means of the single transferable vote. Hyde won just over 1,000 votes, far less than was needed to secure a seat (Coakley, 2005: 249). He became a member of the upper house only after being co-opted to fill the vacancy created by the death of a sitting senator. His main contribution to the Senate debates was on the subject of government funding for the Celtic Congress and of *Amharclann Gaedhealach*. His support for both of these causes reflected his continuing interest in preserving and promoting the Irish language. The Congress, which convened in Dublin in 1925, brought together those who were concerned about the future of the Celtic languages; Hyde addressed the gathering. *Amharclann Gaedhealach*, the Irish theatre, produced Irish language plays. His only other contribution came in the form of a tribute to his old friend George Sigerson, a prominent figure in the Irish literary revival, on the occasion of his death in February 1925. Having no political baggage, Hyde thus satisfied the desire for a candidate outside the political fray. Additionally, as the son of a Church of Ireland clergyman, he had the credentials to appeal to the religious minority and assure them that, despite the special position accorded to the Catholic Church in the new 1937 constitution, there would be no discrimination. This met with the approval of *The Times*, in which it was noted that 'the choice of a Protestant ... as President of a mainly Catholic country has been a practical example of liberalism and tolerance which will not fail to have a great effect in all parts of Ireland and not in Ireland alone' (quoted in *Belfast Telegraph*, 27 June 1938).

Hyde's cultural background also had a further benefit for the presidency: it helped to connect the office with Ireland's cultural heritage. Speaking at the inauguration, Taoiseach Eamon de Valera made reference to the defeat of Gaelic Ireland in the seventeenth century and told Hyde, 'in you we greet the successor of our rightful princes, and in your accession to office we hail the closing of the breach that has existed since the undoing at Kinsale'. De Valera linked Hyde's position to that of the Gaelic chieftains: 'you are ... entitled to the respect which the Gael ever gave to those whom they recognised to be their rightful chiefs, but which for centuries they denied to those whom a foreign law would enforce upon them' (*Irish Independent*, 27 June 1938). Hyde's appointment can thus be seen as part of a broader image-building strategy, and of de Valera's desire to emphasise Irish sovereignty.[2] This was summed up by the *Irish Press*, which noted that 'the two national ideals [of Ireland free and Ireland Gaelic] have been united in one person' (*Irish Press*, 25 June 1938).

VISION OF OFFICE

Hyde's inauguration took place on 25 June 1938; apart from the declaration of office, he made no formal statement. The ceremony in Dublin Castle – the setting for each subsequent inauguration – was conducted in Irish. That Hyde chose to make the declaration in the Irish form indicated that the language would be at the heart of his presidency. This was affirmed by his Christmas broadcast to the United States on 22 December 1938. In this first presidential broadcast, Hyde renewed the contact with America he had first made in person during his extensive lecture tour of 1905–1906. He expressed his pride in now addressing them as President of Ireland, 'a title which indicates the great progress which our beloved country has made'. The greater part of his speech was dedicated to the language question. Though he recognised that the task of restoration was not yet complete, he noted the place of Irish in the constitution, in state services, in the promulgation of laws and in schools.[3]

Despite Hyde's commitment to cultural nationalism, he was keen to be a representative President. This was reflected in the manner in which he established the office at the heart of Irish sporting occasions. This brought him into conflict with the Gaelic Athletic Association (GAA) at the start of his tenure, when he accepted an invitation to attend an international soccer match between Ireland and Poland at Dalymount Park stadium (Moore, 2012). As patron of the GAA, Hyde was considered a member, and members were banned from playing or attending 'foreign' games. Padraig McNamee, president of the GAA, ruled that a patron of the association ceased to be a patron if his duties 'bring him into conflict with the fundamental rules of the Association'. Hyde did not challenge the ruling. Although he ceased to be patron, his support for the organisation and its athletes continued. When his native Roscommon triumphed in the 1943 All-Ireland football final, he took great pride and pleasure in receiving the winning team at the Áras. Similarly, when the Cavan and Kerry teams that participated in the Gaelic football final in New York in 1947 returned, another reception was held at the President's official residence. The connection between the presidency and sport was one continued by Hyde's successor, Seán T. O'Kelly. The rift with the GAA was healed during that time, but not before the organisation refused to be represented at an official welcome for President O'Kelly at the Wexford Feis (festival) because he had attended a soccer match. Following correspondence between the GAA and the Taoiseach's office, the former eventually recognised that 'the President is president of all sections of the community and cannot in any circumstances put himself in a position as to seem by implication or otherwise to discriminate against any section of the community'.[4]

On becoming President, Hyde entered uncharted territory. Although the constitution determined the official functions of the office, the day-to-day operations, procedure and protocol were decided through experience. As secretary to the President, Michael McDunphy – who had served both W.T. Cosgrave and Eamon de Valera in government – played a key role in shaping these matters. McDunphy became so intimately familiar with the proceedings that he would later publish a guide to the functions, powers and duties of the President (McDunphy, 1945). A somewhat bemusing file at the Irish National Archives reveals some of the considerations that the new office demanded: the interior of the presidential car would have to be designed in such a manner as to allow the President, while seated, to take off a top hat in a way that was not undignified. Various models were considered between August 1938 and March 1939, and a burgundy Chrysler limousine with head cushions embroidered with the harp was eventually decided upon.[5]

Article 26.5.2° of the Constitution states that 'the Taoiseach shall keep the President generally informed on matters of domestic and international importance'. Before Hyde even assumed office, it was decided that this provision would be complied with by means of personal conversations; the need for official communications would be considered on the basis of experience. De Valera made his first call to the President on 29 June 1938. Typically, he called late in the evening and usually on a monthly basis. This loose arrangement became more structured during O'Kelly's presidency when it was decided that the Taoiseach would call on the first Friday of each month at 3.30pm; this was changed to Mondays when John A. Costello became Taoiseach in 1948, and reverted to Fridays when de Valera returned to office in 1951.[6] However, as Kevin Rafter shows, this level of contact between the head of government and the President of the day was not always maintained, particularly in the case of Taoiseach Liam Cosgrave and President Cearbhall Ó Dálaigh (see Chapter 6).

Though it was a ceremonial office, there were huge demands on the new President. For the first month, interviews were scheduled for both the morning and afternoon, and the President could undertake up to six a day. With this demanding schedule, the 78-year old President became 'very fatigued', prompting McDunphy to confine interviews to an hour in the morning, leaving afternoons, as well as the whole of Mondays and Saturdays, free. Generally, though, McDunphy observed Hyde to be 'active both physically and intellectually'.[7] Personal time was set aside in his schedule for Hyde to continue reading and writing, and during the presidency he completed *Sgéalta Thomáis Uí Chathasaigh* [Stories of Thomas Casey] (Dunleavy and Dunleavy, 1991: 399).

The supporting role of spouses is one frequently commented upon, and the early Presidents were no exception. Douglas Hyde's wife, Lucy, did not move to Áras an Uachtaráin due to ill-health, and he regularly made the trip home to visit her until her death in December 1938. However, he was not without a strong supporting figure. This role was filled by his younger sister, Annette whose husband had died in 1932. At ease with public figures and dignitaries, she filled the role of hostess, and Hyde often shared with her details of correspondence received at the Áras. Hyde suffered a mild stroke on 13 April 1940 and this, along with the experience of the Second World War – referred to in Ireland as 'the Emergency' – changed the pattern of his working day. On the advice of Dr William Boxwell, President of the Royal College of Physicians in Ireland, his activity was restricted to simple matters such as the signing of official documents. Hyde was confined to his room until 6 June 1940, after which he spent portions of the day on a specially-constructed veranda. By September, he was well enough to receive callers, although the visit of David Gray, the US Ambassador to Ireland, left Hyde 'very much fatigued', with the consequence that the proposed visit of a French government minister was postponed.[8]

POLITICAL ROLE

The fear that the Taoiseach of the day would be able to manipulate the office of the President proved unfounded. Hyde set a number of important precedents. In May 1937, de Valera explained how he had envisaged the role of the office-holder 'to guard the people's rights and mainly to guard the Constitution, maintaining the mastery of the people and safeguarding their rights between elections' (*Dáil Debates*, 67: 51, 11 May 1937). In explaining the duty and functions of the office to Hyde, McDunphy had used the analogy of a referee in a football match: 'There were rules by which the game should be played and

the referee should not interfere unless he saw an infringement of those rules'
(Dunleavy and Dunleavy, 1991: 395).

Article 26 of the constitution provides that the President can refer bills or
sections thereof to the Supreme Court to test their constitutionality, but must
first consult with the Council of State, an advisory body with some similarities
to the old Privy Council. The President is free to disregard their advice. The
first occasion on which the Council met was in January 1940, to discuss the
bill designed to amend the Offences Against the State Act, 1939. The proceedings took place behind closed doors and there is no available record of the discussion, apart from a formal statement signalling the President's intent to refer
the legislation to the Supreme Court. The Bill was found to be constitutional
and Hyde thus signed it into law. Subsequently, in February 1943, he referred
the School Attendance Bill, 1942, and asked for a judgement on Section 4.
He had been prompted to do so by the case made in a letter from Fine Gael's
John A. Costello, who argued that the section in question was repugnant to
Article 42 of the Constitution. That article 'acknowledges that the primary and
natural educator of the child is the Family and guarantees to respect the inal-
ienable right and duty of parents to provide, according to their means, for the
religious and moral, intellectual, physical and social education of their children'. Costello argued that section 4 of the new bill gave the authority to decide
on the nature of a child's education to the Minister for Education, rather than
the parents. The Supreme Court found section 4 to be unconstitutional, effectively undoing the entire piece of legislation (McCullagh, 2010: 143).

In May 1944, de Valera's government was narrowly defeated on the second
stage of the Transport Bill. The Dáil adjourned at 9.20pm and, following a mid-
night meeting of the government, the Taoiseach visited Áras an Uachtaráin,
where he outlined the situation to Hyde. The outcome – a dissolution of the
Dáil – was heavily criticised by the opposition. Much was made of de Valera's
late-night visit to the Áras, and Hyde's age and the status of his health became
a factor in the opposition's criticism that claimed that the Fianna Fáil leader
had effectively coerced the elderly President into accepting his views. Fine
Gael's Tom O'Higgins suggested that de Valera 'took advantage of the failing
health of a great figure in order to cheat parliament', for which he found himself admonished by the Ceann Comhairle, who interpreted the argument as
an implicit criticism of the President. Labour's William Norton declared the
Taoiseach's action 'high treason', and criticised him for exploiting 'an aged man
whom everyone knows to be in anything but a perfect state of health' (*Dáil
Debates*, 93: 2474, 10 May 1944). Despite the inferences of the opposition, Hyde
had not been manipulated; he had consulted with McDunphy, who had

travelled specially to the Áras that night, before consenting to a dissolution (Dunleavy and Dunleavy, 1991: 428). Hyde's independent thinking during his term in office confirmed that the President was not the servant of the government of the day.

SEAN T. O'KELLY, 1949–1959

Seán T. O'Kelly succeeded Hyde in 1945, becoming the first President to be elected directly. Although there was continuity between the cultural interests of the two men, their religious and political backgrounds differed greatly. Born in Dublin in 1882, O'Kelly's childhood education by the Christian Brothers imbued him with a strong sense of religion. He remained a devout Catholic and was a member of the Knights of Columbanus, a secretive Catholic organisation. Among the various decorations that he received was the Grand Cross of the Order of St Gregory the Great, a papal honour, in 1933 (he was granted the Grand Cross of Charles III – the highest Spanish civil decoration – by General Franco in 1950). During his presidency, he made an official visit to Rome, one that the official files reveal he had 'long planned as a private citizen'.[9]

O'Kelly had joined the IRB in 1902 and was a founder-member of the Irish Volunteers, formed to defend Home Rule and in response to the Ulster Volunteers, which sought to prevent the introduction of the settlement that would have granted Ireland a parliament to look after its domestic affairs. His commitment to the separatist movement was such that he resigned as junior assistant at the National Library, feeling that a position under the British government was incompatible with his views (Maume, 2009b). He fought in the Easter Rising and was later active in the independence struggle (1919–1921). Although he was a member of the revolutionary Dáil, he initially boycotted the Free State parliament along with the other Sinn Féin TDs who opposed the 1921 Anglo-Irish Treaty. As discussed below, the political split and ensuing Civil War caused by the Treaty directly affected his family, and he would later use the presidency as a time of atonement. He finally took his seat in Dáil Éireann alongside his, by then, Fianna Fáil colleagues in 1927. After the party came to power in 1932, he subsequently held several ministries and at the time of his election he was Minister for Finance and Tánaiste (deputy prime minister). An Irish language enthusiast, he was one of the politicised members who had changed the complexion of the Gaelic League. His commitment to Irish was obvious during his presidency and indicated a line of continuity with his predecessor.

EMERGENCE AS PRESIDENT

O'Kelly was unanimously chosen at a special meeting of the Fianna Fáil National Executive on 23 April 1945 to contest the forthcoming presidential election. Opposing him was Fine Gael's Seán Mac Eoin, a former Chief of Staff of the Free State army. Mac Eoin was first elected to the Dáil in 1921, but chose not to contest the 1923 general election to focus his attentions on the army. He later resigned that position on re-entering the Dáil in 1929 following a successful campaign in the Sligo–Leitrim by-election. Patrick McCartan, an independent republican, also entered the fray, supported by Labour, Clann na Talmhan and a number of independents. He was a former editor of *Irish Freedom*, newspaper of the IRB, and had been a Sinn Féin organiser. Although O'Kelly himself did not campaign, de Valera and the Fianna Fáil ministers were active on the canvass and they ran the election as a vote of confidence in the government – a tactic that drew the ire of *The Irish Times*. Given that the newspaper had advocated keeping the presidency above politics in 1938, it was unsurprising to find criticisms of the party political dimension to the 1945 campaign. Expressed among its pages was the hope that 'seven years hence ... the office of President will not be dragged into the political gutter' (*The Irish Times*, 19 June 1945). O'Kelly was elected on the second count following the elimination of McCartan and the distribution of his transfers. The slender victory pointed to a degree of unhappiness with the incumbent Fianna Fáil government, while the destination of McCartan's transfers, which went principally to Mac Eoin, foreshadowed the trend at the subsequent general election in 1948 that would unseat de Valera's government.

VISION OF OFFICE

O'Kelly's inauguration was held on 25 June 1945, and the day's proceedings largely followed the procedure adopted for Hyde. Like his predecessor, O'Kelly made the declaration in Irish. In a new development, he gave a short speech in which there were indications as to his priorities. He pledged to continue the work of his predecessor with regard to the restoration of the Irish language. That Irish would be central to his presidency was further reflected in his decision that the Gaelic form of his name – Seán T. Ó Ceallaigh – would be used for official purposes.

O'Kelly was clearly not a President without political baggage, and there were glimpses of the influences that had guided his political thinking.

As President, he instituted the policy of sending official Christmas cards; Hyde had previously gifted copies of his poetry to a selection of friends at Christmas. O'Kelly chose as the subject of his cards a different signatory of the 1916 proclamation of the Irish republic, and by 1953, once all seven signatories had been depicted, he discontinued the practice. But despite having been the Fianna Fáil candidate, his was not a Fianna Fáil presidency. Rather, his time in office was a period of reconciliation. As Anne Dolan observed, 'the 1950s were apparently [his] time to reflect on his past, time to make amends'. In his official capacity, he unveiled statues and monuments across the country to those who had participated in the independence struggle, and at the unveilings spoke of unity and the passage of time. He also became patron of a fund to purchase a bust of the revolutionary leader and pro-Treatyite Michael Collins for the state (Dolan, 2003: 81). *The Irish Times*, reflecting on some of the concerns that had been voiced at the time of his election, observed that 'Seán T. O'Kelly ... has been impartial beyond reproach in his attitude towards the classes, creeds and parties of his country' (*The Irish Times*, 11 April 1965).

O'Kelly had personal experience of the divisions that the civil war had caused. For example, his own family had been divided by the split relating to the treaty. His sister-in-law had married General Richard Mulcahy, a commander of the Free State forces and later Cumann na nGaedheal Minister for Defence, and it was only at his mother-in-law's funeral in 1927 that the two sides of the family were brought back together.[10] Perhaps with his own family's troubled history in mind, he spoke at Newcastle West in County Limerick of 'bringing together again the friends and comrades sundered by the divisions of 1922' (*Irish Independent*, 11 April 1955). Though the term was not used, this early form of 'building bridges' in some respects foreshadows the themes explored in later presidencies (see Chapter 7). Such remarks by the President were broadly welcomed. For example, Liam Skinner of the *Sunday Independent* noted that 'the country is being roused, as seldom before in recent years. From Belfast to Cork and from Galway to Dublin come messages of support for the President's appeal and for the reunification of the movement which achieved so much for Ireland between 1919 and 1921' (*Sunday Independent*, 26 October 1952).

Many of the comments relating to unity were also made in the context of ending partition. At the unveiling of a memorial at Bandon in 1953, O'Kelly spoke of how 'the obligation is still upon us to win back for Ireland the six partitioned counties ... We should not look on complacently, or stand idly by while Britain keeps our brothers of the North divided from us'. Through unity of the old republican ranks, he argued, 'the possibility of progress towards the abolition of partition would be many times multiplied' (*Irish Press*, 3 August 1953). Though the President refrained from wandering into domestic politics, he was clearly not above discussing national issues and his position was in harmony with that of the Fianna Fáil government. De Valera, his former party leader, had used a rare spell in opposition between 1948 and 1951 as an opportunity to travel abroad to communicate the anti-partition message to international audiences. In a similar manner, O'Kelly used his address to the United States Congress, discussed below, as an opportunity to repeat his domestic pronouncements on partition.

POLITICAL ROLE

Unlike Hyde, O'Kelly did not exercise his discretionary powers, although he did convene a meeting of the Council of State to discuss an aspect of the Health Bill, 1947. However, the most important development in the presidency during the early years came during O'Kelly's first term in office when a new, international dimension was added. As is so often repeated, de Valera's constitution had made Ireland a republic in everything but name. Despite the absence of any reference to the monarch in the document (see Chapter 4), in the eyes of the international community the King was nonetheless seen as head of the state. The constitution had not addressed the functions of the President in the realm of external affairs. As late as 1941, British Prime Minister Winston Churchill observed of Ireland, 'her international status is undefined and anomalous' (Canning, 1985: 306). In 1948 Taoiseach John A. Costello signalled Ireland's intent to withdraw from the Commonwealth and to declare a republic. This was to have an important implication for the powers of the President. Section 3 of the resulting Republic of Ireland Act, 1948, stated that 'the President, on the authority and on the advice of the Government, may exercise the executive power or any executive function of the State in or in connection with its external relations'.

It was an important clarification that upgraded the status of the President. As Dunleavy and Dunleavy have noted in their biography of Douglas Hyde, when US Ambassador David Gray arrived in 1940 he came with the obvious assumption that Hyde did not count. He considered Hyde a spent force and identified de Valera, as Taoiseach, as being more important (Dunleavy and Dunleavy, 1991: 422). This, of course, was a product of the constitutional status of both offices – possibly influenced, too, by Hyde's weakened state as he recovered from his stroke – but it was also arguably a result of the ambiguity regarding the head of state. In terminating the King's role as head of state and transferring his powers to the President, Costello's Act allowed the Irish President to play an international role. Previously, the credentials of Irish diplomats were issued by the King on the advice of the Irish government, and the credentials of foreign diplomats were addressed to the King. The President also played no role in the signing of international treaties. Subsequent to the Republic of Ireland Act coming into effect in 1949, the role of the President was transformed. The first letters of credence signed by O'Kelly were those of Leo MacCauley, the new Irish envoy to Spain (McCabe, 1991: 91).

This international role emerged gradually. O'Kelly made two foreign trips of note during his time in office, the first to Rome in April 1950 (on the return from which he paid an unofficial visit to Paris) and the second to the United States. Both visits set important precedents. In the case of Rome, it was the first instance since the formation of the presidency that an office holder had left the State; the protocol followed set the template for future trips. In America, O'Kelly followed in the footsteps of Charles Stewart Parnell, W.T. Cosgrave and John A. Costello in delivering an address to Congress. However, he had the distinction of being the first Irish President to make such a speech. Moreover, unlike his predecessors, who spoke to only one chamber, he was the first Irish leader to address a joint meeting of Congress.

These trips, particularly the latter in March 1959, were important in 'selling Ireland' to an international community and developing the state's reputation abroad, a feature more generally associated with more recent presidencies. Though O'Kelly spoke of the continued problem of partition and outlined Ireland's goal to be 'united and free' in his address to the US Senate and House of Representatives, interwoven through his American speeches was an emphasis on the positive transformation of Ireland. Speaking to the Irish Societies of New York City, O'Kelly aimed to show that 'real progress has been made'. He spoke at length of 'substantial progress' in the economic field, and dealt with developments in housing, the merchant marine, scientific exploitation of peat resources, increased electric power and 'noteworthy advances in important basic sectors of the economy such as sugar, cement, steel and mineral development'.[11] This was a theme replicated in many of his other addresses. O'Kelly's American visit also had a more immediate importance: building on John A Costello's in 1956, his demonstrated a continuing improvement in the relationship between America and Ireland, which had been damaged by Ireland's official policy of neutrality in the Second World War, even though the behind-the-scenes relationship told a different story.

EAMON DE VALERA, 1959–1973

On 25 June 1959, Eamon de Valera entered the final phase of his political career when he was elected the third President of Ireland. Born in New York in 1882, he came to Ireland in April 1885 with his uncle, Edward Coll. A scholarship later permitted him access to Blackrock College where, it has been noted, unlike such contemporaries as the novelist and short-story writer Pádraic Ó Conaire, he showed no interest in the language revival movement and did not attend Irish language classes. The year 1908 has been identified as pivotal in his attitude towards the language. By then, de Valera was teaching at the teacher training college in Carysfort in South Dublin. The creation of the National University of Ireland (NUI) and the introduction of an Irish language requirement for matriculation there had an impact on the curriculum on offer at Carysfort. De Valera resolved to learn the language, and subsequently joined the Gaelic League. He later married his teacher, Sinéad Flanagan, who was four years his senior (Fanning, 2009).

De Valera was strongly committed to the nationalist movement, and attended the inaugural meeting of the Irish Volunteers in 1913. When the Easter Rising occurred, he had charge of the battalion stationed at Boland's Mill – one of the key strategic points seized by the rebels in Dublin city – and his indecisive leadership has since been the subject of much comment. The only surviving senior commander of 1916, he was elected president of the newly-created revolutionary parliament, Dáil Éireann, in 1919. His departure to the United States in June of that year to seek American recognition of an Irish republic and to secure funding meant that he was absent for part of the military campaign for independence. His return to Dublin in December 1920 was followed by the disastrous IRA assault, at his direction, on the Custom House in May 1921, which replicated the failed pitched-battle model of 1916 and damaged the military standing of the IRA. The truce that followed shortly afterwards led to inconclusive talks between de Valera and the British Prime Minister David Lloyd George in July 1921. De Valera's decision not to attend the second round has since been a source of speculation and controversy. He rejected the resulting Treaty, signed on 6 December 1921, and later resigned as president of Dáil Éireann. Over the following years, de Valera became increasingly frustrated at the futility of being on the political margins – his party, Sinn Féin, abstained from attending the Free State Dáil – prompting him to form his own party, Fianna Fáil, in 1926. It too was initially an abstentionist party, but the risk of being cast in the same irrelevant mould as Sinn

Féin, together with some adroit manoeuvring on de Valera's part that allowed him to reinterpret the contentious oath as an 'empty formula', resulted in the Fianna Fáil deputies taking their seats in the Dáil in August 1927.[12] From the outset, the party acted as a government-in-waiting, and in 1932 de Valera led his deputies onto the government benches where he remained almost continuously in power, with the exception of two brief interludes (1948–1951 and 1954–1957), until his election to the presidency.

EMERGENCE AS PRESIDENT

O'Kelly had been re-elected unopposed in 1952. There had been some privately expressed hope within Fianna Fáil that the outgoing President would stand aside, paving the way for de Valera to depart to the Áras and allowing Seán Lemass to become Taoiseach (Whelan, 2011: 94). O'Kelly, in fact, had no real desire to serve a second term, expressing the view in April 1950 that he would not seek re-election 'if I have my way' (*Evening Mail*, 26 April 1950). However, the possibility of de Valera retiring from active politics at that stage was unlikely, and, consequently, as the *Irish Independent* reported, O'Kelly was 'prevailed upon' (*Irish Independent*, 4 April 1952). As the constitution allows for two seven-year terms only, the next presidential election was scheduled for 1959. Given the private discussions that had seemingly taken place in 1952, when Fianna Fáil looked for a candidate seven years later it was hardly surprising that de Valera was the obvious choice. But although his retirement as Taoiseach had been the subject of speculation for some time, there was still shock at a meeting of the parliamentary party on 15 January 1959 when he announced his intention to resign as Taoiseach and to make himself available for the forthcoming presidential election: 'several members, including government ministers, left the meeting with tears in their eyes' (Whelan, 2011: 114). Clearly, the concept of a Fianna Fáil party not led by its founding father was one with which it was difficult for many to come to terms.

De Valera was twice successful in presidential contests, making him the only candidate in the history of the presidency to have won two contested elections. But that he still had the potential by 1959 to be divisive was reflected in the narrowness of his victory over Fine Gael's Seán Mac Eoin, emphasised again seven years later when he defeated Fine Gael's Tom O'Higgins in 1966 by a slender margin of just over 10,000 votes. Of the second election, his official biographers noted that some people thought that it should be unanimously agreed that de Valera remain as President, but he was 'still too controversial a figure to be allowed this honour' (Longford and O'Neill, 1970: 461).

Of the three presidents examined in this chapter, de Valera was by far the most partisan. In nominating himself for a second term, O'Kelly had emphasised the political neutrality of the office. In contrast, de Valera's intention to stand for a second term was announced at a political forum – the Fianna Fáil *ard-fheis* (annual convention) – by Seán Lemass, and his endorsement by that party politicised his candidacy. He had also remained active behind the scenes. That an outgoing President opted to use the Oireachtas nomination process rather than self-nominate provided yet another 'first' in the presidency and presented its own set of challenges. A discussion emerged as to whether an outgoing President *could* be nominated by the Oireachtas or members of the councils.[13] The episode serves as a further example of how procedure was settled during the early presidencies.

The theme of youth was to the forefront of the 1966 campaign. Although the 1960s celebrated a signature date in Ireland's history, they were also a decade of change. A survey conducted on behalf of *The Irish Times* by Vincent Browne and Seán Barrett found that O'Higgins was most popular with younger voters, while de Valera polled best among those over 55. Though one must be careful not to place too much emphasis on a single opinion poll – which came with the caveat of a Dublin bias and an under-representation of lower-income earners – that de Valera's support base appeared to be among older voters was arguably a reflection of changing attitudes.[14] As the dynamic of Irish politics shifted, his departure for the Áras seemed appropriate. Part of Fine Gael's appeal in that election – which explains why the party came so close to defeating a senior commander of 1916 in the year of the golden jubilee – was the emphasis that was placed on youth and energy, and the alternative offered. According to the Fine Gael handbook for canvassers, the men of 1916 were progressive and forward-looking, as was O'Higgins. In the year of the 50th anniversary, it would be appropriate to elect someone who encapsulated those virtues.[15]

The 1966 election provided the first hint of a new type of President. Though unsuccessful, Tom O'Higgins appeared to offer an alternative to the older Presidents. At 49, he was the youngest candidate yet to stand, and his age was very much emphasised throughout the campaign as a point of contrast with the ageing de Valera. On the occasion of his selection, party leader Liam Cosgrave had spoken of how the President symbolised the nation, and that, as such, the occupant should be 'young and active'.[16] The theme of an active President was emphasised throughout his campaign. Echoing his party leader, Tom O'Donnell spoke of the necessity for a 'young, able and energetic'

President, and foresaw a more engaged role in which, for example, the President would promote the country's trading relations.[17] O'Higgins came tantalisingly close to victory; in 13 of the 38 constituencies he out-polled de Valera, while in a further five, de Valera's margin of victory was less than one thousand votes (in the case of Wexford, there were as little as 65 in the difference).

VISION OF OFFICE

The themes of de Valera's inaugural speeches represented continuity with his predecessors: he spoke of the importance of restoring the Irish language and, like O'Kelly, also hoped for an end to partition. These were themes replicated in various speeches he gave during his two terms in office. Speaking at a Fianna Fáil dinner five days after being elected, for example, de Valera expressed the view that the people should not be satisfied until everybody could speak the tongue. This, apart from the question of unity, was the big challenge facing the state (*The Irish Times*, 22 June 1959). Initially de Valera found it difficult to adjust to his new role with reduced political responsibilities. Having had a constant presence for much of the first half of the twentieth century, it must have been peculiar, if not unsettling, for him to have made the transition from a politician accustomed to receiving the seal of office to the man presenting that seal to new ministers. Fears of dictatorship had long since passed, as de Valera took on the role of elder statesman. By the time that he retired from public life in 1973 the working day of the President 'included listening to radio bulletins, dealing with correspondence, attending daily mass in the Áras oratory, signing documents and messages to heads of state, receiving presentations of letters of credence, visiting friends in hospital, chatting with the Taoiseach once a month, and occasionally walking in the grounds and attending cultural events in an official capacity' (Ferriter, 2007: 202). In some respects little had changed since Douglas Hyde took office in 1938.

POLITICAL ROLE

De Valera, like his predecessors, was not an inactive President and there were a number of developments. He referred the Electoral (Amendment) Bill, 1961 to the Supreme Court. He was influenced to do so by the High Court decision on a 1959 electoral bill that had sought to redistribute Dáil seats, and was allegedly designed to give an unfair advantage to Fianna Fáil. That bill was successfully challenged in the High Court by Fine Gael's John O'Donovan, although the decision of Mr Justice Budd was not delivered until 1961. When the new bill introduced by Neil Blaney, Minister for Local Government, passed all its parliamentary stages in 1961, de Valera referred it to the Supreme Court, though there is evidence that this course of action was not unwelcome to the Government (O'Leary, 1979: 61–2). The Supreme Court deemed it to be constitutional. The position of the presidency at the heart of major occasions was also further developed at this time. De Valera's time at the Áras coincided with the 50th anniversaries of 1916 and of the inaugural meeting of the first Dáil in 1919, though he had actually missed the latter because of his imprisonment in Lincoln Jail. The latter occasion afforded him the opportunity to address a joint meeting of the Oireachtas, making him the first President to use this constitutional power. The prominent role that de Valera played at these events helped place the presidency at the centre of major state ceremonies, and followed on from the position at sporting fixtures that had begun during Hyde's term in office.

The visit of American President John F. Kennedy in 1963 was one of the highlights of de Valera's first term and it increased the visibility of the office to the international press that covered the event. The following year – and just six months after Kennedy's assassination – de Valera returned the visit and, like O'Kelly before him, addressed a joint session of Congress. The subject of partition, touched on in his predecessor's speech, was more forcefully to the fore of de Valera's. In tracing the history of the Irish struggle, he made reference to his 1919 visit to America, lamenting that Ireland's unity had since been sundered. Several of the assembled members of the Congress commented on how de Valera had spoken from the heart, but the general reaction was summed up by John McCormack, the Irish-American speaker of the House of Representatives, who said that the American government could do nothing to influence Britain's position on Northern Ireland (*The Irish Times*, 29 May 1964). Nonetheless, that de Valera chose to make partition the keynote of his speech was unsurprising and was in keeping with the views of his long political career.

As already mentioned, de Valera was the most party political of the three presidents under examination. For example, he was called upon to mediate and advise during the arms crisis, a difficult juncture in Fianna Fáil's history. Civil servant Peter Berry learnt on 17 April 1970 of a plan to bring arms and ammunition into Dublin airport. He subsequently consulted with de Valera as to whether he should inform the Taoiseach of a potential security issue (Whelan, 2011: 165). De Valera later intervened when Kevin Boland threatened to resign from the cabinet. He was duly summoned to the Áras where, according to his own account, the President 'foresaw a change to a

Fine Gael-controlled government and pointed out the seriousness of this in the circumstances that existed' (Collins, 2000: 56). Though de Valera was no longer an active politician, he kept a watchful eye over developments within Fianna Fáil.

CONCLUSION

To use the description of Brian Lenihan, Senior, the presidency was seen by many by the 1970s as a 'totem pole', an ancestral symbol to which members of the tribe could pay homage (Walsh, 2008: 412). Between 1938 and 1973, incumbents did little to push the boundaries of the office, and the only significant evolution of its functions came from the legislature rather than the office holder. However, given the fears of dictatorship that surrounded the creation of the office, the manner in which Douglas Hyde conducted his tenure was important in allaying such concerns. By using his discretionary power of referral to the Supreme Court, he demonstrated that the presidency was not a weak office, open to manipulation. Furthermore, the exercising of such powers by both Hyde and de Valera, and the convening of the Council of State by O'Kelly, show that the Presidents were not as inactive as is sometimes suggested. Furthermore, there were hints of themes – such as pluralism and bridge building – that would be to the forefront of later presidencies. In refusing to adhere to the expectations of the GAA, Hyde had shown himself to be a president of all the people, while O'Kelly sought to bridge the civil war divide.

Despite the existence of a somewhat comparable office in the Lord Lieutenant and Governor-General, the presidency brought with it a new set of procedures and it was during these first presidencies that protocol was decided. From placing the President at the heart of major occasions, to the office holder leaving the country for the first time during the O'Kelly years, to de Valera choosing to use the Oireachtas nomination route to contest a second term, all presented a set of challenges to be decided. All three Presidents helped to define the office by fulfilling the role as it had been envisaged. Though some wondered about the necessity for the office, the first three Presidents essentially helped to establish an unknown quantity on firm footing, and won the support and confidence of the ordinary person and political community alike.

NOTES

1. Article 41.2.1 of the Constitution located the place of the woman 'within the home', a position reinforced by article 41.2.2 which stated that mothers 'shall

not be obliged by economic necessity to engage in labour to the neglect of their duties in the home'.

2. De Valera's comments, naturally, were not well received among the loyalist community in Northern Ireland. The *Northern Whig* criticised what it saw as 'certain unmistakably anti-British allusions deliberately introduced by Mr de Valera', while the *Belfast Telegraph* (27 June 1938) claimed that such language served only to deepen the convictions of loyalists opposed to unification in the form of a republic.

3. National Archives of Ireland (hereafter NAI), Office of the President, PRES1/P465, Text of Christmas broadcast, 22 December 1938.

4. NAI, Department of Taoiseach, S13715, Letter from secretary of the GAA to the Taoiseach's office, 21 August 1945.

5. NAI, Office of the President, PRES1/P1238, Correspondence relating to presidential car, August 1983 – March 1939.

6. NAI, Office of the President, PRES1/P464, Protocol, 1938 –1951.

7. NAI, Office of the President, PRES1/P521, Note on President's health and interviews, 22 July 1938.

8. NAI, Office of the President, PRES1/P521, Reception of American Minister, 19 September 1940.

9. NAI, Office of the President, PRES/P4235, Michael McDunphy to Government, 21 February 1949.

10. *Uachtaráin – Séan T Ó Ceallaigh*, TG4 documentary, first aired 25 April 2007.

11. NAI, PRES1/P5418B, Speech at dinner held by Irish Societies of New York, 30 March 1959.

12. Article 4 was the most controversial aspect of the Treaty signed in 1921. It required all elected members of the Irish parliament to swear 'true faith and allegiance to the Constitution of the Irish Free State as by law established and that I will be faithful to H.M. King George V, his heirs and successors'. Republicans interpreted this as an oath of allegiance to the British Crown and argued that it could not be reconciled with their oath of allegiance to the Irish Republic. Those deputies who refused to take the oath were barred from taking their seats in the Dáil.

13. The nomination process requires the support of 20 members of the Oireachtas or the support of four county and/or city councils. An incumbent President can self-nominate.

14. The opinion poll was carried out on O'Connell Street in Dublin city centre on Saturday 21 May 1966 between 2.30pm and 4.30pm and had a sample size of 300 people. University College Dublin Archives (hereafter UCDA), Fine Gael Presidential Election Papers, P39/PR/104, Results of opinion poll, May 1966.

15. UCDA, Fine Gael Presidential Election Papers, P39/PR/87, 'Points for Guidance' handbook.

16. UCDA, Fine Gael Presidential Election Papers, P39/PR/86, Statement by Cosgrave on O'Higgins's selection, 2 February 1966.

17. UCDA, Fine Gael Presidential Election Papers, P39/PR/90, Speech by Tom O'Donnell at Clare convention, 6 March 1966.

6

THE POLITICS OF A 'NON-POLITICAL' OFFICE, 1973–1990

KEVIN RAFTER

INTRODUCTION

This chapter focuses on a period when efforts were made to redefine the office of president while also considering the role of the presidency during a period of considerable party political strife. Each of the three presidencies – Erskine Childers (1973–1974), Cearbhall Ó Dálaigh (1974–1976) and Patrick Hillery (1976–1990) – is examined in terms of the personal background of the incumbent, how they were selected for the position and their role while in office. By its very nature – due to the activism of Childers, the resignation of Ó Dálaigh and Hillery's limited assessment of the role – the discussion will focus on the theme of the power of the president.

The 1973 to 1990 period commenced with the electorate voting into office their preference for president but was followed by two unelected presidencies, a resignation crisis, and a largely unremarkable two-term presidency. The period undoubtedly brought new focus on the office, and two clear areas of difference from the first three presidencies emerge, namely, increased activity as well as issues of presidential cohabitation with the government of the day.

In this first instance Childers's high level of activity in accepting domestic engagements coupled with a willingness to travel abroad was a departure point for the presidency. Ó Dálaigh and Hillery continued with this heightened representation role. Yet, none of these three presidents – in what can be considered the presidency's middle period – set out to radically recast the office. There was a real sense of the status quo prevailing in their respective approaches to the position. The redefinitions that they brought to the position were relatively unambitious, and throughout this period the 'non-political' nature of the office was effectively reinforced by means of limited presidential action. Alongside this 'limited activism' another new challenge emerged in the guise of cohabitation and managing the tricky relationship between governments led by a party leader who differed from the president's party tradition. This was a particular feature when Liam Cosgrave as leader of Fine Gael was Taoiseach between 1973 and 1977 – a four-year period which opened with the latter stages of de Valera's second term and remarkably took in his three immediate successors.

ERSKINE CHILDERS, 1973–1974

Erskine Childers was, in the words of one of his party colleagues, 'a curious paradox, really' (Andrews 2007: 58). His Anglo-Irish accent and English public school education did not make him a natural member of Fianna Fáil. He was on the liberal wing of a conservative parliamentary party (speaking in favour of the public availability of contraception) and was a moderniser in a party not defined by reformers (as health minister he campaigned against excessive alcohol consumption and smoking in public). Following the death of his first wife in 1950, Childers married again two years later, this time to Rita Dudley. Since she was a Catholic and Childers was a Protestant, the Catholic Archbishop of Dublin, John Charles McQuaid, advised against what was a mixed marriage but the couple celebrated at a small, private ceremony in Paris. Childers's long political career was defined by a strong work ethic: 'a man with a single-minded, intense interest in the work assigned to him' (McInerney, 1974). His personality was distant and reserved but colleagues tolerated his eccentricities. On one occasion ahead of a Dáil vote he approached Fianna Fáil Senator Mark Killilea – thinking he was an opposition TD – and asked whether he would mind 'pairing' with him as he had a function to attend.

Childers was born in London in December 1905 and graduated from Cambridge University. Despite this background he had a strong republican pedigree; his father, also Erskine, had been an adviser to the delegation which negotiated the Anglo-Irish Treaty, which he ultimately opposed, and he had been executed during the civil war. After university Childers worked in France prior to being appointed as an advertising executive with the *Irish Press* newspaper in 1931. He held this position until 1935 when he was appointed secretary of the Federation of Irish Manufacturers, a role he retained until 1944 (Young, 1985). Childers was selected to contest the 1938 general election but before the campaign got underway he was keen to resolve the matter of his Irish citizenship. In April 1938 he wrote to de Valera explaining that as his late father had died prior to independence he did not in fact automatically qualify for citizenship through his Irish mother. It was necessary for the government to confirm citizenship for Childers, his brother and his mother following the introduction of new legislation (Section 5 of the Citizenship Act, 1935). Certificates of naturalisation were issued to all three on 25 April 1938 – to Mary Childers, as she herself had rendered distinguished service to the Irish nation, and to her two sons, Robert and Erskine, based on their late father's 'distinguished service'.[1]

Successfully elected as a Dáil deputy in 1938, Childers was returned at 11 national elections representing Athlone-Longford (1938–1948), Longford-Westmeath (1948–1961) and Monaghan (1961–1974). It was said in 1944 that there was 'no more conscientious or hard-working Deputy in Dáil Eireann' (Kenny, 1974). He enjoyed a long ministerial career, serving under de Valera, Lemass and Lynch. A parliamentary secretary from 1944 to 1948, Childers was a cabinet minister in every Fianna Fáil government from 1951 to 1973. He served in a number of different ministries: Posts and Telegraphs (1951–1954; 1966–1969), Lands and Fisheries (1957–1959); Transport and Power (1959–1969) and Health (1969–1973). Lynch appointed him Tánaiste in 1969. His ministerial record has been dismissed as 'spectacularly unsuccessful' (Browne and Farrell, 1981: 39) but another source credited him as Ireland's 'most successful' Minister for Health (Nowlan, 1974).

Childers backed Jack Lynch during the 1969–1970 'Arms crisis' when two government ministers were dismissed from cabinet amid allegations of illegal importation of guns for use in Northern Ireland. At the fractious Fianna Fáil *ard-fheis* (convention) in 1971, when internal divisions were played out in public amid scuffles and fistfights, the cameras captured the image of the dignified Childers sitting at the top table with his head in his hands. During this period he emerged as a strong voice at cabinet in support of Lynch's moderate approach to the nascent crisis. Childers authored two 'thought-provoking' papers in August and September 1969 on the government's policy on Northern Ireland (Keogh, 2008: 197–8). The contents reflected his outright opposition to the use of violence: 'Everything that I had said presumes a tough control of the new IRA. Their incursion will spell disaster. The IRA can only destroy any reputation we have and discourage unity in the Six Counties'.[2] The two papers also show the progressive thoughts of the then 64-year-old Childers on ecumenism and the constitutional ban on divorce.

SELECTION AND ELECTION

Erskine Childers, by now a veteran politician, had effectively withdrawn from frontline activity following Fianna Fáil's electoral defeat in the 1973 general election at the time when Jack Lynch was addressing the uncertainty about candidate selection for an imminent presidential election. Lynch's name was mentioned as a possible candidate but the party leader ruled out moving from the parliamentary arena. Childers had adopted a similar stance while a minister in the outgoing government – and had rung political correspondents and issued a statement indicating his lack of interest in the presidency – but with Fianna Fáil now in opposition it was reported that 'his attitude may have changed' (*The Irish Times*, 4 April 1973).

The request to Childers to contest the presidential election came from Lynch and had the unanimous backing of the Fianna Fáil parliamentary party at a meeting on 6 April 1973. In his first media conference after securing the party nomination Childers laid emphasis on redefining the office: 'I have consented to be candidate, on the understanding that, if I am elected, I will be able to expand the dimension and character of the Presidency, and only on that condition' (*The Irish Times*, 7 April 1973). In this first appearance, prior to having his views shaped by the campaign itself and, indeed, later by the realities of office, Childers mentioned prioritising the place of young people – or 'youth' – and inviting representatives from the two communities in Northern Ireland to the presidential residence, Áras and Uachtaráin. Beyond these two specific areas the other issues identified were general and vague, with Childers promising that he 'would not create division, but would encourage enlightened examination' (*The Irish Times*, 7 April 1973).

In an obvious acknowledgement of the limitations of the role in contemporary politics, he said that the president should look to the future, an area that was no doubt regarded as safe ground, 'to speak about shaping the nation, not dictating solutions but asking for reasoned discussion on new policies.' He saw the presidency outside the Áras in terms of public engagements, while recognising the need to avoid conflict with the government of the day. In this regard, he said, the president should be able to seek out the views of those 'engaged in constructive policy-shaping, and ask that all people should weigh up their proposals without committing the government or any political party to making decisions' (*The Irish Times*, 7 April 1973).

While asserting that the constitutional limitations of the office had previously been too narrowly interpreted, Childers declared that the president 'could not be a personal innovator.' So while setting out to 're-define' the role,

Childers was openly accepting the limitations of the office – and he offered the experience of his long ministerial career as an advantage in avoiding controversy. Grappling with the limitations of the president's powers while attempting to identify new themes for the office – as articulated by Childers on 7 April 1973 – would in many respects become a challenge for all subsequent presidential candidates in seeking to provide this non-political office with added legitimacy and relevance.

During the election campaign Childers expanded on his initial thoughts for the office. The one specific new proposal to emerge was the establishment of a 'think tank' to advise the president on new ideas for the Ireland of the 1990s, to debate long-term development and to help avoid 'all the evils of an industrial society'. Crucially, however, this 'think tank' was to reach conclusions by popular consensus so as to avoid intervening directly in the affairs of government (Walsh, 1973). The Childers campaign undoubtedly borrowed from themes identified by Fine Gael's Tom O'Higgins seven years previously in promising a presidency that was more accessible and more relevant to contemporary life. O'Higgins had been narrowly defeated by de Valera in 1966. He did not contest the 1973 Dáil election as he had already been selected as a presidential candidate in the election due in the same year.

Fianna Fáil ran a high-profile personalised campaign, a template of sorts for its 1977 Dáil election campaign. Childers visited every constituency in what newspapers reported as a 3,000-mile tour, making use of a specially converted bus with its own speaking platform. The campaign bus was mocked by opponents who labelled it 'Wanderly Wagon', a reference to a popular children's programme on the public television station, RTÉ. For such an experienced political figure, however, Childers was not a natural campaigner. David Andrews recalled his arrival in Dun Laoghaire:

> There was quite a good crowd of people out to see him and the famous bus. As he got off the bus he spotted a newspaper seller and bought an evening paper. He then proceeded to walk down the road reading it and completely ignoring the welcoming party, which went down rather badly (Andrews, 2007: 58).

It was an approach that would not have survived the more media-driven presidential campaigns after 1990. Voting took place on 30 May 1973. With a turnout of 62.2 per cent, Childers received 635,867 votes (51.9 per cent) against O'Higgins's total of 587,771 (48.0 per cent).

VISION OF THE OFFICE

The Childers inauguration took place on 25 June 1973, when he became the fourth President of Ireland. Some 450 invited guests attended the 20-minute formal ceremony which was broadcast 'live in colour' by RTÉ television (Grogan, 1973).[3] Security plans for the event noted that it would last for all of 54 minutes, and that included arrival and departure times. Little pomp or ceremony surrounded the presidential speech. In a short address, Childers noted that, 'making a meaningful contribution to the harmony among Irishmen and Irishwomen is all I desire'.[4] He did not attempt to stake out an over-arching theme for his presidency or expand on ideas floated during the campaign. Interestingly, the national newspapers opted to concentrate their coverage on the significance of the interdenominational religious service in St Patrick's Cathedral that had preceded the inauguration ceremony at Dublin Castle. As an editorial in *The Irish Times* put it, 'in religion, as in other things, Erskine Childers has a mind which reaches out, and his choice of readings yesterday was not only an expression of a broad as well as a deep Christian faith, but an appreciation of the faith of others' (*The Irish Times*, 26 June 1973).

Childers died suddenly on 17 November 1974. His short tenure allowed insufficient time to truly define his vision of the presidency or make real in any significant way the promise to add a new dimension to the office. Nevertheless, the immediate and historical assessments of this short-life presidency have been remarkably positive. Newspaper coverage reflected the view that Ireland had lost a highly popular and visible president while with the benefit of greater distance, Dermot Keogh (2008: 380) subsequently described Childers as 'the first of the modern presidents' based on his active diary of public engagements. As President, Childers was undoubtedly visible in a way none of his predecessors had been. For example, his schedule was frequently mentioned in the 'What's on today' noticeboard column in *The Irish Times*. Listings of presidential engagements open to the public included an address delivered in the Metropole Hotel in Cork on the topic 'Ireland in the 1990s' (20 September 1973); a literary festival at the Derryhale Hotel in Dundalk where the President read poetry (25 October 1973); and a lecture on Ireland's architectural heritage at the RDS Concert Hall in Dublin under the auspices of An Taisce, an Irish heritage body (25 September 1974). There were other events which, while adding to the President's public visibility, did not always clearly fit into Childers's desire to redefine the office: opening a cricket festival week in Cork in April 1974, for instance, and opening a new swimming pool in Portarlington in June 1974.

POLITICAL ROLE

This new wave of presidential activism also reached into the international arena. The organisation of the Childers state visit to Belgium in May 1974 by the President's staff (themselves drawn from the civil service) suggests a lack of prior experience in dealing with the logistics and protocol of presidential foreign travel. There were questions about whether the President would need a valet (no) and whether Mrs Childers would need a 'hairdresser in attendance' (yes), while one early official memo observes of travel arrangements: 'for prestige and security purposes [a] special plane chartered by Aer Lingus would seem essential'.[5] This decision to be an active and visible President brought tensions with the civil service staff responsible for ensuring that invitations and speeches met with government approval. Childers's wife, Rita, would later recall that Áras an Uachtaráin was 'rigidly administered by the civil service':

> In the beginning long tedious memoranda appeared on the President's desk practically every day setting out various reasons why such invitations should be accepted or not 'under the Constitution of the Presidency'. Eventually these screeds so infuriated the late President that he went into town himself to buy the largest felt pen on the market to write the words 'over-ruled' on such memoranda. If he had not done so he would have sat in a chair for most of his all too few days there (Childers, 1976).

Garret FitzGerald, Minister for Foreign Affairs in the 1973–1977 Fine Gael–Labour coalition, was aware of the difficulties Childers was experiencing – as FitzGerald put it – 'in coming to terms with the constraints of office as a constitutional president' (FitzGerald, 1991: 254). Within weeks of his election Childers confided in FitzGerald that he was considering resigning. The circumstances arose following communication from Taoiseach Liam Cosgrave that the President could not proceed with his election promise to establish a 'think tank' to consider Ireland's future wellbeing. Childers felt he had been placed in 'an impossible situation' and, according to FitzGerald, it took 'resources of tact and diplomacy' to dissuade him from leaving office (FitzGerald, 1991: 254). With no constitutional issues at stake Childers would most likely have been within his rights in convening such a body. In allowing Cosgrave the power of veto, however, Childers was effectively conceding his own powerlessness in circumstances where the government of the day narrowly interpreted the President's role. It was an experience shared by his two immediate successors in their relations with Cosgrave.

In Dáil tributes following Childers's sudden death in November 1974, the Labour leader Brendan Corish remarked that the fourth president had 'added a new dimension to that office, one which will be quickly imitated and followed by his successors' (*Dáil Debates*, 276: 8, 19 November 1974). In truth, however, Childers had not been long enough in office to deliver on the challenges he set himself when accepting the Fianna Fáil nomination for the 1973 presidential election: to redefine the dimension and character of the presidency. He did not proceed with the idea of using the Áras to bring the two communities in Northern Ireland together, and, surprisingly in light of this promise, no politicians from north of the border received formal invitations to his inauguration.

Childers also showed a reluctance to directly challenge Cosgrave's restrictive attitude to the presidency. This was most clearly evident when plans for the proposed presidential 'think tank' were stymied. The dispute behind closed doors over the 'think tank' is an early example of a pattern of difficult relations that existed between Cosgrave and the presidency. Had Childers lived, it is possible that the strained relationship with Cosgrave might have led to public controversy. Such issues of problematic cohabitation between a head of state and a head of government from a different party political background also featured in the Ó Dálaigh and Hillery presidencies – quite dramatically in the first case. It is arguable that the Fine Gael leader viewed the incumbents from a party political perspective and that this narrowed his regard for the holders of the office. Interestingly, when Childers hosted a dinner for members of the Council of State and their spouses in early 1974, Cosgrave declined an invitation despite this being an innovation by a new President only a short time in office.[6]

Notwithstanding his premature death, through his highly visible presidency Childers succeeded in reconnecting the office with the wider public and commenced an era of presidential activism, though defined in less ambitious terms than by his successors. Noting the 'spontaneous outpouring of affection' when news of the President's death was announced, a leader writer in *The Irish Times* observed that the 'strenuous timetable of what must often have seemed a trivial round of openings and commemorations would daunt many a younger man' (*The Irish Times*, 18 November 1974).

Cearbhall Ó Dálaigh, 1974–1976

Born in February 1911, Cearbhall Ó Dálaigh had been a Fianna Fáil activist in the 1930s. He sought to establish a national political career but was unsuccessful in both Dáil and Seanad contests in 1948 and again in 1951. He worked as Irish language editor with the *Irish Press* newspaper from 1931 to 1940, at the same time as Childers worked there, while also building up his legal career. His first journalistic assignment was – ironically in light of both men's subsequent routes to the Áras – to interview Douglas Hyde on his retirement from University College Dublin. De Valera appointed Ó Dálaigh as Attorney General on two occasions (1946–1948 and 1951–1953) and in 1953 he was appointed to the Supreme Court. He became Chief Justice in 1961, a role he filled until 1973 when he was nominated as Ireland's judicial representative in the European Court.

Selection as President

Following the death of Erskine Childers, speculation focused on the idea of an agreed candidate from the world beyond politics. The Fine Gael–Labour government was keen to avoid an electoral contest. There were differing views within Fianna Fáil about the party's approach, although Jack Lynch's name was widely mentioned. The government prepared a list of possible agreed candidates and this was sent to Lynch for consideration. The coalition favoured Rita Childers, widow of the late President, who had agreed to have her name included on the list. What followed, however, was a bizarre and messy episode. Lynch requested that discussions with Cosgrave remain private until he secured Fianna Fáil backing for Rita Childers. But when the story appeared in the newspapers there was considerable anger in Fianna Fáil circles that the party was being 'bounced' into a decision based on a government 'leak'.

Political correspondent Dick Walsh noted that government support for Mrs Childers was 'looked upon by leading members of the Opposition as a gesture of expediency' (Walsh, 1974a). The unsigned Backbencher column in *The Irish Times* – generally written by John Healy – summarised the outcome: 'while the men were still squaring off the earth on Erskine's grave, Liam takes Jack aside, makes the ritual noises about an agreed candidate – and before Jack can call the lads together to sound them out, Liam leaks the news to the press' (Backbencher, 1974). It subsequently emerged, however, that there had not been a deliberate leak; rather, a government minister had inadvertently confirmed that Mrs Childers was the agreed candidate, believing that an announcement had been made public (FitzGerald, 1991: 315).

Following several hours of discussion at a parliamentary party meeting on 27 November 1974 Lynch publicly confirmed that he would not be a candidate but neither was the party going to acquiesce in the government's preference for Rita Childers. Fianna Fáil figures mooted as possible candidates included George Colley (a prominent former minister), Vivion de Valera (son of the party founder and a long-standing TD) and Joseph Brennan (a former minister and the party's deputy leader). But Lynch had other ideas. He phoned his former cabinet colleague Patrick Hillery, who was now Ireland's European Commissioner. Hillery had been sounded out as a possible candidate for the 1973 presidential election but opted to remain in his European position. As Hillery later recalled of the second request: 'When Childers died, Jack contacted me. He said: "The party wanted to know would you go for the presidency, but I don't think you would want to". I said "I don't". Then Jack asked: "Would you ask Cearbhall Ó Dálaigh?"' (Walsh, 2008: 413). Hillery duly made contact with Ó Dálaigh, who had a Fianna Fáil background but who was now a European Court judge based in Luxembourg. After considering the offer for 24 hours, Ó Dálaigh accepted in a phone call: 'he was reluctant, but in view of the times that were in it he accepted' (Walsh, 2008: 414).

While Fianna Fáil was secretly attempting to confirm a presidential candidate Rita Childers added to public confusion, and surprised many of her supporters, by declaring an interest in being a non-party candidate. The government's attachment to Rita Childers, however, was far less than its desire to avoid an election and, with Fianna Fáil clearly signalling its intent on nominating an alternative candidate, support rapidly ebbed away from the widow of the late president. On 28 November 1974 Labour issued a statement confirming that its parliamentary party had 'empowered the Labour Ministers through the Government to reach agreement with Fianna Fáil on a Presidential candidate' (Walsh, 1974b). Lynch formally wrote to Cosgrave on 28 November 1974 informing him that Fianna Fáil was nominating Ó Dálaigh to fill the presidential vacancy: 'He… is willing to accept nomination if the three parties represented in Oireachtas Eireann will agree' (Walsh, 1974b).

An unedifying game of behind-the-scenes political horse-trading was nearing an end. The government had apparently already rejected Ó Dálaigh as an agreed candidate (Walsh, 1974a). Moreover, correspondence from Cosgrave to Lynch noted the government's regret that agreement could not have been reached on any of the names on the list presented to the Fianna Fáil leader on 21 November 1974.[7] Nevertheless, the Fianna Fáil move, combined with its opposition to Rita Childers and a government desire to avoid an election, ultimately secured the position for Ó Dálaigh, whose nomination papers were signed, as he requested, by representatives of the three main political parties.

Ó Dálaigh's candidacy was confirmed on 29 November 1974. Despite being an agreed candidate, his nomination was widely welcomed: 'unlike so many eminent jurists, his personality has not been dehydrated by his profession' (*The Irish Times*, 30 November 1974). When nominations closed on 3 December 1974 the sole candidate was at his home in Kilquade in County Wicklow. He invited the media for tea and sandwiches before telling the journalists that he had no concerns about securing the position without an election. He also deftly sidestepped controversial questions – for example, about European political unity: 'political means are something outside the line of my activity' – and was sufficiently vague about plans for his term of office: 'a President's contribution is what he endeavours to make himself in the years he has lived before he has attained office' (*The Irish Times*, 4 December 1974).

VISION OF THE OFFICE

Ó Dálaigh clearly accepted the limitations of the office, and in this respect his views were similar to those of his immediate predecessor. He observed in one pre-inauguration interview:

> You cannot take out of a vessel more than there is in it. There are many functions, which I will be called upon to discharge on the advice and instructions of the Government. Necessarily, and quite properly, I shall have no views to offer on the great political decisions, which are being debated in the community. I must be above all that (Ellis, 1974).

Alongside his distinguished legal career, Ó Dálaigh had strong links with cultural organisations and the national council on alcoholism. He was keen to associate with these groups so as to provide 'moral support' for their activities (Ellis, 1974). In this regard, the new president was setting down a path that later presidencies (Robinson, McAleese and Higgins) would follow in strengthening the non-constitutional role of the office.

The inauguration address was wide-ranging and touched on personal and political matters. Ó Dálaigh paid tribute to Flann O'Brien, quoted Standish O'Grady and Oliver Cromwell, and drew laughter in mentioning his 'life-long difficulty with elections'. Contemporary events were also mentioned when Ó Dálaigh expressed the hope that the Provisional IRA's temporary Christmas truce would be 'prolonged indefinitely'. In his inauguration address the fifth president was from the outset also more in tune with the approaches later adopted by Robinson, McAleese and Higgins than with those who had held office previously (or, indeed, with the two Hillery addresses). He set down a template to be followed by several of his successors when he observed that while Irish presidents did not have policies they could have themes, and his would be 'community spirit'.

Unlike his predecessors, Ó Dálaigh's previous career had not involved an active public role. At the time of his inauguration one commentator remarked on his 'awkwardness' in front of the camera (Gray, 1974). He has been described as 'a very sensitive person' (Andrews, 2007: 62) while FitzGerald recorded that although popular Ó Dálaigh 'did not seem entirely happy in the job and did not adjust easily to his new position'. He speculated that Ó Dálaigh and his wife regretted taking the position and that this may have been 'a contributory factor' in his resignation (FitzGerald, 1991: 315). Whatever about the accuracy of this latter assessment, the record shows that the fifth president continued with the highly visible diary of public engagements of his predecessor. He also had a strong international profile, visiting France and Spain, and becoming the first head of state to visit the European institutions.

POLITICAL ROLE

As had been the case during the Childers presidency, Ó Dálaigh was also to experience the dismissive attitude that Liam Cosgrave showed to the office of President. There was infrequent contact. Ó Dálaigh later accused Cosgrave of failing to keep him 'generally informed on matters of domestic and international policy' as required under Article 28.5.2 of the constitution.[8] The two office holders had only four such meetings, described by Ó Dálaigh as 'bright, breezy, chatty, but carefully non-communicative on policy matters. The Taoiseach would gratefully accept an Irish whiskey, [inquired how the President found life in the Áras] and talked of this and that of no constitutional relevance'.[9] Ó Dálaigh admitted that the lack of contact baffled him and was both 'a grave constitutional default on his [Cosgrave's] part' and 'a calculated act of defiance of the protocol'.[10] Cosgrave, however, took a differ-ent view, arguing that he had complied with the constitutional requirement in having met de Valera once, Childers five times and Ó Dálaigh four times. He also noted that in his final 15 months as Taoiseach Jack Lynch had met de Valera on only four separate occasions (*Dáil Debates*, 294: 430, 23 November 1976). The reality of cohabitation, however, might suggest that the Fine Gael leader needed to make a greater effort in a relationship with a President from a Fianna Fáil background than Lynch might have needed to do with a President from his own political tradition.

Tensions with the Cosgrave government were fuelled in part by the President's decision in March 1976 to consult the Council of State on the Criminal Law (Jurisdiction) Bill. The government had said that its advice was that the legislation was constitutional, a view which was subsequently endorsed by the Supreme Court. There was renewed tension when in September 1976 the President decided to consult the Council of State on the Emergency Powers Bill and the Criminal Law Bill. The legislation had been prompted by the heightened security situation related to the conflict in Northern Ireland. Loyalist paramilitaries had set off bombs in Dublin and a number of other locations in the Republic in early July 1976, leaving 34 people dead, while at the end of the same month Provisional IRA landmines outside the British Ambassador's residence in Dublin killed the ambassador and a member of the embassy staff. Ó Dálaigh was on holidays in County Kerry where he heard of the national emergency announcement from read-ing the newspapers.

Following a meeting of the Council of State, Ó Dálaigh signed the Criminal Law Bill into law but opted, quite correctly in one assessment (Lee, 1989: 482), to refer the second piece of legislation to the Supreme Court. The Emergency Powers Bill proposed allowing a person to be detained for up to seven days without charge. Ó Dálaigh's response was criticised in private by some min-isters but there was no public conflict with the President. The Supreme Court ultimately found the legislation to be in keeping with the constitution, and on Saturday 16 October 1976 the President signed the bill into law. Two days later on Monday 18 October 1976 the Minister for Defence Paddy Donegan gave vent to his strongly held view that the President in referring the bill had acted incorrectly. His intervention, and the Taoiseach's subsequent response, led to the single biggest controversy to engulf the office of President. Speaking before a military audience at Columb Barracks in Mullingar, Donegan reportedly described Ó Dálaigh as a 'thundering disgrace' for delaying the legislation, though it is widely acknowledged that the actual words used took a cruder form (Keogh, 2008: 402).

The Minister for Justice, Patrick Cooney, who was present at the same function, clearly understood the import of the intemperate remarks. Cooney immediately phoned Cosgrave. Once the attack was publicised, Donegan, having considered the implications of his words and his own position as Defence Minister in attacking the President, who was the titular commander-in-chief of the defence forces, offered to resign. Cosgrave, however, refused the resignation offer and his attitude over the following days towards Ó Dálaigh, and the office he held, has left a significant blemish on his political record.

Ó Dálaigh heard of Donegan's remarks on the 6.30pm RTÉ radio news. A presidential aide had in fact received a phone call from a journalist alerting the Áras to the news story. 'It was the first item. Short and to the point,' Ó Dálaigh later recalled.[11] The President's response was swift. He issued instructions that no government representative except the Taoiseach was to be admitted to the Áras without his approval. He then prepared some notes, anticipating a phone call from the Taoiseach. Cosgrave made contact with the Áras at 10pm on that Monday evening. Ó Dálaigh recorded that the Taoiseach said that the minister's remarks were 'unofficial'.[12] No apology on Cosgrave's behalf, or on behalf of his government, was offered. Ó Dálaigh said he was prepared to meet with the Taoiseach but he did not wish to discuss the matter over the phone. Cosgrave did not take up the offer and would only speak once more with the President before his resignation four days later. That same evening the Government Information Service issued a statement noting Donegan's regret at the incident and his intention to apologise to the President.

Donegan's formal request for a meeting was made on Tuesday morning 19 October 1976 but Ó Dálaigh declined. Following a cabinet meeting to consider the impasse Cosgrave again briefly spoke with the President by phone at 12 noon to inform him that a written apology from Donegan was being prepared. In what must have registered as a warning Ó Dálaigh informed Cosgrave that he had 'already taken certain preliminary steps'.[13] Donegan's letter – which offered his 'sincere and humble apology' was received at the Áras at 5.45pm on Tuesday 19 October 1976.[14] Ó Dálaigh drafted his reply that same evening but with no typist available in the Áras he opted to sleep on the text. The cabinet met to consider the reply on Wednesday 20 October 1976. Ó Dálaigh, while not threatening resignation, observed that his relationship with the Defence Minister had been 'irreparably breached not only by what you said yesterday but also because of the place where, and the persons before whom, you chose to make your outrageous criticism' (FitzGerald, 1991: 316).[15] The President had chosen his words carefully but as far as he was concerned 'irreparably breached' meant, 'the Minister left/was removed; or I didn't stay. Could I have spelt it out more clearly or more directly?'[16] There was little in the correspondence from which the Fine Gael and Labour ministers could have drawn any comfort. The President had not softened his words in relation to Donegan: 'have you any conception of your responsibilities as a Minister of State and, in particular, as Minister for Defence?'

As the government considered its next move, which appeared to be that the exchange of correspondence had brought the affair to a close, the controversy was raised in the Dáil later that day, Wednesday 20 October 1976. Cosgrave was asked what action he proposed to take in light of Donegan's 'gross insult' (*Dáil Debates*, 293: 35–6, 20 October 1976). Cosgrave noted his regret 'that the Minister should have made any remark which slighted the President' and stated that Donegan had 'offered a full and unreserved apology' (*Dáil Debates*, 293: 35–6, 20 October 1976). It is likely that Donegan's resignation combined with contrition from the government would have ended the controversy at this point. But Cosgrave was apparently intent on protecting his party colleague, and, with little sign of unrest from his coalition partners in Labour, he refused to be drawn in subsequent questioning. Jack Lynch said he was unhappy with the 'taciturn and totally indefensible reply' and duly moved a motion of no confidence in Donegan.

In the Dáil debate on the Fianna Fáil motion on Thursday 21 October 1976 Cosgrave maintained his stance of attempting to see out the controversy from a party political perspective. He repeated his view that his minister had made a full and unreserved apology (*Dáil Debates*, 293: 155–63, 21 October 1976). But the Taoiseach did nothing to ease any slight the President felt either personally or in respect of the office he held, and was, in the words of one of his ministers, 'unwise to the point of provocation' (FitzGerald, 1991: 316). Donegan did not contribute to the debate.

Ó Dálaigh had departed for Wexford late on Wednesday afternoon for a series of official engagements. He returned to the Áras in the early hours of Thursday morning, 21 October 1976, and several hours later received the new ambassador from New Zealand as the Dáil debated the no confidence motion. Garret FitzGerald, who was in attendance at the Áras in his capacity as Minister for Foreign Affairs, admitted to Ó Dálaigh that he was 'personally dismayed at the recent incident'.[17] Ó Dálaigh observed from reading newspaper commentary that 'the matter is over as far as the government was concerned'.[18] He listened to the radio news at 6.30 pm where the Dáil motion dominated the headlines and noted that, 'the matter was disposed of in a short debate'.[19] By a majority of five votes (63 to 58) the motion calling on Donegan to resign was defeated. Cosgrave's sole priority was to protect his party colleague and – in his words and inaction – he showed little understanding of the seriousness of the situation. It seems that he saw a ministerial casualty as having greater party and governmental consequence than the fall-out from presidential embarrassment. Apart from Cosgrave's two brief telephone conversations, there was no further contact. Ó Dálaigh was, however, more than embarrassed. Within 24 hours of the Dáil vote he had tendered his resignation.

Ó Dálaigh's letter of resignation was sealed at 11.35am on Friday 22 October 1976 and timed for 6pm that evening so that he could fulfil a final public engagement. He left Áras an Uachtaráin at 3pm for the final time. About 90 minutes later Cosgrave – having received news of the arrival of the resignation letter – called an impromptu meeting of several cabinet members. The government's poor handling of the entire episode was only further emphasised by an unsuccessful last-minute attempt to minimise the political fallout by having Donegan finally resign before news of the President's decision was publicly announced (FitzGerald, 1991: 317). A second letter from Donegan – 'of no relevance' according to Ó Dálaigh – was delivered to the President as he was driven with his wife to their home in County Wicklow.[20]

Ó Dálaigh's reason for resigning – 'to protect the dignity and independence of the presidency as an institution' – was a direct rebuke to Cosgrave, who had dismissed such a notion in the previous day's Dáil debate. FitzGerald concluded that Cosgrave had been 'fatally betrayed by his own excessive loyalty' to Donegan (FitzGerald, 1991: 317). Cosgrave undoubtedly acted in a partisan manner and must ultimately share the greatest responsibility for the presidential resignation. As mentioned previously there is sufficient evidence to conclude that the Fine Gael leader had difficulty dealing with presidents from the Fianna Fáil tradition and, more specifically, in the case of Ó Dálaigh he was dealing with someone whom he had not even wanted as President. Childers had encountered difficulties with Cosgrave while Ó Dálaigh's successor, Patrick Hillery, who was only in office for a short period before Cosgrave departed as Taoiseach, also recorded that the Fine Gael–Labour government displayed 'a policy of hostility and accorded the presidency low political status' (Walsh: 2008: 430–1). Interestingly, this assessment of Cosgrave's attitude was supported by the acting British ambassador in Dublin in a report on the controversy submitted to the Foreign Office. In this report – released in 2006

– it was concluded that Cosgrave's response to Donegan's outburst was driven by his 'tough and partisan approach to politics in general … [and an] … over-tender feeling of loyalty to a colleague' (Rapple, 2006).

One final aspect of the controversy is worthy of comment: the implications of Ó Dálaigh's route to the Áras. He had addressed his non-elected status in his inauguration address when being an agreed candidate was not considered a serious issue. It is only possible to speculate about how the affair would have played out had Ó Dálaigh secured the office through a vote of the people. As a directly elected President he might have felt greater personal security in his role and might therefore, through an implicit threat of resignation, have had the potential to cause greater difficulty for Cosgrave's two-party coalition. In this regard, it is interesting to note Ó Dálaigh's subsequent conclusion that he was 'a substitute for an elected President' – an apparent admission that in succeeding Childers as an agreed candidate he lacked a degree of popular legitimacy.[21]

PATRICK HILLERY, 1976–1990

Born in County Clare in 1923, Patrick Hillery was a medical doctor by training, having studied at University College Dublin. He was first elected a TD in 1952 on a Fianna Fáil ticket in Clare that also included Eamon de Valera. A member of Dáil Éireann for 21 years, he spent 12 of those years at the cabinet table in a ministerial career that included Education (1959–1965), Industry and Commerce (1965–1966), Labour (1966–1969) and Foreign Affairs (1969–1973). His frontline political career was relatively unremarkable, judged to have been low key and lacking any sense of urgency (Kennedy, 1976). One obituary writer following Hillery's death in April 2008 observed: 'As a minister, he had ability and ideas but lacked the drive necessary to push his proposals through cabinet or the civil service' (*Daily Telegraph*, 16 April 2008).

The outbreak of conflict in Northern Ireland led to Hillery's most noted interventions. His statement in 1969 that 'we do regard all 32 counties as our territory' raised 'howls of outrage' from the British government, and 12 months later he again offended the British government by crossing the border without informing them that he was going to visit Belfast (McHardy, 2008). His career is also remembered for his strong public support for Jack Lynch at the Fianna Fáil *ard-fheis* in 1971. Hillery was appointed Ireland's first European Commissioner in 1973 but with the Fine Gael–Labour government not offering a second term he was contemplating prolonging his public career through membership of the European Parliament when the first direct elections were held in Ireland. Instead, he found himself the sole nominee to become Ireland's sixth President.

SELECTION AS PRESIDENT

Following the Ó Dálaigh resignation Liam Cosgrave had moved quickly to minimise the ongoing controversy by approaching the Fianna Fáil leader to find an agreed candidate. While there was once more speculation that Jack Lynch would take the position he, in fact, favoured Patrick Hillery as the Fianna Fáil nominee. Hillery's term as Ireland's European Commissioner was coming to an end, and the coalition government had confirmed that he was not going to be reappointed. It was the third time in as many years that Hillery was presented with the opportunity of being Fianna Fáil's presidential nominee. As, when approached at the end of de Valera's second term, and later after Childers's death, Hillery's initial reaction to the idea of succeeding Ó Dálaigh was negative: 'it is very flattering but I would not like to spend seven years a prisoner in the Phoenix Park especially from the point of view of my children' (Walsh, 2008: 418). Following a meeting between the two men, Lynch publicly confirmed Hillery's negative response on 25 October 1976.

The name of the outgoing European Commissioner, however, continued to be mentioned in newspaper reports along with other senior Fianna Fáil figures, including, once again, Vivion de Valera and Joseph Brennan. With continued Fianna Fáil pressure coming on Hillery, Fine Gael and Labour ministers let it be known that they would support his candidacy. Hillery – a 'profoundly reluctant' candidate – acquiesced on 3 November 1976 (Walsh, 2008: 421). The selection was made by a vote of the Fianna Fáil parliamentary party, with Hillery defeating Brennan by 55 votes to 15. His election was thereafter a mere formality; he was the only candidate when nominations closed on 9 November 1976.

VISION OF THE OFFICE

Hillery took the oath of office on 3 December 1976. The inauguration, the third in as many years, was, according to one newspaper report, met by 'international indifference' with no heads of state in attendance (*The Irish Times*, 1 December 1976). The conflict in Northern Ireland was one of the main issues touched upon in Hillery's inauguration address; 'Hillery stresses law and liberty in first speech as President' was the somewhat uninspiring headline in *The Irish Times* (O'Brien, 1976). The address did little to connect the new President with the public, who had once more been denied an opportunity to decide who occupied the Áras. Moreover, Hillery made no attempt to identify his presidency with a specific theme or set of ideas. Seven years later, in marking the start of his second term, again as an agreed candidate, Hillery's inauguration address focused on the prevailing poor economic situation and the use of illegal drugs at a ceremony considered to have been on a 'smaller scale' than previous events (Pyle, 1983).

Hillery was 'a reluctant but safe' choice (Arnold, 2001: 193). In light of Ó Dálaigh's resignation the initial challenge was to keep the presidency out of controversy: in his own words, 'I saw my task as one of restoring the presidency' (Walsh, 2008: 438). That Hillery achieved this objective was supported by Brian Cowen's graveside oration for Hillery in April 2008 when he noted that 'his time in Áras an Uachtaráin was calm and dignified' (Cowen, 2008). A less flattering assessment concluded that stability had been restored 'largely through invisibility and silence' (*Daily Telegraph*, 16 April 2008). In the short term, Hillery's low-key approach assisted in achieving equilibrium, although it may ultimately have undermined perceptions of his own presidency, and even the office itself.

When he started his first term as President, Hillery, at 53 years of age, was younger that the five other men who had served as President. Yet this relative youth mattered little as Hillery adopted a conservative approach. He openly accepted the constraints of the office and he had little inclination to seek to give his presidency a 'theme'. He displayed no ambition to re-orientate or to redefine the role – as he saw it, there were 'no policies to carry out' (Walsh, 2008: 439). Nevertheless, there was continuity, as the activist role pioneered by Childers and followed by Ó Dálaigh was continued. The new President had a busy schedule of domestic engagements but what was novel under his two immediate predecessors now became the norm. There was also a succession of high-profile international trips, with seven state visits in his first term alone, with increased emphasis on the 'trade envoy' role for the President when abroad. The second term deviated little from this routine of domestic engagements combined with foreign travel.

Walsh has argued that Hillery had neither the inclination nor the opportunity to expand significantly the role and profile of the presidency. While essentially correct in the former respect, particularly in light of Hillery's limited ambition for the role, the latter interpretation is open to challenge. As

President, Hillery did little to give his two terms wider public relevance. He worked within a narrow interpretation of the role, as the novelty of the limited activism adopted by his two immediate predecessors lessened over time. In a profile assessment as Hillery's first term came to an end one commentator wrote: 'One way or the other, with a [golf] handicap of seven the President of Ireland has the lowest handicap of any European head of state. So the past six-and-a-half years haven't been entirely wasted' (Kerrigan, 1983). Hillery believed that media coverage of his activities was inadequate and felt aggrieved at the government's failure to provide him with a full-time press officer. Yet, he actually had access to the media should he have wanted to use it. He was embroiled in a bizarre episode in 1979 that saw him bring senior journalists to the Áras to deny that he was experiencing marital difficulties, following rumour and speculation that he would resign because of extra-marital affairs.

In many respects Hillery's two terms resembled an amalgam of the first three low-key presidencies with the increased public activity of his two immediate predecessors. Despite being reluctant to accept the presidency in December 1976 – followed by a sense of frustration in the role and a desire to leave public life – Hillery was returned unopposed for a second seven-year term. As he put it, 'I changed my mind against my better judgement and against my feelings' (Walsh, 2008: 487). The opportunity presented by a second term was not grasped.

POLITICAL ROLE

During the 14 years that he spent as President, Hillery avoided political conflict. For example, he acceded to a government request not to attend the installation of the new Church of Ireland Archbishop of Armagh in April 1980. In November of the same year he declined – again on advice from the Department of the Taoiseach – an invitation to attend a Remembrance Day service organised by the British Legion. It was the first time the President had received an invitation to the service, which commemorated Irish members of the British defence forces who lost their lives in the two world wars. These events were, however, genuine opportunities to provide a wider narrative for the presidency but Hillery failed to take advantage. Alongside these areas for symbolic expansionism Hillery was also presented with the possibility of exercising a previously unused presidential power – described as one that is 'potentially the greatest' available to a President (Gallagher, 1977: 374). The President may 'in his absolute discretion' refuse to dissolve the Dáil leading to a general election on the advice of a Taoiseach 'who has ceased to retain the support of a majority' in parliament.

On 27 January 1982 the minority Fine Gael–Labour coalition was defeated on a Dáil vote on the annual budget. Garret FitzGerald's government had only been in power since the previous summer. Following the Dáil vote, Fianna Fáil publicly indicated its interest in forming a new government without recourse to a general election. Such an eventuality would have required the President to use his constitutional power to refuse dissolution to allow an alternative administration to be formed. Given that it was only eight months since the previous general election – and if a stable Fianna Fáil-led government was a possibility – there was justification in seeing this as the type of scenario envisaged by the framers of the constitution when providing the President with this power.

Hillery had, however, decided from the outset not to exercise this constitutional power (Walsh, 2008: 474–6). His rationale was that to do otherwise would ultimately embroil the President in party politics. He also adopted an exceptionally narrow interpretation of the President's role in being unwilling to consult on the issue; nor was he prepared to offer any public explanation for his decision. Following the government's parliamentary defeat, Hillery instructed his staff that he would only speak to the Taoiseach. The fact that FitzGerald as the defeated Taoiseach did not travel immediately to the Áras created space for additional uncertainty. Charles Haughey contacted the Áras to inform the President that he was available to form a government without a general election being called. With Hillery unwilling to speak to anyone other than FitzGerald, or to explain his stance, other Fianna Fáil figures contacted the Áras, as did independent TD Sean Loftus. Hillery was angry at what he considered political interference with his office and saw the contacts as part of a 'gang mentality' seeking to influence his decision (Walsh, 2008: 480). It subsequently emerged that the President's staff had been verbally threatened as Haughey and his colleagues sought access to Hillery.[22]

Nevertheless, if the President had publicly explained his thinking – and the decision he had already taken – room for any form of pressure, political or otherwise, would have been limited. Moreover, it does not seem an unreasonable action for a President, in determining the appropriateness of using the constitutional provision, to formally consult the outgoing Taoiseach and the individual who might be able to form an alternative administration. By deciding that he would only act through the outgoing Taoiseach, Hillery believed that he was avoiding any personal intervention in the political process. But it is also possible to see Hillery's very decision as itself an inherently political action. Interestingly, when Haughey's minority coalition collapsed later in 1982, Hillery was apparently happy to receive indirect communication from Haughey's opponents in Fianna Fáil who wanted the President to know that dissolving the Dáil could be prevented by a leadership change in the party (Walsh, 2008: 482). In the aftermath of the 1987 general election – when it was unclear that the first meeting of the reconvened Dáil would lead to the election of a new Taoiseach – Hillery had no difficulty in offering advice to the outgoing Taoiseach, Garret FitzGerald (Walsh, 2008: 493). According to Walsh, this tactical approach was intended to 'exert increasing pressure on the Dáil to resolve the deadlock' (Walsh, 2008: 493) but it was nonetheless the type of political intervention Hillery had sought to avoid in February 1982. Hillery's relationship with Haughey was poor and this may have influenced his decision and approach in opening up a direct line of contact. Moreover, Haughey's hostile and threatening communication with Áras staff as the political situation developed would only have reinforced Hillery's viewpoint about Haughey's suitability for office. Nevertheless, the type of situation that existed when FitzGerald's coalition collapsed in February 1982 is precisely that in which the constitution allows for presidential intervention. Had Hillery played a proactive role – and had an election been prevented – it is possible that his influence on the office and its standing, and on those who succeeded him in the position, would be far greater than the limited historical legacy that exists today.

CONCLUSION

The presidencies of Erskine Childers, Cearbhall Ó Dálaigh and Patrick Hillery contributed to the emergence of a new activism in the Irish presidency, most evident in public engagements and foreign travel. This activity created a tangible difference from the early presidents and has become a hallmark of more recent presidential terms. Yet, despite higher public visibility, none of the three presidents considered in this chapter had any radical plan to reinvent this non-political office or to push the boundaries of presidential power. There were some limited ideas for role expansion – such as Childers's idea for a 'think tank' – but there was no desire to counter governmental restrictions or to seriously challenge the narrow interpretation accepted by the first three presidents. If anything, the Childers – Ó Dálaigh – Hillery era is defined by an implicit acceptance of the weakness of the office and the view that activity in the political arena clashed with a desire to be 'above politics' (Gallagher, 1977: 382). There was a very strong desire to avoid all possibility of political conflict without carefully distinguishing between engagement in the 'political arena', defined primarily as party political, and an enhanced role in the 'public arena'. There was nothing to prevent Childers from pursuing his 'think tank' proposal so long as its agenda was carefully managed, although once Cosgrave rejected the idea it was apparently meekly abandoned.

Of the three Presidents in the 1973–90 period Hillery, in particular, was presented with the greatest opportunity to reorientate the position, but he was the one with least ambition for the role. Following Ó Dálaigh's resignation there was a serious opportunity to consider the role anew, and certainly as Taoiseach Garret FitzGerald was open to change, and would, he later recorded, 'happily have provided him [Hillery] with further assistance had he wished to pursue more actively some suggestions that came up in discussion between us' (FitzGerald, 1991: 604). Hillery was also presented in February 1982 with a scenario to legitimately exercise new powers but he was unwilling to consider constitutional intervention to prevent a general election. Overall, with these three presidents we see more than the 'hints of themes' (see Chapter 5) evident in earlier terms but the increased activity is still framed against a continuation of conservatism relating to the role itself.

Cohabitation is the second significant issue that can be identified from these three presidential terms. In this 17-year period three presidents from Fianna Fáil backgrounds were in office at a time when Fine Gael and Labour enjoyed three terms in government (1973–1977, 1981–1982 and 1982–1987, with 1982 broken by a short Fianna Fáil interregnum). The issue of cohabitation emerges as a strong theme, primarily due to the attitude and actions of Liam Cosgrave, whose relationship with each of the three Presidents was difficult, and, in one case, was ultimately responsible for a presidential resignation. It might have been expected that a leader from a party different to that from which the President emerged would have shown greater sensitivity in developing good working relations. It has been suggested here, however, that Cosgrave viewed these Presidents through a party political prism and against their Fianna Fáil backgrounds. Interestingly, in light of the Cosgrave experience, another Fine Gael Taoiseach adopted a very different approach. Garret FitzGerald ensured regular communication with the President, including providing updates on political events and offering information on key government initiatives including the 'developing plans for an Anglo-Irish Agreement' (FitzGerald, 1991: 604).

The issue of cohabitation was also a reality during later presidential terms, most particularly during the Robinson presidency (Reynolds, 2009: 299–300). Such difficulty as did emerge between Robinson and the four Taoisigh who were in office in the 1990 to 1997 period (Charles Haughey, Albert Reynolds, John Bruton and Bertie Ahern) fell short of those discussed in this chapter. It seems that there has been little, if any, serious contention arising from presidents and governments from differing political persuasions. Indeed, such differences of opinion as did emerge on a small number of issues were as likely to have involved the President and members of her former party, Labour, which was in office from 1992 to 1997.

NOTES

1. National Archives of Ireland (NAI), Office of the President, PRES 10564 2005/7/570.
2. NAI, 2000/6/659 D/T 93610, Childers memo. 26 August 1969.
3. NAI 2004/27/5, Details on Childers inauguration plans.
4. NAI, 2004/27/5, Text of Childers inauguration address.
5. NAI 2005/24/01, Organisation of state visit to Belgium, May 1974.
6. NAI 2005/160/38, Council of State dinner.
7. NAI 2004/25/48, Cosgrave to Lynch, 21 November 1974.
8. University College Dublin Archives (UCDA), Cearbhall Ó Dálaigh papers, P51/216 4–5.
9. UCDA P51/216 171-172, 182, Notes prepared by Ó Dálaigh.
10. UCDA P51/216 12-13, Notes prepared by Ó Dálaigh.
11. UCDA P51/217 23, Ó Dálaigh papers: 'The Last Days of a President'
12. UCDA P51/217 26, Ó Dálaigh papers: 'The Last Days of a President'
13. UCDA P51/217 23, Ó Dálaigh papers: 'The Last Days of a President'
14. UCDA P51/211 23, Ó Dálaigh papers: 'The Last Days of a President'
15. UCDA P51/217 45, Ó Dálaigh papers: 'The Last Days of a President'
16. UCDA P51/217 45, Ó Dálaigh papers: 'The Last Days of a President'
17. UCDA P51/217 176, Ó Dálaigh papers: 'The Last Days of a President'
18. UCDA P51/217 59, Ó Dálaigh papers: 'The Last Days of a President'
19. UCDA P51/217 61, Ó Dálaigh papers: 'The Last Days of a President'
20. UCDA P51/217 84, Ó Dálaigh papers: 'The Last Days of a President'
21. UCDA P51/209 9 Notes prepared by Ó Dálaigh.
22. UCDA P205/145, Patrick Hillery papers: Áras an Uachtaráin telephone log record, 27 January 1982.

7

ACTIVIST PRESIDENTS AND GENDER POLITICS, 1990–2011

YVONNE GALLIGAN

INTRODUCTION

The outcome of the 1990 and 1997 presidential elections brought two women into Áras an Uachtaráin, heralding a discernable change of pace, tone and focus in the office. The relatively staid backwater that was the received image of the Irish presidency became charged with a new political energy. This transformation rested on the personalities of Mary Robinson and Mary McAleese. However, personal disposition alone does not fully explain their development of a more activist presidency. Their respective political agendas motivated much of this new interpretation of the office. So too did their differing conceptions of the role of the President. While staying within constitutional boundaries, both women sought to add content to a political institution that in the public mind had become apolitical, even irrelevant. Their lasting achievement was to reconstruct the nature of the presidency from being a sinecure for elder statesmen, to being a political institution that evoked public pride in its representative function.

This chapter traces the transformation of the Irish presidency between 1990 and 2011. It takes each President in turn, and, following discussion of personal background, it looks at the path to the presidency, vision of office and political role. It analyses their inaugural speeches to uncover the defining themes of each presidency, and discusses the extent to which each woman fulfilled this self-chosen agenda in subsequent years. The inaugural address marks a significant moment in a presidential term of office. It allows space for the newly-installed incumbent to reassure voters that they have made the right choice of President. It gives the new President the opportunity to acknowledge the democratic link between the people and the office, and it provides a formal public stage for the incoming President to indicate the nature of the relationship she hopes to foster with the people. It also allows the new office-holder to indicate priorities and set the tone for the next seven years of the presidency. In the third section, the discussion moves to evaluating the transformative extent of the Robinson and McAleese presidencies. It concludes by reflecting on the cultural symbolism of the office and the contributions of the two women to refashioning the presidency for modern times.

MARY ROBINSON, 1990–1997

In this section, Mary Robinson's path from her early years to the presidency is discussed, followed by an analysis of her vision for the office and an overview of her presidential term. Born in Ballina, County Mayo on 21 May 1944, Mary Bourke (her pre-marriage surname) was the middle child and only girl in a family of five children. Coming from a prosperous professional family, the Bourke children were encouraged to achieve, and given every material and emotional support to do so. In 1963, on securing permission from Catholic church authorities to attend the Protestant-ethos Trinity College Dublin, Mary Bourke commenced her studies in legal science.[1] She became auditor of Trinity's Law Society in 1967 and chose as the theme of her inaugural address the separation of church and state. In this speech she raised two of the issues that would later become important motifs in her political and legal career, divorce and contraception (O'Leary and Burke, 1998: 30–32). Graduating with first-class honours in 1967, she commenced a fellowship at Harvard Law School. Mary Bourke immersed herself in this environment where the questioning of the relationship between law, politics and society provoked passionate debate. She returned to Ireland with a first-class Masters degree. A year later, in 1969, as an apprentice barrister and part-time law tutor at University College Dublin (UCD), she was elected to one of the three Trinity seats in the Seanad and began a 30-year career in Irish politics. In 1970 she married Nicholas Robinson, whom she met during her student years.

Robinson's legal and political careers fused on human rights and law reform issues. She has attributed her abiding sense of justice and human rights to the influence of her father and grandfather, and the experience of growing up in a medical practice household (Horgan 1997:14; O'Leary and Burke

1998: 15–16). One of her first legislative acts was to introduce a private member's bill in the Seanad on reproductive rights in 1971 that sought to make contraception legally available. In 1976 she joined the Irish Labour Party and the following year ran for election to the Dáil in the Dublin south city constituency of Rathmines. She failed to win a seat by 400 votes and resumed her Seanad career. Another Dáil election attempt, this time in the Dublin West constituency in 1981, was also unsuccessful. Robinson again resumed her Seanad career while maintaining an academic position and a legal practice. In 1985 she resigned from Labour in protest at the Anglo-Irish agreement which she described as 'fatally flawed', as it was based on intergovernmental structures negotiated between the Irish and British governments without the input of unionist political leaders (Horgan, 1997: 113–115).[2] In 1989 Robinson took the decision to concentrate on her academic and legal career. Less than one year later, she was a candidate for the presidency.

EMERGENCE AS PRESIDENT

In 1990, President Hillery's second term was coming to a close. The name of Brian Lenihan, a popular Fianna Fáil minister and ally of Taoiseach and party leader Charles J. Haughey, began to circulate informally in late 1989 as the party's choice to succeed Hillery (Horgan, 1997: 125). At the same time, Labour's strong 1989 election result encouraged Labour leader Dick Spring to announce in early January that the party would contest the presidential election for the first time (Finlay, 1990: 12). Although Spring had no one person in mind at that time, Mary Robinson's name quickly came to the fore. After some negotiation, Robinson expressed a willingness to accept a nomination, but as an independent candidate. In April 1990, her candidacy was officially endorsed by Labour after the alternative possibility of Noel Browne, canvassed by the party's radical wing, disappeared (Horgan, 1997: 129–30; Finlay, 1990: 18–24). Robinson's candidacy quickly drew support from two other small left-leaning parties, the Green Party and the Workers' Party. She launched her campaign in May with a low-key tour of the country, visiting remote and island communities as well as small towns and urban areas, listening to their expectations of a President.

In June, Lenihan saw off a challenge from party colleague and former Minister for Education John Wilson to become the Fianna Fáil presidential candidate. Meanwhile, there were problems with Fine Gael's efforts to secure a nominee. Former leader Garret FitzGerald and former Tánaiste

Peter Barry refused invitations to put their names forward. Eventually, in September, the party nominated a former Northern Ireland politician, Austin Currie, who was then a Fine Gael TD in Dublin West.[3] Fine Gael leader Alan Dukes, whose authority had already been undermined by the poor party showing at the 1989 election, lost further standing over the candidacy debacle (O'Sullivan, 1991: 87–90).

Robinson's early campaign start gave her time to meet people and groups across the country, engaging them in a discussion about the role of the President in modern Ireland. She integrated these views with her own vision for the office and encapsulated the combined views in the campaign slogan 'a president with a purpose'. The other candidates, responding to her redefinition of the office, also promised an activist presidency: Lenihan as a 'people's president' offered to promote Ireland's heritage and culture at home and abroad; Currie imagined the President as a 'reconciling figure' (O'Sullivan, 1991: 90–91).

In addition to being the first candidate in the field to articulate a clear and modern vision for the office, Robinson also gained from the mistakes of her opponents during the campaign. Lenihan stumbled when he was forced to clarify, and then retract, a claim that he had sought to influence President Hillery not to dissolve the Dáil in 1982. In brief, Lenihan had publicly denied that he had asked President Hillery to refuse a dissolution of parliament to the incumbent Taoiseach, Garret FitzGerald during a period of political crisis. However, his statements were challenged when a tape recording was made public on which Lenihan admitted to having made persistent phone calls to Áras an Uachtaráin, and claimed to have spoken with the President, for that purpose. Lenihan repeated his denial that the phone calls took place, explaining that he had been under heavy medication at the time of the interview that had affected his recollection of events. The affair undermined Lenihan's credibility as a candidate. The controversy soured relations between the governing parties, Fianna Fáil and the Progressive Democrats (PDs), and ultimately leaked into parliamentary politics. The PDs insisted on Lenihan's resignation from cabinet as a condition for their support of Fianna Fáil in a no-confidence vote tabled by the opposition. Lenihan refused to resign and was removed from office by Haughey. Ironically, the Lenihan campaign gained renewed impetus after this episode and he began to claw back much of the support he had earlier lost to Robinson during the controversy (Finlay, 1990: 122–125, 127; O'Sullivan, 1991: 91–94).

Robinson's own campaign came under pressure in the final days. Her commitment to social justice was cast as 'red' politics by Fianna Fáil. In a similar vein, Fianna Fáil cabinet minister Padraig Flynn on a radio current affairs programme launched a personalised attack on Robinson, accusing her of being an opportunistic socialist candidate with no empathy for the lives of ordinary people, while masquerading as a caring politician. In a blistering tirade, Flynn went on to criticise her 'new clothes and her new look and her new hairdo and she has the new interest in family, being a mother and all that kind of thing', adding 'None of us who knew Mary Robinson very well in previous incarnations ever heard her claiming to be a great wife and mother' (Finlay, 1990: 135). The sexist attack was immediately roundly countered by PD representative Michael McDowell, a panellist on the same radio programme. Although Flynn offered a profuse apology soon thereafter, his outburst spectacularly backfired on the Lenihan campaign and pushed voters towards Robinson. On the eve of the election, Lenihan and Robinson were evenly matched in public support – and it is likely that this incident contributed to consolidating Currie transfers to Robinson. Although Lenihan won 44 per cent of the first preference vote while Robinson garnered 39 per cent, more than three-quarters of Currie's votes transferred to Robinson, handing her victory on the second count (O'Sullivan, 1991: 95–6).

VISION OF OFFICE

Robinson's electoral victory was described at the time as 'mould-breaking': the first woman to hold the office, the first time the position was held by a politician from a party other than Fianna Fáil. Robinson's shaping of the presidential office as a purposeful one, which began during the election, continued during her tenure. Her campaign slogan was carefully crafted to the image of a president prepared to use the soft power of the office to validate individual and collective efforts to improve the quality of civic and democratic life in Ireland and further afield. Robinson knew that her election was a reflection of the changes taking place in Irish society and political culture. It was, as Stephen Lucas put it, a 'moment of consequence'[4] and her inaugural address gave the new President an opportunity to define her vision of the state and nation in response to her mould-breaking election. Previous incumbents of the office, by and large, had been content to interpret their presidential role in a conventional manner – as defenders of the constitution (Ó Dálaigh, Hillery) and low-key supporters of volunteerism and social good works (Childers, Hillery). Robinson was at pains to stress her break with the received interpretation of the institution.

In her inaugural address (Robinson, 1990; see Appendix 2), the new President made extensive reference to aspects of 'new' and 'modern' Ireland

and her desire to support empowering civic and social values and activities. For Robinson, this new sense of Irishness was inextricably bound to closer integration with Europe and underpinned by the liberal norms of 'respect for human rights, pluralism, tolerance and openness to new ideas', which were, for her, core political values.

Although her electoral victory was decisive, Robinson also acknowledged in her address that not all of her electors endorsed her political views. Thus, one of the purposes of her inaugural speech was to create a bond of friendship between her as President and the people, so as to consolidate the legitimacy of her presidency. She intended to create this connection through emphasising her office as a focus for local and community attention in all its forms, promising that 'As President I will seek to the best of my abilities to promote this growing sense of local participatory democracy'.

By recognising the diversity of political views among her electors, and binding all, including herself, to promoting 'a new Ireland, open, tolerant, inclusive', she went on during her presidency to be a 'witness' to these impulses. She carefully chose the events she supported, by her presence drawing attention to instances of civic action and multi-cultural engagement across the island. As Bresnihan (1999: 250–265) observed, Robinson set out to symbolise a politics based on 'strong democracy' and 'nurturing reason'.

POLITICAL ROLE

Robinson explicitly spelled out her interpretation of the head of state's representative function in her inaugural address, and in the following years developed the office according to the values she articulated on taking office. Her active interpretation of this representative office led to conflict in the early years with Taoiseach Charles J. Haughey and officials in the Department of the Taoiseach who were accustomed to working with a more traditional, low-key interpretation of the presidency. A defining moment in this relationship came with the visit of the Dalai Lama to Ireland in 1991, and Robinson's intention to recognise him, given her advocacy of human rights in Tibet while senator (O'Leary and Burke, 1998: 154–156; Robinson 2013: 162–165). Haughey repeatedly sought to deter her from meeting the Dalai Lama, but finally backed down when Robinson stood her ground (O'Leary and Burke, 1998: 154–156). From that point onwards, Robinson grew in confidence and skill in using the symbolic power of her office to recognise, support and validate the 'new, pluralist Ireland' of her inaugural speech.

One aspect of her presidential agenda to which she applied considerable thought and diplomacy was in building a relationship with Queen Elizabeth II as a symbol of the growing friendship between the two states. This began in April 1991 with the breaking of an unwritten convention – that Irish Presidents do not visit Britain – and culminated in June 1996 with an official visit to Britain. In between came the symbolically important reconciliatory event on 27 May 1993 when the Irish President paid a personal visit to the Queen, the first meeting of an Irish President and a British monarch (Siggins, 1997: 164).

Robinson skilfully used her gender as a woman to political effect, recognising marginalised women and their efforts to create better lives for their communities across the island. It was the wedge that unblocked another barrier to the scope of the presidency, this time a visit to Northern Ireland. Until Robinson accepted an invitation from women's groups from both communities in Belfast in February 1992, Irish Presidents had confined their cross-border visits to events of a religious nature in Armagh, seat of the Catholic Church in Ireland. This visit helped to pave the way for her controversial visit to west Belfast in June 1993, on the invitation of community representatives. This initiative was strenuously objected to by the British government, the Northern Ireland Office and Northern unionists. The British government went so far as to hint that it might not be able to guarantee her personal safety while in the jurisdiction (Siggins, 1997: 166). The Irish government, too, was unhappy with the visit – independently of the British view – with concerns that Sinn Féin would hijack the event for propaganda purposes, and sought to deter Robinson. Dick Spring, then Minister for Foreign Affairs in the Fianna Fáil–Labour coalition government, was tasked with conveying this disquiet, along with conveying the negative view of the British government, to the planned visit. Increasing heat marked the exchanges between President and Government leaders on the matter. No official prohibition on the President's travel arrangements came, and although Spring remained opposed to it, the Taoiseach was more sanguine in his view. On 18 June 1993, three weeks on from the symbolic meeting with the Queen, President Robinson attended the Whiterock Road campus of the Belfast Institute of Further and Higher Education and shook hands with representatives from over 50 community and civic organisations (nationalist and unionist), local councillors, Joe Hendron of the SDLP and Gerry Adams, President of Sinn Féin. Photographers were excluded from the venue. This did not prevent an outbreak of condemnation for her actions from political leaders, Irish and British media commentators, Fine Gael, and the Northern Ireland Office (O'Leary and Burke, 1998:

208–218). The public, however, viewed the visit and the Adams handshake differently, with an Irish Independent poll showing 77 per cent approval of the President's action (*Fortnight*, 320, Sept. 1993: 30). The public response indicated that there was general support in the Republic of Ireland for a peace process that included Sinn Féin.

In her inaugural address, Robinson had sought to represent Ireland in the promotion of human rights on the international stage. As President, she sought to realise this promise through visiting famine-stricken Somalia. Irish aid agencies working in Somalia organised the visit, and Robinson's emotionally powerful response to her experiences brought the grim reality of poverty and hunger to world attention. She was to follow the Somalia visit with three visits to Rwanda, forming a view of the political and practical action required to address human rights and development needs in these countries. These visits, and her international advocacy for a rights-based development agenda, laid the foundations of her later career in the United Nations. While President, her actions in this area showed that Ireland, a small country, could make a significant contribution to international affairs in humanitarian terms. Although she was by then growing out of the presidential role and into a new international one, Robinson skilfully used the presidency to keep her inauguration promise.

By the time Mary Robinson announced she would not seek a second term as President, she enjoyed over 92 per cent support in opinion polls (Marsh, 1999: 217). She had accepted thousands of invitations to local official events, supported the work of the traveller community, women's groups, and social justice organisations. She had played a central part in normalising the political relationship between Ireland and Britain, and between north and south in Ireland. She had represented Ireland extensively abroad, including 10 state visits. She worked with three different prime ministers and two different administrations. In the course of her presidential term, Robinson tackled the constitutional limitations of the office by negotiating her role with successive Taoisigh, finding the spaces on which the constitution was silent and using these opportunities to represent aspects of Irish cultural and social values. Robinson had lived up to her vow to be a 'president with a purpose'.

MARY MCALEESE, 1997–2011

Mary McAleese emerged from a fraught electoral campaign to succeed Mary Robinson to the presidency. The contrast between the two women's backgrounds is striking. While their political views and ambitions for the office were also different, both shared an ambition to maximise the President's representative role. The following sections discuss these matters in more detail. Mary Leneghan was born in Belfast on 27 June 1951, the eldest of nine children. Her parents were small business owners in the mixed-community Ardoyne area of north Belfast. As the family enlarged, the Leneghans moved to a mainly Protestant part of Ardoyne, where the young Mary Leneghan was taunted occasionally on account of her religious background. Her father's keen interest in local history and her mother's family interest in republican politics shaped her Catholic nationalist identity.[5] She also inherited a strong sense of social justice and commitment to peace from her parents (McGarry, 2008: 51–2).

A high-achieving student in the all-girls St Dominic's High School, in 1969 Leneghan went on to study law in Queen's University Belfast. Her time at Queen's coincided with the beginning of the communal conflict, from which the family was not immune. Over the course of the following years, her brother and sister were injured in separate sectarian attacks, Mary was caught in crossfire between the British Army and the IRA, and a car bomb destroyed her father's public house business on the Falls Road. A machine gun attack on the Leneghan home during the night of 7 December 1972 instigated a family move away from north Belfast and eventually to the more peaceful seaside town of Rostrevor, County Down.

During that troubled period, Mary Leneghan continued her legal studies, and graduated with honours in 1974. She briefly practised at the Northern Ireland Bar and in 1975 was appointed Reid Professor of Criminal Law at Trinity College Dublin,[6] succeeding Mary Robinson in the post. In 1976 she married Martin McAleese. In Dublin she became involved in some of the controversial social issues of the day, founding the campaign for homosexual law reform with David Norris, supporting the introduction of divorce, and championing moves to ban abortion in Ireland (McGarry, 2008: 78-83). Indeed, she advocated a strong and inclusive notion of marriage and family throughout her public life, supporting gay marriage independently of Catholic doctrine (McGarry, 2012).

In 1979 she joined the state broadcasting service, RTÉ, as a journalist, working on the flagship television current affairs programme, *Today Tonight*. Her nationalist roots and personal experience of the conflict became quickly at odds with the anti-nationalist viewpoint of the current affairs editor and producers. A defining moment came when the *Today Tonight* editor, Joe Mulholland, refused to cover the funeral of IRA hunger striker Bobby

Sands on the grounds that it would constitute propaganda for the republican movement. McAleese argued that the hunger strikes were radicalising the nationalist community, with deep implications for Northern Ireland's politics, and that this event could not be ignored. She resigned from RTÉ after an unhappy three years, and resumed her Trinity College position, although in 1983 she returned to RTÉ as a freelance reporter and broadcaster, while continuing to lecture in law in Trinity. By all accounts a consummate presenter, McAleese became embroiled in a quarrel ostensibly over 'double jobbing' with the National Union of Journalists (NUJ). A union rule required members to earn at least two-thirds of their salary from journalism, and it was alleged that McAleese breached that rule. For her part, McAleese argued that the charge against her was politically motivated and stemmed from her appearance with the Catholic bishops at the New Ireland Forum. She challenged the NUJ to take a stance on all broadcasters with second careers, to no avail. On 31 March 1984 McAleese was suspended from the NUJ's Dublin Broadcasting Branch, though this did not prevent her from continuing her part-time broadcasting activities with RTÉ (McCarthy, 1999: 64–7; Mac Mánais, 2004: 203–6).

Shortly before the spat with the NUJ, McAleese was invited to join the Catholic Church delegation to the New Ireland Forum in 1984. In this capacity she debated the merits of integrated education versus denominational schooling with then Senator Mary Robinson (O'Leary and Burke, 1998: 91–2). Like Robinson, she did not support the 1985 Anglo-Irish agreement because 'the people who were obliged to work it had not bought into it. And they hadn't been asked to buy into it' (McGarry, 2008: 101–2). In 1984, having previously turned down approaches from Fine Gael, she joined Fianna Fáil. In the early years of her party membership, McAleese shared views on a range of issues with her party leader, Charles J. Haughey. Indeed, her imposition as a candidate for the party in the liberal Dublin South East constituency for the 1987 general election, after failing to win a place on the ticket at the selection convention, was due to Haughey. Her initial foray into electoral politics was unsuccessful (McCarthy, 1999: 79, 81–5). As Haughey began to shift towards acceptance of the Anglo-Irish Agreement, and support for the extradition of Irish republican terrorist suspects to Britain, her disillusionment with him and Fianna Fáil grew. Soon after the 1987 election, the family returned to Northern Ireland and to a new chapter in the public life of Mary McAleese (McCarthy, 1999: 90–94).

McAleese successfully applied for the position of Director of the Institute of Professional Legal Studies at her alma mater, Queen's University Belfast. She beat rival candidate, Queen's law lecturer and member of the Ulster

Unionist Party, David Trimble, for the position. The surprise choice of out-sider McAleese (a Catholic woman, and nationalist, who had carved political, journalistic and academic careers in the Republic) led to unionist allegations of political interference by Haughey in her selection (McCarthy, 1999: 102–105). Trimble supporters called for a debate in the House of Commons – and the bitterness over the matter lingered for over a decade. In the years following her Queen's appointment, McAleese advanced her career, held a number of directorships, and in 1994 was appointed pro-vice chancellor of the University – the first woman and second Catholic to hold the post. She made a rare high-profile foray into public debate in 1992 on the three-part abortion referendum proposed by the Fianna Fáil–Labour government led by Albert Reynolds. Away from the glare of publicity, she maintained close professional and per-sonal ties to the Catholic hierarchy, and in 1996 became active in the efforts of the Clonard monastery's peace initiative in west Belfast to re-establish the IRA ceasefire. Yet, she remained a strong critic of the doctrinaire, traditional, Catholic hierarchy, especially for its dismissive attitude towards women's role in the Church.[7] McAleese's career trajectory in academia had reached a pla-teau by then, but the Irish presidency was not on her mind when Robinson announced her early departure from office on 12 March, 1997.[8]

EMERGENCE AS PRESIDENT

Robinson's resignation announcement some months before her term came to a close was unexpected. With her continued high popularity it was generally believed that she would seek a second term. Preparations for candidate selec-tion in all parties were stalled while SDLP leader and peace process architect John Hume considered putting his name forward. Hume delayed clarifying his intentions until 9 September, when he backed away from seeking the office. In the meantime, having been persuaded by close friend Harry Casey[9] to seek a nomination for the office, Mary McAleese began an informal canvass of the Fianna Fáil membership, building support among influential grassroots net-works within the party. This low-key campaign continued through the gen-eral election campaign and into the summer. While her candidacy was first suggested in early April by Fr Alec Reid of Clonard Monastery to Martin Mansergh, Fianna Fáil's special adviser on Northern Ireland, the response to it was muted.[10] With Fianna Fáil returned to office in June 1997, McAleese decided to test interest in her nomination for the presidency with her old friend and Fianna Fáil deputy leader, Mary O'Rourke. The seasoned politician was supportive of McAleese's ambitions, and conveyed this to her party leader, Bertie Ahern.

The summer of 1997 was defined by overt and covert campaigning for the Fianna Fáil nomination. Former Taoiseach Albert Reynolds had already publicly declared his interest and had put his considerable financial resources into becoming the party's flagbearer. In mid-August former EU Commissioner Michael O'Kennedy announced his intention to seek the nomination. In the meantime, McAleese party supporters, mobilised by Harry Casey, undertook a concerted letter-writing campaign to their elected representatives advocating her nomination.

With eight days to the Fianna Fáil selection convention, McAleese wrote to Taoiseach Bertie Ahern indicating her interest in being a candidate. At a meeting to informally interview the putative candidate, Ahern revealed little of his personal view on her candidacy, but indirectly encouraged her to continue seeking support from the party's elected representatives. During the following days, Reynolds, O'Kennedy and McAleese intensively canvassed the Fianna Fáil parliamentary party. Addressing the parliamentary party the night before the selection meeting, Ahern indicated that in an ideal world having a presidential candidate with a track record of service in Fianna Fáil was preferable. However, he reminded the meeting that this outcome might not be the right one if the party were to have a realistic prospect of regaining the office. He advised his colleagues to vote for the best candidate at the party's selection convention the following day (McCarthy, 1999: 178).

On 17 September 1997, Ahern supporters were openly canvassing for McAleese, convinced that a Reynolds candidacy would be divisive and would fail to return the presidency to the party. The first round of voting was inconclusive, with no nominee winning the necessary 57 votes that would constitute an overall majority. On the second round, Kennedy's votes went en bloc to McAleese, giving her 62 votes to 48 for Reynolds, and making her the Fianna Fáil presidential nominee (McCarthy, 1999: 185). The outsider had defeated one of the most senior and experienced Irish politicians.[11] The outcome was reported as a 'political earthquake'. When asked about her vision for the office, McAleese said that she would use the role of President 'for bringing people to each other simply and solely in friendship'.

The drama of the Fianna Fáil contest was not reflected to the same extent in the other parties. Mary Banotti, a member of the European Parliament since 1984 and from a distinguished political family, was proposed as a candidate by the Fine Gael leadership in July, but was not ratified until 16 September when she defeated seasoned politician and former minister Avril Doyle by a narrow margin. Surprisingly, Labour was slow to nominate a candidate, and on 16 September – the day before Fianna Fáil's landmark decision – the party ratified Adi Roche, anti-nuclear campaigner and director of a children's charity. She was backed by Dick Spring, even though a party stalwart was available – Michael D. Higgins, who was to become Ireland's ninth President in 2011 (Doyle, 1998: 135–6; Marsh, 1999: 217–221).

The low-key selection of the Fine Gael and Labour candidates stood in contrast to the cliff-edge search for a nomination by singer and former Eurovision Song Contest winner Dana Rosemary Scallon, followed by former Garda (Irish police) representative Derek Nally, from the local councils. This was the first time that the constitutionally-provided local government power to nominate a presidential candidate was employed. Although the councils were controlled by the main parties, Scallon mounted a sufficiently convincing case for support based on the argument that she was merely seeking the right to stand for election, and that the voters would be the final arbiters. The main parties did not view her as a major threat to their own candidates, and so assisted in her nomination, as also that of Derek Nally (Doyle, 1998: 136–7).

The election campaign began with Roche in a commanding lead of 38 per cent in the opinion polls, but early criticisms from co-workers about her abrasive management style dented her support (Marsh, 1999: 224). The campaign quickly became a two-person contest between Banotti and McAleese, with McAleese assuming a commanding position in the polls which was never seriously challenged (Doyle, 1998: 142). A defining moment in the campaign came in mid-October with publication of leaked documents from the Department of Foreign Affairs that were used to suggest that McAleese was "'pushing a Sinn Féin agenda" and should not be trusted'.[12] This allegation, which had first surfaced during her RTÉ days, was turned into a political weapon by her opponents. Her capacity to be a 'proper' President on this basis was challenged by Derek Nally. He was joined in this theme by Fine Gael leader John Bruton, who alleged that McAleese was the 'Sinn Féin endorsed candidate' (Doyle, 1998: 140–41). Eoghan Harris, media commentator and key player in the Robinson presidential victory, went further and in an intemperate news interview described McAleese as a 'tribal time bomb' – an ironic echo of the Padraig Flynn slur on Robinson's character seven years previously (McCarthy, 1999: 200–201; McGarry, 2008: 173–180). The effect was to swing public support in favour of McAleese while damaging the campaigns of the other candidates. McAleese also countered these attacks, speaking for the first time in public about her involvement in the peace initiative in west Belfast. The attacks also provoked the Belfast-based *Irish News* to robustly defend McAleese and castigate Bruton for his insensitive remarks (McGarry, 2008: 179). Even the Unionist politician John Taylor, who had bitterly opposed her appointment at Queen's University some years earlier, came out in support of McAleese, declaring her 'by no means a Republican sympathiser' (McCarthy, 1999: 196–214).

This political storm worked to the benefit of McAleese in a number of ways. It cemented the allegiance of Fianna Fáil and mobilised party members into campaigning for her. It brought her to public attention, turning a relatively unknown candidate into a household name. Finally, it enabled her to campaign in a more confident and self-assured manner. She turned the allegations into a positive peace-building theme, in keeping with her campaign slogan 'Building Bridges'. Banotti's support fell further after Bruton's attack, and the media attention on McAleese deprived Banotti of an essential platform to press home her claim to the office. The controversial allegations resulted in the collapse of Nally's campaign, and Dana's support remained marginal throughout, despite her competent and professional media performances.

The result reflected the poll patterns from mid-October onwards: McAleese secured over 45 per cent of first preferences, with Banotti securing over 29 per cent and the other candidates trailing some distance behind. With the support of transferred votes, McAleese won convincingly on the second count, with 59 per cent – the first northern nationalist to hold presidential office in the Republic (Doyle,1998: 143). On Tuesday 11 November 1997, Mary McAleese succeeded Mary Robinson as President of Ireland. Seven years later, she was again inaugurated as President, having been returned unopposed for a second term.

VISION OF OFFICE

As a noted American political communication expert has observed, 'democracy is based on empathy, that is, on citizens caring about each other and acting on that care, taking responsibility not just for themselves but for their families, communities, and their nation' (Lakoff, 2011). This empathic understanding of democracy was evident in the McAleese presidency, from her inaugural address through to the end of her 14 years in office. In contrast to the directness of Robinson, her first inaugural speech was dominated by poetic imagery of caring, offering to 'point the way to a reconciliation of these many tensions and to see Ireland grow ever more comfortable and at ease with the flowering diversity that is all around us' (McAleese, 1997; Appendix 2).

By the time of her second inaugural speech, McAleese, still with a poetic turn of phrase, had consolidated this empathic, facilitatory style with more precision while retaining the caring aspect, as she sought to 'nurture and celebrate commitment to community and to responsible citizenship and to encourage self-belief among the most marginalised' (McAleese, 2004; Appendix 2).

In her first inaugural address, McAleese voiced a preoccupation with the peace process in Northern Ireland, an issue with which she was closely associated and a defining issue during the electoral contest. In announcing the theme of her presidency as 'Building Bridges', McAleese sought to reassure her critics that she would facilitate consensus-building and peace-making as 'work I want to help in every way I can.'

McAleese also conveyed her own religious faith unambiguously in this inaugural speech – a counterpoint to Robinson's humanistic beliefs. In doing so, she was affirming a sense of national bonding through shared Christian values. This was a difficult issue to raise in a political setting, yet for her presidency to be widely accepted, McAleese had to give a signal that she would be a non-sectarian head of state. Thus, her references to religion were carefully crafted to appeal to the faithful of all beliefs. When publicly berated by then Archbishop of Boston, Cardinal Bernard Law, in 1998 for supporting the ordination of women and being a 'poor Catholic president', McAleese replied: 'I am not a Catholic president. I'm President of Ireland ... I happen to be Catholic' (McGarry, 2012). Indeed, as an event early in her presidency would show, McAleese was not afraid to challenge Catholic orthodoxy in a clash of religion, ethics and politics. On the invitation of the Church of Ireland (Anglican) Archbishop of Dublin, she took communion in an inter-faith service and was strongly criticised for so doing by the Catholic Archbishop of Dublin. Her actions were rewarded with 78% popular support.[13]

By the time of her second inaugural address in 2004, the peace process was well established. As she accomplished her first-term agenda, and gained experience of being a head of state, McAleese became more comfortable in situating Ireland in a wider context. She saw that the country could make a distinctive contribution to global development:

> Ireland's fortunes are linked to global politics as never before and though we are a small peripheral island we have a fascinating and exceptional engagement with the world that spans every conceivable connection ... As President I have a key role in the renewal and development of ties to our global Irish family (McAleese, 2004; Appendix 2).

1. President Hyde (in back of car, holding top hat), leaving Dublin Castle following his inauguration as Ireland's first president on 25 June 1938. The new president stopped outside the GPO on O'Connell Street before continuing to his new home at Áras an Uachtaráin (formerly the Viceregal Lodge, home of the Lord Lieutenant of Ireland) in the Phoenix Park. Credit: National Library of Ireland.

2. President Hyde with participants in the Cumann Drámaídheachta na Sgol competition at an awards ceremony in Áras an Uachtaráin, 30 March 1939. Credit: *The Irish Times*.

3. President O'Kelly outside Áras an Uachtaráin with (right to left) Lord Rugby (Lord Loader Maffey, 1st Baron Rugby, United Kingdom representative to Ireland), British Prime Minister, Clement Attlee, and Michael McDunphy, Secretary to the President, October 1948. Credit: *The Irish Times*.

4. President O'Kelly inspecting a guard of honour outside the GPO 1957. Credit: *The Irish Times*.

5. President de Valera welcomes US president John F. Kennedy to Ireland on 26 June 1963. Credit: *The Irish Times*.

6. President de Valera unveiling a plaque to the memory of Seán MacDermott on the then *Irish Times* building in D'Olier Street in Dublin, May 1967. Photographer: Tommy Collins, *The Irish Times*.

7. President Childers and his wife Rita being driven from Dublin Castle after his inauguration ceremony, 26 June 1973. Photographer: Paddy Whelan, *The Irish Times*.

8. President Childers greeting his predecessor, Eamon de Valera, at the Easter Rising commemoration ceremonies at Arbour Hill in Dublin, 9 May 1974. Also pictured: the Minister for Transport and Power Peter Barry, and Taoiseach Liam Cosgrave. Photographer: Tom Lawlor, *The Irish Times*.

9. Installation of Cearbhall
Ó Dálaigh as Ireland's fifth
president following the
death of President Childers,
20 December 1974. Credit:
Dermot O'Shea, *The Irish Times*.

10. Behind the scenes at Áras an Uachtaráin in 2009. Members of the household staff
Therese Robinson (left) and Aisling McBride setting a table for dinner under portraits
of presidents Patrick Hillery and Cearbhall Ó Dálaigh. Credit: Frank Miller, *The Irish Times*.

11. President Hillery painting in the grounds of Áras an Uachtaráin, November 1990. Credit: Pat Langan, *The Irish Times*.

12. Mary Robinson, Ireland's first woman president, at her inauguration ceremony in St Patrick's Hall in Dublin Castle, 3 December 1990. Credit: Matt Kavanagh, *The Irish Times*.

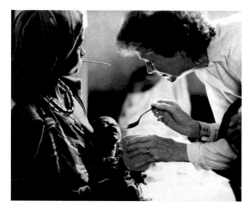

13. President Robinson visiting a Concern feeding centre at Baidoa in Somalia, October 1992. Credit: Eric Luke, *The Irish Times*.

14. President Robinson with Queen Elizabeth II at Buckingham Palace, May 1993. Credit: Eric Luke, *The Irish Times*.

15. President McAleese at the inauguration ceremony for her second term in office, November 2004. Credit: Dara Mac Dónaill, *The Irish Times*.

16. President McAleese watched by her husband Martin planting a tree in front of Áras an Uachtaráin in July 1999 to commemorate the anniversary of the death of Douglas Hyde; the tree was grown from a cutting taken from the original Douglas Hyde tree which had to be cut down after being affected by Dutch Elm Disease. Credit: David Sleator, *The Irish Times*.

17. Michael D. Higgins at the Dublin Castle count centre. Credit: Alan Betson, *The Irish Times*.

18. A single non-transferrable vote for Michael D. Higgins. Credit: Frank Miller, *The Irish Times*.

This was a similar perspective to that of Robinson, who was acutely aware of promoting Ireland's role in a global context. McAleese more frequently acknowledged a new, modern and diverse Ireland – echoing another strong theme in Robinson's presidency. She also drew attention to the challenges to social well-being brought by Ireland's newly acquired prosperity. Tackling these new problems, embedding the peace process, and contributing to global challenges were identified as priorities for her second term. While individually significant issues, they were fragmented, lacking the unifying power of the 'building bridges' theme that had lent normative coherence to her activities in the first term and informed her reconciliatory agenda in the second term.

The similarity in value emphasis, coming from women of very different ideological dispositions, seems to indicate that as McAleese became familiar with being a symbol of the nation – a role that the politically-experienced Robinson had appreciated – she placed greater emphasis on modern Ireland's contribution at home and abroad to universalist social values of solidarity and inclusion. However, it is open to interpretation as to whether McAleese gave effect to these universalist values in a global context as she worked through her second term.

POLITICAL ROLE

In the initial weeks of her first term as President, Mary McAleese travelled to Northern Ireland on the first of many official visits. On arrival at Belfast City Airport, she was greeted in Irish by the Deputy Lord Lieutenant of Belfast, Col. Charles Hogg. Later that day, Danny Kennedy of the Ulster Unionist Party welcomed her to Newry, and in west Belfast she met and shook hands with Sinn Féin leader Gerry Adams (McGarry, 2008: 196–7). This unity in welcome, presaged by Taylor's endorsement of her candidacy during the campaign, suggests that the northern interest in building a new relationship with the south was shared across the communities. By the end of her 14-year period as President, McAleese had officially visited Northern Ireland on over 100 occasions, only one of which was the subject of protest.

The theme of reconciliation emerged as the dominant motif of her first term of office. It was characterised by a Twelfth of July garden party at the Áras where representatives from both communities in Northern Ireland mingled with invited groups and politicians. Her husband, Martin McAleese, worked behind the scenes with former loyalist paramilitary leaders and communities to bring these marginalised representatives into the peace process. Indeed, the

President symbolically used the office to emphasise the shared aspects of history between Britain and Ireland. The joint inauguration in 2006 of the Island of Ireland Peace Park at Messines, Belgium, by President McAleese, Queen Elizabeth II and King Albert II of Belgium, in memory of all soldiers from Ireland who served in World War I, was a powerful moment of reconciliation. The last taboo in Anglo-Irish relations was broken towards the end of her presidency, with the visit of the UK monarch to Ireland in 2011. The personal warmth between the two women, and the responsive welcome of Irish people, was a fitting celebratory capstone to the normalisation of Anglo-Irish relations fostered by Robinson and continued by McAleese.

Mary McAleese's complex relationship with the Catholic Church continued, especially during her first term: on the one hand, she continued to profess a strong personal religious faith and commitment to Catholic orthodox teaching, while on the other, she was critical of Church structures and exclusionary practices. Her regular attendance at ecumenical services, and her welcoming of liberal Church-related groups such as BASIC (Brothers and Sisters in Christ)[14] to Áras an Uachtaráin illustrates her commitment as head of state to recognising religious plurality.

The other major dimension of her two terms in office was her representation of Ireland abroad as a place of business and trade, a feature of earlier presidential terms. This aspect of McAleese's activity, however, became more prominent in her second term. Many of her state visits were undertaken with a view to the economic advantage to Ireland, with her visit to China in June 2010 of particular interest. Concerns about human rights in that emerging economic superpower were soft-pedalled during her visit in favour of the commercial benefits to Ireland, a contrasting emphasis to that represented by Robinson. Yet, woven within those economic promotional trips were instances of recognition of the Irish diaspora and the work of Irish missionaries. The tackling of global challenges promised in the second inaugural speech did not materialise to any extent.

In her second term, with the political drama of the Irish peace process settling into routine political activity, McAleese placed a greater emphasis on the social problems of the day – increases in suicide, drug misuse, poverty and social alienation. Many of the visitors received by McAleese in the Áras, and visited by her in their communities, were from organisations working to alleviate social problems and integrate marginalised groups, such as representatives of the Traveller community, disability action groups, special Olympics interests, and suicide and drug prevention activists, among others. Like Robinson, her vision of a democratic polity was an inclusive one, and in this term, too, she continued her predecessor's practice of valuing the public commitment displayed by groups and individuals in marginalised communities.

Yet, writing a mid-term assessment of the McAleese presidency, journalist Justine McCarthy (2007: 2) expressed the critical view that the incumbent had lost her way in the second term:

> the peace process is as good as complete, rendering redundant her mission to build bridges ... within the narrow confines of cross-border bonding, as she has defined it ... in the afterglow of Ian Paisley's benign power grab and his avuncular handshake with Bertie Ahern at Farmleigh, the North has receded as a significant national issue.

There is some truth in this assertion. McAleese had finally conformed to the political status quo, losing her essential radicalism once the peace process became embedded in regular democratic politics. She continued to carry out the duties of her office with commitment and care, but without the guidance of a new narrative or an all-encompassing slogan. The promise of meaningful engagement on a global stage was not substantively realised. It could be argued that in assuming a second term of office without going through the scrutiny of an election process, McAleese unwittingly lost an opportunity to carve out a fresh political agenda, settling instead for the relative comfort of modest and by now familiar public expectations. She continued to speak out on the social ills of society while continuing to be the 'primary ambassador' for Ireland on trade delegations abroad.[15] As the fiscal and economic crisis became apparent from 2007 onwards in Ireland, McAleese drew more attention to initiatives with economic and employment potential. In addition, the historic state visit of Queen Elizabeth II to Ireland in May 2011 marked an important moment of reconciliation between the two states. However, without a new value-based theme to add to that of reconciliation, the power of symbolic leadership that had characterised her first term declined.

TRANSFORMING THE OFFICE OF PRESIDENT

Robinson and McAleese brought a fresh energy to what had become a staid office. They sought to refashion the Irish presidency in line with the themes and issues they identified in the course of their election campaigns. The vision offered for the office by each woman is encapsulated in her inaugural address.

From this formal speech penned by the incoming President and untainted by the influence of party political priorities, one can glean much about the agenda to follow. In both instances, it was a vehicle for expressing the nature of the relationship that the new President wished to foster with the public, be it one of bonding (that is, using the commonality of 'Irishness' to connect people of differing backgrounds) or bridging (that is, reconciling people of different cultural, political persuasions). Given, too, that the island of Ireland was a chronically divided polity during each President's terms of office, the inaugural address affords an insight into the presidential approach to this concern. The addresses also convey the intention of the new President in defining the place of Ireland on a world stage. Each woman took the opportunity of her inaugural address to articulate her position on these matters, using her new authority as head of state to map her future role and her relationship with the people of Ireland.

At the time of her election, Robinson was not representative of mainstream public opinion. Aware of this fact, she chose to emphasise the similarities among Irish people, and in doing so sought to bridge the divide between her, as President, and the people. She therefore had to reassure the public that she acknowledged differences in their respective views, while suggesting that these differences were positive, and part of a modern society.

McAleese had fewer 'firsts' to contend with. Ideologically and culturally, she conformed to the dominant values of Irish politics and society to a greater extent than Robinson. She was the second female President, so her gender no longer held as much 'novelty value'. She was a devout Catholic, which reassured conservative groups that had been uneasy with Robinson's humanist orientation. In addition, she was the candidate of the dominant party of the time, Fianna Fáil. McAleese, then, did not present the same perceived potential for destabilising the office as had Robinson. Yet, she was also different: the first President to come from Northern Ireland. McAleese's 1997 inaugural address shows awareness of the need for her to identify with the nation, while promoting peace on the island. In her second inaugural address in 2004, McAleese has already defined her presidential relationship with the people, and spent less time on this point. Nonetheless, she repeated the importance of bridging the divide in understanding between the communities on the island and in building a 'shared future'.

The more muted concern with trust-building among and between communities in the second McAleese address is replaced by a stronger focus on Ireland's relations with the wider world – reflecting her experience in representing the state abroad over the previous seven years. In contrast, Robinson sought to firmly place Ireland in a wider context on a number of occasions in her inaugural speech: as part of a 'new integrated Europe', and with a role as 'a moral and political conscience in world affairs'. Robinson developed this theme in a more substantial manner than her successor, locating Ireland's role in the wider world in terms of 'respect for human rights, pluralism, tolerance and openness to new ideas'. She held out the prospect of a relevant role for the country in a wider context, with 'something "strange and precious" to contribute to the sea-change presently sweeping through the entire continent of Europe'.

Robinson's relationship as head of state to Northern Ireland was equally explicit. She sought to 'encourage mutual understanding and tolerance between all the different communities sharing this island'. McAleese, too, sought to foster peace-making efforts, to 'do my best to make us comfortable in each other's company and unafraid of a shared future'. The direct manner in which both women addressed the Northern issue was a departure from past presidential practice. While context may have shaped their thoughts and words, addressing the conflict and its legacy for relationships on the island was a sign that they were going to use their presidential term in pursuit of a political objective. Although ostensibly 'above politics', both Robinson and McAleese declared an intention to find a way to act presidentially in a political context.

As each woman worked through her presidency, she gave content to these inaugural address themes in innovative ways, while staying within the constitutional boundaries of the office. Thus, both women contributed to transforming the office through utilising the soft, persuasive and symbolic powers vested in the presidency.

CONCLUSION

Irish presidents have a distinctive role as cultural signifiers of the nation – a role that the first President of Ireland (1938–45), Douglas Hyde, fulfilled. Hyde was a figure of reconciliation in a society seeking to establish its newly-won independent status while bearing the recent memory of internal conflict (see Chapter 5). This role was revived by Robinson and McAleese in different ways. Both women were highly conscious of the symbolic content, and potential, of the presidential office. In their inaugural speeches, they conveyed how they intended to use this symbolic power. As activists by inclination, both women understood the importance of valuing and fostering social engagement. Instinctively, they gravitated towards local, community and grassroots endeavours, appreciating that recognition by the President endowed these efforts with authority and validity in the wider society, and, indirectly, in politics. That validation would be used in different ways, with different purposes, by Ireland's two female presidents. Robinson would use her presidency to create a sense of shared identity and communal endeavour; McAleese would emphasise the importance of reconciling different identities in a shared understanding, and mutual respect, of different traditions.

Robinson's presidential role fitted that of a classical 'representative', employing to effect the aspects of delegate and trusteeship that this concept implies. McAleese fashioned her role around the concept of 'facilitator' – a looser definition than that employed by her predecessor. It served her well during her first term when the sensitive process of peace-building dominated politics, but underminded her capacity to exploit the soft power of the presidency later in her second term. However, McAleese had a personal quality of empathy, seen at its best in unscripted and compassionate responses to the 1998 Omagh bombing and the attack on the World Trade Center in New York in September 2001 (O'Dowd, 2011). Both presidents defined, and were defined by, the manner in which they interpreted the office and the personality they brought to this task. They left a combined legacy of an activist presidential role, endowed with heightened public visibility and renewed sense of relevance for the people and for the politics of the time. It is a measure of their success that towards the end of their terms of office, each woman was more popular with the public than they were on their presidential election day.

NOTES

1. At the time, Catholic students wishing to study in Trinity College Dublin required special permission from their local bishop. Mary Bourke's two older brothers were already at Trinity studying medicine, having been granted permission in this way. When her parents sought the same permission for their daughter, the necessary letter of recommendation from Bourke's school principal to the local bishop was not forthcoming. Her parents instead sought and received permission from the Archbishop of Dublin, John Charles McQuaid (Siggins 1997: 37–8). The ban on Catholics attending Trinity College was lifted in 1970.
2. For unionist reaction, see also http://cain.ulst.ac.uk/events/aia/reaction.htm.
3. The SDLP was founded in 1970 by Currie, John Hume and others as a constitutional nationalist party in Northern Ireland. It sought a peaceful solution to the economic, social and political discriminations suffered by nationalists under

unionist-dominated rule. Currie held an SDLP seat in the Northern Ireland Assembly from 1973 to 1974, and briefly held a ministerial position in the power-sharing executive until its collapse in May 1974. He relocated to Dublin in 1989 and in the same year was elected to the Dáil for Fine Gael (O'Sullivan 1991: 89–90).

4. Stephen E. Lucas, quoted in CBS News, 'The Power of Oratory', 11 February 2009. Available at http://www.cbsnews.com/2100-3445_162-3732704.html (accessed 6 September 2012).

5. John McManus, her maternal grandfather, joined the IRA in 1921 and fought in the War of Independence. He returned to his home town of Dromara, County Down after the 1921 Anglo-Irish Treaty brought hostilities to an end (Mac Mánais, 2005: 20–21).

6. The Reid professorship is an early-career position, combining lecturing and academic activity with practice at the Irish Bar.

7. Interview with Mary McAleese: Vincent Browne, Sunday 1 February 1998. Available at http://politico.ie/component/content/article/221-politics/5004-interview-with-mary-mcaleese.htm (accessed 15 Mar 2012).

8. http://news.bbc.co.uk/2/hi/europe/1680695.stm (accessed 2 Dec 2011).

9. Harry Casey taught religion and English at second level in Navan, County Meath. He shared the deep religious faith of the McAleese couple, and became their close friend and confidante. He was her director of elections in 1987 (Mac Mánais, 2005: 302–303).

10. Mansergh, who had a distinguished career in the Irish Department of Foreign Affairs, became special adviser on Northern Ireland to successive Fianna Fáil leaders. He was closely connected with the Irish peace process.

11. RTE news report on McAleese nomination: http://wn.com/Mary_McAleese_beats_Albert_Reynolds_for_Fianna_Fail_Presidential_Nomination,_September_1997 (accessed 29 July 2011)

12. *The Sunday Times*, 19 October 1997 'SDLP linked McAleese to Sinn Féin', quoted in http://sluggerotoole.com/2011/09/27/from-aras97-to-aras11-has-the-media-decommissioned/ (accessed 16 August 2012)

13. *The Independent*, 23 December 1997 'Faith: Catholics angered by Irish president taking Protestant communion', available at http://www.independent.co.uk/news/faith-catholics-angered-by-irish-president-taking-protestant-commun-ion-1290292.html (accessed 16 August 2011).

14. McAleese received members of BASIC to the Áras on 9 November 1998.

15. Self-description of her representative functions as head of state accompanying delegations to market Ireland in other parts of the world; Paul Clarkson, 'I want another seven years: President Mary's poll dream', *The Mirror*, 15 October 2003, available at http://www.thefreelibrary.com/I+want+another+SEVEN+years%3B+PRESIDENT+MARY'S+POLL+DREAM.-a0108861156 (accessed 6 September 2012).

8

PRESIDENTIAL ELECTIONS: THE COLLAPSE OF PARTISANSHIP?

GARY MURPHY AND THERESA REIDY

INTRODUCTION

Much public debate regarding presidential elections in Ireland has focused on the limitations of the office. In the 2011 contest this led to a rather stultifying political situation where the candidates, desperate to distinguish themselves from each other, searched for any slight point of difference to gain public approval. While the President might be mainly a symbolic figure (see Chapter 3), the holder of the office nevertheless fills a political role. This chapter focuses on the seven presidential elections in Ireland between 1945 and 2011 and argues that the contests can be split into two distinct categories: the four contests from 1945 to 1973 and the three contests from 1990 to 2011. The first category of presidential elections reflects the entirely stable and predictable pattern of party competition that represented politics in Ireland since Fianna Fáil first came to power in 1932. In essence, this comprised a dominant Fianna Fáil party, assured of practically 45 per cent of the vote, and a strong Fine Gael party, equally assured of about a third of the popular vote, and a variety of smaller parties with a range of causes which could at times help Fine Gael to oust Fianna Fáil from power but which were not homogenous enough to do this on a consistent basis. The second category reflects a different type of politics in Ireland: one where presidential elections took place against the backdrop of a changing party system and an increasingly volatile electorate.

Fianna Fáil's dominance in Dáil elections remained until the party's rout at the 2011 general election, but the presidential contests of 1990, 1997 and 2011 all show evidence of increasing voter disconnect from the party system, and a shift away from the defining features of previous presidential elections. This trend is seen not only through an analysis of the Fianna Fáil performance but also by assessing the nature of the Fine Gael vote, which substantially weakens in presidential elections after 1973. The performance of the Labour Party and the increased number of independent candidates, and their performance since 1973, are also signals of a striking change in the dynamic of the three most recent presidential elections.

The constitution sets down that elections to the presidency, with its seven-year term, are to be conducted using proportional representation by means of the single transferable vote, although with just one position available the process is more accurately described as election using the alternative vote system. The focus of this chapter will be an examination and discussion of the nomination processes, election campaigns and outcomes of presidential elections. The chapter is divided into three sections addressing each of these elements. The conduct and outcomes of elections are examined using the analytical lens of the party system. The evaluation of election results draws on changes in the party system and on the Reif and Schmitt (1980) second order election framework.

With Douglas Hyde taking office in 1938 as an agreed candidate, the first direct election to the presidency took place in 1945. In all, the position has come vacant on 13 occasions and there have been seven elections (see Appendix 1 for results). All incumbent presidents who have sought a second term have been elected unopposed, apart from Eamon de Valera, who was challenged in 1966. Fianna Fáil dominated the early election contests for the presidency, winning in 1945, 1959, 1966 and 1973. Predictability was, however, ended in 1990 when Mary Robinson, albeit nominally an independent candidate, won with substantial backing from the Labour Party. Party competition has become more volatile and unstable, and in that context the presidential elections of 1990, 1997 and 2011 were played out in a much more politically febrile, and unpredictable, atmosphere than previous ones.

THE NOMINATION PROCESS

There are three entry routes into presidential elections in Ireland. Retiring or former presidents may nominate themselves for re-election on one occasion. As the position of President is intended to be above day-to-day politics, the self-nomination route allows incumbents to seek re-election without needing to return to their supporting political party for endorsement. While incumbents have a non-partisan route into the race in seeking a second term, all other candidates must go through a highly politicised process. Candidates can be nominated by 20 members of the Houses of the Oireachtas or by four city or county councils. Both the Oireachtas and council routes give political parties a central and controlling influence over which candidates can secure a place on the ballot paper.

Political parties, or groups of independents within the Oireachtas, may nominate candidates if they have sufficient numbers. Apart from the first presidential election in 1945 when there were three candidates[1], two candidate races, in essence Fianna Fáil versus Fine Gael, became the norm until 1990. Three candidates contested in 1990, five in 1997 and seven in 2011. Smaller political parties and independent members of the Oireachtas have become more active in the nomination process in recent campaigns. But it is the local council route, first successfully used by candidates in 1997, which has become the main mechanism for increasing the number of candidates. This option has been particularly attractive to candidates from outside the three main political parties, Fianna Fáil, Fine Gael and Labour.

Political parties employ different selection processes when making decisions on candidate nomination, and these have evolved over the decades. At early elections, decision making was largely located within the party hierarchy, often with a controlling role for the party leader. Frequently, only one candidate sought the nomination. More recent elections have brought devolution of decision making and a more competitive candidate selection environment.

Within Fianna Fáil, the decision on presidential candidate selection rests with the parliamentary party. While the party leader's wishes may be taken account of informally, it is the parliamentary party which selects the candidate, or decides not to nominate, as the party did in 2011, the first occasion that Fianna Fáil did not contest a presidential election. When the presidency has been contested, Fianna Fáil traditionally opted for candidates who were veteran politicians with longstanding cabinet experience, as was the case with Sean T. O'Kelly, Eamon de Valera, Erskine Childers and Brian Lenihan.

There was a change of approach in 1997 when Mary McAleese, a lawyer and academic, and an unsuccessful Dáil candidate in 1987, won the nomination, defeating former Taoiseach Albert Reynolds by 62–48 in a vote of the Fianna Fáil parliamentary party. McAleese was widely seen as the preferred candidate of party leader Bertie Ahern, although the selection process was noteworthy for the way in which Ahern went out of his way during the voting to show Reynolds that he had given him his support. Reynolds had notable achievements to his credit, including the nascent peace process in Northern Ireland, but he had led Fianna Fáil to its worst general election result to that point in 1992, and had presided over the break-up of two coalition governments. As a party grandee, Reynolds met the criteria of past Fianna Fáil candidates for the Áras, but internal opposition to his candidacy was deep rooted (Murphy, 2003: 6). Fianna Fáil's coalition partners, the Progressive Democrats, also made it clear that they would not support him.[2] The decision in essence to back a political outsider was a significant departure from party tradition. It was, however, rooted in the simple political fact that Fianna Fáil could not be assured of winning the 1997 presidential election if Reynolds was its candidate.

Fine Gael operates a college-based system for selecting its candidate. There are three groups in the electoral college, members of the national executive, city and county councillors and members of the parliamentary party. There are some shared features in the candidate selection strategies adopted by Fine Gael and Fianna Fáil. At early elections, selection decisions were taken on a more ad-hoc basis, but over time parliamentary parties and the executive branches of parties have become more involved. Like Fianna Fáil, Fine Gael has tended to look to party grandees and senior figures as natural candidates, especially in the early elections when General Sean MacEoin (1945 and 1959) and Tom O'Higgins (1966 and 1973) represented the party. In its troubled search for a candidate in 1990 Fine Gael initially turned to party standard-bearers, including former leader Garret FitzGerald. When this route proved unsuccessful, former Northern Ireland politician Austin Currie – who had moved to the Republic and had been elected as a Fine Gael TD – was prevailed upon to be the party's candidate. Since the 1990 contest, there has been a significant broadening of the net for presidential candidates. More recent line-ups have contained a mixture of senior political figures and other lesser-known candidates from beyond the world of politics, who potentially present a more attractive image than that of a party grandee looking to Áras an Uachtaráin as a retirement home. Yet, despite this overall change in candidate profile, Fine Gael's candidates in 1997 and 2011 had strong party pedigrees as longstanding public representatives.

The Labour Party mooted participation in the presidential election on a number of occasions, and some consideration was given to contesting the 1966 election, as a step towards consolidating advances in the preceding general election. Decisions to remain out of presidential contests were informed in part by the financial implications of contesting a national election, and, more importantly, by the knowledge that any prospective candidate would have little or no chance of actually winning (Gallagher, 1982: 59–60).

Thus, it was not until 1990 that Labour first entered a presidential campaign. The party leader, Dick Spring, played a decisive role in the strategy of seeking a candidate beyond the parliamentary party fold, and was seen as instrumental in approaching Mary Robinson (although she ultimately contested the election as an independent candidate). He was again involved in the decision to approach Adi Roche in 1997, though ultimately with far less success than seven years previously. In 2004 party leader Pat Rabbitte toyed with the idea of nominating a candidate. There was some discussion within the party of challenging Mary McAleese, and Michael D. Higgins's attempt to secure the support of the party's ruling council failed by one vote, leading to some internal discontent. In the end the party decided not to run against the popular incumbent (Murphy, 2008: 10). Although the Labour Party leader is at the centre of decision making, formally the process of presidential candidate selection is a function of the parliamentary party and the executive board of the party, acting jointly. This was the case in 2011 when Michael D. Higgins secured the Labour nomination by defeating former party adviser Fergus Finlay and former public representative Kathleen O'Meara. Fifty-two members of the parliamentary party and 14 executive council members decided the outcome, with Higgins securing 37 votes against 18 for Finlay and seven for O'Meara (RTE, 2011).

Independent members of the Oireachtas and those aligned with smaller political parties all have nominating rights, although these have only been invoked on a few occasions. Involvement in the presidential nomination processes is arranged on a more ad-hoc basis among these members of the Oireachtas and coordination is organised on a case-by-case basis. The decision to nominate a candidate will be informed by a variety of factors. Presidential elections are potentially an opportunity to raise party profile. Having a candidate in the race ensures that the party is given broadcast time and media coverage to promote individual personnel and, to a degree, party policy. However, smaller parties must also balance the cost of running in a presidential election against the reality that victory is unlikely. Patrick McCartan contested as a non-party candidate in 1945, but independents and small parties did not exercise their nominating powers again until 2011, when a number of independent TDs joined with Sinn Féin to nominate Martin McGuinness. McGuinness was a high-profile candidate for Sinn Féin, as Deputy First Minister in the Northern Ireland Executive (he stepped down as Deputy First Minister for the duration of the presidential election campaign) and Sinn Féin's chief negotiator during the peace talks which led to the Good Friday Agreement. David Norris (a longstanding senator, elected from the University of Dublin panel) abandoned the Oireachtas nomination route in 2011 amidst significant controversy over letters he had written some years earlier in support of his former partner, who had been charged with sexual offences in Israel. Norris re-entered the race just weeks later and used the council nomination route to get onto the ballot, but his earlier difficulty in securing the required 20 Oireachtas nominations underlines the challenge which non-party candidates face if they select this particular route – one that is highly politicised, and historically the preserve of the three larger parties, which not unreasonably wanted to exclude other candidates from the contest. In that context, party political outsiders have in recent years been more successful using the council nomination process.

The prospect of nominations from this source had arisen earlier. In 1959 a number of councils considered nominating Dr McCartan, who was keen to run again; one council, Wicklow County Council, formally nominated him. But it was alleged that the election date had been deliberately set to limit the scope of city and county councils to make nominations (see letters page, *The Irish Times*, 7 March 1959). The local council route was considered again in 1990, when the then Lord Mayor of Dublin, Carmencita Hederman, expressed an interest in being a presidential candidate. Hederman, however, failed to get the backing even of her own council, and was forced to abandon her attempt to contest the election (O'Sullivan, 1991).

Seven years later the position changed: two independent candidates, Dana Rosemary Scallon and Derek Nally, entered the presidential contest through the council nomination process. The councils were active again in using their nomination powers in 2011, when four candidates entered the race through this route. The council option has opened up nomination opportunities for candidates wishing to go forward, although it still favours candidates with a political background. Independents need to achieve a majority vote in a council to get a nomination. Consequently, a benign approach is required from any political party with a possible blocking majority. In many cases, the larger political parties on the councils abstained from the decision to nominate candidates, particularly at the 2011 contest. While these party councillors were not active in recommending candidates, their abstention was a tacit endorsement of the decision of other council members to play a role in the nominating process. Many commentators were skeptical of Scallon's chances of getting on the ballot in 1997, but she secured the backing of councils with reasonable ease. This was true also in 2011, when she entered the race quite late in the day. The council route was seriously pursued by four candidates (Dana Rosemary Scallon, Mary Davis, Seán Gallagher and David Norris), all of whom eventually got onto the ballot paper.

It is difficult to determine precisely why councils have become more active in nominating presidential candidates. Allegations of party control and attempts to prevent independents from securing nominations date back to the mooted McCartan candidacy in 1959. Increasing autonomy in local politics (Katz and Mair, 1995: 21), wider media coverage of the nomination process and opinion poll evidence (at least in 2011) indicating that the public was in favour of opening up the race to independent candidates provided the opportunity for councillors to play a larger role in national politics. Many of the candidates used the idea of broadening the field in their speeches to councils when seeking nomination. Since councillors view themselves as starved of political influence, the nomination route was a mechanism for addressing a perceived imbalance in the distribution of power.[3] There was evidence of a similar motivation in respect of the 1997 contest (Doyle, 1998). Many councillors seem to have believed that it was unlikely that the party head office or hierarchy would take action against councillors who ignored the party directive, and that the rules could be bent or ignored. As the number of councils nominating a presidential candidate grew in 2011, a cascade effect was created. Councils even convened last-minute meetings just days before the close of nominations, underscoring their enthusiasm to play a part in the presidential nomination process.

Alleged deficiencies in the nomination process have been the subject of vigorous debate during election campaigns. Alternative nomination routes, such as the Finnish and Portuguese systems of requiring a nomination to be made by several thousand voters, have been canvassed (see Chapter 2). Such alternatives maintain a requirement for candidates to achieve a critical mass of support as a condition for entry into the race. However, the Irish political system has shown little evidence of enthusiasm for reform of the nomination process. In early 2011, when reform of the entire political system was the subject of a serious national debate, in advance of the Dáil general election, many of the parties produced extensive political reform manifestoes; but the presidential nomination process did not feature (Suiter and Farrell, 2011). A Fine Gael proposal to reduce the term of office from seven to five years was their sole suggestion about the presidency. Nevertheless, with the more extensive use of the local authority power to nominate, and the increasingly fragmented nature of parliament in the wake of the 2011 general election result, it is probably unlikely that any serious candidate would be prevented from running in the future.

PRESIDENTIAL ELECTION CAMPAIGNS

Presidential elections are clearly different from other contests in Ireland, since they offer the only opportunity for citizens to vote for a national candidate as distinct from constituency ones. As only a small number of candidates participate, the campaign is much more intensely focused; personal characteristics are stressed, as all aspects of the candidates' lives are scrutinised. There is no formal policy role for the Irish President; Marsh (1999: 222) described the position as one of 'being rather than doing'. This leaves candidates in the somewhat invidious position of having to participate in an intensely focused campaign where there is little to discuss apart from their own personal suitability for the position and a vision, however nebulous, of how they would operate as president. The elections of 1959, 1966 and 1973 were clearly straightforward political contests between Fianna Fáil and Fine Gael, but there was no question of the President filling anything other than a 'father of the nation', ceremonial type role. In contrast, the Robinson candidacy in 1990 was much more 'political', as she articulated a different vision for the presidency. The candidates in 1997 and 2011 also offered their respective visions for the presidency. In that context while the presidency itself may be constraining in terms of its direct political power, there clearly have been political candidacies.

PROJECTING THE CANDIDATES

The limited policy role and constrained constitutional position of the President has featured in all presidential campaigns. Allegations that candidates did not understand the role of the President have appeared from the first campaign in 1945, with then Tánaiste Seán Lemass noting that 'if Dr McCartan had taken the trouble to study the Constitution, he would see that the President's powers could do nothing to influence the general policy of the state' (*The Irish Times*, 12 June 1945). Since 1990, candidates have constantly had to face criticisms that they simply do not understand the limits of the role of president, given that they have for the most part campaigned on operating a different type of presidency. O'Malley (Chapter 9) discusses the persistent claims throughout the 2011 campaign that several candidates were ill-informed about the specific responsibilities and powers of the role.

With so few candidates in the race, campaigning techniques are also quite different from other Irish elections, which often draw on a type of military rhetoric, with discussion of territory, battlegrounds and strategy. A distinction has been made between 'direct' campaigning techniques, including canvassing and postering, and 'indirect' techniques, including radio and television appearances, campaign literature, social media and newspaper coverage (LeDuc et al, 2002). Indirect methods have come to dominate Irish presidential election campaigns. A single candidate will be able to meet only a small number of voters from a national constituency, so the campaign is largely conducted through the airwaves. As media outlets have multiplied, the media campaign has become the defining aspect of presidential elections. Candidates use local radio, national television and radio, and local and national newspapers to project their candidacies. Interviews and debates have grown in number. The direct campaigning elements see candidates traversing the country 'pressing the flesh'. Early elections were organised around mass rallies, campaign events and church gate addresses (see Chubb, 1992: 145–6). By the end of the twentieth century, candidates had taken to travelling in buses with their images emblazoned across them. Candidates attend sporting occasions and fairs; and the biggest event in the agricultural calendar, the national ploughing championships, has become a favourite for presidential candidates.

There is contradictory evidence on the use of posters in campaigns. In 1997 the Fine Gael candidate Mary Banotti vowed not to use any posters in furtherance of a green agenda but her campaign quickly changed its mind once it became clear in polls that her candidacy was languishing far behind Fianna Fáil's Mary McAleese. There is little evidence that the change made any difference to the campaign. In 2011 the independent candidate Seán Gallagher also took the decision not to use posters – with remarkably different results, as he looked set for victory until his strategy unravelled in the last week of that tumultuous campaign. Although the 'ground war' is a feature of every presidential candidate's campaign, there is a growing sense that the 'air war' is displacing it in connecting with voters.

The idea of a presidential theme was identified by Cearbhall Ó Dálaigh in his inaugural address in 1974. Ó Dálaigh – an agreed candidate for the office – observed that 'Presidents under the Irish Constitution don't have policies. But ... a president can have a theme' (see Chapter 6). In recent elections, some of the winning candidates have successfully employed campaign themes as a mechanism for communicating their priorities. The strategy was used effectively by Robinson in 1990 when she promised to have a permanent light in the window of Áras an Uachtaráin as a symbol of her engagement with the Irish diaspora. Mary McAleese also delivered a strong message with her 1997 slogan 'Building Bridges', which correlated with the Northern Ireland peace process. It also played upon McAleese's background as a moderate nationalist from Belfast. The candidates in 2011 also had clearly crafted messages to go along with their campaign slogans – none more than Seán Gallagher's view that he would use the presidency as a vehicle to create jobs.

The individual campaigns have in common their intensely personalised nature and their focus on the suitability of the individual to become President of Ireland. This candidate focus is evident as early as 1945, although with the multiplication of media outlets and modes, the intensity of the campaigns has been greatly amplified. Early presidential campaigns were somewhat muted affairs, and press coverage largely focused – perhaps inevitably – on reporting the activities and speeches of the individual candidates. The prominence given to presidential elections, however, has grown substantially in recent contests, with a notable shift in 1990, as will be seen in the following subsections.

THE EARLY CAMPAIGNS

Much of the 1945 presidential election coverage was overshadowed by the ending of World War II, which dominated all of the papers. However, this did not prevent some occasional outbursts on the part of candidates or their parties. Fianna Fáil minister Seán Lemass questioned the credentials of the Fine Gael candidate, arguing that General Seán MacEoin had toured the country campaigning against the 1937 Constitution and was therefore unsuited to become the guardian of that very document. Lemass was also critical of the independent candidate: 'Then there is the spectacle of Dr McCartan … who after voting for the Treaty, went to America, where he has been selling sweepstake tickets, and then he comes back here to be elected President, no less' (*The Irish Times*, 12 June 1945). Perhaps the most astringent comments came from Fine Gael leader General Richard Mulcahy, who claimed that 'the object of the Government in nominating a member of Fianna Fáil is to raise the swastika of Fianna Fáil over the residence of the President' (*The Irish Times*, 12 June 1945). Allegations of dictatorship surfaced across the campaign and were strongly refuted by de Valera at a series of election rallies the week before polling (*The Irish Times*, 2 June 1945). The Fianna Fáil attacks may be interpreted as political charges from the party that had dominated Irish politics for over a decade and which wanted to ensure that it won the first contest for the presidency. Mulcahy's comments, however, suggest that Fine Gael, too, did not hesitate to engage in robust attack.

The 1959 contest represented in many respects a revival of Civil War animosities, and the campaign speeches of the candidates, Eamon de Valera and Seán MacEoin, were focused on their respective roles in the War of Independence and the Civil War. Newspaper coverage was moderate, appearing occasionally on the front page but mostly consigned to short articles in the middle pages. *The Irish Times* complained about the conduct of the campaign, finding fault with the various personal attacks on candidates (see, for example, *The Irish Times*, 29 May 1959). Indeed the most notable feature was the lack of real substantive coverage of the candidates, the campaign or the presidency itself. In essence, the campaign was dominated by de Valera and whether his move from Taoiseach to President would make any difference to public policy in Ireland.

The 1966 campaign was the first – and to-date the last – to involve an incumbent president. The advantages of incumbency have been demonstrated clearly across the election literature (Erikson, 1971; Ferejohn, 1977). De Valera was re-elected but it was the closest presidential election in history with just 10,717 votes separating the candidates on election day, as de Valera gained 50.5 per cent of the vote. The closeness of de Valera's victory certainly came as a shock to Fianna Fáil. While one could speculate that incumbency certainly did him no harm in the election, it is also valid to argue that the Fine Gael candidate, the relatively youthful Tom O'Higgins, was aided by campaigning on the idea that it was time for a modern Ireland to have a modern president (O'Higgins was 49, de Valera was 83). The election year was also noteworthy as the jubilee celebrations for the 1916 Easter Rising took place just two months before the presidential election. The commemorations were a highly charged political event, and the direct involvement of the President raises the challenge which presidents face in staying out of daily politics while presiding over them. While there were some grumblings from Fine Gael about the enhanced public profile of Eamon de Valera in advance of the election, the fundamental feature of the 1966 election was that it was clearly a partisan Fianna Fáil versus Fine Gael affair.

The 1973 campaign was the first presidential election in which the broadcast media played a significant role. Candidates made a small number of appearances on television, and there was more extensive use of radio.

Interestingly, Fine Gael declined Fianna Fáil requests for a televised presidential debate. The dynamic of presidential election campaigns was largely unchanged, with a partisan contest between Erskine Childers of Fianna Fáil and Tom O'Higgins of Fine Gael, who was contesting the presidency for a second time. Since O'Higgins had come so close to beating de Valera in 1966, he had been widely expected to win the contest, capitalising on the victory of Fine Gael and Labour in the Dáil election just three months previously. The campaign lacked some of the vitriol and rancour of the earlier elections. Although still a direct contest between Fianna Fáil and Fine Gael, it was the first without divisive figures from the civil war era. Hostility had declined with the passage of five decades, and both Childers and O'Higgins refrained from personalised attacks. In any event Childers won a close contest, ensuring that Fianna Fáil retained control of the presidency.

The partisanship that characterised presidential elections from 1945 to 1973 was followed by a period of apparent apathy towards the office amongst people and politicians alike. There were few complaints about the 17 years that were to elapse without a presidential election: the vacancy created by Childers's sudden death in 1974 was filled by an agreed candidate (Ó Dálaigh), and when he resigned two years later he was succeeded by another agreed candidate (Hillery). When Patrick Hillery was chosen as the agreed candidate for the Áras in 1976, he was both unwilling to seek the nomination and profoundly reluctant to accept the position (Walsh, 2008: 421–2), in what can only been be interpreted as a testament to the weakness of the office. Fianna Fáil was happy to have the office; Fine Gael and the Labour Party were happy to let them have it, with considerations of cost and the apparent inevitability of a Fianna Fáil victory no doubt contributing towards this attitude. This would all change dramatically in 1990.

THE LATER CAMPAIGNS

The 1990 campaign marks a significant number of turning points in presidential elections. The first contest in 17 years excited the media, and the campaign took centre stage in the front and inside pages of all the main newspapers. The Labour Party took the lead in ensuring that there would be a contest when its leader Dick Spring declared in January 1990 that Labour would contest a presidential election and he would be the candidate, if he had to be (Collins, 1993: 174–5). In fact, Spring soon found himself a much stronger candidate outside his parliamentary party fold. This was part of a deliberate strategy to raise the profile of the party with a view to enhancing its performance in future general elections. Television and radio programmes gave extensive coverage to the campaign. While elections up to this point had at times involved personal attacks on the candidates from other candidates or within parties, the focus had been exclusively on the public personae of the candidates. Their private lives and those of their family members did not feature in the public commentary. This changed in 1990 and became much more pronounced in 1997. Probably most crucially of all, the 1990 presidential campaign saw a woman stand for the first time for Ireland's highest office. While initially Mary Robinson's entry into the fray was not seen by Fianna Fáil as a major threat to its hold on the presidency, this view began to change as Robinson's campaign gained traction.

By 1990, radio and television appearances were expected, and debates and interviews with the candidates had become a central feature of the campaign. Generally, candidate debates are not seen as being all that decisive in determining election outcomes, although much of the research supporting that assertion is drawn from the analysis of US presidential debates (Shaw, 1999). It is more difficult to assess the wider impact of media coverage. Nevertheless the 1990 campaign included a number of decisive broadcast moments.

Brian Lenihan, Tánaiste in the Fianna Fáil–Progressive Democrat coalition and a senior member of Fianna Fáil, was selected as his party's candidate, and continued the long-standing tradition of Fianna Fáil grandees bearing the party's standard at presidential election time. He was, however, put on the defensive during the campaign when, participating in a popular discussion programme on RTE television, he denied making phone calls in 1982 to President Hillery asking him not to dissolve the Dáil following the collapse of the Fine Gael–Labour coalition. He was further embarrassed when a student produced a recording in which he admitted making the calls. While Lenihan downplayed the controversy, describing it as a 'storm in a teacup' (*The Irish Times*, 27 October 1990), it was to overshadow the remainder of his campaign, culminating in his dismissal as Tánaiste under pressure from the Progressive Democrats, although he remained Fianna Fáil's candidate for President. In the same campaign, a casual remark by EU Commissioner Pádraig Flynn that seemed to cast aspersions on Robinson's maternal qualities has been identified by observers as having swayed many female voters to support Robinson (O'Sullivan, 1991: 94). Increasingly desperate attempts to portray Robinson as some sort of radical feminist foundered. The 1990 campaign affirms an old political adage; the campaign matters. Lenihan had entered the race as the clear front runner but a series of events saw

Robinson's public support rise, and a *Sunday Press* poll placed her in the lead just days before the election (*The Irish Times*, 10 November 1990).

The marginalisation of Fine Gael has been one of the more remarkable features of recent presidential elections. The candidacy of former SDLP MP and Northern Ireland civil rights activist Austin Currie in 1990 proved to be a major disappointment to the party; he had agreed to run only after several Fine Gael grandees had refused the nomination, but he won only 17 per cent of the first preference vote. The election result led to the ousting of Alan Dukes as party leader just days after the election (Gallagher and Marsh, 2002: 33). The 1997 election proved a second dispiriting contest for Fine Gael as its candidate, Mary Banotti, who had edged out Avril Doyle at Fine Gael's selection convention, never managed to gain significant support, and eventually carried only the core Fine Gael vote of just over 29 per cent. The party experienced another disappointing presidential outcome in 2011 when Fine Gael veteran politician Gay Mitchell not only failed to capture the public's imagination but also failed to deliver even his party's core supporters (see Chapter 9).

While 1990 marked the move towards more media focused attacks on candidates, 1997 was to witness a significant intensification of this development. Adi Roche, the Labour Party candidate, was the first to be targeted. She had been chosen by party leader Dick Spring as a candidate in the Robinson mould, and was widely known and admired for her work with a Chernobyl children's charity. She immediately faced suggestions that she had bullied colleagues within her charity, and long-standing allegations against her brother, who was dismissed from the army in 1969 for allegedly being in the company of members of various republican splinter groups, were also aired. Roche, who had been an early front runner in opinion polls, saw her campaign slide into disarray. Mary McAleese, the Fianna Fáil candidate, also faced personal attacks. During the campaign, confidential documents from the Department of Foreign Affairs were leaked to the *Sunday Business Post*, and were used to suggest that she was an IRA sympathiser. This seems, however, to have backfired, with a widespread perception that the allegations, and the manner in which they were made public, were unfair. Personal scrutiny and personal attack were of course important features of the 2011 campaign (see Chapter 9).

OPINION POLLS

In addition to intensification of media coverage, presidential election campaigns have also adapted to the increased prevalence of opinion polls. The first experiment in presidential polling occurred in 1945 when *The Irish Times* carried out a 'straw vote' – 9,974 sample ballots were circulated and just under 3,000 were returned by post over a two-week period (*The Irish Times*, 9 June 1945). The poll prediction was famously incorrect. It suggested that the transfers from the elimination of McCartan would put MacEoin well ahead of O'Kelly. The poll incurred the ire of many government ministers, including Sean Lemass and Frank Aiken, who both indicated that they viewed it as an attempt by *The Irish Times* to influence the outcome of the election. *The Irish Times* refuted the criticism in a sharply worded rejoinder on 12 June 1945:

> Apparently [Fianna Fáil] have been annoyed by the result of our 'straw vote'. The Minister ... who no longer can use his dagger against this newspaper through Censorship got in a few half hearted stabs in his speech. ... His colleague [Sean Lemass] ... declared that this newspaper was anxious to secure the return of General MacEoin; but not for the first time and certainly not for the last time, Mr Lemass was utterly wrong.

Despite the prominence given to the straw vote, there was no further indication of a swing away from O'Kelly, in any of the coverage or commentary on the election in either *The Irish Times*, the *Cork Examiner* or the *Irish Independent*. This seems to suggest that it was not a rogue poll per se, but more a clumsy attempt at a survey that was simply not scientifically accurate. In fact, *The Irish Times*'s political standpoint in the period just after the end of the 'Emergency' (as the Second World War was called in Ireland) was more agnostic than simply anti-Fianna Fáil, and its favoured form of solution to Ireland's problems was to call for a national government (O'Brien, 2008: 154–5; Murphy, 2009: 161–2). In that context, while there may have been no overt bias in *The Irish Times* poll, the newspaper was unlikely to view a Fianna Fáil president allied to a Fianna Fáil government as a good thing in itself.

After this inauspicious start to opinion polling at presidential elections, polls were not to return to centre stage until the 1990 election, when several polls were produced by *The Irish Times*, the *Sunday Press* and the *Sunday Independent*, among others, to track the dramatic race. So numerous were the polls that *The Irish Times*, in a look back on the election, headlined their article 'A Case of for Whom the Opinion Polls' (*The Irish Times*, 10 November 1990). Since 1990, opinion polls have become a kind of fulcrum around which presidential campaigns revolve.

An examination of all of the presidential campaigns confirms that the contests are intensely personal, with a central focus on the suitability of the candidates for the position of President, along with their personality traits and behaviours. Campaigns have changed dramatically in character since the first presidential contest in 1945. Not only has politics in Ireland become more professionalised, but the broadcast media have moved centre stage and have become the main mechanism which candidates use for communicating their message to voters. The broadcast media have also provided some of the critical moments in recent elections with opinion polls tracking the rise and fall of candidates in the course of the campaign. We can see a distinct shift in campaign strategies and media coverage between the first four presidential contests and the three more recent elections. However, the intensified media element to campaigns from 1990 onwards serves to amplify the dynamic of elections rather than significantly altering their trajectory. Campaigns had always been personal; they became more so with the advent of more media outlets. It seems that the media recorded the changing fortunes of Fianna Fáil rather than shaping them.

DECIPHERING THE RESULTS

Michael Marsh (1999: 226) has argued that 'to win an Irish election any candidate or party must either be Fianna Fáil or beat it'. This statement captures the reality of Irish presidential elections particularly well until 2011 when for the first time Fianna Fáil did not even nominate a candidate. The presidential scorecard technically reads Fianna Fáil seven, independents one and the Labour Party one. Mary Robinson contested as an independent and has always maintained that she was an independent candidate who was supported not only by the Labour Party, which nominated her, but also by the Green Party, Workers Party and many in the Progressive Democrats, although that party was in coalition with Fianna Fáil at the time and did not formally endorse her or have any official role in her campaign. Robinson's share of the vote in 1990, at 38.9 per cent, was nearly 30 per cent more than the Labour Party received in the 1989 general election and close to 20 per cent more than it would receive in 1992; it would, then, be an exaggeration to see her victory as one for the Labour Party. Moreover, she had not been a member of the party since 1985, when she resigned over her opposition to the Anglo-Irish agreement. Her victory can be attributed to many factors, not least the implosion of the Fine Gael vote, the controversy over Brian Lenihan's campaign, and the fact that she was the first woman to stand for the office – but the fact that she ran an excellent campaign may have been the most important factor of all (O'Reilly, 1991). Up to Robinson's victory the office was the preserve of Fianna Fáil candidates and would return to that party with Mary McAleese's victory in 1997. But the 1990 presidential contest decisively signalled the end to the two-party dualism in presidential elections (for full results, see Appendix 1).

How are we to explain turnout in presidential elections? The 'second order election' model is a useful approach and supports the overall analysis in this chapter: it predicts that turnout will be lower at these types of contests since the stakes are lower (Reif and Schmitt, 1980). Presidential elections in Ireland conform to this expectation. It is clear from Figure 8.1, which reports turnout in Dáil and presidential elections since the 1940s, and local and European elections more recently, that there has been a downward trend especially since the late twentieth century. There may have been some recovery from the middle of the first decade of the twenty-first century, when turnout levels improved at all types of elections. Concerns about the quality and accuracy of the electoral registers at Irish elections have persisted for some years, making it to difficult to arrive at final conclusions on turnout at any of the recent elections. Nevertheless, it is clear that turnout in presidential elections has been much lower than in Dáil elections, and this was particularly obvious in 1997

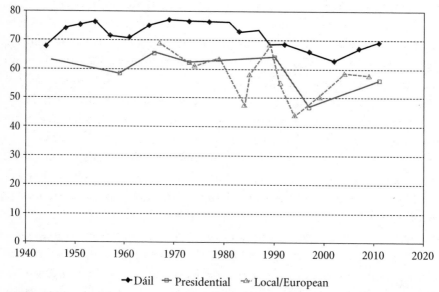

+ Dáil — Presidential — Local/European

FIGURE 8.1   Turnout in Dáil, presidential, local and European elections, 1944–2011

and 2011, when turnout at presidential elections was significantly lower than at Dáil elections in the same years.

In explaining the outcome of presidential elections there are a number of explanatory frameworks in the comparative literature; yet, apart from the second order election model, none of them work very well in the Irish case. Magalhães (2007) and Magalhães and Gómez Fortes (2008) suggest that one step in examining results in presidential elections requires consideration of the concept of government gains and losses. The second order literature predicts a curvilinear pattern (Marsh 1998; Ferrara and Weishaupt 2004). But applying this analysis makes little sense in the Irish context as the governing party has won all but two of the presidential elections. Only Mary Robinson and Erskine Childers won the presidency when their respective parties were not in government. Incumbency is frequently considered in the analysis of presidential elections. It is clear that it can confer an advantage, and estimates of the extent of the advantage vary, depending on the political and institutional context (Fiorina, 1977; Ferejohn, 1977). However, with just one incumbent president having contested an Irish presidential election, analysis of incumbency is pretty pointless in the Irish case.

Two possible explanations remain: parties and candidates. The evidence from second order contests suggests that party identification as a determinant of voting behaviour may be in decline. Marsh (2000) considers the candidate and party dichotomy and argues that while candidate effects might be expected to be significant under the single transferable vote, the evidence suggests that party labels are quite influential. Indicating that campaigns can have two strands, with a national campaign on party political lines working alongside a more personalised candidate centred element, he also describes much of the dynamic of presidential elections. Later, Marsh (2007) provides support for party-based voting hypotheses, and indicates that perceptions of candidate centred effects may have been overstated, although he does demonstrate that candidate voting was relevant for a sizeable minority. Similarly, Mair and Weeks (2005: 156), in analysing voting at Dáil elections, note that one future scenario 'might envisage many voters turning away from party politics as such, and relying more heavily on competing personal appeals of the party leaders or even the local candidates, which could lead to even greater successes for independent, single-issue candidates'. In effect this is how the 1990 presidential election played out, with enough voters being persuaded that Robinson's personal appeal was a sufficiently strong reason to vote for her (though ultimately Lenihan received more first preference votes). Transfers from Fine Gael's Austin Currie were the deciding factor and went to Robinson over Lenihan in a ratio of 6:1 (O'Sullivan 1991). The 2011 presidential election saw similar personal appeals made by all the candidates during that campaign and, of course, that contest was most noteworthy for the decision of Fianna Fáil not to run a candidate.

Mair and Weeks (2005: 154) identify 1989 as a turning point in the Irish party system, pointing to the decision of Fianna Fáil to enter coalition government as a step towards becoming 'just another party'. While Fianna Fáil remained the dominant player in party competition for several years to come, still winning the majority of votes and seats at all national elections until 2011, its share of first preference votes had already begun to decline. Fianna Fáil has come close to winning 50 per cent of all votes at presidential elections, securing a higher percentage than it has achieved at Dáil elections (see Figure 8.2). Figure 8.2 also shows that while Fine Gael has challenged Fianna Fáil through the decades, and even though it has secured marginally more votes at presidential elections over Dáil elections, it came close to securing the office only once, in 1966. Indeed, the party share of the vote at presidential elections has been in significant decline since 1973, culminating in the shockingly low 6.4 per cent it received in 2011.

Fine Gael has competed vigorously with Fianna Fáil for decades. Evaluations have often pointed out that in contrast to Fianna Fáil, it has a

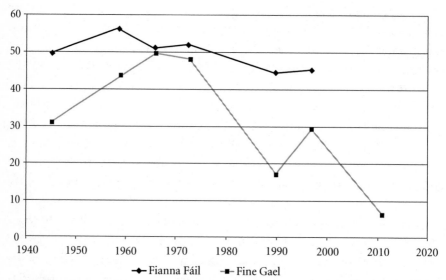

FIGURE 8.2 Support for Fianna Fáil and Fine Gael in presidential elections, 1945–2011

top-down structure, a weaker organisational base and, in recent decades, it has displayed an inability to recover from the defining influence of the Garret FitzGerald leadership period (Gallagher and Marsh, 2002; O'Malley and Kerby, 2004). From the late 1980s, it drifted through a succession of leaders and often seemed to grasp at short-term solutions to its difficulty in connecting with the electorate. Nowhere is this more in evidence than in its approach to presidential elections. Although candidate selection has become a more open process with several candidates competing for the nomination, the party has opted for one electorally unappealing candidate after another, with Gay Mitchell bringing the party to its lowest point in 2011. Mitchell, who had been a very successful vote getter in another second order contest (European Parliament elections in Dublin) never connected with the public and was unable to even attract a core Fine Gael vote. Resources do not appear to have been a problem as Fine Gael has invested significant amounts of money in campaigns through the years. In fact, the absence of Fine Gael's long-standing partisan opponent, Fianna Fáil, seems to have worsened its performance, and the party's candidate did not even secure the regular partisan quota of votes. With Fianna Fáil out of the race, it seems, many Fine Gael voters felt free to opt out of the party political approach to voting. When personality, gender or specific issues trump partisanship in presidential elections, Fine Gael is the big loser. It is unable to connect with voters in presidential elections and now cannot even rely on a core vote.

It is hard to dismiss party as a major determinant of voting behaviour based on the trends in Figure 8.2. Garvin (1978) used variables which characterised rural society to explain Fianna Fáil support in the early presidential elections, while Sinnott (1995) found that support for the divorce referendum worked best to explain the Robinson vote in 1990. However, party support appears pretty stable across the decades. The 1990 presidential election continued in the tradition of the 'Fianna Fáil versus the rest' dynamic of electoral politics. What was different was that a strong third candidate, with a wide appeal, entered the fray and took non-core Fianna Fáil voters away from potentially supporting the Fianna Fáil candidate. Brian Lenihan still received 44 per cent of the first preference vote. Seven years later, the Fianna Fáil candidate Mary McAleese received 45 per cent of the first preference vote. The graphical analysis of results at elections indicates that the traditional dominance of Fianna Fáil in party politics also held for presidential elections until 2011, when it did not run a candidate after its catastrophic showing in the general election. A simple correlation analysis also confirms this: correlating party share of the vote at the previous Dáil elections with the share of the first preference vote secured by the party candidates at presidential elections produces a coefficient of 0.705 for Fianna Fáil with a weaker 0.495 for Fine Gael. This brings us back to the opening statement of this section – 'to win an Irish election any candidate or party must either be Fianna Fáil or beat it'.

CONCLUSION

Irish presidential elections are rather unusual, and the electoral tools used to explain outcomes in other jurisdictions have limited applicability. The elections themselves are infrequent and are often avoided through inter-party agreement, itself an unusual outcome. The nature of party competition in Ireland renders it difficult to apply models based on notions of incumbency, reward and punishment, and cultural conflicts. The electoral dominance of Fianna Fáil is the simple explanation for that party's success at all presidential elections until 1990. After that point, there is a pattern of slow decline in the Fianna Fáil vote, underpinning the changed nature of competition at presidential elections. The Robinson victory in 1990 can be seen as an early indication of the changing nature of Irish politics, with the partisanship of the first 70 years of the Irish state eventually giving way to a more fluid and aggressive era of political competition. While this election conforms to Marsh's thesis of beating Fianna Fáil, it seems pretty clear that it is the first step in a changing electoral landscape. This would take over 20 years to manifest itself fully, at the general and presidential elections of 2011, but it can be traced back, not simply to the Robinson election, but also to the decision of Fianna Fáil to enter coalition in 1989. The stability and size of the Fianna Fáil vote kept it in power for the greater part of the state's history, and, it could be argued, delivered it victory in the 1997 presidential election. Growing instability and partisan de-alignment have, however, opened up all Irish elections, and the volatility at the 2011 Dáil election raises very serious questions about the long-term future of Fianna Fáil, with its decision not to contest the 2011 presidential elections reflecting its transformed position.

For its part, Fine Gael's dramatic performance in the 2011 general election was perversely mirrored by its spectacularly disastrous collapse in the presidential election. While Labour might appear as the big political winners of 2011, the reality is that its presidential election victory was won on a soft vote when the Gallagher campaign imploded in the last week, and there can be no guarantee that at the next general election it will sustain its 2011 result. In that context it can take no comfort into the future from the victory of Michael D. Higgins in the presidential election.

All of the nomination routes to get onto the ballot paper have now been used, with the majority of candidates getting onto the ballot through the council mechanism in 2011. While dissatisfaction with the nomination processes has grown, it appears unlikely that any changes will materialise in the near future. Presidential election campaigns are characterised by intensely personal contests. Media proliferation has contributed to this phenomenon and the modern campaign is professional and expensive. In that context we can clearly say that the Ireland of the presidential elections of 1945 to 1973, with its predictable political stability, has been replaced by an Ireland in which partisan voting is weakening, as candidates come under more and more public scrutiny. In that context presidential elections can evince no certainties into the future in an Ireland where politics has substantially changed over the past two decades and where party loyalty is now but a distant memory of earlier elections.

NOTES

1. Dr Patrick McCartan, an independent republican and Sinn Féin representative in the First Dáil, was nominated by a number of Labour TDs and Senators and some Clann na Talmhan TDs in 1945 and contested the first presidential election.
2. The fact that Reynolds presided over Fianna Fáil's lowest ever vote in the 1992 general election and that he was widely blamed for the break up of both the Fianna Fáil – Progressive Democrat coalition of 1989-1992 and the Fianna Fáil – Labour coalition of 1992–4 had tainted him in the minds of many within Fianna Fáil itself. Reynolds was also embroiled in contested allegations of wrong-doing in the 1994 Report of the Tribunal of Inquiry into the Beef Processing Industry (the Beef Tribunal).
3. Six interviews undertaken by Dr Reidy with local council members in Munster confirmed this view.

9

THE 2011 PRESIDENTIAL ELECTION: EXPLAINING THE OUTCOME

EOIN O'MALLEY

INTRODUCTION

The 2011 Irish presidential election was notable for the number and diversity of candidates, the volatility of the patterns of support and the negativity of the campaign. One of the candidates was previously best known for his part in a reality TV show, and this election resembled reality television in that each of the candidates was subject to a great deal of personal scrutiny and some were seemingly eliminated from contention in voters' minds. The ultimate front-runners, Seán Gallagher, an independent candidate with a background in Fianna Fáil, and long-time Labour parliamentarian, Michael D. Higgins, then fought an essentially head-to-head contest in the final two weeks, during which Gallagher's integrity and honesty were called into question. His support dropped sharply in the last week, and Higgins benefited from the shift from Gallagher. In the end Higgins was elected comfortably.

This chapter argues that while underlying ideology and partisan preferences will influence many voters' choices, the presidential election is part personality contest and in part suitability test for the office. Voters consider the appropriateness of the person for the position, and it was revelations about candidates' past lives and their personal characteristics that influenced a volatile electorate in 2011 more than policy concerns. The following sections describe in turn the main potential explanations of voting behaviour in the presidential election, the nominations for candidacy, the campaign, and the result of the 2011 Irish presidential election. The discussion looks briefly at what Irish people see as important in a President before using constituency level and opinion poll data – taken before, during and immediately after the 2011 election – to establish support for the various potential explanations. This analysis is discussed in the concluding section.

EXPLAINING PRESIDENTIAL ELECTION OUTCOMES

If, as Marsh and Mikhaylov (2010: 6) put it, 'elections are meaningful only when political parties present voters with serious policy alternatives', Irish presidential elections might be thought meaningless. In fact they are probably meaningful in some other way. Not much being at stake, presidential elections are second-order elections (Reif and Schmitt, 1980), and they follow the second-order election model where voters behave differently than they would in first-order elections. For instance, turnout is lower than in the more important general elections (turnout was significantly lower in the presidential elections of 1997 and 2011 compared to the general elections held the same year). Voters could be influenced by their attitude to something completely removed from the ostensible object of the election. In a second-order election voters may be more likely to focus on issues that are not the direct subject of the election, deviate from their partisan loyalties, choose candidates on the basis of non-political attributes, or use the election as a way to reward, punish or pressurise government parties (Tilley, Garry and Bold, 2008). If voters have no need to vote in a self-interested, instrumental way, in order to achieve some specific policy that brings policy closer to their ideal point, then on what basis are they voting? We can identify four possible explanations for voters' decisions.

a.   'Culture war' – position on a liberal/conservative dimension
b.   Partisan preferences – basic party attachment
c.   Valence issues – the intrinsic psychological attraction to candidates
d.   Rewards and punishment – satisfaction with government.

Though having very limited formal powers, the office of President is of some symbolic importance. Cearbhall Ó Dálaigh noted in his inauguration speech in 1974 that 'Presidents under the Irish Constitution don't have policies. But ... a president can have a theme' (see Appendix 2). The themes might be thought to be platitudinous – Ó Dálaigh's was 'community spirit' – so vote choice could be based on the competing ideological background of each candidate. We might see that voters choose the candidate whose ideological profile fits with their own. There is anecdotal evidence for this. In the aftermath of the 1997 presidential election some car stickers were seen to show 'Pro-Life 1, Abortionists 0' (Marsh, 1999: 215). This suggests that if liberal Ireland had won in 1990 with the election of an unashamedly liberal anti-national-ist in Mary Robinson, the other side won in 1997 with the election of Mary McAleese, a committed Catholic and a traditional Northern Irish nationalist.

During the 2011 Irish presidential election the *Sunday Independent*, Ireland's largest circulation broadsheet, characterised the contest as a 'battle for the soul of Ireland' (9 October 2011). So we might think of the 2011 presi-dential election, much like the elections of 1990 and 1997, as a battle with lines drawn on cultural values. Presidential elections might be a theatre in which voters could express their opinions on a 'culture war' between secularists and conservatives. Many of Higgins's voters might have been hoping that if elected he would make speeches excoriating social conservatism, thereby reflecting their views to the country and wider world. The culture war explanation is used by many in the USA to explain voting trends there (see for instance Frank, 2004).

As well as being above policy, the presidency is meant to be a non-par-tisan office. Indeed party labels are not displayed on the ballot paper. But as Murphy and Reidy show (see Chapter 8), parties have dominated presidential elections. Another possible explanation for people's vote choice is that the vote is a reflection of underlying partisan identifications, so a Fine Gael supporter will vote for a Fine Gael candidate, a Labour Party supporter will vote for the Labour Party candidate, and so forth, regardless of the ideological position of that candidate on the culture war. Establishing a partisan basis for voting may not be that clear because it is certain that the candidates' ideological positions will be related to the party that nominates them. So it is unlikely that Fine Gael would nominate a candidate who does not share its ideological positions.

Or are these presidential elections more about selecting an individual who is suitable for the job, regardless of their party or position in any culture war? Because little is at stake, valence issues may become important (Clarke et al., 2004: 8). Valence is the intrinsic psychological attractiveness of a per-son, object or event. It was introduced to electoral studies by Stokes (1963). Especially where parties or candidates are ideologically close or their ideology is irrelevant, judgement and not just values are important in voters' evalua-tions. In these cases voters might support the candidate who appears to offer the best chance of a competent performance, might have more integrity or be most charismatic. Ideological stances may of course influence assessments as to who is a suitable candidate. For valence to be truly important we should see that the evaluation of candidates on these issues is independent of ideological position or partisan judgement.

Alternatively, voters might be influenced by their temporary attitude to the government rather than by long-term partisan attitudes. Satisfaction with the government was mentioned as a core covariant with vote choice in 1997 (Gormley and Murphy, 2008), and there is some evidence that some referendums in Ireland have been barometers of government popularity (Garry, Marsh and Sinnott, 2005). Voters might use the election as an opportunity to punish a poorly performing government by withholding support from the governing parties' candidates. This may come in the form of voting for other parties or not participating in the election.

It is most likely that people's choices are a varying combination of all these elements: committed party supporters would vote for their party's candidate, almost regardless of the quality of the candidate, but other supporters might choose to withdraw their support if the candidate was ideologically or personally unattractive. If partisan or ideological positions were the key determinants we would expect to see limited volatility in the late stages of the campaign as the ideological and partisan position of each candidate would be reasonably well established.

The 2011 election is a good test for these competing explanations because Fine Gael, the most popular party in the state as evident in the results of the general election in February of that year, against the wishes of the leadership, selected a candidate who was highly partisan. He was also someone whom commentators found personally brusque. There were also several candidates who were clearly on one side or the other of the 'cultural' divide, and there were two candidates from the governing parties.

THE NOMINATIONS

Twenty-nine names were mentioned in the media in the year before the election as potential presidential candidates, including the final seven candidates.[1] To be nominated, a candidate needs to receive the endorsement of 20 members of the Oireachtas or four city or county councils. The nomination process, which had been the preserve of the political parties, was opened up in 1997 when independent Dana Rosemary Scallon was nominated by local authorities. It was likely that the local authorities would be eager to use this right again in 2011, and given the large number of independents elected to the Dáil in 2011 and the fact that Sinn Féin came close to having

20 Oireachtas members, a large field was a possibility. Polling day was set for 27 October and the nomination period ran from 1 to 28 September. A nominated candidate could withdraw his or her nomination at any time before the completion of the ruling on nominations but not thereafter. This was the 'short' nomination process. In fact, Michael D. Higgins had advertised his intention to seek the Labour nomination about a year before Mary McAleese's second term was due to end.

FINE GAEL

Having overtaken Fianna Fáil as the largest party in the 2011 general election, senior members of Fine Gael were said to be have been eager to win the presidential election. The party hoped to persuade former Taoiseach John Bruton to run. He was never very eager for the position and he eventually ruled himself out in late May. In the meantime a number of other names had been mentioned as possible Fine Gael candidates, including MEPs Mairéad McGuinness and Seán Kelly and former MEP Pat Cox. The party leadership was thought to favour the candidacy of Pat Cox (*Sunday Independent*, 10 July 2011), who only became a member of the party less than a month before the nominations. He had been a Progressive Democrat TD and MEP, later became an independent MEP, and had served as President of the European Parliament. Mairéad McGuinness, who was well-known as a broadcaster, was thought to have been likely to attract votes beyond the party supporters. Avril Doyle, a former MEP and junior minister also announced her candidacy, but withdrew before the convention as she felt she had no chance of securing the party's nomination.

Gay Mitchell sought the Fine Gael nomination quite late, seemingly in reaction to Cox's entry. As a long-serving TD and MEP for Dublin he could have been regarded as the most 'Fine Gael' of the three who survived into the final stage of the contest. The party held a special convention to select a candidate on 9 July. The electorate for the convention was over 600 people, including about 500 councillors, 99 members of the parliamentary party and 29 members of the party's executive. Each group's vote was weighted, with the parliamentary party carrying 70 per cent of the total vote, the local authority members 20 per cent and the executive council 10 per cent (*The Irish Times*, 30 June 2011). The result of the vote was not released, but it was reported that Cox was eliminated in the first count and that Mitchell beat McGuinness by 54 to 46 per cent. In choosing the most partisan of the three, Fine Gael also chose someone who was openly conservative – he frequently referred to his Christian Democratic principles – and the most politically combative. He was not a typical presidential candidate, and the Fine Gael leadership did not hide its annoyance at the party's choice (*The Irish Times*, 11 July 2011).

LABOUR

There were three candidates for the Labour Party nomination. Michael D. Higgins, an elder statesman and former president of the party, had sought the nomination in 1997 and 2004 (Quinn, 2005: 369). In 1997 Labour nominated a party outsider in the hope of repeating the formula with which Mary Robinson had won in 1990. In 2004 Labour's leader, Pat Rabbitte, decided that there was no point in the party contesting the election because it was felt that the incumbent, Mary McAleese, was too popular. Rabbitte did, however, suggest that Éamon Ryan, a Green TD, might be a good candidate (O'Malley and Marsh, 2005).

Higgins was always the favourite to receive the nomination were the party members to decide, though there were some concerns about his age (he was 70 at the time of the election) and health (he had had an accident which restricted mobility in his legs). Higgins was challenged by Fergus Finlay and Kathleen O'Meara. Finlay was well known in the party and in political circles but perhaps less prominent among the public. His background was that of a special adviser to Dick Spring and later to Pat Rabbitte, but latterly he became head of a children's charity and a newspaper columnist. O'Meara was a former journalist and senator, but had retired from politics in 2007. The Labour parliamentary party and the executive board met on 19 June, and the result, announced on the Labour Party twitter account, had Higgins on 37 votes, Finlay on 18 votes and O'Meara with seven votes.

FIANNA FÁIL

Fianna Fáil nominees, with one exception, had won every contested presidential election. It would have seemed natural for the party to contest the election, but in the aftermath of the 2011 general election the party leadership was unsure whether it should do so. There were concerns that the party did not have the resources to fight an election that it was unlikely to win, nor would the campaign do much to help it to recover from the disastrous general election result earlier that year, though some argued it had little to lose in contesting (Gallagher, 2011). It seemed clear that the leader, Micheál Martin, was disinclined to nominate a candidate, but there were offers from party members, most plausibly Brian Crowley, the Cork-based MEP, who was popular within his Munster constituency. He was a well-tried and successful candidate, not associated with the previous Fianna Fáil-led governments.

Fianna Fáil took some time to make a final decision. When the name of the popular broadcaster, Gay Byrne, was mentioned, Martin was reported to have contacted him to indicate that Fianna Fáil would facilitate his nomination as an independent candidate. Byrne revealed this conversation publicly, causing some problems within Fianna Fáil as it suggested that Martin had made a decision on the party strategy without the endorsement of the parliamentary party. In mid-August Martin set up a six-man sub-committee to make a recommendation to the parliamentary party. It recommended not running a candidate or supporting any other candidate, and on 31 August this proposal was accepted by the Fianna Fáil parliamentary party. There were rumours of divisions over this strategy between Martin and his deputy leader, Éamon Ó Cuív, who was also rumoured to have an interest in standing. The party decided to wait until after the close of nominations to adopt a position in respect of any other candidate. Martin's authority was further questioned when a Fianna Fáil senator indicated he would seek a nomination from Fianna Fáil Oireachtas members, but at a later meeting of the parliamentary party it was decided that members of the parliamentary party would not endorse or nominate any other candidates (*The Irish Times*, 21 September 2011).

SINN FÉIN

Sinn Féin had considered supporting an independent candidate with strong nationalist leanings. Fianna Fáil's decision not to contest – and the absence of an obvious front runner at the time – offered the party an opportunity to increase its profile and support base in the Republic, in particular at the expense of Fianna Fáil. At a meeting of the officer board of the party on 16 September, it decided that the Deputy First Minister of Northern Ireland and a former leading member of the Provisional IRA, Martin McGuinness, should be the Sinn Féin candidate. This was later accepted by the party's *Ard Comhairle* (national executive). The party was still short of the 20 Oireachtas members needed to nominate a candidate, but McGuinness sought and received the support of three independent TDs.

INDEPENDENT CANDIDATES

At the same time as Sinn Féin announced McGuinness's candidacy, another candidate announced that he would seek a nomination, having earlier opted out of the contest. David Norris, who was an independent senator elected by graduates of Trinity College and a prominent gay rights activist, had led the opinion poll race for most of the first half of the year. A Red-C poll in January 2011 gave him 27 per cent support. In March he formally launched his campaign and had put together a professional and well-organised campaign structure. His supporters were confident that he would receive a nomination, but his campaign stumbled in late May when comments he made in an interview in 2002 in which he appeared to defend pederasty resurfaced. His reaction to the issue in a radio interview was less than convincing, but an opinion poll with fieldwork split between the weeks before and after the controversy showed that it had little impact on his first preference support.[2] An *Irish Times*/Ipsos MRBI poll – reported on 20 July – also had Norris in the lead of a speculative field of candidates with 25 per cent of first preference vote. However, in late July it emerged that Norris had lobbied on behalf of his former partner, who had been convicted of statutory rape of a minor in Israel (*The Irish Times*, 3 August 2011). Key members of his campaign team, dismayed that he had not warned them and feeling that he was unsuitable to hold the office of President, resigned. On 2 August Norris withdrew from the race, but later changed his mind. He re-emerged in mid-September, when he announced on a popular entertainment television programme, the *Late Late Show*, that he would again be seeking a nomination. Many of those initially willing to support his nomination had indicated they were now unwilling, so he appealed to county councils to facilitate his candidacy. On the day before nominations closed Norris was supported by a fourth county council and so secured his position on the ballot.

Dana Rosemary Scallon, best known by her stage name Dana from the time she represented Ireland and won the Eurovision Song Contest, also made a surprise entry in mid-September to say that she would seek a nomination. Though it was not clear whether she had any organisation or financial resources, the fact that she had received 14 per cent in the 1997 presidential contest and had been elected an MEP in 1999 gave her plausibility as a candidate to represent a conservative, Eurosceptic part of Irish society. She comfortably secured the backing of four rural local authorities.

Two other independent candidates had been in the race for much longer than Dana. Mary Davis had become well known as the organiser of the Special Olympics when it was held in Ireland in 2003. She had been appointed to the Council of State (an advisory council for the President) and had indicated in 2010 that she might seek a nomination from one of the parties (*Sunday Business Post*, 15 August 2010). She then decided to run as an independent and received nominations from 13 local authorities by mid-September. Businessman and television personality Seán Gallagher also comfortably received a nomination from four local authorities by July, becoming the first independent to secure a nomination. He had been a member of Fianna Fáil for most of his adult life and up until January 2011 was on the party's national executive. But he decided to seek a nomination as an independent, and given Fianna Fáil's unpopularity at the time that probably made sense.

THE CAMPAIGN

Though David Norris had been consistently the most popular candidate in the opinion polls in which he featured, almost as soon as he was formally nominated and the prospect of his presidency became real potential voters turned away. Before the short campaign, opinions had been quite volatile. For instance, when Gay Byrne was suggested as a candidate, he immediately got 28 per cent support in one poll. Michael D. Higgins had consistently polled well, being the second or third favourite candidate, and emerged as the leading candidate soon after the short campaign started.

Presidential election campaigns differ from general and local elections in that there is much less focus on door-to-door canvassing. Candidates cannot expect to meet as large a proportion of voters as they do in general elections (see for instance Marsh, 2004). Consequently, the campaign is primarily fought in the media. Seán Gallagher's decision not to use posters may have been made because of financial constraints, but, if so, he managed to make a virtue of this by criticising other candidates for the cost imposed upon the exchequer (of course, his decision did nothing to save money for taxpayers; he just spent it on other items). Gallagher possibly also realised that posters are useful in low information elections where candidates get little other coverage. As all candidates agreed to a large number of joint appearances and debates on radio and television stations, it became clear that the media would play a central role in the 2011 campaign. In presidential elections the broadcast media are obliged to give each candidate equal coverage, and because it is a national election, candidates can expect to get plenty of coverage. It would be the nature of the coverage that mattered.

The media set the tone and determined the nature of the campaign. It was one where each candidate was thoroughly questioned on what might be perceived as his or her weak points. Gay Mitchell's poor poll ratings, and the fact that so few of his party's supporters planned to vote for him, was immediately seized upon. Fine Gael gave little impression of being convinced that he was a potentially winning candidate, and it was reported that the party scaled back its spending toward the end of the campaign. Yet Mitchell spent more money than any other candidate (over €0.5m), all of which appears to have come from Fine Gael (SIPO, 2011). The Mitchell campaign team claim that the candidate did not have a plan for the campaign, yet rejected its advice (*Irish Independent*, 31 October 2011). The campaign strategy seemed to be centred on attacking Martin McGuinness and his membership of the IRA. In so doing Mitchell's message was overtly negative, and his candidacy steadily lost support (see Figure 9.1). When questioned on this repeatedly the Fine Gael candidate got tetchy, and towards the end of the campaign shouted at the moderator in a TV debate.

Martin McGuinness, the target of Mitchell's attentions, was also questioned vigorously in the media. For him it was on his membership of and role in the IRA. In a debate on the privately-owned television station, TV3, the moderator Vincent Browne quoted a number of books which alleged he was a leader of the IRA up to five or six years earlier; he had said he left in 1974 (see Table 9.1 below). In a debate on the popular current affairs programme, *Prime Time,* on state-owned RTÉ, McGuinness was asked how he could reconcile his religious beliefs with the fact that he 'was involved in the murder of so many people'. He complained about this 'disgraceful comment', but this was an issue which dogged his campaign. Earlier in the campaign, the son of a soldier murdered by the IRA in the early 1980s confronted McGuinness, demanding that he provide information on the identity of his father's killers. McGuinness claimed not to have any information and he also repeated his claim to have left the IRA in 1974. Although not many may have believed his answers, the responses were unlikely to have had an impact. In the negative campaign against McGuinness he was being attacked for something he freely admitted to or of which most people already knew. It did not seem to take any support away from him, but may have prevented increases in his vote. As one of the most polarising of the candidates (40 per cent of voters expressing an opinion said he was the candidate they least wanted elected President; Red C poll for Paddy Power, 6 October 2011) he may have had the impact of boosting turnout among people wishing to vote 'against' him.

Mary Davis's campaign seemed to be professionally run, and in early opinion polls she performed reasonably well; she was the best placed of the independent candidates in early October. Her campaign's theme was one of social entrepreneurship and volunteerism while her experience in organising

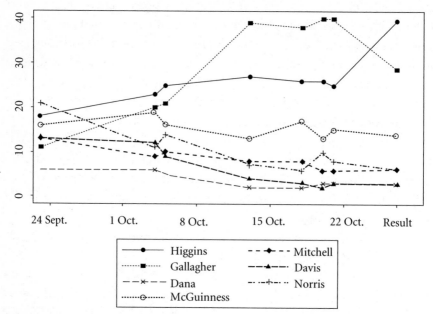

FIGURE 9.1 The short campaign opinion polls and final result, presidential election, 2011

the Special Olympics also no doubt helped her reputation. But when repeatedly questioned about the number of state and private boards she sat on, her answers were used by critics to label her the 'Quango Queen'. Her links with the controversial businessman Denis O'Brien were also used against her. She revealed her salary as head of Special Olympics Europe and her income from board memberships, which seemed high given her claim to be a champion of the voluntary sector.

Dana's campaign appeared the least well organised and least professional. She spent less than €60,000 on the campaign, by far the lowest amount of all the candidates (SIPO, 2011). Many observers took the view that her campaign was descending into farce when during a presidential election TV debate she read a statement about a 'vile and false allegation' made against a member of her family. Before that, testimony from a court case involving her and her sister was raised, revealing the fact that Dana was a US citizen, which she struggled to reconcile with her desire to be Ireland's first citizen. An accident caused when a tyre in the car in which she was travelling blew out led her husband to speculate about an assassination attempt (*The Irish Times*, 20 October 2011). There was even a suggestion that she would simply stop campaigning.

By comparison to most other candidates, Michael D. Higgins appears to have been subjected to much less media scrutiny. There were some questions about his age, his religious beliefs, or lack of them, and his attitude to abortion. But he rarely received the sustained questioning that his rivals endured. He also dealt effectively with these questions by evading them or, in the case of questions on his mobility, making self-deprecating remarks which reflected more poorly on the questioner than on Higgins. He never lost his temper and did not engage in the increasingly fractious debates about the suitability of other candidates. He tried instead to concentrate on his theme of inclusive citizenship. His support was steady throughout the campaign, polling consistently in the low to mid-20s. He remained the second favourite for a plurality of opinion poll respondents throughout the campaign. In a tight election this would have seen him overtake the leader, and indicated that he was a sort of default option for uncertain voters. By contrast to McGuinness, Higgins offended very few people – fewer than one in 20 cited him as their least favoured option (Red C poll, 6 October 2011).

Seán Gallagher also avoided being embroiled in negative campaigning, and he concentrated on a simple theme of entrepreneurship. Perhaps by not being a front-runner for the early part of the campaign he, too, avoided the sustained attacks that others received. His membership of Fianna Fáil was raised, and he was shown to have not told the truth about when he left the party's national executive. He prevaricated when asked to criticise the policies pursued by Fianna Fáil in government. It was only when his support doubled in the polls in early October – to show him to be clearly the best-supported independent candidate – and then doubled again in polls published a week later that there was sustained media questioning on these issues. His success as an entrepreneur was also questioned, as was the probity of some of his business practices, which were repeatedly raised but appeared to have limited public impact as he maintained his lead up to the final week of the campaign.

Gallagher's success in the campaign is interesting. He was arguably the least well-known of the candidates, and only his appearance on a reality TV show may have given him exposure to the public. His association with Fianna Fáil and the construction industry should have made him an odd choice for voters in the wake of the economic crisis. Gallagher may have benefited from being the best placed independent; perhaps voters concentrated on him as the best placed alternative to Higgins. For his own campaign team this appeared to be the 'strategy' – to stay ahead of the other independents (*Sunday Times* [Irish edition], 13 November 2011). It was not clear whether he wanted to be associated with Fianna Fáil or not – his media adviser, Richard Moore, describes trying in vain to get a photo opportunity with Micheál Martin. Moore's description of the campaign was one in which they got lucky – when

TABLE 9.1   TV debates and viewing figures, presidential election, 2011

Programme	Station	Date	Peak audience	Average audience
Late Late Show	RTÉ	30 September	723,000	654,000
Big Presidential Debate	TV3	4 October	443,000	367,000
Prime Time	RTÉ	12 October	702,000	654,000
Presidential Debate	TG4	18 October	175,000	123,000
Frontline	RTÉ	24 October	899,000	787,000

Source: Nielsen TAM Ireland.

a poll was published putting Gallagher at 39 per cent he noted '[n]obody on the campaign could believe it'. But it led to increased volunteer numbers, up to 2,000 (*Sunday Times* [Irish edition], 13 November 2011).

One poll in early October showed that, unlike McGuinness, Dana or Norris, almost no one disliked Gallagher enough to make him their least preferred candidate (Red-C poll, 6 October 2011). He was much younger and more energetic than the other candidates, in particular Higgins. His focus on a single message and irrepressible positive outlook gave him the air of a self-help guru, but it was one which struck a chord with people. His experience in television may have also helped in what was essentially a campaign carried out in television studios (see Table 9.1).

Election debates are not thought to have big effects in US presidential elections – about 1-2 per cent (Shaw, 1999) – mainly because they are so well-rehearsed that candidates cancel out any gains made by each other. However, they might be a determining factor where a candidate is less well-known, an election is close, large numbers of voters are undecided, and/or party allegiances are weak (Chaffee, 1978: 342). The first TV debate in the British general election of 2010 catapulted the Liberal Democrat leader, Nick Clegg, from relative obscurity into a prominent position, transforming the rest of the campaign. The TV debates in the Irish presidential election similarly allowed the character of candidates to emerge.

There was wide agreement that the final TV debate on RTÉ's popular discussion programme, *Frontline*, had a major impact on the outcome of the election. Seán Gallagher was again questioned about his business practices and then forced to spend much of his time explaining a trail of financial accounting errors in which the member of the audience who did the questioning sounded more convincing than Gallagher. The audience was left incredulous when he gave a less than assured response to the assertion that he had mislaid a cheque for €89,000. He was later questioned on his fundraising activities for Fianna Fáil. Martin McGuinness, standing beside him, put it directly to him that he had evidence that Gallagher had lied in denying having received cheques for Fianna Fáil fundraisers. Gallagher then said he had 'no recollection of getting a cheque from this guy', at which the audience jeered. His inability or unwillingness to categorically deny receiving a cheque would have made for uncomfortable viewing for a Gallagher supporter. Then Gallagher decided to concede that he might have received a cheque: 'I may well have delivered a photograph; if he gave me an envelope [laughter]…if he gave me a cheque, it was made out to Fianna Fáil Headquarters and had nothing to do with me'. At home almost 900,000 watched the *Frontline* debate, about half of the number who eventually voted. For many this was the moment Gallagher lost the election. His performance in the debate became the centre of media coverage in the last two days of the campaign, and all of his appearances centred on these issues. The presence of the live studio audience may have also been important. Most in the studio would have been associated with one of the candidates and as such, more politically aware than most. Their reaction would have helped 'interpret' Gallagher's performance for those at home.

The *Frontline* programme was the subject of an appeal to the Broadcasting Authority of Ireland (BAI) and of an internal RTÉ review (RTÉ, 2012). The BAI upheld the allegation in respect of a tweet which led to questions of whether Gallagher had accepted a cheque on behalf of Fianna Fáil from Hugh Morgan, a Northern Ireland businessman. The tweet, said to have come from the official Martin McGuinness campaign twitter account, asserted that Morgan would present himself to the media alleging that Gallagher was wrong in his recollections. The BAI upheld the appeal that the tweet should not have been broadcast. The RTÉ review found that there were other problems with the programme. It was noted that Seán Gallagher was asked three direct and challenging questions, and that Martin McGuinness was asked two. This was defensible, the report concluded, on the basis that frontrunners might get more attention. However, the fact that Michael D. Higgins received no direct or challenging questions, even where one was available, was seen as a flaw in the programme. In January 2013 Gallagher announced that he would take legal proceedings against RTÉ seeking a declaration that the debate was 'unfair' and 'seriously damaged' Mr Gallagher's electoral prospects. This was something the editor of the debate had earlier conceded.

EXPLAINING THE RESULT

As soon as the first ballot boxes were open it was clear that Higgins would win the presidency comfortably. The number and consistency of the polls in the final two weeks indicates that they were an accurate reflection of public opinion. Higgins received almost 40 per cent of the vote (see Appendix 1), up 15 points from the last opinion poll of the campaign. Gallagher got 28.5 per cent, down from 40 per cent in the final polls. Of the other candidates, only Martin McGuinness won a sufficient share of the votes to secure the reimbursement of a portion of his electoral expenses from the state.[3] Fine Gael's result was particularly disappointing, coming after its success in the general election only eight months previously. Higgins was elected on the fourth count, with 73 per cent of collective transferable votes from candidates as diverse as McGuinness and Mitchell going to him.[4]

The amount of money a candidate spent turned out to be unrelated to the candidate's proportion of the vote. The highest spenders were among the worst performers. Of course, the candidate who spent by far the least, Dana, also did poorly. Presumably, a candidate who spent no money would not have been taken seriously in the media. But because the campaign is an 'air war' rather than a 'ground war', the rules that guarantee equal treatment by the broadcast media might mean that money is of less relevance in these campaigns.

It is obvious that there were massive shifts in voter support in the final week of the campaign, in which Gallagher lost over 10 points. Fieldwork for the final opinion poll had taken place up to the Friday before the election. Gallagher had come under significant pressure during this period, with vigorous questioning arising from the issues raised in the *Frontline* debate. In the absence of polls the betting markets can offer some clues. Immediately after the *Frontline* debate Paddy Power cut the odds on Michael D. Higgins, indicating that the betting market thought it was much more likely that Higgins would win, and that a Gallagher victory would be much less probable as a result of that TV debate (see O'Malley, 2011). This would suggest that earlier media attention had little direct impact. The proximate cause of the massive shift may seem obvious, but exploring it further may inform us as to what the electorate takes into account in presidential elections, and in particular which of the four hypothesised explanations discussed above has most support.

There are some problems with the 'culture war' explanation. Did Ireland, having made a liberal turn in 1990, take a step towards social conservatism in

1997? It seems unlikely, when all the evidence shows that people's opinions on social issues were compatible with a trend towards liberalism (Lyons, 2008: 146). There is no evidence of the emergence of discrete groups in Irish society in these areas; Irish people tend towards the centre in most polls on these issues. If the election represented a simple choice between liberalism and conservatism, we might not have expected to see so much volatility among the electorate, except perhaps between the candidates that represented these positions.

Others have, however, found some evidence to support the 'culture war' explanation (Gallagher and Marsh, 1993; Marsh, 1999). The evidence came primarily from constituency-level correlations of results in different elections and referendums. From the early 1980s, when social liberalism started to become an issue beyond an intellectual elite, social issues have divided Irish society, and these divisions have manifested themselves in referendums more than in general elections. Constituency-level correlations between party support at general elections and referendum outcomes tend to be weaker than those between presidential candidate and referendum support. This was because parties tended to avoid making social issues general election issues, and were content for them to be debated in the relative safety of a referendum campaign.

The 'culture wars' in Ireland might be a combination of social conservatism and anti-Europeanism. The leaders of the anti-EU debate in recent constitutional referendum campaigns were a combination of neo-conservatives such as Declan Ganley's Libertas, Christian conservatives represented by groups such as Cóir, and the nationalist populist Sinn Féin, whose supporters have been shown to be socially conservative (O'Malley, 2008). The Irish National Election Study 2011 data shows that there is a *very* weak, if statistically significant, correlation (coefficient=.061, p=0.014) between attitude towards further European integration and attitude to abortion.

The relationship between Higgins's vote and opposition to restricting abortion appears remarkably strong, and the opposite pattern appears with Gallagher's (see Table 9.2). Gallagher's and Higgins's constituency support levels seem to reflect those of McAleese and Banotti in 1997 and Robinson and Lenihan in 1990. When we partition these data between cities (Dublin, Cork and Limerick) and other areas the correlation weakens greatly and is not significant *within* cities. This suggests that the relationship between Higgins's support and attitude to abortion has more to do with general support for the two in urban areas. The correlation between Higgins's vote and the 'yes' vote on the first Lisbon Treaty European referendum in urban areas is 0.93

TABLE 9.2   Constituency level correlations between support for presidential candidates and party and referendum votes, 1986-2011

Candidate	pro-divorce (1986/1995)	restrict abortion (2001)	pro-Nice/Lisbon (2001/2008)	supporting parties
1990:				
Robinson	0.86***	–	–	0.70***
Lenihan	–0.69***	–	–	0.64***
1997:				
McAleese	–0.79***	0.77***	–0.13	0.49**
Banotti	0.77***	–0.86***	0.34*	–0.10
2011:				
Higgins	-	–0.71***	0.50***	0.42**
Gallagher	-	0.78***	–0.10	0.52***
McGuinness	-	0.42**	–0.75***	0.86***
Mitchell	-	0.12	0.10	0.32*

Note: For the divorce referendums the correlations are with the 1986 referendum for the 1990 election candidates and 1995 for the 1997 candidates. For Nice I and Lisbon I Treaty referendums the correlations reported refer to the 1997 and 2011 candidates' support respectively. The supporting parties correlation is with the percentage vote the party or parties that nominated the candidate received in the previous general election. For Gallagher the reported correlation is with Fianna Fáil vote in 2011. * indicates a coefficient is significant at the .05 level, ** indicates significance at the .01 level and *** at the .001 level.

(p<.0001), which suggests that the urban, educated middle classes who support European integration also supported Higgins.

The evidence for partisan voting is more mixed. Higgins's vote is correlated with the Labour constituency vote, but not strongly. In fact, Gallagher's vote is more strongly correlated with Fianna Fáil's vote in 2011. We would expect that correlations for the winning candidates would be weaker than this, as they also draw on support from other sources (Higgins's support, for example, extended well beyond Labour Party voters). Higgins's vote correlates reasonably well with the combined support of the government parties at constituency level (coefficient =0.42, p=0.006), but this does not suggest that Higgins became the unofficial government candidate. Support for Mitchell was only weakly related to Fine Gael support. Only McGuinness's vote trends are supportive of the partisan hypothesis (in mirroring the distribution of

Sinn Féin support). There is also a clear link with his support and that of the Lisbon referendum in which Sinn Féin campaigned clearly for a 'no' vote.

There are problems in using aggregate data to make inferences about individual voters; survey data can help to answer these questions. When considering what they want in a president, people overwhelmingly mentioned personal characteristics rather than partisan or policy ones. In a survey asking potential voters to identify the two most important qualities in a president, the most mentioned characteristics in a survey in April-June were coded as honesty and integrity (22 per cent) and ability to represent Ireland abroad (21 per cent).[5] Other important attributes included being a statesperson (12 per cent), a good speaker (12 per cent), likeable (9 per cent), and a leader (8 per cent). Being independent of party politics (2 per cent) did not appear to be very important, nor were policy or ideological issues mentioned by respondents (for instance, being 'liberal' was mentioned by less than 1 per cent of respondents).

A Red-C/*Sunday Business Post* survey carried out a week before polling day reported Mitchell as the preferred candidate among less than 19 per cent of those intending to vote Fine Gael (compared to 26 and 31 per cent for Higgins and Gallagher respectively). Even Higgins only secured 50 per cent from putative Labour Party voters. The implications of the aggregate data analysis mentioned above are borne out: Gallagher and McGuinness secured 60 per cent support from Fianna Fáil and Sinn Féin supporters respectively. There is also limited support for the 'punishment' hypothesis. Satisfaction with the government during the campaign was at 36 per cent (*Sunday Times* [Irish edition], 23 October 2011). But if we use 'intention to vote for a government party' as a proxy for government satisfaction, then Fine Gael's status as most popular party does not support the idea that government satisfaction negatively affected Mitchell's performance. Furthermore of the two parties in government satisfaction was higher for Fine Gael leader and Taoiseach, Enda Kenny (58 per cent) than Labour leader and Tánaiste, Éamon Gilmore (46 per cent). Yet the Fine Gael candidate performed much worse than Labour's.

A Red-C recall poll for RTÉ provides useful additional individual level data. This was limited in size and scope; there were few questions beyond vote choice and demography. Recall polls have not been used extensively in Ireland so it is worth noting that the responses closely reflect the actual result (see Table 9.3). The poll also provided an accurate assessment of support in the 2011 general election, though somewhat overestimating Fine Gael support and underestimating Sinn Féin support. Using self-reported switching

TABLE 9.3 Comparison of recall poll result and actual first preference, presidential election, 2011

Candidate	Red-C Recall poll	Actual result
Higgins	40.2	39.6
Gallagher	27.4	28.5
McGuinness	13.9	13.7
Mitchell	6.7	6.4
Norris	7.7	6.2
Dana	2.2	2.9
Davis	2.0	2.7

n= 1080

Note: 'Results of a phone survey carried out by Red-C Research for RTÉ on the evening of the election and early the following morning. See http://redcresearch.ie/news/innovation-accuracy-in-rte-recall-poll for details.'

in votes, it is also consistent with the earlier Red-C opinion polls. An analysis of the recall poll data reveals that almost 30 per cent of voters changed their mind on how to vote, and of those 82 per cent did so in the last two or three days of the campaign, after the *Frontline* debate.

The main focus of the poll was on voters' perceptions of desirable characteristics in candidates. Table 9.4 reports the mean scores and spread in respect of each of these characteristics. It is striking that independence, or being nonpartisan, is less important than many commentators felt during the campaign. The least important trait is agreement with political views, suggesting that ideological position on, say, the 'culture war' was not an important determinant of vote choice. By contrast, valence issues, honesty and 'best candidate to represent Ireland abroad', are rated most highly.

Figure 9.2 reports an analysis of the most important covariates of vote choice in multivariate models, where we look at the factors influencing candidate choice in four ways. The first is by looking at those who voted for Higgins (coded as 1) compared to voters for other candidates (coded as 0). The second model studies voters for Gallagher (1) compared to voters for other candidates (0). Then we look at those who prefer Higgins (1) to Gallagher (0), and finally those who switched either to Gallagher (1) or away from him (0) in the days before polling. Binary variables are used because there is some evidence that voters centred on the top two candidates. Though demographic factors

TABLE 9.4   Importance of candidate characteristics for vote choice, presidential election, 2011

Characteristic	Mean Score	Standard Deviation
Honesty and integrity	8.81	1.68
Candidate to represent Ireland	8.56	1.81
Experience/ qualifications	7.80	2.09
Good for jobs/ economy	6.93	2.71
Independence	6.54	2.75
Agree with political views	6.42	2.63

Note: mean scores are out of 10.   Source: Red-C RTÉ Recall poll.

are significant when tested on their own, when we include the characteristic variables, none are significant for choosing Higgins as opposed to one of the other six candidates (see Figure 9.2a). Having voted for Labour significantly increases the likelihood of voting for Higgins. Holding all other variables constant at their mean, almost 60 per cent of Labour voters supported Higgins, compared to just 30 per cent for those who voted for other parties. Those rating honesty and experience highly were more likely to choose Higgins rather than any other candidates (50 per cent of those rating as 10 the importance of honesty and integrity voted for him, compared to about seven per cent of those who rated it six or less, everything else being equal). Higgins was significantly less popular among those who cited agreement with the candidate's political views, which indicates that voters for Higgins were less interested in his policy or ideological position.

For Gallagher voters, honesty and experience were much less important criteria. Voting for Fianna Fáil in 2011 was a significant indicator of voting for Gallagher, and unsurprisingly rating highly whether a candidate would be good for the economy is a significant factor in explaining Gallagher's vote. Those who were looking for the best candidate to represent Ireland abroad were more likely to choose Gallagher. Other models not reported here show that the votes for McGuinness and Mitchell were *much* more partisan and that their support was based on whether a voter agreed with the candidate's political views.

Another model (not displayed) tests the choice between the obviously liberal candidates (Higgins and Norris) and those who were obviously

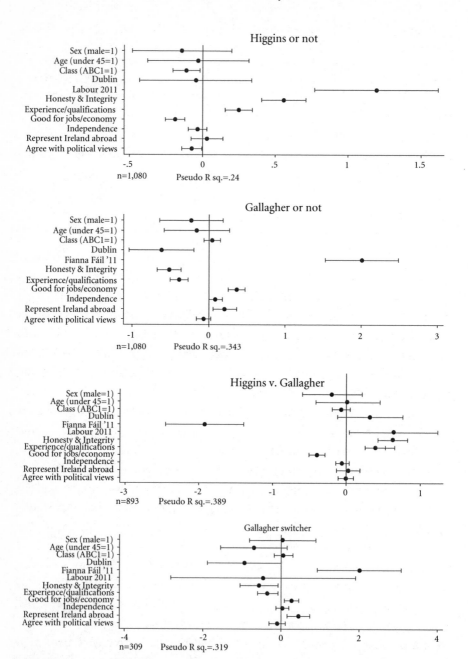

FIGURE 9.2   Logit models explaining candidate support, presidential election, 2011

Note: These figures give the point estimations for model coefficients and the 95% confidence intervals around these estimates. Where the lines do not cross over the vertical zero line they are statistically significant. The position of the point estimate does not indicate the strength of the relationship, but is determined by the measurement of the independent variables. The first five to six variables are dummy variables, whereas the bottom six are on a ten-point scale.

conservative (Mitchell and Dana). This demonstrates the validity of the method as we see those covariates we would expect to be important for liberalism/conservatism such as age emerge as significant. We can also see that those who voted for the conservative candidates such as Mitchell and Dana were much more likely to consider the political views of the candidates, whereas those rating experience highly chose Higgins or Norris.

By looking at the first and second preference votes of the 1,080 interviewed, in the case of 893 respondents we can tell whether they favoured Higgins over Gallagher or vice versa (see Figure 9.2c). Of these, 64.5 per cent favour Higgins. Unsurprisingly those who voted Fianna Fáil in 2011 are significantly less likely to prefer Higgins over Gallagher. When the importance of different candidate traits is introduced these show that Higgins was probably perceived as more honest and better qualified. Neither candidate does better among those who think agreeing with the candidate's political views is important.

Of the almost 30 per cent of respondents who reported having changed their mind in the last week of the campaign, a majority switched away from Gallagher, and a majority of these moved to Higgins. The net gain to Higgins from Gallagher was just less than ten percentage points. Gallagher's reported net loss in the final week of the campaign was 13.4 percentage points (which tallies with the reported last opinion polls estimates of support for each candidate). The final model (Figure 9.2d) looks at those who report having changed their minds and moved to or from Gallagher in the last week.

Support for Gallagher seems to have become more partisan as a result of the last week of the campaign. He had had broad backing from supporters of many political parties. In an earlier poll 38 per cent of those who reported voting for Fine Gael in 2011 said they supported Gallagher. A quarter of Labour and Sinn Féin voters also supported him, as did about a third of those who voted for independents. In the recall poll of those who switched, Fianna Fáil voters were much more likely to switch to Gallagher. Labour and Fine Gael voters switched to Higgins at Gallagher's expense. If discrete voting blocks existed, they only emerged in the last week. Before that point, transfers between Gallagher and Higgins were reasonably high, and they remained high from Gallagher to Higgins in the election. If there were voting blocks, they do not appear to have had an ideological basis. Gallagher was seen by many as a good candidate, but for too many others there were questions about his integrity and his experience for the office. His reaction to pressure on his links to Fianna Fáil and his business practices appears to have been crucial.

Conclusion

The 2011 Irish presidential election was notable for the extent of negativity and close attention to each candidate's character and temperament. Many of the candidates were eliminated from contention in voters' minds as the campaign progressed. The available data does not allow us to test competing hypotheses as thoroughly as we would like, but some points can be made.

Partisanship is somewhat important in determining voting choice at presidential elections, but to be successful a candidate must appeal beyond party loyalties. However, while we know that Mitchell's vote was highly partisan, he could not mobilise a great deal of his party's support. 'Culture' may not be irrelevant for presidential elections, but it does not appear to decide elections, especially where there are multiple candidates for each 'block'. In 2011 any 'blocks' were less obvious, but the shift in the final week of the campaign occurred across what blocks there were, not within them as we would have expected had ideology been important. Some candidates' support, in particular that of Dana and Mitchell, appears to have been more ideologically-based than the vote for Higgins. In 2011 candidate characteristics emerge as most important. Voters sought someone appropriate for the office with less emphasis on partisan heritage or ideological position. It also appears that Higgins was the least unacceptable option rather than someone whom voters voted 'for'. Whether Gallagher would have won had there not been a *Frontline* debate or had it been conducted differently is impossible to say, but even had he maintained the lead that he took into the final week, it is possible that Higgins could have overtaken him in later counts.

Of the parties involved, Sinn Féin may have expected that this would be a breakthrough election, especially given Fianna Fáil's absence. Its support grew only slightly, though, and its candidate struggled to pick up transfers. This may have been because of the unique nature of the candidate, but if this was the case, then it represented a strategic error. However, its strategy might not have been winning the presidency at all. It could have been that the party, by nominating a former IRA leader, hoped to make northern nationalist opinion mainstream in the Republic and normalise involvement in the 'armed struggle' in the same way as partaking in the War of Independence was normalised. The election shows that people were not afraid to vote for a Fianna Fáil candidate. They shied away when he started to resemble what people did not like about Fianna Fáil, but Gallagher polled a very creditable 28.5 per cent, which one suspects Fianna Fáil would be very happy to secure in the next general election.

In the presidential election due to take place in 2018 parties may continue to move away from overtly party candidates, but there is less evidence that this is important. A candidate with a party nomination has won all presidential contests since 1945. While there is no evidence that parties push the party label in a presidential campaign strongly, party label is not a problem if the candidate is suitable. Parties may find it more difficult to get good candidates as the campaigns appear more gruelling than most experienced politicians would be used to. Calls for a relaxation of the rules for nomination may recede, since on this occasion it was possible for seven candidates to be nominated, and it is unlikely that anyone would have wanted a system that produced more.

ACKNOWLEDGEMENTS

The author would like to thank Ed Mulhall of RTÉ, Pat Leahy of the *Sunday Business Post* and Richard Colwell of Red-C for permission to use and for supplying the data from the recall poll and campaign polls, and to Stephen O'Brien of the *Sunday Times* [Irish edition] for supplying other poll results. He also thanks David Doyle, editors John Coakley and Kevin Rafter, and two anonymous reviewers for useful comments and suggestions.

NOTES

1. Others mentioned were: Gerry Adams, Bertie Ahern, Robert Ballagh, John Bruton, Gay Byrne, Pat Cox, Brian Crowley, Avril Doyle, Fergus Finlay, Michelle Gildernew, Mary Hanafin, Seamus Heaney, Seán Kelly, Justin Kilcullen, Mairéad McGuinness, Pádraig Ó Céidigh, Éamon Ó Cuiv, Niall O'Dowd, Kathleen O'Meara, Micheál Ó Muircheartaigh, Labhrás Ó Murchú, and Mary White.
2. Ipsos MRBI poll for the *We the Citizens* project carried out between April and June 2011 (held by the author).
3. Candidates who received at least a quarter of the quota (12.5 per cent) in the final count in which they were involved could claim a refund of up to €200,000 in election expenses.
4. Even if 100 per cent of available transfers from Mitchell went to Higgins, almost 60 per cent of McGuinness's transfers would have been needed to account for so large an advantage for Higgins over Gallagher.
5. These are data from a survey carried out between April and June 2011 by Ipsos MRBI for *We the Citizens*. These data are from an open-ended question.

10

CONCLUSION: THE PRESIDENT OF IRELAND: PAST, PRESENT AND FUTURE

JOHN COAKLEY AND KEVIN RAFTER

INTRODUCTION

In the introduction to this book, we discussed the confusion and disagreement that was generated by the new office of President of Ireland while the 1937 constitution was being debated in the Dáil. Three-quarters of a century later, Irish political leaders appear to share a much clearer and more positive interpretation of the value of the office. This was unanimously expressed in the Dáil on the occasion of the retirement of President McAleese in 2011. In the words of the Taoiseach, Enda Kenny, she was leaving behind 'a country so much better for her being its President'; for the Tánaiste, Eamon Gilmore, she was 'a true embodiment of [the] ideal of public service'; and for Fianna Fáil leader Micheál Martin she was 'a President who has made the people proud'. This cross-party unanimity in warmth of endorsement of President McAleese's contribution also showed a continuing appreciation of the subtle character of the President's office, one that defies explicit description. As the Tánaiste observed, 'the office of President is hard to define', adding that 'a President is as much a moral as a political leader', while Micheál Martin expressed the thoughtful but enigmatic view that 'many say the Presidency is above politics, but that is not the case. It is a highly political office, but it is removed from party politics'.[1]

As well as discussing the office as constitutionally defined, we have attempted in this book to probe some of these difficult issues, about which the constitution and the law are silent: what is the real function of the President in the Irish political system, and in Irish society more generally? The various chapters have explored a range of themes relating to the presidency, including the comparative and historical dimensions and the electoral process. More specifically, they have traced the evolution of the office from the inauguration of Douglas Hyde as first President in 1938 to that of Michael D. Higgins in 2011, offering a sense of the presidency's contribution to Irish society notwithstanding the obvious absence of real political power. In this concluding chapter we attempt to draw the strands of discussion together by focusing on a number of themes: the contribution of the presidency to date, its contemporary role, and, more speculatively, what the future may have in store for it.

THE EVOLUTION OF THE PRESIDENCY

One theme that emerges clearly from the chapters that make up the core of this book is the process of steady development of the office of President. The starting point was not a particularly auspicious one. Reactions to the creation of the office in the 1937 constitution were, as we have seen, divided. Quite apart from the debate about the powers that would be associated with the office, there were questions about its legitimacy. For some, it represented the return of the Governor-General in a new guise. But even if it did not, for close observers it could be seen as demonstrating the continuation of Ireland's ambiguous relationship of dependency on Great Britain. The President was not declared to be head of state; indeed, the typical functions of head of state were partitioned between the King (external affairs) and the President (internal affairs). The King never visited his Irish realm, nor was his role visible; but it was only in 1949 that the functions of accrediting Irish ambassadors and receiving the credentials of incoming ambassadors, as well as of representing Ireland internationally more generally, were transferred from the King to the President (Coakley, 2012a).

The process by which the first President took office may have been consensual, but the fact that there was only one candidate deprived him of the consecration of direct election – or even of indirect election, since the procedure was close to one of appointment. This also set the trend for subsequent presidential accessions, as Gary Murphy and Theresa Reidy show in Chapter 8. Of the 13 that have taken place, on six occasions there has been no election (though on three of these a President was being returned, without opposition, for a second term). On a further three occasions, only the two largest parties put forward candidates; on two more occasions, a third politically-nominated candidate ran; and on only two occasions, in 1997 and 2011, was the election more 'open', with additional candidates securing nomination from county councils. Undoubtedly, the fact that early presidents had been returned at the behest of politicians compromised their freedom of action and their independence. By contrast, the intensity with which presidential elections have been contested since 1990 has given the winning candidate a particular legitimacy.

The selection process may also have been responsible for the age profile of presidents, given the fact that, at least in the past, it has tended to favour established political figures. Presidents have ranged in age on accession from 46 (the two women presidents) to 78 (Douglas Hyde), though all were, of course, older by the time they completed their term, with the record held by de Valera, at 91. Unless age-related illness or frailty prevents a President from discharging public duties fully, however, it is not clear why the age of a President should matter. Nevertheless, elderly presidents have been accused of being out of touch with contemporary issues, an argument that can be used by their opponents as a stick with which to beat them.

In respect of professional background, most presidents (O'Kelly, de Valera, Childers, Hillery and Higgins) were best known as active and experienced politicians who had spent decades in public life, lending credence to the cynical description of Áras an Uachtaráin as a retirement home. It is clear, though, that each was selected by his party as a candidate with the capacity to win against stiff opposition, a choice that would not have been made had the candidate not had impressive vote-pulling power (though Hillery was not put to the test on this). Three others were prominent lawyers, with Ó Dálaigh having led a distinguished career in the Irish Supreme Court and the European Court of Justice, Robinson combining an academic legal position with an active career in the Seanad, and McAleese moving between university legal positions, university administration and journalism. Douglas Hyde was a Professor of Modern Irish, a language activist and an independent senator. All had achieved sufficient distinction and acquired enough experience before being inaugurated as President to be in a position to discharge the duties of the office with dignity and discretion.

The early presidents shared a relatively narrow perception of the nature of the presidency. This may have been shaped by its obvious role as successor to the office of Governor-General, a post associated with the legacy of British rule, as John Coakley argues in Chapter 4. The pace of change was slow. Ciara Meehan points out in Chapter 5 that, following an initial period during which new procedures were worked out and implemented, the presidency was marked by little innovation from the accession of Douglas Hyde in

1938 to the end of Eamon de Valera's second term in 1973. Over this 35-year period, the presidency was marked by a limited vision for the office coupled with relative inactivity in the performance of the role. A period of activism followed under the presidencies of Erskine Childers and Cearbhall Ó Dálaigh, but, as Kevin Rafter argues in Chapter 6, during the two-term presidency of Patrick Hillery there was a reversion to the earlier period as regards perception of the limited potential of the office.

Early presidents were also conscious of the restricted content of the presidential role. In his inauguration address in December 1974 Cearbhall Ó Dálaigh spoke perceptively of the President as having a theme rather than having policies. With his deep constitutional knowledge as a former Chief Justice, Ó Dálaigh was well positioned to assess the role of President of Ireland. This recognition of the constitutional limitations on the office, and its relative powerlessness, was explicitly addressed by Patrick Hillery's official biographer who described the office as 'symbolic, silent and almost entirely powerless' (Walsh, 2008: 429).

The presidencies of Mary Robinson and Mary McAleese, as described by Yvonne Galligan in Chapter 7, have been defined by much greater efforts to make the office a more meaningful institution with a subtle political dimension (using this term in the broadest, nonpartisan sense). President Michael D. Higgins has followed the same approach. In particular, the three most recent Presidents have shown a willingness to utilise the presidency's symbolic potential and 'soft power' to enhance its political relevance.

Evidence of this expanded activism can be seen in Mary Robinson's focus on the famine in Somalia in 1992, as well as her role in relation to Northern Ireland. Her successor, Mary McAleese, was similarly active, and her visit to Omagh the day after the August 1998 bombing gave presidential expression to national outrage at the attack. The remarks by President Higgins during the controversy about the legal position in relation to abortion in Ireland would have been considered major political interventions during earlier presidencies, but now raise few eyebrows. President Higgins's critical remarks on the economic policies being pursued in the European Union, however, did attract some criticism, with one influential journalist describing these as 'a direct intervention into political debate probably unprecedented in the history of the office', and as bringing the President into the political arena (Collins, 2013).

More typically, however, presidents tend to confine themselves to a symbolic role, one that is reinforced by the attention that presidents pay to the elderly, the disadvantaged, the marginalised, and members of minority groups in Irish society, who are frequently guests at Áras an Uachtaráin. Whether by their physical presence or through carefully chosen words, presidents have found it possible to make the influence of their office felt, and in three successive elections voters have indicated their preference for candidates committed to expanded presidential activism.

These new interpretations of the presidency were reflected in stances taken by the candidates during the presidential election campaigns. Thus, in the 1990 campaign Mary Robinson's two main slogans pledged her to be 'a president with a purpose' and 'a president for all the people', and in her election literature she identified the presidency with 'standing up for people who have no-one else to represent them' and with 'fighting for our heritage and our environment'. She committed herself to bringing 'a new dimension' to the office, and her aim of making a break with the 'quiet' presidency of Patrick Hillery has been seen as one of her key selling points with the electorate. Seven years later, Mary McAleese campaigned under the slogan 'building bridges', with a promise to give the presidency a role in ending division between the two communities in Northern Ireland, and between the unionist and nationalist traditions on the island of Ireland. Her election literature stressed that she would 'bring a cool head to protecting the Constitution'. During the 2011 presidential contest Michael D. Higgins promised to be 'a president who can promote Ireland on the international stage', and campaigned with the slogan 'a president who will do us proud'.

President Higgins, however, offered the most significant tangible proposal for developing the office of President since the campaign pledge of Erskine Childers in 1973 to establish a 'presidential think tank'. Outright rejection of this idea by Taoiseach Liam Cosgrave in 1973 fatally undermined this earlier attempt to involve the presidency more actively in national life. In the absence of hostility of this kind, Higgins was able to proceed with a similar initiative: the hosting of presidential seminars, which would 'reflect and explore' such themes as the restoration of trust in national institutions, the ethical connection between economy and society and the future of Europe. The process began in May 2012. Over the following six months at Áras an Uachtaráin, and at a number of regional locations, President Higgins met with groups of young people to develop the first in a series of such seminars. The outcome of this deliberative process was a report published in November 2012 (Áras an Uachtaráin, 2012). While unremarkable in its content and recommendations, the very fact that a published document directly associated with the presidency emerged from the process perhaps points to the potential for future development.

THE POLITICS OF THE PRESIDENCY

We set ourselves three related questions about the office of President of Ireland in the introduction to this book. The first has to do with its comparative standing: its similarity to the post of head of state in other jurisdictions. The second question addresses the range of functions of the President as defined in the constitution, but in particular as modified by the collective contribution of individual presidents. The third raises the impact of the selection and election processes on the character of the office, and the extent to which direct election actually matters. What answers does this book offer to these questions?

The first of these questions is tackled directly by Robert Elgie in Chapter 2. He uses five criteria to set the Irish President in the context of other heads of state and, in particular, of those who are directly elected but endowed with limited powers. Elgie concludes that in respect of two of these criteria Ireland was once unusual, but is now much closer to the global norm: the *selection principle* (direct election by the people) was very unusual in 1937 in the case of ceremonial heads of state, but is now extremely common; and the President's clearly *subordinate position in relation to the government*, once a rare status, now occurs widely. In respect of *constitutional powers*, the Irish President was for long extremely weak, but is no longer by any means unique in this respect; Elgie argues that weaker presidents, even directly elected ones, are to be found. On a fourth criterion, *electoral formula and term of office*, the standing of the Irish President is more unusual than ever: the single transferable vote system continues to be unique as an electoral system in a world where the two-ballot system is the norm, and the President's seven-year term of office, once commonly to be found elsewhere, is now unusual, since most presidents are elected for five years. Finally, the *reform debate* in relation to the Irish President now focuses mainly on minor matters, unlike the position in other countries, where more fundamental changes to the president's position are often contemplated, with a tendency to move towards the principle of direct election and restricted powers – a position characteristic of the Irish President from the very beginning. Elgie's conclusion is, then, that while the office of President of Ireland is unusual in several respects, it is by no means unique, as has sometimes been argued.

The second major question concerns the functions of the President. As Michael Gallagher points out in Chapter 3, the President's freedom of action is

highly circumscribed in constitutional theory. Most functions are purely ceremonial, to be carried out 'on the advice' of the Government. Of the two major
areas where the President has been given discretion, one has been actively
used. On 27 occasions the President has overtly considered referring a bill to
the Supreme Court because of doubts about its compatibility with the constitution; on 25 occasions the Council of State has met to advise the President as
to whether the bill should indeed be referred (including two occasions when
two bills were considered); on 15 occasions the President then proceeded to
refer the bill; on eight of these occasions the Supreme Court cleared the bill;
and on the remaining seven occasions the bill's life came to an end when the
Supreme Court found it not to be fully compatible with the constitution.

As Gallagher also shows, although no President has ever refused to withhold a dissolution of the Dáil from a Taoiseach who had lost its confidence,
thus triggering a general election, this power remains a real one. No Taoiseach
can take it for granted any more that a general election can be called in all
circumstances. When Albert Reynolds's Fianna Fáil–Labour coalition collapsed in 1994, President Robinson let it be known obliquely that she would
not necessarily grant a dissolution, a message strong enough to discourage the
Taoiseach from asking for one, resulting in the formation of a new Fine Gael–
Labour–Democratic Left coalition that was to last until 1997. This raises two
further questions about presidential functions: the extent to which they have
changed over time, and the degree to which constitutional provisions offer a
full description of the reality of the President's role.

It will be clear from the three chapters that explore the role of individual
presidents that, even in the absence of constitutional change, there has been
very marked progression over time in the manner in which presidents have
discharged their functions. The limited role and low public profile of the first
three presidents, Hyde, O'Kelly and de Valera, emerges clearly from Ciara
Meehan's analysis in Chapter 5, and Kevin Rafter shows in Chapter 6 that the
position was similar during the Hillery presidency. It is true, as Rafter points
out, that Childers and Ó Dálaigh each sought to expand the role of the presidency during their brief terms of office (1973–1976); but each came up against
determined opposition from a Taoiseach, Liam Cosgrave, whose understanding of his relationship with the President appears to have been shaped more by
political hostility than by a willingness to adhere to constitutional proprieties.
It is not surprising that Childers contemplated resignation, or that Ó Dálaigh
actually resigned; but the question arises as to why, in similar circumstances
at the beginning of her presidency, Mary Robinson stood her ground, forcing

a Taoiseach as strong-willed as Charles Haughey to back down. She ended the practice by which the government had exercised a veto on the content of presidential speeches and, as Yvonne Galligan shows in Chapter 7, the government felt powerless to stop her from engaging in such independent gestures as meeting the Dalai Lama in 1991 and shaking hands with Gerry Adams in 1993. It seems clear that the relative freedom of expression and freedom of movement that Mary Robinson achieved for the President allowed her successors to play a similarly active role.

But is the tussle over the constitutional functions of the office of President of Ireland the whole story? The manner in which the office has evolved since 1990 suggests that it is not. There can be little doubt about their relative powerlessness in a narrow political sense, but presidents also play a much broader social role. During the three most recent presidential campaigns all of the candidates appeared to recognise the tension between these two dimensions. In many respects the various candidates' 'visions' for the office were a reaction to perceived presidential weakness. Candidates tended to summarise their 'visions' in shorthand terms through slogans and campaign themes, offering a signal of intent in addressing the presidential power deficit.

Analysis of presidential inauguration addresses allows us to see what precisely incoming presidents had to say about the office itself (see Appendix 2). The addresses share certain features. Little is said about presidential power; nothing is proposed as regards reform. Within this, though, we may see an evolution in the vision of the presidency. Early presidential inauguration speeches were short and unspecific, and took the form of a response to the Taoiseach, who made the initial speech following the formal swearing-in. In 1938, 1945 and 1952, the Taoiseach, Eamon de Valera, engaged in fulsome tribute to the incoming President, describing Hyde in 1938 as symbolising the incarnation of the Irish nation, 'our President, our head, freely chosen under our own laws', and O'Kelly as 'the first citizen of the state, elected by the people of their own free will in accordance with the democratic laws of the country' (1945) and as 'the successor of our native chiefs, the guardian of the constitution of Ireland and the protector of its laws' (1945).[2] This set the tone for remarks by the subsequent Taoisigh, though these were sometimes more prosaic.

Presidents' responses were initially very brief, beginning with some words of thanks. They went no further than invoking God's blessing in the case of Hyde (1938), but O'Kelly committed himself to support for the Irish language (1945) and to Irish unity and to harmonious relations between parties (1952).

In 1959 de Valera made a very brief speech, but in 1966 he went much further, not just stressing 'the two cherished aims which have not yet been realised – the unity of our country and the restoration of our language', but making a specific proposal for a national convention on the restoration of the Irish language. The short addresses by Childers (1973) and Hillery (1976, 1983) were studiously non-political; the much longer one by Ó Dálaigh (1974), in three languages (with a portion in French), included extensive personal reminiscences, but also veered into political terrain, expressing hope for a truce in Northern Ireland.

More recent presidents have followed a similar model, tending to refer to the presidency only in general terms, but offering a more elaborate 'vision' of the office. Mary Robinson stressed the need to promote a 'growing sense of local participatory democracy', to encourage a confident sense of Irishness in an increasingly integrated Europe, and to protect human rights. Mary McAleese focused on the theme of reconciliation in her first inauguration address in 1997, and at the beginning of her second term in 2004 she identified particular pressing social problems as requiring attention (youth suicide, racism, binge-drinking, street crime and corruption), in the context of the goal of achieving overall prosperity and security. Michael D. Higgins committed himself to a 'presidency of transformation' in his inaugural address, seeing his office as 'of assistance and encouragement to investment and job creation, to innovation and original thinking'.

The third big question about the nature of the contemporary Irish presidency has to do with the impact of the selection and election processes. The traditional route to Áras an Uachtaráin was exemplified by the characteristics of the early office holders: all were essentially political grandees, and backed by Fianna Fáil in either their election campaign or in elevation to the office without a contest. O'Kelly, de Valera and Childers were elected at the ballot box as Fianna Fáil nominees; Hyde, Ó Dálaigh and Hillery secured the office without an election, but only after receiving the backing of Fianna Fáil. The profile of the candidates for the office changed dramatically in 1990 with the Labour Party's decision to contest and to nominate Mary Robinson. In the two subsequent election campaigns we see more non-party candidates with different life experiences and from varying political backgrounds. As Gary Murphy and Theresa Reidy argue in Chapter 8, the breakdown in partisan loyalty in Irish party politics has been a crucial driver of recent presidential nomination outcomes, with local councillors abandoning their traditional deference to party headquarters and displaying a surprising willingness to endorse non-party candidates, such as Dana Rosemary Scallon and Derek Nally in 1997 and Seán Gallagher, Mary Davis and David Norris in 2011 (with Dana also once again securing a place on the ballot paper). The 2011 presidential election, as Eoin O'Malley shows in Chapter 9, illustrates the extent to which this breakdown in partisanship has coloured the outcome of the election campaign. The expansion of candidate numbers illustrates the kind of striking evolution that can take place even in the absence of any change in the nomination system laid down in the 1937 Constitution.

It seems clear that presidential election contests have a considerable political impact. The creditable performance of Patrick McCartan in 1945 was seen as an important stage in preparing the ground for the upsurge in support for a new party, Clann na Poblachta, in the 1948 general election. The poor performance of the Fine Gael candidate in 1990 led to the resignation of Alan Dukes as party leader, and Dick Spring resigned as leader of the Labour Party in 1997 following the very weak showing of the party candidate in the presidential election. Of more central interest, however, is the impact of the electoral process on the presidential office. Until the early 1990s, the fact that the President was in practice more likely to have been nominated than elected meant that the office was taken less seriously by the government, and was certainly not seen as a rival power base (Duffy, 1993: 137). Cearbhall Ó Dálaigh questioned the strength of his authority in having assumed office as an agreed candidate, while Mary Robinson drew specific attention to the importance of endorsement by universal suffrage in conferring great moral authority on the President – a position that not even the Taoiseach can rival. Subsequent presidents, and, indeed, Taoisigh, have been conscious of this moral and social psychological reality, giving the President much greater freedom of action than in the past.

THE FUTURE OF THE PRESIDENCY

While presidential candidates have spoken extensively about the future of the office, they have tended to confine themselves to suggesting what is possible within the limits of the provisions currently defined in the constitution. Nevertheless, the future of the office has been considered in some depth as part of three major constitutional review processes over the last half century. The first was the Committee on the Constitution, a 12-member all-party group of TDs and senators chaired by George Colley, Minister for Industry and Commerce. Established in August 1966, it completed its work in a little over a year, publishing its report in December 1967. The second was the Constitution Review

Group, comprising 15 non-political experts, including academics, lawyers and others, chaired by a former leading civil servant, T.K. Whitaker. Established in April 1995, it reported in July 1996. The recommendations of this body were then considered by an all-party Oireachtas committee that was established in 1996 during the term of the Fine Gael–Labour–Democratic Left coalition, with Fine Gael TD Jim O'Keeffe as chairperson. With the change of government the following year the new Fianna Fáil–Progressive Democrat coalition nominated Brian Lenihan Junior of Fianna Fáil as chairperson. The renewed committee, comprising eight TDs and four senators, continued to produce periodic reports on specific constitutional issues; its third progress report in November 1998 was devoted to the office of President. The most fundamental question explored by the three committees was the very existence of the presidency – whether the office should remain in the constitution at all. Aside from this, the committees explored the desirability of reform in the President's functions, and in the arrangements for selecting the President.

It is striking that none of the three committee reports made a strong case for the presidency itself – a reflection, no doubt, of the relatively poor standing of the office in the past, but surprising, given that two of the reports were published during the activist period that commenced with Mary Robinson's election in 1990. The Colley committee succinctly outlined arguments for and against outright abolition of the presidency, and it is clear from the text that the committee contained few, if any, real champions of the office. The reasons advanced for abolishing the office included the view that it was largely a figurehead one, the formal duties of which could 'without difficulty' be assigned to the Taoiseach, and abolishing it would deliver 'substantial financial savings' (Committee on the Constitution, 1967: 8). The committee accepted, however, that these two points could be reversed: it would be unrealistic for the Taoiseach to undertake the work of head of state as well as head of government given the heavy burden that this would impose, and combining the two offices would not actually deliver real cost savings. The only positive argument offered for retaining the office was the need to maintain the President's role as 'guardian of the constitution'.

The Whitaker committee noted that the President 'serves as a personification of the State' and is an individual in whom the people 'seek a reflection of their highest values and aspirations' (Constitution Review Group, 1996: 25). Despite these vague and rather grandiose claims, the members were divided on the question of whether or not the office should continue in existence. They settled on the not very flattering conclusion that there was 'no public demand or good reason for abolition of the office' (Constitution Review Group, 1996: 26). This sense of preserving the presidency – but not because of any great enthusiasm for the office – was also a feature of the Lenihan committee report in 1998. It accepted the earlier Whitaker assessment that there was no public demand or good reason to abolish the office, noting lamely that it was proper to have a head of state separate from the executive (All-Party Oireachtas Committee, 1998: 5).

The report of the Colley committee made no recommendation on enhancing the role of the President, nor did it suggest giving the holder of the office any new powers (Committee on the Constitution, 1967: 9). The Whitaker group looked at the idea of expanding the presidency's discretionary powers to embrace certain appointive functions, for example in the selection of judges. But ultimately it concluded that this move would become problematic as it would involve a President in party politics and there would also be problems of reduced accountability, as the President could not be answerable to parliament for these decisions (Constitution Review Group, 1996: 29–30). The Lenihan Committee also concluded that the President's discretionary powers should not be extended, noting that 'the symbolic value of the office derives from the detachment of the holder from partisan politics' (All-Party Oireachtas Committee, 1998: 10). Thus, it took the view that there was no need to alter the President's power in the area of withholding a dissolution of the Dáil from a Taoiseach who had lost its confidence. On the other hand, it proposed one innovation: giving the President responsibility for administering a new national honours system.[3] Such a system had been proposed by Taoiseach Bertie Ahern in June 1998. The committee backed the idea, and proposed giving the Council of State a consultative role in the process of selecting those to be honoured. In light of the committee's previous concerns about involving the presidency in the political domain, it seems surprising that it did not address the question as to whether giving the President a role in the allocation of national honours would involve the holder of the office in 'partisan politics'. The committee concluded that 'leaving decisions on the honours systems to the President would elevate the system above partisan claims as well as give it the prestige which attaches to the elected office of the President' (All-Party Oireachtas Committee, 1998: 10). The idea of an honours system received a lukewarm response from the main opposition parties, and was not ultimately carried further.

The three reports considered the method of election and the nomination system in some detail. The Colley committee examined the arguments for and against moving to an electoral college based largely on Oireachtas membership, though its members were divided on the issue (Committee on the Constitution, 1967: 9). Almost 30 years later, the Whitaker group concluded that, as there was no public demand for change – although no evidence was provided to support this conclusion – it was possible to 'infer that the people wish to retain their right to vote for a President' (Constitution Review Group, 1996: 29). The Lenihan committee repeated this latter recommendation without any elaboration.

As regards the nomination process, the Colley committee had merely recommended deleting the constitutional provision (12.4.4) that allowed former or retiring presidents to self-nominate (Committee on the Constitution, 1967: 9). The Whitaker group felt that the nomination system was 'too restrictive and in need of democratisation' (Constitution Review Group, 1996: 29). Its main proposal, however, was fairly conservative, merely suggesting a reduction in the number of Oireachtas members required to nominate a presidential candidate below its existing level of 20 TDs and senators. The Lenihan committee considered the nomination process in greatest depth. This was not surprising given that the committee's deliberations followed the 1997 presidential election, when the ballot paper included a record five candidates, two of whom (Dana Rosemary Scallon and Derek Nally) had made a piece of political history in securing a nomination via the local authority route. At that time there had been public discussion about expanding the nomination process, and Fine Gael, then in opposition, published proposals to facilitate nomination by the public.[4]

The Lenihan committee proposed amending the system of candidate nomination by reducing the number of Oireachtas members whose support was needed from 20 to ten. The minimum number of county and county borough councils was, however, to be left at four. In what was probably the most significant proposal in relation to any aspect of the presidency to arise out of the three reports, the Lenihan committee backed the idea of popular nomination, though drawbacks were acknowledged: 'it leaves open the possibility that the office of President could be demeaned by the nomination of frivolous candidates or endangered by the nomination of inadequately qualified ones' (All-Party Oireachtas Committee, 1998: 6). The committee's deliberations on procedures for nominating appropriate candidates offer a fascinating insight into the characteristics seen as desirable in a President:

> The President must have the presidential skills that will allow him or her to represent the state with style and dignity both within the state and

outside it. The President must have the analytical skills to allow him or her to exercise the discretionary powers, which bear upon important legal and political matters; and the President must have the firmness to assert and sustain the status of the office of President against the encroachment of any of the other national institutions (All-Party Oireachtas Committee, 1998: 6).

While there was support for a new nomination route, and one that allowed the public a direct say, this was matched by concern that the political parties would lose their veto over the type of candidate who secured a nomination.

As part of its work the Lenihan committee examined the popular nomination systems used in other countries, including Finland and Portugal. The objective was to find a system characterised by a strict but practical regime for validating nominations (All-Party Oireachtas Committee, 1998: 7). The committee concluded that an appropriate system would need a high threshold of signatures to secure a nomination, as well as a rigorous system to ensure that all signatures were registered voters. In the end, it recommended a figure of 10,000 nominators alongside a validation system whereby each nominator would have to attend a designated public office with a signed nomination form and proof of identification. The idea was not subsequently taken further by governments and, more surprisingly given the renewed emphasis on greater public participation in the democratic process, it did not feature in any of the more recent political reform discussions until the Convention on the Constitution offered the unsolicited view in 2013 that the nomination process should be more open (Convention on the Constitution, 2013: [7]).

Two related matters were considered by the Whitaker and Lenihan committees. The Whitaker group was divided on the question of reducing the age of eligibility of the President, but on balance recommended no change (Constitution Review Group, 1996: 30). The Lenihan committee, however, saw no logical reason for the 35-year threshold, and recommended aligning candidate eligibility with the voting age of 18 years (All-Party Oireachtas Committee, 1996: 13). The two committees also considered the case for reducing the presidential term of office, but recommended retaining the seven-year term, with the Whitaker group concluding that 'a shorter term than seven years could tend to associate the presidency more with party political change' (Constitution Review Group, 1996: 33).[5]

While the office of President has, then, been examined at considerable length by successive committees, no consensus has emerged as to any changes that might need to be made in the definition of its powers and functions. The report of the Convention on the Constitution (2013) may result in efforts to broaden the nominating process being put on the political agenda. But the fact that there is such limited momentum behind reform of the office suggests that no radical change is likely in the immediate future, and implies broad public and political satisfaction with the manner in which incumbents have discharged their duties.

CONCLUSION

Perhaps the most striking of all of the themes running through this book has been that of change. Of course, any institution that has lasted for three quarters of a century is unlikely to remain static, as norms adjust to new social and political realities and as offices are redefined by new personalities. But the transformation of the Irish presidency was exceptionally extensive and abrupt. The abruptness is to be seen in the manner in which the significance of this office changed in a single year, 1990. In January of that year, as President Hillery entered his last few months in office, the presidency was recognisably similar to the office established more than 50 years earlier. Within a year that had changed. A new President, a woman and a political outsider, took office after a hard-fought election, and used her popular mandate to face down Taoisigh and other political leaders who in earlier years would have brooked no independence of speech or action from her predecessors.

On the day that Douglas Hyde was inaugurated as President of Ireland in 1938, his office issued a message that signalled the quiet role that he intended to play. This announced that the President had made it a general rule 'that in his official capacity he will be present only at functions of a State or national character, or of such a special nature as to make it desirable, in his opinion, that he should attend'.[6] The much more assertive role of contemporary presidents was articulated in an *Irish Times* editorial 75 years later that paid tribute to President Higgins's activism as expressed in his recent speeches – an editorial that would never have been written about any of the early presidents:

> The President has enjoyed a good relationship with the Government and Opposition parties. But his forthright comments have brought rumblings of concern that traditional boundaries might be breached and lead to a confrontation with Government. That response appears to be unnecessarily apprehensive, in view of the diplomatic way in which Mr Higgins

conducts himself. … As Ireland prepares to exit the EU-IMF bailout, presidential comments that were once shrugged off by politicians have increasing relevance. … The President has an important role to play in promoting debate on the kind of society that should emerge from the wreckage of the Celtic Tiger.[7]

The Irish presidency has at times been a silent and forgotten office. But over its first 75 years, as the various contributors to this book have shown, the office – notwithstanding its limited constitutional powers – has gained a high level of visibility, and perceptions of its relevance are now much more positive than in the past. When given a choice (as in 1990, 1997 and 2011), Irish voters ultimately opted for candidates to push the office to greater limits in its symbolic power. In these three highly contested – and hugely political – electoral contests, the presidency was seen as an office worth fighting for, and worth engaging with. After 75 years, the reservations of political leaders, the confusion of observers and the relative indifference of the public – so prominent a feature of attitudes towards this office in the late 1930s – appear by now to have been well and truly banished.

NOTES

1. *Dáil Debates*, 10 November 2011, vol. 746, cols 263–70.
2. *The Irish Times*, 27 June 1938, 26 June 1945, 26 June 1952.
3. This national honours system would have been separate from 'Gaisce: the President's Awards' launched in 1985 to recognise the achievements of young people aged between 15 and 25. See http://www.gaisce.ie/about.aspx (accessed 1 March 2013).
4. Fine Gael TDs Jim O'Keeffe and Paul McGrath sponsored a private member's bill, which was discussed in the Dáil; see *Dáil Debates*, 30 September–1 October 1997, Vol. 470, cols 954–75, 1349–72.
5. Other issues discussed by these two committees included removing the religious aspects of the President's inauguration declaration (both in agreement), while the Lenihan committee proposed extending membership of Council of State to include two members of the Dáil who belonged to parties not in government. Amendments of a technical nature were also proposed.
6. *The Irish Times*, 27 June 1938.
7. *The Irish Times*, 27 April 2013.

APPENDIX 1

RESULTS OF PRESIDENTIAL ELECTIONS, 1938–2011

NOTE ON DATA AND SOURCES

The following tables give full information on electoral participation and votes by candidate at each presidential election. Counting of votes took place by Dáil constituency, except in 1945, when the presidential election coincided with local elections and counting took place by administrative county. Results have been summarised by province (as these were defined originally for purposes of European elections). Information on the electorate and on turnout in 1945 is unofficial and approximate. In 1945, the counting of votes in the second count took place jointly for the county and country borough of Limerick; the data reported here for the county refer to both administrative areas.

The main source for the raw data presented here is the official report on presidential elections (Ireland, 2011) and its predecessors. Percentages and provincial summaries have been computed separately. For 1945, the only officially available information on the electorate was (1) total electorate and (2) turnout in Clare and Kerry. Estimates were derived as follows: a preliminary estimate of the electorate in 1945 was made by interpolating from the electorate on 1 June 1944 and 15 April 1946, available in *Annual Reports of the Department of Local Government* 1944–5 (p. 136) and 1945–7 (p. 96); this was checked against unofficial and often conflicting figures published in the *Irish Press*, *Irish Independent*, *Irish Times* and *Roscommon Champion*, various dates, June 1945; the most likely figure was selected in cases of discrepancy; and the result was rounded to the nearest thousand to indicate that it is an estimate. The figures for Clare and Kerry were further adjusted to ensure that the turnout figure is correct. Due to rounding error, figures in this column will not sum exactly to the reported total. No invalid votes were reported for Kildare in 1973.

In the summary tables that follow, candidates are listed in order of first preference votes, and the candidate who was elected is indicated in bold. The parties, if any, with which candidates were associated are also indicated by standard party abbreviations. In the detailed tables, the first percentage column refers to turnout (all votes cast as a percentage of the electorate) and the second to invalid votes as a percentage of all votes cast. Percentages reported for the first count refer to candidates' first preferences as a percentage of valid votes. For second and later counts, 'tr.' refers to votes transferred and 'total' to the sum of this figure and the votes already allocated to the respective candidates. On the last count, the percentage figures refer to the votes allocated to the remaining candidates as a percentage of all votes except those reported as non-transferable at that point. 'NT' designates non-transferable votes (note that in the third and fourth counts in 2011 this refers only to non-transferable votes arising on those counts, not to the cumulative number). Names have been abbreviated in some places because of constraints of space. 'CB' designates county borough.

FINAL RESULTS, 1938–2011

Year	Successful candidate	Total candidates	Election date	Inauguration
1938	Dubhglas de hÍde	1	n.a.	25 June
1945	Seán T. O'Kelly	3	14 June	25 June
1952	Seán T. O'Kelly	1	n.a.	25 June
1959	Eamon de Valera	2	17 June	25 June
1966	Eamon de Valera	2	1 June	25 June
1973	Erskine Childers	2	30 May	25 June
1974	Cearbhall Ó Dálaigh	1	n.a.	19 December
1976	Patrick Hillery	1	n.a.	3 December
1983	Patrick Hillery	1	n.a.	3 December
1990	Mary Robinson	3	7 November	3 December
1997	Mary McAleese	5	30 October	11 November
2004	Mary McAleese	1	n.a.	11 November
2011	Michael D. Higgins	7	27 October	11 November

CONTESTED ELECTIONS, 1945–2011: SUMMARY

1945 (THURSDAY 14 JUNE)

Electorate:	1,803,463	Total poll:	1,136,625	(63.0%)
Valid votes:	1,086,338	Invalid votes:	50,287	(4.4%)
Quota:	543,170			

	Count 1		**Count 2**	
Candidate	**Votes**	**(%)**	**Transfers**	**Total**
O'Kelly, Seán T. (FF)	537,965	(49.5)	27,200	565,165
Mac Eoin, Seán (FG)	335,539	(30.9)	117,886	453,425
McCartan, Patrick	212,834	(19.6)	−212,834	.
non-transferable	-	-	67,748	67,748

1959 (WEDNESDAY 17 JUNE)

Electorate:	1,678,450	Total poll:	979,628	(58.4%)
Valid votes:	955,539	Invalid votes:	24,089	(2.5%)
Quota:	477,770			

Candidate	**Votes**	**(%)**
de Valera, Eamon (FF)	538,003	(56.3)
Mac Eoin, Seán (FG)	417,536	(43.7)

1966 (WEDNESDAY 1 JUNE)

Electorate:	1,709,161	Total poll:	1,116,915	(65.3%)
Valid votes:	1,107,005	Invalid votes:	9,910	(0.9%)
Quota:	553,503			

Candidate	**Votes**	**(%)**
de Valera, Eamon (FF)	558,861	(50.5)
O'Higgins, Thomas F. (FG)	548,144	(49.5)

1973 (WEDNESDAY 30 MAY)

Electorate:	1,977,817		Total poll:	1,230,584	(62.2%)
Valid votes:	1,223,638		Invalid votes:	6,946	(0.6%)
Quota:	611,820				

Candidate	Votes	(%)
Childers, Erskine (FF)	635,867	(52.0)
O'Higgins, Thomas F. (FG)	587,771	(48.0)

1990 (WEDNESDAY 7 NOVEMBER)

Electorate:	2,471,308		Total poll:	1,584,095	(64.1%)
Valid votes:	1,574,651		Invalid votes:	9,444	(0.6%)
Quota:	787,326				

Candidate	Count 1 Votes	(%)	Count 2 Transfers	Total
Lenihan, Brian (FF)	694,484	(44.1)	36,789	731,273
Robinson, Mary (Lab)	612,265	(38.9)	205,565	817,830
Currie, Austin(FG)	267,902	(17.0)	−267,902	.
non-transferable	–	–	25,548	25,548

1997 (THURSDAY 30 OCTOBER)

Electorate:	2,739,529		Total poll:	1,279,688	(46.7%)
Valid votes:	1,269,836		Invalid votes:	9,852	(0.8%)
Quota:	634,919				

Candidate	Count 1 Votes	(%)	Count 2 Transfers	Total
McAleese, Mary (FF)	574,424	(45.2)	131,835	706,259
Banotti, Mary (FG)	372,002	(29.3)	125,514	497,516
Scallon, Dana Rosemary	175,458	(13.8)	−175,458	.
Roche, Adi (Lab)	88,423	(7.0)	−88,423	.
Nally, Derek	59,529	(4.7)	−59,529	.
non-transferable	–	–	66,061	66,061

2011 (THURSDAY 27 OCTOBER)

Electorate:	3,191,157	
Valid votes:	1,771,762	
Quota:	885,882	

Total poll:	1,790,438	(56.1%)
Invalid votes:	18,676	(1.0%)

Candidate	Count 1 Votes	(%)	Count 2 Transfers	Total	Count 3 Transfers	Total	Count 4 Transfers Total	Total
Higgins, Michael D. (Lab)	701,101	(39.6)	29,379	730,480	62,648	793,128	213,976	1,007,104
Gallagher, Seán	504,964	(28.5)	24,437	529,401	18,972	548,373	79,741	628,114
McGuinness, Martin (SF)	243,030	(13.7)	9,581	252,611	12,585	265,196	−265,196	.
Mitchell, Gay (FG)	113,321	(6.4)	14,036	127,357	8,952	136,309	−136,309	.
Norris, David	109,469	(6.2)	7,057	116,526	−116,526	.	.	.
Scallon, Dana Rosemary	51,220	(2.9)	−51,220	.	.	.	.	.
Davis, Mary	48,657	(2.7)	−48,657	.	.	.	.	.
non-transferable	-	–	15,387	15,387	13,369	28,756	107,788	136,544

1945: ELECTORAL PARTICIPATION

County	Electorate (see note)	Total votes		Invalid votes		Valid votes
		no.	%	no.	%	
Carlow	20,000	13,993	70.0	780	5.6	13,213
Cavan	44,000	31,341	71.2	1,926	6.1	29,415
Clare	54,250	40,968	75.5	1,283	3.1	39,685
Cork County	172,000	119,684	69.6	6,873	5.7	112,811
Cork CB	46,000	28,546	62.1	932	3.3	27,614
Donegal	86,000	50,023	58.2	4,053	8.1	45,970
Dublin County	74,000	38,155	51.6	469	1.2	37,686
Dublin CB	294,000	158,142	53.8	4,065	2.6	154,077
Galway	96,000	59,734	62.2	3,372	5.6	56,362
Kerry	86,500	36,758	42.5	489	1.3	36,269
Kildare	38,000	22,126	58.2	1,011	4.6	21,115
Kilkenny	42,000	26,162	62.3	1,091	4.2	25,071
Laoighis	30,000	20,482	68.3	969	4.7	19,513
Leitrim	29,000	21,574	74.4	1,171	5.4	20,403
Limerick County	61,000	42,816	70.2	2,150	5.0	40,666
Limerick CB	24,000	17,302	72.1	715	4.1	16,587
Longford	23,000	16,975	73.8	311	1.8	16,664
Louth	41,000	28,803	70.3	1,055	3.7	27,748
Mayo	95,000	57,670	60.7	3,233	5.6	54,437
Meath	40,000	25,027	62.6	754	3.0	24,273
Monaghan	35,000	25,873	73.9	1,891	7.3	23,982
Offaly	32,000	20,891	65.3	976	4.7	19,915
Roscommon	47,000	33,929	72.2	1,688	5.0	32,241
Sligo	41,000	27,283	66.5	1,379	5.1	25,904
Tipperary NR	36,000	25,497	70.8	1,544	6.1	23,953
Tipperary SR	46,000	33,124	72.0	1,530	4.6	31,594
Waterford County	30,000	19,284	64.3	625	3.2	18,659
Waterford CB	15,000	11,581	77.2	281	2.4	11,300
Westmeath	33,000	22,395	67.9	715	3.2	21,680
Wexford	56,000	36,977	66.0	2,027	5.5	34,950
Wicklow	37,000	23,510	63.5	929	4.0	22,581
Dublin	*368,000*	*196,297*	*53.3*	*4,534*	*2.3*	*191,763*
Rest of Leinster	*392,000*	*257,341*	*65.6*	*14,598*	*5.7*	*332,229*
Munster	*570,750*	*375,560*	*65.8*	*12,442*	*3.3*	*273,632*
Connacht-Ulster	*473,000*	*307,427*	*65.0*	*18,713*	*6.1*	*288,714*
Total	1,803,463	1,136,625	63.0	50,287	4.4	1,086,338

1945: FIRST PREFERENCE VOTES

County	Number of votes			Percentage of votes		
	McCartan	MacEoin	O'Kelly	McCartan	MacEoin	O'Kelly
Carlow	1,838	5,197	6,178	13.9	39.3	46.8
Cavan	3,032	11,883	14,500	10.3	40.4	49.3
Clare	5,979	10,796	22,910	15.1	27.2	57.7
Cork County	24,163	38,911	49,737	21.4	34.5	44.1
Cork CB	4,714	9,025	13,875	17.1	32.7	50.2
Donegal	7,834	13,137	24,999	17.0	28.6	54.4
Dublin County	9,815	11,665	16,206	26.0	31.0	43.0
Dublin CB	44,027	39,273	70,777	28.6	25.5	45.9
Galway	11,153	12,713	32,496	19.8	22.6	57.7
Kerry	8,500	7,180	20,589	23.4	19.8	56.8
Kildare	2,958	6,731	11,426	14.0	31.9	54.1
Kilkenny	3,476	8,158	13,437	13.9	32.5	53.6
Laoighis	4,884	5,683	8,946	25.0	29.1	45.8
Leitrim	2,995	9,344	8,064	14.7	45.8	39.5
Limerick County	4,758	13,183	22,725	11.7	32.4	55.9
Limerick CB	2,538	4,731	9,318	15.3	28.5	56.2
Longford	646	10,170	5,848	3.9	61.0	35.1
Louth	4,668	9,395	13,685	16.8	33.9	49.3
Mayo	12,505	14,672	27,260	23.0	27.0	50.1
Meath	3,406	6,784	14,083	14.0	27.9	58.0
Monaghan	4,062	6,878	13,042	16.9	28.7	54.4
Offaly	4,136	5,199	10,580	20.8	26.1	53.1
Roscommon	5,140	11,747	15,354	15.9	36.4	47.6
Sligo	3,590	12,026	10,288	13.9	46.4	39.7
Tipperary NR	3,946	7,530	12,477	16.5	31.4	52.1
Tipperary SR	5,155	10,499	15,940	16.3	33.2	50.5
Waterford County	2,481	5,198	10,980	13.3	27.9	58.8
Waterford CB	2,135	3,267	5,898	18.9	28.9	52.2
Westmeath	1,636	9,741	10,303	7.5	44.9	47.5
Wexford	8,488	10,082	16,380	24.3	28.8	46.9
Wicklow	8,176	4,741	9,664	36.2	21.0	42.8
Dublin	*53,842*	*50,938*	*86,983*	*28.1*	*26.6*	*45.4*
Rest of Leinster	*58,029*	*108,375*	*165,825*	*17.5*	*32.6*	*49.9*
Munster	*50,652*	*83,826*	*139,154*	*18.5*	*30.6*	*50.9*
Connacht-Ulster	*50,311*	*92,400*	*146,003*	*17.4*	*32.0*	*50.6*
Total	212,834	335,539	537,965	19.6	30.9	49.5

1945: SECOND COUNT (DISTRIBUTION OF MCCARTAN'S VOTES)

County	MacEoin			O'Kelly			NT
	tr.	total	%	tr.	total	%	
Carlow	810	6,007	47.6	437	6,615	52.4	591
Cavan	1,523	13,406	47.2	510	15,010	52.8	999
Clare	3,106	13,902	37.0	758	23,668	63.0	2,115
Cork County	13,777	52,688	50.2	2,613	52,350	49.8	7,773
Cork CB	2,602	11,627	44.5	629	14,504	55.5	1,483
Donegal	3,107	16,244	38.6	882	25,881	61.4	3,845
Dublin County	6,881	18,546	51.7	1,111	17,317	48.3	1,823
Dublin CB	28,674	67,947	47.2	5,342	76,119	52.8	10,011
Galway	5,075	17,788	34.6	1,157	33,653	65.4	4,921
Kerry	4,419	11,599	34.9	1,038	21,627	65.1	3,043
Kildare	1,645	8,376	41.4	443	11,869	58.6	870
Kilkenny	1,982	10,140	42.1	484	13,921	57.9	1,010
Laoighis	2,254	7,937	45.4	594	9,540	54.6	2,036
Leitrim	1,282	10,626	55.6	433	8,497	44.4	1,280
Limerick C and CB	3,914	21,828	39.7	1,084	33,127	60.3	2,298
Limerick CB	-	-	-	-	-	-	-
Longford	316	10,486	63.7	126	5,974	36.3	204
Louth	2,592	11,987	45.6	627	14,312	54.4	1,449
Mayo	6,023	20,695	42.1	1,158	28,418	57.9	5,324
Meath	1,896	8,680	37.2	572	14,655	62.8	938
Monaghan	1,549	8,427	38.1	629	13,671	61.9	1,884
Offaly	1,745	6,944	37.3	1,092	11,672	62.7	1,299
Roscommon	2,760	14,507	47.8	499	15,853	52.2	1,881
Sligo	1,650	13,676	55.7	569	10,857	44.3	1,371
Tipperary NR	2,130	9,660	42.5	605	13,082	57.5	1,211
Tipperary SR	3,032	13,531	44.8	756	16,696	55.2	1,367
Waterford County	1,460	6,658	37.2	271	11,251	62.8	750
Waterford CB	1,266	4,533	42.2	317	6,215	57.8	552
Westmeath	807	10,548	49.8	317	10,620	50.2	512
Wexford	4,983	15,065	46.7	829	17,209	53.3	2,676
Wicklow	4,626	9,367	46.0	1,318	10,982	54.0	2,232
Dublin	*35,555*	*86,493*	*48.1*	*6,453*	*93,436*	*51.9*	*11,834*
Rest of Leinster	*31,544*	*139,919*	*44.5*	*8,788*	*174,613*	*55.5*	*17,697*
Munster	*27,818*	*111,644*	*43.5*	*6,122*	*145,276*	*56.5*	*16,712*
Connacht-Ulster	*22,969*	*115,369*	*43.2*	*5,837*	*151,840*	*56.8*	*21,505*
Total	117,886	453,425	44.5	27,200	565,165	55.5	67,748

1959: ELECTORAL PARTICIPATION

Constituency	Electorate	Total votes no.	%	Invalid votes no.	%	Valid votes
Carlow-Kilkenny	56,117	35,078	62.5	534	1.5	34,544
Cavan	36,762	24,904	67.7	323	1.3	24,581
Clare	47,227	29,809	63.1	444	1.5	29,365
Cork City	62,647	35,454	56.6	724	2.0	34,730
Cork East	35,193	21,743	61.8	331	1.5	21,412
Cork North	33,805	23,869	70.6	322	1.3	23,547
Cork South	35,238	22,993	65.3	717	3.1	22,276
Cork West	32,290	21,368	66.2	272	1.3	21,096
Donegal East	40,863	22,789	55.8	334	1.5	22,455
Donegal West	30,850	15,501	50.2	185	1.2	15,316
Dublin North (Central)	24,940	13,093	52.5	278	2.1	12,815
Dublin North (East)	62,241	34,539	55.5	676	2.0	33,863
Dublin North (West)	31,441	17,012	54.1	364	2.1	16,648
Dublin South (Central)	50,045	24,335	48.6	506	2.1	23,829
Dublin South (East)	35,845	20,790	58.0	393	1.9	20,397
Dublin South (West)	61,631	32,372	52.5	626	1.9	31,746
Dublin County	74,084	37,713	50.9	972	2.6	36,741
Dun L.-Rathdown	61,716	32,631	52.9	738	2.3	31,893
Galway North	28,588	14,720	51.5	315	2.1	14,405
Galway South	28,318	17,798	62.9	220	1.2	17,578
Galway West	29,882	14,933	50.0	251	1.7	14,682
Kerry North	43,718	22,030	50.4	1,989	9.0	20,041
Kerry South	30,631	13,242	43.2	289	2.2	12,953
Kildare	36,552	22,543	61.7	1,958	8.7	20,585
Laoighis-Offaly	56,583	34,513	61.0	409	1.2	34,104
Limerick East	45,980	29,223	63.6	2,274	7.8	26,949
Limerick West	31,999	21,933	68.5	1,216	5.5	20,717
Longford-Westmeath	49,243	34,312	69.7	544	1.6	33,768
Louth	40,209	25,059	62.3	337	1.3	24,722
Mayo North	32,358	16,180	50.0	1,310	8.1	14,870
Mayo South	46,460	23,864	51.4	401	1.7	23,463
Meath	37,686	23,951	63.6	301	1.3	23,650
Monaghan	29,370	18,852	64.2	463	2.5	18,389
Roscommon	38,658	23,087	59.7	300	1.3	22,787
Sligo-Leitrim	57,271	31,289	54.6	759	2.4	30,530
Tipperary North	32,467	20,669	63.7	312	1.5	20,357
Tipperary South	41,196	29,042	70.5	574	2.0	28,468
Waterford	42,777	25,746	60.2	352	1.4	25,394
Wexford	50,150	31,493	62.8	536	1.7	30,957
Wicklow	35,419	19,156	54.1	240	1.3	18,916
Dublin	*401,943*	*212,485*	*52.9*	*4,553*	*2.1*	*207,932*
Rest of Leinster	*361,959*	*226,105*	*62.5*	*4,859*	*2.1*	*221,246*
Munster	*515,168*	*317,121*	*61.6*	*9,816*	*3.1*	*307,305*
Connacht–Ulster	*399,380*	*223,917*	*56.1*	*4,861*	*2.2*	*219,056*
Total	1,678,450	979,628	58.4	24,089	2.5	955,539

1959: FIRST PREFERENCE VOTES

Constituency	Number of votes		Percentage of votes	
	de Valera	MacEoin	de Valera	MacEoin
Carlow-Kilkenny	20,023	14,521	58.0	42.0
Cavan	13,912	10,669	56.6	43.4
Clare	19,095	10,270	65.0	35.0
Cork City	19,390	15,340	55.8	44.2
Cork East	12,117	9,295	56.6	43.4
Cork North	12,754	10,793	54.2	45.8
Cork South	11,909	10,367	53.5	46.5
Cork West	10,235	10,861	48.5	51.5
Donegal East	15,521	6,934	69.1	30.9
Donegal West	9,616	5,700	62.8	37.2
Dublin North (Central)	6,133	6,682	47.9	52.1
Dublin North (East)	16,417	17,446	48.5	51.5
Dublin North (West)	7,707	8,941	46.3	53.7
Dublin South (Central)	11,819	12,010	49.6	50.4
Dublin South (East)	10,363	10,034	50.8	49.2
Dublin South (West)	16,195	15,551	51.0	49.0
Dublin County	19,449	17,292	52.9	47.1
Dun Laoghaire-Rathdown	16,911	14,982	53.0	47.0
Galway North	9,037	5,368	62.7	37.3
Galway South	11,710	5,868	66.6	33.4
Galway West	10,134	4,548	69.0	31.0
Kerry North	12,361	7,680	61.7	38.3
Kerry South	7,472	5,481	57.7	42.3
Kildare	10,794	9,791	52.4	47.6
Laoighis-Offaly	20,059	14,045	58.8	41.2
Limerick East	15,942	11,007	59.2	40.8
Limerick West	12,918	7,799	62.4	37.6
Longford-Westmeath	16,234	17,534	48.1	51.9
Louth	13,646	11,076	55.2	44.8
Mayo North	9,219	5,651	62.0	38.0
Mayo South	12,925	10,538	55.1	44.9
Meath	13,940	9,710	58.9	41.1
Monaghan	11,028	7,361	60.0	40.0
Roscommon	12,188	10,599	53.5	46.5
Sligo-Leitrim	16,081	14,449	52.7	47.3
Tipperary North	12,253	8,104	60.2	39.8
Tipperary South	16,568	11,900	58.2	41.8
Waterford	15,679	9,715	61.7	38.3
Wexford	17,290	13,667	55.9	44.1
Wicklow	10,959	7,957	57.9	42.1
Dublin	*104,994*	*102,938*	*50.5*	*49.5*
Rest of Leinster	*122,945*	*98,301*	*55.6*	*44.4*
Munster	*178,693*	*128,612*	*58.1*	*41.9*
Connacht-Ulster	*131,371*	*87,685*	*60.0*	*40.0*
Total	538,003	417,536	56.3	43.7

1966: ELECTORAL PARTICIPATION

Constituency	Electorate	Total votes no.	%	Invalid votes no.	%	Valid votes
Carlow-Kilkenny	58,319	40,643	69.7	586	1.4	40,057
Cavan	34,360	25,126	73.1	153	0.6	24,973
Clare	48,138	31,272	65.0	148	0.5	31,124
Cork City	58,751	37,657	64.1	247	0.7	37,410
Cork Mid	51,337	36,844	71.8	297	0.8	36,547
Cork North-East	59,196	41,794	70.6	415	1.0	41,379
Cork South-West	34,929	24,841	71.1	120	0.5	24,721
Donegal North-East	34,813	22,849	65.6	342	1.5	22,507
Donegal South-West	36,035	23,886	66.3	301	1.3	23,585
Dublin North-Central	38,903	22,017	56.6	159	0.7	21,858
Dublin North-East	75,960	49,337	65.0	361	0.7	48,976
Dublin North-West	41,006	24,367	59.4	170	0.7	24,197
Dublin South-Central	54,328	31,354	57.7	251	0.8	31,103
Dublin South-East	40,981	26,529	64.7	134	0.5	26,395
Dublin South-West	57,612	34,782	60.4	326	0.9	34,456
Dublin County	71,601	44,429	62.1	219	0.5	44,210
Dun Laoghaire-Rathdown	60,009	37,190	62.0	376	1.0	36,814
Galway East	54,409	36,862	67.7	290	0.8	36,572
Galway West	33,787	19,648	58.2	181	0.9	19,467
Kerry North	35,318	20,501	58.0	151	0.7	20,350
Kerry South	35,832	20,038	55.9	196	1.0	19,842
Kildare	45,485	31,130	68.4	403	1.3	30,727
Laoighis-Offaly	56,074	39,581	70.6	460	1.2	39,121
Limerick East	46,501	32,262	69.4	438	1.4	31,824
Limerick West	33,121	24,195	73.1	214	0.9	23,981
Longford-Westmeath	44,337	30,051	67.8	360	1.2	29,691
Louth	37,126	25,205	67.9	163	0.6	25,042
Mayo North	31,634	18,081	57.2	107	0.6	17,974
Mayo South	42,535	26,082	61.3	323	1.2	25,759
Meath	35,615	23,410	65.7	151	0.6	23,259
Monaghan	32,813	23,311	71.0	203	0.9	23,108
Roscommon	44,287	30,575	69.0	274	0.9	30,301
Sligo-Leitrim	43,210	26,548	61.4	379	1.4	26,169
Tipperary North	34,287	23,094	67.4	296	1.3	22,798
Tipperary South	46,057	33,437	72.6	392	1.2	33,045
Waterford	36,986	24,343	65.8	96	0.4	24,247
Wexford	47,359	30,623	64.7	152	0.5	30,471
Wicklow	36,110	23,021	63.8	76	0.3	22,945
Dublin	*440,400*	*270,005*	*61.3*	*1,996*	*0.7*	*268,009*
Rest of Leinster	*360,425*	*243,664*	*67.6*	*2,351*	*1.0*	*241,313*
Munster	*520,453*	*350,278*	*67.3*	*3,010*	*0.9*	*347,268*
Connacht-Ulster	*387,883*	*252,968*	*65.2*	*2,553*	*1.0*	*250,415*
Total	1,709,161	1,116,915	65.3	9,910	0.9	1,107,005

1966: First preference votes

Constituency	Number of votes		Percentage of votes	
	de Valera	O'Higgins	de Valera	O'Higgins
Carlow-Kilkenny	21,332	18,725	53.3	46.7
Cavan	12,542	12,431	50.2	49.8
Clare	19,992	11,132	64.2	35.8
Cork City	18,129	19,281	48.5	51.5
Cork Mid	17,532	19,015	48.0	52.0
Cork North-East	21,204	20,175	51.2	48.8
Cork South-West	11,590	13,131	46.9	53.1
Donegal North-East	13,540	8,967	60.2	39.8
Donegal South-West	12,781	10,804	54.2	45.8
Dublin North-Central	9,842	12,016	45.0	55.0
Dublin North-East	20,300	28,676	41.4	58.6
Dublin North-West	10,202	13,995	42.2	57.8
Dublin South-Central	13,954	17,149	44.9	55.1
Dublin South-East	10,554	15,841	40.0	60.0
Dublin South-West	14,764	19,692	42.8	57.2
Dublin County	19,656	24,554	44.5	55.5
Dun Laoghaire-Rathdown	13,869	22,945	37.7	62.3
Galway East	20,621	15,951	56.4	43.6
Galway West	11,793	7,674	60.6	39.4
Kerry North	11,334	9,016	55.7	44.3
Kerry South	11,083	8,759	55.9	44.1
Kildare	16,022	14,705	52.1	47.9
Laoighis-Offaly	19,046	20,075	48.7	51.3
Limerick East	17,002	14,822	53.4	46.6
Limerick West	13,719	10,262	57.2	42.8
Longford-Westmeath	14,951	14,740	50.4	49.6
Louth	13,519	11,523	54.0	46.0
Mayo North	9,878	8,096	55.0	45.0
Mayo South	12,598	13,161	48.9	51.1
Meath	13,368	9,891	57.5	42.5
Monaghan	11,700	11,408	50.6	49.4
Roscommon	15,655	14,646	51.7	48.3
Sligo-Leitrim	13,251	12,918	50.6	49.4
Tipperary North	12,589	10,209	55.2	44.8
Tipperary South	19,300	13,745	58.4	41.6
Waterford	13,334	10,913	55.0	45.0
Wexford	15,268	15,203	50.1	49.9
Wicklow	11,047	11,898	48.1	51.9
Dublin	*113,141*	*154,868*	*42.2*	*57.8*
Rest of Leinster	*124,553*	*116,760*	*51.6*	*48.4*
Munster	*186,808*	*160,460*	*53.8*	*46.2*
Connacht-Ulster	*134,359*	*116,056*	*53.7*	*46.3*
Total	558,861	548,144	50.5	49.5

1973: ELECTORAL PARTICIPATION

Constituency	Electorate	Total votes		Invalid votes		Valid votes
		no.	%	no.	%	
Carlow-Kilkenny	64,997	45,005	69.2	316	0.7	44,689
Cavan	40,553	27,558	68.0	158	0.6	27,400
Clare	43,589	26,826	61.5	79	0.3	26,747
Clare-South Galway	37,961	25,490	67.1	74	0.3	25,416
Cork City North-West	40,146	24,938	62.1	153	0.6	24,785
Cork City South-East	40,404	26,744	66.2	201	0.8	26,543
Cork Mid	54,713	40,812	74.6	198	0.5	40,614
Cork North-East	54,674	38,370	70.2	230	0.6	38,140
Cork South-West	40,985	29,016	70.8	169	0.6	28,847
Donegal North-East	41,518	21,759	52.4	177	0.8	21,582
Donegal-Leitrim	41,760	26,156	62.6	141	0.5	26,015
Dublin City Central	50,263	25,653	51.0	187	0.7	25,466
Dublin City North-Central	52,450	29,413	56.1	239	0.8	29,174
Dublin City North-East	63,809	34,988	54.8	294	0.8	34,694
Dublin City North-West	50,396	25,341	50.3	258	1.0	25,083
Dublin City South-Central	56,307	30,760	54.6	244	0.8	30,516
Dublin City South-East	41,759	23,438	56.1	200	0.9	23,238
Dublin City South-West	46,764	23,734	50.8	169	0.7	23,565
Dublin County North	68,947	37,855	54.9	237	0.6	37,618
Dublin County South	53,102	32,374	61.0	227	0.7	32,147
Dun Laoghaire-Rathdown	62,302	37,859	60.8	167	0.4	37,692
Galway North-East	36,886	23,864	64.7	103	0.4	23,761
Galway West	42,115	23,499	55.8	121	0.5	23,378
Kerry North	40,534	23,372	57.7	128	0.5	23,244
Kerry South	39,517	23,494	59.5	143	0.6	23,351
Kildare	46,626	28,980	62.2	0	0.0	28,980
Laoighis-Offaly	61,339	41,994	68.5	176	0.4	41,818
Limerick East	53,307	35,009	65.7	160	0.5	34,849
Limerick West	40,579	28,901	71.2	116	0.4	28,785
Longford-Westmeath	51,677	33,524	64.9	150	0.4	33,374
Louth	44,210	26,358	59.6	227	0.9	26,131
Mayo East	37,970	23,501	61.9	70	0.3	23,431
Mayo West	37,530	22,641	60.3	100	0.4	22,541
Meath	44,150	27,253	61.7	177	0.6	27,076
Monaghan	39,647	26,119	65.9	152	0.6	25,967
Roscommon-Leitrim	40,632	27,124	66.8	113	0.4	27,011
Sligo-Leitrim	41,171	25,799	62.7	138	0.5	25,661
Tipperary North	38,494	27,595	71.7	124	0.4	27,471
Tipperary South	50,694	36,544	72.1	203	0.6	36,341
Waterford	43,876	29,034	66.2	133	0.5	28,901
Wexford	55,078	35,289	64.1	132	0.4	35,157
Wicklow	44,386	26,601	59.9	162	0.6	26,439
Dublin	*546,099*	*301,415*	*55.2*	*2,222*	*0.7*	*299,193*
Rest of Leinster	*412,463*	*265,004*	*64.2*	*1,340*	*0.5*	*263,664*
Munster	*581,512*	*390,655*	*67.2*	*2,037*	*0.5*	*388,618*
Connacht-Ulster	*437,743*	*273,510*	*62.5*	*1,347*	*0.5*	*272,163*
Total	1,977,817	1,230,584	62.2	6,946	0.6	1,223,638

1973: FIRST PREFERENCE VOTES

Constituency	Number of votes		Percentage of votes	
	Childers	**O'Higgins**	**Childers**	**O'Higgins**
Carlow-Kilkenny	23,231	21,458	52.0	48.0
Cavan	14,001	13,399	51.1	48.9
Clare	16,412	10,335	61.4	38.6
Clare-South Galway	14,470	10,946	56.9	43.1
Cork City North-West	15,589	9,196	62.9	37.1
Cork City South-East	15,918	10,625	60.0	40.0
Cork Mid	21,603	19,011	53.2	46.8
Cork North-East	20,887	17,253	54.8	45.2
Cork South-West	13,745	15,102	47.6	52.4
Donegal North-East	12,253	9,329	56.8	43.2
Donegal-Leitrim	14,326	11,689	55.1	44.9
Dublin City Central	12,081	13,385	47.4	52.6
Dublin City North-Central	14,012	15,162	48.0	52.0
Dublin City North-East	16,613	18,081	47.9	52.1
Dublin City North-West	12,102	12,981	48.2	51.8
Dublin City South-Central	15,117	15,399	49.5	50.5
Dublin City South-East	11,540	11,698	49.7	50.3
Dublin City South-West	10,924	12,641	46.4	53.6
Dublin County North	18,625	18,993	49.5	50.5
Dublin County South	15,561	16,586	48.4	51.6
Dun Laoghaire-Rathdown	18,037	19,655	47.9	52.1
Galway North-East	12,005	11,756	50.5	49.5
Galway West	12,920	10,458	55.3	44.7
Kerry North	12,206	11,038	52.5	47.5
Kerry South	12,280	11,071	52.6	47.4
Kildare	15,689	13,291	54.1	45.9
Laoighis-Offaly	21,078	20,740	50.4	49.6
Limerick East	17,897	16,952	51.4	48.6
Limerick West	16,013	12,772	55.6	44.4
Longford-Westmeath	17,324	16,050	51.9	48.1
Louth	14,556	11,575	55.7	44.3
Mayo East	11,290	12,141	48.2	51.8
Mayo West	10,983	11,558	48.7	51.3
Meath	14,542	12,534	53.7	46.3
Monaghan	13,706	12,261	52.8	47.2
Roscommon-Leitrim	12,884	14,127	47.7	52.3
Sligo-Leitrim	12,832	12,829	50.0	50.0
Tipperary North	14,723	12,748	53.6	46.4
Tipperary South	20,002	16,339	55.0	45.0
Waterford	15,785	13,116	54.6	45.4
Wexford	16,279	18,878	46.3	53.7
Wicklow	13,826	12,613	52.3	47.7
Dublin	*144,612*	*154,581*	*48.3*	*51.7*
Rest of Leinster	*136,525*	*127,139*	*51.8*	*48.2*
Munster	*213,060*	*175,558*	*54.8*	*45.2*
Connacht-Ulster	*141,670*	*130,493*	*52.1*	*47.9*
Total	635,867	587,771	52.0	48.0

1990: ELECTORAL PARTICIPATION

Constituency	Electorate	Total votes		Invalid votes		Valid votes
		no.	%	no.	%	
Carlow-Kilkenny	79,921	53,138	66.5	335	0.6	52,803
Cavan-Monaghan	76,800	47,670	62.1	333	0.7	47,337
Clare	64,802	43,603	67.3	233	0.5	43,370
Cork East	56,601	38,260	67.6	160	0.4	38,100
Cork North-Central	63,121	39,155	62.0	265	0.7	38,890
Cork North-West	41,146	30,569	74.3	150	0.5	30,419
Cork South-Central	79,302	53,926	68.0	270	0.5	53,656
Cork South-West	42,917	29,750	69.3	136	0.5	29,614
Donegal North-East	45,583	23,348	51.2	159	0.7	23,189
Donegal South-West	47,579	25,363	53.3	167	0.7	25,196
Dublin Central	64,765	38,614	59.6	365	0.9	38,249
Dublin North	52,372	34,586	66.0	206	0.6	34,380
Dublin North-Central	55,566	37,763	68.0	289	0.8	37,474
Dublin North-East	53,598	33,941	63.3	230	0.7	33,711
Dublin North-West	48,008	27,973	58.3	327	1.2	27,646
Dublin South	84,423	56,979	67.5	282	0.5	56,697
Dublin South-Central	71,725	43,152	60.2	333	0.8	42,819
Dublin South-East	56,869	33,579	59.0	216	0.6	33,363
Dublin South-West	66,618	37,115	55.7	288	0.8	36,827
Dublin West	79,041	48,482	61.3	284	0.6	48,198
Dun Laoghaire	81,410	52,944	65.0	198	0.4	52,746
Galway East	42,435	27,644	65.1	89	0.3	27,555
Galway West	77,999	46,217	59.3	260	0.6	45,957
Kerry North	47,585	30,461	64.0	218	0.7	30,243
Kerry South	42,943	28,608	66.6	151	0.5	28,457
Kildare	80,619	50,889	63.1	162	0.3	50,727
Laois-Offaly	75,270	51,153	68.0	257	0.5	50,896
Limerick East	67,546	42,818	63.4	210	0.5	42,608
Limerick West	43,829	30,958	70.6	182	0.6	30,776
Longford-Westmeath	62,413	41,551	66.6	234	0.6	41,317
Louth	63,585	39,975	62.9	359	0.9	39,616
Mayo East	39,828	26,985	67.8	177	0.7	26,808
Mayo West	39,712	25,823	65.0	98	0.4	25,725
Meath	77,946	49,265	63.2	313	0.6	48,952
Roscommon	40,575	28,297	69.7	138	0.5	28,159
Sligo-Leitrim	58,899	38,608	65.5	237	0.6	38,371
Tipperary North	41,731	29,309	70.2	188	0.6	29,121
Tipperary South	55,262	37,528	67.9	233	0.6	37,295
Waterford	61,142	38,918	63.7	163	0.4	38,755
Wexford	72,314	47,192	65.3	295	0.6	46,897
Wicklow	67,508	41,986	62.2	254	0.6	41,732
Dublin	*714,395*	*445,128*	*62.3*	*3,018*	*0.7*	*442,110*
Rest of Leinster	*579,576*	*375,149*	*64.7*	*2,209*	*0.6*	*372,940*
Munster	*707,927*	*473,863*	*66.9*	*2,559*	*0.5*	*471,304*
Connacht-Ulster	*469,410*	*289,955*	*61.8*	*1,658*	*0.6*	*288,297*
Total	2,471,308	1,584,095	64.1	9,444	0.6	1,574,651

1990: FIRST PREFERENCE VOTES

Constituency	Number of votes			Percentage of votes		
	Currie	Lenihan	Robinson	Currie	Lenihan	Robinson
Carlow-Kilkenny	9,941	23,808	19,054	18.8	45.1	36.1
Cavan-Monaghan	10,049	25,365	11,923	21.2	53.6	25.2
Clare	7,956	21,669	13,745	18.3	50.0	31.7
Cork East	7,048	16,928	14,124	18.5	44.4	37.1
Cork North-Central	6,038	15,020	17,832	15.5	38.6	45.9
Cork North-West	8,414	13,843	8,162	27.7	45.5	26.8
Cork South-Central	9,254	18,176	26,226	17.2	33.9	48.9
Cork South-West	8,623	11,957	9,034	29.1	40.4	30.5
Donegal North-East	3,958	12,834	6,397	17.1	55.3	27.6
Donegal South-West	4,794	13,344	7,058	19.0	53.0	28.0
Dublin Central	4,711	17,855	15,683	12.3	46.7	41.0
Dublin North	3,931	14,812	15,637	11.4	43.1	45.5
Dublin North-Central	4,752	16,658	16,064	12.7	44.5	42.9
Dublin North-East	3,690	13,939	16,082	10.9	41.3	47.7
Dublin North-West	2,795	11,611	13,240	10.1	42.0	47.9
Dublin South	9,646	17,948	29,103	17.0	31.7	51.3
Dublin South-Central	5,578	16,847	20,394	13.0	39.3	47.6
Dublin South-East	5,528	10,573	17,262	16.6	31.7	51.7
Dublin South-West	3,661	15,340	17,826	9.9	41.7	48.4
Dublin West	6,439	21,987	19,772	13.4	45.6	41.0
Dun Laoghaire	8,957	14,974	28,815	17.0	28.4	54.6
Galway East	5,629	13,883	8,043	20.4	50.4	29.2
Galway West	8,094	18,885	18,978	17.6	41.1	41.3
Kerry North	5,192	13,896	11,155	17.2	45.9	36.9
Kerry South	4,891	14,230	9,336	17.2	50.0	32.8
Kildare	7,701	21,388	21,638	15.2	42.2	42.7
Laois-Offaly	8,690	25,635	16,571	17.1	50.4	32.6
Limerick East	7,498	14,583	20,527	17.6	34.2	48.2
Limerick West	5,955	16,055	8,766	19.3	52.2	28.5
Longford-Westmeath	7,716	21,860	11,741	18.7	52.9	28.4
Louth	5,588	20,134	13,894	14.1	50.8	35.1
Mayo East	5,023	11,838	9,947	18.7	44.2	37.1
Mayo West	4,706	12,114	8,905	18.3	47.1	34.6
Meath	8,174	23,960	16,818	16.7	48.9	34.4
Roscommon	6,482	14,454	7,223	23.0	51.3	25.7
Sligo-Leitrim	7,794	18,917	11,660	20.3	49.3	30.4
Tipperary North	5,822	14,373	8,926	20.0	49.4	30.7
Tipperary South	7,227	17,317	12,751	19.4	46.4	34.2
Waterford	6,160	17,236	15,359	15.9	44.5	39.6
Wexford	7,906	21,790	17,201	16.9	46.5	36.7
Wicklow	5,891	16,448	19,393	14.1	39.4	46.5
Dublin	*59,688*	*172,544*	*209,878*	*13.5*	*39.0*	*47.5*
Rest of Leinster	*61,607*	*175,023*	*136,310*	*16.5*	*46.9*	*36.6*
Munster	*90,078*	*205,283*	*175,943*	*19.1*	*43.6*	*37.3*
Connacht-Ulster	*56,529*	*141,634*	*90,134*	*19.6*	*49.1*	*31.3*
Total	267,902	694,484	612,265	17.0	44.1	38.9

1990: SECOND COUNT (DISTRIBUTION OF CURRIE'S VOTES)

Constituency	Lenihan			Robinson			NT
	tr.	total	%	tr.	total	%	
Carlow-Kilkenny	1,295	25,103	48.4	7,679	26,733	51.6	967
Cavan-Monaghan	1,431	26,796	57.7	7,741	19,664	42.3	877
Clare	1,046	22,715	53.2	6,259	20,004	46.8	651
Cork East	908	17,836	47.9	5,314	19,438	52.1	826
Cork North-Central	914	15,934	41.6	4,514	22,346	58.4	610
Cork North-West	1,053	14,896	50.3	6,549	14,711	49.7	812
Cork South-Central	1,240	19,416	36.8	7,075	33,301	63.2	939
Cork South-West	1,127	13,084	45.6	6,606	15,640	54.4	890
Donegal North-East	550	13,384	59.4	2,765	9,162	40.6	643
Donegal South-West	571	13,915	56.5	3,672	10,730	43.5	551
Dublin Central	793	18,648	49.5	3,359	19,042	50.5	559
Dublin North	646	15,458	45.4	2,926	18,563	54.6	359
Dublin North-Central	736	17,394	47.0	3,521	19,585	53.0	495
Dublin North-East	598	14,537	43.6	2,690	18,772	56.4	402
Dublin North-West	448	12,059	44.1	2,041	15,281	55.9	306
Dublin South	1,382	19,330	34.6	7,370	36,473	65.4	894
Dublin South-Central	896	17,743	42.0	4,123	24,517	58.0	559
Dublin South-East	785	11,358	34.7	4,156	21,418	65.3	587
Dublin South-West	554	15,894	43.6	2,747	20,573	56.4	360
Dublin West	972	22,959	48.2	4,896	24,668	51.8	571
Dun Laoghaire	1,319	16,293	31.4	6,712	35,527	68.6	926
Galway East	603	14,486	53.4	4,608	12,651	46.6	418
Galway West	990	19,875	43.8	6,494	25,472	56.2	610
Kerry North	773	14,669	49.3	3,941	15,096	50.7	478
Kerry South	582	14,812	52.8	3,902	13,238	47.2	407
Kildare	1,105	22,493	45.0	5,829	27,467	55.0	767
Laois-Offaly	1,105	26,740	53.3	6,826	23,397	46.7	759
Limerick East	1,006	15,589	37.3	5,708	26,235	62.7	784
Limerick West	779	16,834	55.7	4,614	13,380	44.3	562
Longford-Westmeath	1,021	22,881	56.3	6,054	17,795	43.7	641
Louth	936	21,070	53.9	4,159	18,053	46.1	493
Mayo East	524	12,362	46.6	4,215	14,162	53.4	284
Mayo West	452	12,566	49.5	3,940	12,845	50.5	314
Meath	1,162	25,122	52.2	6,219	23,037	47.8	793
Roscommon	731	15,185	54.9	5,272	12,495	45.1	479
Sligo-Leitrim	989	19,906	52.7	6,222	17,882	47.3	583
Tipperary North	746	15,119	52.9	4,557	13,483	47.1	519
Tipperary South	982	18,299	50.1	5,463	18,214	49.9	782
Waterford	934	18,170	47.8	4,521	19,880	52.2	705
Wexford	1,200	22,990	49.9	5,857	23,058	50.1	849
Wicklow	905	17,353	42.1	4,449	23,842	57.9	537
Dublin	*9,129*	*181,673*	*41.7*	*44,541*	*254,419*	*58.3*	*6,018*
Rest of Leinster	*8,729*	*183,752*	*50.1*	*47,072*	*183,382*	*49.9*	*5,806*
Munster	*12,090*	*217,373*	*47.0*	*69,023*	*244,966*	*53.0*	*8,965*
Connacht-Ulster	*6,841*	*148,475*	*52.4*	*44,929*	*135,063*	*47.6*	*4,759*
Total	36,789	731,273	47.2	205,565	817,830	52.8	25,548

1997: Electoral participation

Constituency	Electorate	Total votes		Invalid votes		Valid votes
		no.	%	no.	%	
Carlow-Kilkenny	85,696	43,422	50.7	358	0.8	43,064
Cavan-Monaghan	83,185	40,198	48.3	309	0.8	39,889
Clare	71,113	35,184	49.5	240	0.7	34,944
Cork East	63,489	33,622	53.0	208	0.6	33,414
Cork North-Central	71,865	32,674	45.5	260	0.8	32,414
Cork North-West	46,884	28,136	60.0	202	0.7	27,934
Cork South-Central	84,458	44,126	52.2	318	0.7	43,808
Cork South-West	47,966	27,710	57.8	237	0.9	27,473
Donegal North-East	52,723	20,970	39.8	190	0.9	20,780
Donegal South-West	51,661	21,599	41.8	185	0.9	21,414
Dublin Central	63,899	22,024	34.5	234	1.1	21,790
Dublin North	63,916	29,541	46.2	208	0.7	29,333
Dublin North-Central	66,431	31,348	47.2	278	0.9	31,070
Dublin North-East	59,258	24,817	41.9	183	0.7	24,634
Dublin North-West	60,172	23,910	39.7	208	0.9	23,702
Dublin South	89,955	45,021	50.0	263	0.6	44,758
Dublin South-Central	67,985	28,737	42.3	281	1.0	28,456
Dublin South-East	63,476	28,632	45.1	258	0.9	28,374
Dublin South-West	75,760	26,198	34.6	197	0.8	26,001
Dublin West	66,462	26,351	39.6	166	0.6	26,185
Dun Laoghaire	87,091	42,217	48.5	282	0.7	41,935
Galway East	61,331	30,984	50.5	248	0.8	30,736
Galway West	78,266	35,238	45.0	267	0.8	34,971
Kerry North	51,190	23,295	45.5	181	0.8	23,114
Kerry South	47,420	23,180	48.9	195	0.8	22,985
Kildare North	52,290	23,124	44.2	145	0.6	22,979
Kildare South	47,880	20,205	42.2	112	0.6	20,093
Laois-Offaly	84,815	41,588	49.0	295	0.7	41,293
Limerick East	77,122	35,779	46.4	223	0.6	35,556
Limerick West	47,974	24,849	51.8	218	0.9	24,631
Longford-Roscommon	64,002	32,922	51.4	266	0.8	32,656
Louth	71,215	31,477	44.2	251	0.8	31,226
Mayo	88,031	42,106	47.8	394	0.9	41,712
Meath	90,336	39,709	44.0	279	0.7	39,430
Sligo-Leitrim	64,738	32,349	50.0	274	0.8	32,075
Tipperary North	54,135	28,583	52.8	210	0.7	28,373
Tipperary South	51,618	27,081	52.5	177	0.7	26,904
Waterford	70,571	31,789	45.0	255	0.8	31,534
Westmeath	49,104	23,256	47.4	143	0.6	23,113
Wexford	83,900	39,760	47.4	387	1.0	39,373
Wicklow	80,146	35,977	44.9	267	0.7	35,710
Dublin	*764,405*	*328,796*	*43.0*	*2,558*	*0.8*	*326,238*
Rest of Leinster	*709,384*	*331,440*	*46.7*	*2,503*	*0.8*	*328,937*
Munster	*785,805*	*396,008*	*50.4*	*2,924*	*0.7*	*393,084*
Connacht-Ulster	*479,935*	*223,444*	*46.6*	*1,867*	*0.8*	*221,577*
Total	2,739,529	1,279,688	46.7	9,852	0.8	1,269,836

1997: FIRST PREFERENCE VOTES

Constituency	Number of votes					Percentage of votes				
	Banotti	McAleese	Nally	Roche	Scallon	Ban.	McA.	Nal.	Ro.	Sc.
Carlow-Kilkenny	11,962	19,949	3,040	2,936	5,177	27.8	46.3	7.1	6.8	12.0
Cavan-Monaghan	9,299	21,749	1,122	1,373	6,346	23.3	54.5	2.8	3.4	15.9
Clare	8,353	17,970	1,637	1,889	5,095	23.9	51.4	4.7	5.4	14.6
Cork East	8,859	15,598	1,063	3,444	4,450	26.5	46.7	3.2	10.3	13.3
Cork North-Central	8,348	14,322	1,194	4,808	3,742	25.8	44.2	3.7	14.8	11.5
Cork North-West	8,214	13,086	776	2,291	3,567	29.4	46.8	2.8	8.2	12.8
Cork South-Central	12,609	19,410	1,894	5,434	4,461	28.8	44.3	4.3	12.4	10.2
Cork South-West	8,808	12,616	825	2,208	3,016	32.1	45.9	3.0	8.0	11.0
Donegal North-East	3,313	11,008	575	748	5,136	15.9	53.0	2.8	3.6	24.7
Donegal South-West	3,958	11,060	545	826	5,025	18.5	51.6	2.5	3.9	23.5
Dublin Central	6,864	9,226	1,175	1,605	2,920	31.5	42.3	5.4	7.4	13.4
Dublin North	10,161	12,599	1,291	1,918	3,364	34.6	43.0	4.4	6.5	11.5
Dublin North-Central	10,789	12,949	1,342	1,946	4,044	34.7	41.7	4.3	6.3	13.0
Dublin North-East	8,728	10,132	1,114	1,770	2,890	35.4	41.1	4.5	7.2	11.7
Dublin North-West	7,806	9,910	1,180	1,769	3,037	32.9	41.8	5.0	7.5	12.8
Dublin South	18,766	16,053	1,990	2,589	5,360	41.9	35.9	4.4	5.8	12.0
Dublin South-Central	10,900	10,636	1,375	1,909	3,636	38.3	37.4	4.8	6.7	12.8
Dublin South-East	12,692	9,338	1,056	1,885	3,403	44.7	32.9	3.7	6.6	12.0
Dublin South-West	8,879	10,366	1,539	1,833	3,384	34.1	39.9	5.9	7.0	13.0
Dublin West	8,965	10,678	1,504	1,675	3,363	34.2	40.8	5.7	6.4	12.8
Dun Laoghaire	18,415	14,310	1,632	2,696	4,882	43.9	34.1	3.9	6.4	11.6
Galway East	7,352	15,979	1,076	1,285	5,044	23.9	52.0	3.5	4.2	16.4
Galway West	9,495	16,707	1,437	2,012	5,320	27.2	47.8	4.1	5.8	15.2
Kerry North	5,266	10,753	689	3,039	3,367	22.8	46.5	3.0	13.1	14.6
Kerry South	5,384	11,586	778	2,075	3,162	23.4	50.4	3.4	9.0	13.8
Kildare North	7,657	9,496	1,242	1,483	3,101	33.3	41.3	5.4	6.5	13.5
Kildare South	6,052	9,204	1,039	1,426	2,372	30.1	45.8	5.2	7.1	11.8
Laois-Offaly	10,878	20,398	1,739	2,090	6,188	26.3	49.4	4.2	5.1	15.0
Limerick East	11,529	15,080	1,714	2,235	4,998	32.4	42.4	4.8	6.3	14.1
Limerick West	6,999	11,823	886	1,201	3,722	28.4	48.0	3.6	4.9	15.1
Longford-Roscommon	8,212	15,654	1,456	1,159	6,175	25.1	47.9	4.5	3.5	18.9
Louth	7,322	16,356	1,228	1,983	4,337	23.4	52.4	3.9	6.4	13.9
Mayo	10,923	21,174	1,348	1,666	6,601	26.2	50.8	3.2	4.0	15.8
Meath	11,338	18,584	1,487	2,123	5,898	28.8	47.1	3.8	5.4	15.0
Sligo-Leitrim	7,909	16,162	1,044	1,670	5,290	24.7	50.4	3.3	5.2	16.5
Tipperary North	7,547	13,316	1,550	2,158	3,802	26.6	46.9	5.5	7.6	13.4
Tipperary South	6,928	11,865	832	4,187	3,092	25.8	44.1	3.1	15.6	11.5
Waterford	8,243	15,769	1,406	2,229	3,887	26.1	50.0	4.5	7.1	12.3
Westmeath	5,969	10,653	1,160	1,561	3,770	25.8	46.1	5.0	6.8	16.3
Wexford	8,779	16,713	7,405	2,415	4,061	22.3	42.4	18.8	6.1	10.3
Wicklow	11,532	14,187	2,144	2,874	4,973	32.3	39.7	6.0	8.0	13.9
Dublin	*122,965*	*126,197*	*15,198*	*21,595*	*40,283*	*37.7*	*38.7*	*4.7*	*6.6*	*12.3*
Rest of Leinster	*89,701*	*151,194*	*21,940*	*20,050*	*46,052*	*27.3*	*46.0*	*6.7*	*6.1*	*14.0*
Munster	*107,087*	*183,194*	*15,244*	*37,198*	*50,361*	*27.2*	*46.6*	*3.9*	*9.5*	*12.8*
Connacht-Ulster	*52,249*	*113,839*	*7,147*	*9,580*	*38,762*	*23.6*	*51.4*	*3.2*	*4.3*	*17.5*
Total	372,002	574,424	59,529	88,423	175,458	29.3	45.2	4.7	7.0	13.8

1997: SECOND COUNT (DISTRIBUTION OF NALLY'S, ROCHE'S AND SCALLON'S VOTES)

Constituency	Banotti			McAleese			NT
	tr.	total	%	tr.	total	%	
Carlow-Kilkenny	4,512	16,474	40.4	4,346	24,295	59.6	2,295
Cavan-Monaghan	2,860	12,159	31.9	4,266	26,015	68.1	1,715
Clare	3,189	11,542	34.7	3,796	21,766	65.3	1,636
Cork East	3,346	12,205	38.8	3,620	19,218	61.2	1,991
Cork North-Central	3,853	12,201	40.2	3,817	18,139	59.8	2,074
Cork North-West	2,473	10,687	40.3	2,739	15,825	59.7	1,422
Cork South-Central	4,412	17,021	41.1	5,027	24,437	58.9	2,350
Cork South-West	2,518	11,326	42.9	2,440	15,056	57.1	1,091
Donegal North-East	1,531	4,844	25.6	3,105	14,113	74.4	1,823
Donegal South-West	1,615	5,573	28.4	3,000	14,060	71.6	1,781
Dublin Central	2,276	9,140	44.6	2,123	11,349	55.4	1,301
Dublin North	2,852	13,013	46.2	2,550	15,149	53.8	1,171
Dublin North-Central	3,114	13,903	46.7	2,894	15,843	53.3	1,324
Dublin North-East	2,386	11,114	47.3	2,242	12,374	52.7	1,146
Dublin North-West	2,531	10,337	45.9	2,270	12,180	54.1	1,185
Dublin South	4,670	23,436	54.2	3,726	19,779	45.8	1,543
Dublin South-Central	2,987	13,887	51.3	2,546	13,182	48.7	1,387
Dublin South-East	3,011	15,703	57.6	2,230	11,568	42.4	1,103
Dublin South-West	2,855	11,734	47.6	2,554	12,920	52.4	1,347
Dublin West	2,883	11,848	47.3	2,521	13,199	52.7	1,138
Dun Laoghaire	4,330	22,745	56.3	3,368	17,678	43.7	1,512
Galway East	2,651	10,003	34.1	3,339	19,318	65.9	1,415
Galway West	3,479	12,974	38.9	3,711	20,418	61.1	1,579
Kerry North	2,676	7,942	37.0	2,793	13,546	63.0	1,626
Kerry South	2,247	7,631	35.1	2,523	14,109	64.9	1,245
Kildare North	2,552	10,209	46.5	2,245	11,741	53.5	1,029
Kildare South	1,924	7,976	41.9	1,835	11,039	58.1	1,078
Laois-Offaly	3,607	14,485	36.9	4,363	24,761	63.1	2,047
Limerick East	3,679	15,208	45.1	3,413	18,493	54.9	1,855
Limerick West	2,083	9,082	38.9	2,454	14,277	61.1	1,272
Longford-Roscommon	3,004	11,216	36.4	3,901	19,555	63.6	1,885
Louth	2,693	10,015	33.9	3,171	19,527	66.1	1,684
Mayo	3,420	14,343	36.0	4,377	25,551	64.0	1,818
Meath	3,688	15,026	40.1	3,846	22,430	59.9	1,974
Sligo-Leitrim	2,820	10,729	35.0	3,750	19,912	65.0	1,434
Tipperary North	2,828	10,375	38.8	3,057	16,373	61.2	1,625
Tipperary South	3,201	10,129	40.2	3,200	15,065	59.8	1,710
Waterford	2,827	11,070	37.1	2,991	18,760	62.9	1,704
Westmeath	2,393	8,362	38.5	2,694	13,347	61.5	1,404
Wexford	5,364	14,143	39.1	5,351	22,064	60.9	3,166
Wicklow	4,174	15,706	46.8	3,641	17,828	53.2	2,176
Dublin	*33,895*	*156,860*	*50.3*	*29,024*	*155,221*	*49.7*	*14,157*
Rest of Leinster	*33,911*	*123,612*	*39.8*	*35,393*	*186,587*	*60.2*	*18,738*
Munster	*39,332*	*146,419*	*39.4*	*41,870*	*225,064*	*60.6*	*21,601*
Connacht-Ulster	*18,376*	*70,625*	*33.6*	*25,548*	*139,387*	*66.4*	*11,565*
Total	125,514	497,516	41.3	131,835	706,259	58.7	66,061

2011: ELECTORAL PARTICIPATION

Constituency	Electorate	Total votes no.	%	Invalid votes no.	%	Valid votes
Carlow-Kilkenny	106,810	59,328	55.6	591	1.0	58,737
Cavan-Monaghan	98,952	58,518	59.1	554	0.9	57,964
Clare	81,419	47,417	58.2	405	0.9	47,012
Cork East	82,731	45,462	55.0	509	1.1	44,953
Cork North-Central	75,622	41,602	55.0	576	1.4	41,026
Cork North-West	62,113	37,784	60.8	371	1.0	37,413
Cork South-Central	91,716	53,710	58.6	662	1.2	53,048
Cork South-West	60,248	35,941	59.7	370	1.0	35,571
Donegal North-East	58,579	28,582	48.8	328	1.1	28,254
Donegal South-West	64,158	31,068	48.4	352	1.1	30,716
Dublin Central	54,500	28,236	51.8	351	1.2	27,885
Dublin Mid-West	64,370	34,113	53.0	396	1.2	33,717
Dublin North	69,347	39,731	57.3	401	1.0	39,330
Dublin North-Central	51,929	33,239	64.0	381	1.1	32,858
Dublin North-East	57,627	34,462	59.8	400	1.2	34,062
Dublin North-West	50,410	25,361	50.3	358	1.4	25,003
Dublin South	104,145	64,492	61.9	514	0.8	63,978
Dublin South-Central	77,688	41,604	53.6	529	1.3	41,075
Dublin South-East	55,533	30,780	55.4	295	1.0	30,485
Dublin South-West	69,977	36,669	52.4	474	1.3	36,195
Dublin West	61,583	36,319	59.0	370	1.0	35,949
Dun Laoghaire	82,033	49,191	60.0	428	0.9	48,763
Galway East	81,896	47,092	57.5	411	0.9	46,681
Galway West	94,700	50,688	53.5	414	0.8	50,274
Kerry N.-W. Limerick	63,068	34,525	54.7	391	1.1	34,134
Kerry South	57,776	31,969	55.3	356	1.1	31,613
Kildare North	76,623	43,463	56.7	329	0.8	43,134
Kildare South	57,933	31,295	54.0	333	1.1	30,962
Laoighis-Offaly	107,023	59,365	55.5	517	0.9	58,848
Limerick	66,345	36,876	55.6	359	1.0	36,517
Limerick City	66,421	34,725	52.3	363	1.0	34,362
Longford-Westmeath	85,911	45,543	53.0	484	1.1	45,059
Louth	102,941	58,126	56.5	673	1.2	57,453
Mayo	97,714	53,627	54.9	567	1.1	53,060
Meath East	65,477	35,453	54.2	309	0.9	35,144
Meath West	63,111	33,071	52.4	324	1.0	32,747
Roscommon-S.Leitrim	60,416	36,486	60.4	394	1.1	36,092
Sligo-North Leitrim	62,152	34,251	55.1	361	1.1	33,890
Tipperary North	62,603	38,381	61.3	439	1.1	37,942
Tipperary South	56,295	32,618	57.9	348	1.1	32,270
Waterford	78,960	42,731	54.1	471	1.1	42,260
Wexford	108,490	58,629	54.0	627	1.1	58,002
Wicklow	93,812	57,915	61.7	591	1.0	57,324
Dublin	*799,142*	*454,197*	*57.9*	*4,897*	*1.1*	*449,300*
Rest of Leinster	*868,131*	*482,188*	*54.1*	*4,778*	*1.0*	*477,410*
Munster	*905,317*	*513,741*	*54.0*	*5,620*	*1.1*	*508,121*
Connacht-Ulster	*618,567*	*340,312*	*61.7*	*3,381*	*1.0*	*336,931*
Total	3,191,157	1,790,438	56.1	18,676	1.0	1,771,762

2011: FIRST PREFERENCE VOTES: NUMBERS

Constituency	Davis	Gallagher	Higgins	McGuin.	Mitchell	Norris	Scallon
Carlow-Kilkenny	1,143	19,846	21,574	7,257	4,511	2,792	1,614
Cavan-Monaghan	1,071	26,150	11,471	11,940	4,109	1,636	1,587
Clare	890	14,779	20,828	4,950	2,545	1,707	1,313
Cork East	923	15,455	16,435	6,193	2,678	1,921	1,348
Cork North-Central	693	11,526	15,427	8,201	1,911	2,090	1,178
Cork North-West	561	14,362	12,836	4,329	2,836	1,380	1,109
Cork South-Central	1,080	13,224	23,861	7,496	2,488	3,423	1,476
Cork South-West	770	12,449	12,047	4,608	3,035	1,534	1,128
Donegal North-East	598	7,978	6,516	9,085	1,384	788	1,905
Donegal South-West	660	9,912	7,093	8,738	1,620	916	1,777
Dublin Central	820	4,577	12,267	4,485	1,392	3,588	756
Dublin Mid-West	1,039	7,436	13,594	5,374	2,176	3,428	670
Dublin North	1,253	10,014	17,630	4,097	1,742	3,868	726
Dublin North-Central	1,148	6,603	15,230	3,678	1,953	3,434	812
Dublin North-East	1,491	7,138	14,956	4,484	1,727	3,512	754
Dublin North-West	915	5,069	9,709	4,985	1,111	2,638	576
Dublin South	2,100	12,814	32,673	4,146	4,684	6,265	1,296
Dublin South-Central	1,116	6,154	16,391	6,803	4,971	4,703	937
Dublin South-East	975	4,179	16,315	2,289	2,486	3,574	667
Dublin South-West	1,127	7,947	14,530	6,006	2,345	3,482	758
Dublin West	1,174	8,677	15,539	4,278	1,916	3,632	733
Dun Laoghaire	1,711	8,626	25,616	3,355	3,424	4,973	1,058
Galway East	1,053	13,473	21,554	4,849	2,905	1,177	1,670
Galway West	900	9,281	28,970	5,392	2,326	1,660	1,745
Kerry N.-W. Limerick	757	9,909	12,947	5,739	2,221	1,301	1,260
Kerry South	838	9,668	11,604	4,723	2,302	1,246	1,232
Kildare North	1,198	11,615	19,775	3,796	2,364	3,490	896
Kildare South	937	9,733	12,447	3,553	1,681	1,966	645
Laoighis-Offaly	1,181	22,115	18,686	7,663	3,891	3,547	1,765
Limerick	819	12,238	14,134	3,854	2,864	1,369	1,239
Limerick City	648	7,643	16,935	4,150	1,917	2,065	1,004
Longford-Westmeath	945	15,166	15,987	5,885	3,372	2,154	1,550
Louth	1,316	17,027	20,844	11,499	2,359	3,141	1,267
Mayo	4,981	13,370	20,329	6,300	4,878	1,483	1,719
Meath East	995	11,300	13,397	4,095	2,199	2,340	818
Meath West	831	10,972	11,280	4,865	1,982	1,928	889
Roscommon-S.Leitrim	1,070	13,011	11,480	5,286	2,334	1,322	1,589
Sligo-North Leitrim	1,112	9,943	12,363	5,464	2,360	1,349	1,299
Tipperary North	890	13,491	13,197	4,459	3,121	1,385	1,399
Tipperary South	761	11,003	11,411	4,188	2,517	1,415	975
Waterford	918	13,107	16,340	5,737	2,489	2,451	1,218
Wexford	1,462	19,685	21,010	8,112	3,459	2,797	1,477
Wicklow	1,787	16,299	23,873	6,644	2,736	4,599	1,386
Dublin	*14,869*	*89,234*	*204,450*	*53,980*	*29,927*	*47,097*	*9,743*
Rest of Leinster	*11,795*	*153,758*	*178,873*	*63,369*	*28,554*	*28,754*	*12,307*
Munster	*10,548*	*158,854*	*198,002*	*68,627*	*32,924*	*23,287*	*15,879*
Connacht-Ulster	*11,445*	*103,118*	*119,776*	*57,054*	*21,916*	*10,331*	*13,291*
Total	48,657	504,964	701,101	243,030	113,321	109,469	51,220

2011: FIRST PREFERENCE VOTES: PERCENTAGES

Constituency	Davis	Gallagher	Higgins	McGuinn.	Mitchell	Norris	Scallon
Carlow-Kilkenny	1.9	33.8	36.7	12.4	7.7	4.8	2.7
Cavan-Monaghan	1.8	45.1	19.8	20.6	7.1	2.8	2.7
Clare	1.9	31.4	44.3	10.5	5.4	3.6	2.8
Cork East	2.1	34.4	36.6	13.8	6.0	4.3	3.0
Cork North-Central	1.7	28.1	37.6	20.0	4.7	5.1	2.9
Cork North-West	1.5	38.4	34.3	11.6	7.6	3.7	3.0
Cork South-Central	2.0	24.9	45.0	14.1	4.7	6.5	2.8
Cork South-West	2.2	35.0	33.9	13.0	8.5	4.3	3.2
Donegal North-East	2.1	28.2	23.1	32.2	4.9	2.8	6.7
Donegal South-West	2.1	32.3	23.1	28.4	5.3	3.0	5.8
Dublin Central	2.9	16.4	44.0	16.1	5.0	12.9	2.7
Dublin Mid-West	3.1	22.1	40.3	15.9	6.5	10.2	2.0
Dublin North	3.2	25.5	44.8	10.4	4.4	9.8	1.8
Dublin North-Central	3.5	20.1	46.4	11.2	5.9	10.5	2.5
Dublin North-East	4.4	21.0	43.9	13.2	5.1	10.3	2.2
Dublin North-West	3.7	20.3	38.8	19.9	4.4	10.6	2.3
Dublin South	3.3	20.0	51.1	6.5	7.3	9.8	2.0
Dublin South-Central	2.7	15.0	39.9	16.6	12.1	11.4	2.3
Dublin South-East	3.2	13.7	53.5	7.5	8.2	11.7	2.2
Dublin South-West	3.1	22.0	40.1	16.6	6.5	9.6	2.1
Dublin West	3.3	24.1	43.2	11.9	5.3	10.1	2.0
Dun Laoghaire	3.5	17.7	52.5	6.9	7.0	10.2	2.2
Galway East	2.3	28.9	46.2	10.4	6.2	2.5	3.6
Galway West	1.8	18.5	57.6	10.7	4.6	3.3	3.5
Kerry North-W.Limerick	2.2	29.0	37.9	16.8	6.5	3.8	3.7
Kerry South	2.7	30.6	36.7	14.9	7.3	3.9	3.9
Kildare North	2.8	26.9	45.8	8.8	5.5	8.1	2.1
Kildare South	3.0	31.4	40.2	11.5	5.4	6.3	2.1
Laoighis-Offaly	2.0	37.6	31.8	13.0	6.6	6.0	3.0
Limerick	2.2	33.5	38.7	10.6	7.8	3.7	3.4
Limerick City	1.9	22.2	49.3	12.1	5.6	6.0	2.9
Longford-Westmeath	2.1	33.7	35.5	13.1	7.5	4.8	3.4
Louth	2.3	29.6	36.3	20.0	4.1	5.5	2.2
Mayo	9.4	25.2	38.3	11.9	9.2	2.8	3.2
Meath East	2.8	32.2	38.1	11.7	6.3	6.7	2.3
Meath West	2.5	33.5	34.4	14.9	6.1	5.9	2.7
Roscommon-S.Leitrim	3.0	36.0	31.8	14.6	6.5	3.7	4.4
Sligo-North Leitrim	3.3	29.3	36.5	16.1	7.0	4.0	3.8
Tipperary North	2.3	35.6	34.8	11.8	8.2	3.7	3.7
Tipperary South	2.4	34.1	35.4	13.0	7.8	4.4	3.0
Waterford	2.2	31.0	38.7	13.6	5.9	5.8	2.9
Wexford	2.5	33.9	36.2	14.0	6.0	4.8	2.5
Wicklow	3.1	28.4	41.6	11.6	4.8	8.0	2.4
Dublin	*3.3*	*19.9*	*45.5*	*12.0*	*6.7*	*10.5*	*2.2*
Rest of Leinster	*2.5*	*32.2*	*37.5*	*13.3*	*6.0*	*6.0*	*2.6*
Munster	*2.1*	*31.3*	*39.0*	*13.5*	*6.5*	*4.6*	*3.1*
Connacht-Ulster	*3.4*	*30.6*	*35.5*	*16.9*	*6.5*	*3.1*	*3.9*
Total	2.7	28.5	39.6	13.7	6.4	6.2	2.9

2011: SECOND COUNT (DISTRIBUTION OF DAVIS'S AND SCALLON'S VOTES)

Constituency	Gallagher tr.	Gallagher total	Higgins tr.	Higgins total	McGuinness tr.	McGuinness total	Mitchell tr.	Mitchell total	Norris tr.	Norris total	NT
Carlow-Kilk.	685	20,531	808	22,382	240	7,497	404	4,915	183	2,975	437
Cavan-Mon.	822	26,972	614	12,085	335	12,275	363	4,472	164	1,800	360
Clare	560	15,339	745	21,573	202	5,152	265	2,810	151	1,858	280
Cork East	608	16,063	596	17,031	200	6,393	344	3,022	138	2,059	385
Cork NC	447	11,973	472	15,899	206	8,407	274	2,185	145	2,235	327
Cork NW	432	14,794	441	13,277	141	4,470	266	3,102	110	1,490	280
Cork SC	605	13,829	740	24,601	196	7,692	394	2,882	202	3,625	419
Cork SW	481	12,930	512	12,559	168	4,776	318	3,353	100	1,634	319
Donegal NE	661	8,639	519	7,035	541	9,626	245	1,629	123	911	414
Donegal SW	683	10,595	542	7,635	420	9,158	246	1,866	119	1,035	427
Dublin Central	306	4,883	447	12,714	146	4,631	249	1,641	174	3,762	254
Dublin MW	370	7,806	502	14,096	155	5,529	239	2,415	162	3,590	281
Dublin North	440	10,454	614	18,244	160	4,257	252	1,994	205	4,073	308
Dublin NC	423	7,026	542	15,772	187	3,865	317	2,270	163	3,597	328
Dublin NW	526	7,664	688	15,644	196	4,680	280	2,007	218	3,730	337
Dublin NW	339	5,408	414	10,123	157	5,142	222	1,333	127	2,765	232
Dublin South	723	13,537	1,169	33,842	196	4,342	596	5,280	295	6,560	417
Dublin SC	393	6,547	524	16,915	213	7,016	412	5,383	195	4,898	316
Dublin SE	318	4,497	571	16,886	113	2,402	269	2,755	164	3,738	207
Dublin SW	423	8,370	526	15,056	151	6,157	286	2,631	171	3,653	328
Dublin West	446	9,123	543	16,082	141	4,419	260	2,176	189	3,821	328
Dun Laoghaire	599	9,225	901	26,517	182	3,537	510	3,934	265	5,238	312
Galway East	665	14,138	906	22,460	259	5,108	337	3,242	139	1,316	417
Galway West	558	9,839	910	29,880	273	5,665	398	2,724	148	1,808	358
Kerry N-W.Lim.	510	10,419	574	13,521	215	5,954	254	2,475	116	1,417	348
Kerry South	500	10,168	649	12,253	199	4,922	249	2,551	117	1,363	356
Kildare North	522	12,137	648	20,423	161	3,957	287	2,651	169	3,659	307
Kildare South	409	10,142	492	12,939	134	3,687	195	1,876	123	2,089	229
Laois-Offaly	810	22,925	752	19,438	279	7,942	370	4,261	236	3,783	499
Limerick	515	12,753	566	14,700	184	4,038	302	3,166	125	1,494	366
Limerick City	355	7,998	504	17,439	138	4,288	253	2,170	137	2,202	265
Long.-Westmth	646	15,812	661	16,648	281	6,166	351	3,723	153	2,307	403
Louth	582	17,609	771	21,615	302	11,801	307	2,666	215	3,356	406
Mayo	1,755	15,125	2,503	22,832	611	6,911	866	5,744	228	1,711	737
Meath East	439	11,739	537	13,934	134	4,229	259	2,458	146	2,486	298
Meath West	430	11,402	477	11,757	149	5,014	251	2,233	141	2,069	272
Rosc.-S.Leitrim	688	13,699	710	12,190	303	5,589	331	2,665	185	1,507	442
Sligo-N.Leitrim	654	10,597	766	13,129	268	5,732	300	2,660	106	1,455	317
Tipperary North	597	14,088	627	13,824	180	4,639	359	3,480	126	1,511	400
Tipperary S.	438	11,441	523	11,934	156	4,344	230	2,747	118	1,533	271
Waterford	478	13,585	629	16,969	191	5,928	278	2,767	159	2,610	401
Wexford	804	20,489	759	21,769	242	8,354	402	3,861	195	2,992	537
Wicklow	792	17,091	985	24,858	276	6,920	446	3,182	212	4,811	462
Dublin	*5,306*	*94,540*	*7,441*	*211,891*	*1,997*	*55,977*	*3,892*	*33,819*	*2,328*	*49,425*	*3,648*
Rest of Leinst.	*6,119*	*159,877*	*6,890*	*185,763*	*2,198*	*65,567*	*3,272*	*31,826*	*1,773*	*30,527*	*3,850*
Munster	*6,526*	*165,380*	*7,578*	*205,580*	*2,376*	*71,003*	*3,786*	*36,710*	*1,744*	*25,031*	*4,417*
Connacht-Ulst.	*6,486*	*109,604*	*7,470*	*127,246*	*3,010*	*60,064*	*3,086*	*25,002*	*1,212*	*11,543*	*3,472*
Total	24,437	529,401	29,379	730,480	9,581	252,611	14,036	127,357	7,057	116,526	15,387

2011: THIRD COUNT (DISTRIBUTION OF NORRIS'S VOTES)

Constituency	Gallagher tr.	Gallagher total	Higgins tr.	Higgins total	McGuinness tr.	McGuinness total	Mitchell tr.	Mitchell total	NT
Carlow-Kilk.	558	21,089	1,537	23,919	386	7,883	180	5,095	314
Cavan-Mon.	407	27,379	750	12,835	234	12,509	216	4,688	193
Clare	364	15,703	977	22,550	213	5,365	125	2,935	179
Cork East	359	16,422	1,097	18,128	222	6,615	124	3,146	257
Cork NC	363	12,336	1,199	17,098	298	8,705	128	2,313	247
Cork NW	335	15,129	750	14,027	168	4,638	82	3,184	155
Cork SC	574	14,403	2,010	26,611	377	8,069	243	3,125	421
Cork SW	274	13,204	912	13,471	167	4,943	120	3,473	161
Donegal NE	183	8,822	401	7,436	123	9,749	73	1,702	131
Donegal SW	181	10,776	467	8,102	141	9,299	93	1,959	153
Dublin Central	409	5,292	2,269	14,983	417	5,048	237	1,878	430
Dublin MW	559	8,365	1,810	15,906	466	5,995	313	2,728	442
Dublin North	729	11,183	2,154	20,398	421	4,678	283	2,277	486
Dublin NC	491	7,517	2,020	17,792	373	4,238	280	2,550	433
Dublin NW	589	8,253	1,973	17,617	391	5,071	283	2,290	494
Dublin NW	433	5,841	1,363	11,486	386	5,528	204	1,537	379
Dublin South	940	14,477	3,975	37,817	437	4,779	552	5,832	656
Dublin SC	565	7,112	2,698	19,613	578	7,594	516	5,899	541
Dublin SE	374	4,871	2,476	19,362	264	2,666	298	3,053	326
Dublin SW	588	8,958	1,813	16,869	452	6,609	336	2,967	464
Dublin West	618	9,741	1,992	18,074	407	4,826	263	2,439	541
Dun Laoghaire	688	9,913	3,264	29,781	317	3,854	444	4,378	525
Galway East	198	14,336	678	23,138	187	5,295	100	3,342	153
Galway West	268	10,107	1,068	30,948	210	5,875	116	2,840	146
KN-WL	270	10,689	695	14,216	194	6,148	101	2,576	157
Kerry South	222	10,390	755	13,008	155	5,077	84	2,635	147
Kildare North	644	12,781	2,016	22,439	319	4,276	268	2,919	412
Kildare South	400	10,542	1,055	13,994	207	3,894	172	2,048	255
Laois-Offaly	804	23,729	1,775	21,213	438	8,380	308	4,569	458
Limerick	302	13,055	801	15,501	153	4,191	100	3,266	138
Limerick City	338	8,336	1,270	18,709	221	4,509	143	2,313	230
Long.-Westmth	362	16,174	1,180	17,828	294	6,460	183	3,906	288
Louth	543	18,152	1,784	23,399	434	12,235	225	2,891	370
Mayo	269	15,394	887	23,719	197	7,108	144	5,888	214
Meath East	475	12,214	1,292	15,226	250	4,479	196	2,654	273
Meath West	373	11,775	1,031	12,788	227	5,241	182	2,415	256
Rosc.-.Leitrim	291	13,990	721	12,911	218	5,807	94	2,759	183
Sligo-N.L	229	10,826	808	13,937	179	5,911	108	2,768	131
Tipperary N.	280	14,368	768	14,592	155	4,794	130	3,610	178
Tipperary S.	292	11,733	710	12,644	185	4,529	126	2,873	220
Waterford	473	14,058	1,310	18,279	341	6,269	179	2,946	307
Wexford	567	21,056	1,474	23,243	329	8,683	240	4,101	382
Wicklow	791	17,882	2,663	27,521	454	7,374	360	3,542	543
Dublin	*6,983*	*101,523*	*27,807*	*239,698*	*4,909*	*60,886*	*4,009*	*37,828*	*5,717*
Rest of Leinst.	*5,517*	*165,394*	*15,807*	*201,570*	*3,338*	*68,905*	*2,314*	*34,140*	*3,551*
Munster	*4,446*	*169,826*	*13,254*	*218,834*	*2,849*	*73,852*	*1,685*	*38,395*	*2,797*
Connacht-Ulst.	*2,026*	*111,630*	*5,780*	*133,026*	*1,489*	*61,553*	*944*	*25,946*	*1,304*
Total	18,972	548,373	62,648	793,128	12,585	265,196	8,952	136,309	13,369

2011: FOURTH COUNT (DISTRIBUTION OF McGUINNESS'S AND MITCHELL'S VOTES)

Constituency	Gallagher			Higgins			NT
	tr.	total	%	tr.	total	%	
Carlow-Kilkenny	2,616	23,705	43.2	7,217	31,136	56.8	3,145
Cavan-Monaghan	5,041	32,420	61.5	7,474	20,309	38.5	4,682
Clare	1,468	17,171	38.3	5,169	27,719	61.7	1,663
Cork East	2,001	18,423	44.3	5,067	23,195	55.7	2,693
Cork North-Central	2,015	14,351	38.9	5,462	22,560	61.1	3,541
Cork North-West	1,568	16,697	47.4	4,486	18,513	52.6	1,768
Cork South-Central	1,995	16,398	33.4	6,026	32,637	66.6	3,173
Cork South-West	1,844	15,048	45.5	4,553	18,024	54.5	2,019
Donegal North-East	2,644	11,466	49.7	4,159	11,595	50.3	4,648
Donegal South-West	2,619	13,395	52.0	4,256	12,358	48.0	4,383
Dublin Central	1,171	6,463	25.8	3,558	18,541	74.2	2,197
Dublin Mid-West	1,590	9,955	32.7	4,623	20,529	67.3	2,510
Dublin North	1,336	12,519	34.0	3,881	24,279	66.0	1,738
Dublin North-Central	1,157	8,674	28.6	3,864	21,656	71.4	1,767
Dublin North-East	1,341	9,594	30.7	4,006	21,623	69.3	2,014
Dublin North-West	1,370	7,211	32.6	3,397	14,883	67.4	2,298
Dublin South	1,823	16,300	26.8	6,816	44,633	73.2	1,972
Dublin South-Central	2,329	9,441	25.9	7,360	26,973	74.1	3,804
Dublin South-East	899	5,770	20.1	3,582	22,944	79.9	1,238
Dublin South-West	1,919	10,877	33.4	4,861	21,730	66.6	2,796
Dublin West	1,390	11,131	33.7	3,839	21,913	66.3	2,036
Dun Laoghaire	1,409	11,322	24.5	5,090	34,871	75.5	1,733
Galway East	1,517	15,853	35.9	5,184	28,322	64.1	1,936
Galway West	1,448	11,555	24.2	5,332	36,280	75.8	1,935
Kerry North-W.Limerick	1,525	12,214	39.5	4,489	18,705	60.5	2,710
Kerry South	1,428	11,818	40.6	4,299	17,307	59.4	1,985
Kildare North	1,345	14,126	34.6	4,237	26,676	65.4	1,613
Kildare South	1,243	11,785	40.7	3,153	17,147	59.3	1,546
Laoighis-Offaly	2,877	26,606	48.9	6,608	27,821	51.1	3,464
Limerick	1,413	14,468	42.2	4,352	19,853	57.8	1,692
Limerick City	1,090	9,426	29.3	4,011	22,720	70.7	1,721
Longford-Westmeath	2,101	18,275	43.8	5,616	23,444	56.2	2,649
Louth	3,154	21,306	41.0	7,250	30,649	59.0	4,722
Mayo	2,170	17,564	35.6	8,024	31,743	64.4	2,802
Meath East	1,414	13,628	41.5	4,000	19,226	58.5	1,719
Meath West	1,583	13,358	44.3	3,981	16,769	55.7	2,092
Roscommon-S.Leitrim	1,947	15,937	48.0	4,372	17,283	52.0	2,247
Sligo-North Leitrim	1,817	12,643	40.6	4,594	18,531	59.4	2,268
Tipperary North	1,778	16,146	45.6	4,672	19,264	54.4	1,954
Tipperary South	1,454	13,187	44.1	4,041	16,685	55.9	1,907
Waterford	1,845	15,903	40.8	4,781	23,060	59.2	2,589
Wexford	2,777	23,833	44.5	6,514	29,757	55.5	3,493
Wicklow	2,270	20,152	37.7	5,720	33,241	62.3	2,926
Dublin	*17,734*	*119,257*	*28.8*	*54,877*	*294,575*	*71.2*	*26,103*
Rest of Leinster	*21,380*	*186,774*	*42.2*	*54,296*	*255,866*	*57.8*	*27,369*
Munster	*21,424*	*191,250*	*40.6*	*61,408*	*280,242*	*59.4*	*29,415*
Connacht-Ulster	*19,203*	*130,833*	*42.6*	*43,395*	*176,421*	*57.4*	*24,901*
Total	79,741	628,114	38.4	213,976	1,007,104	61.6	107,788

APPENDIX 2

PRESIDENTIAL INAUGURATION ADDRESSES, 1938–2011

NOTE ON DATA AND SOURCES

Article 12.8 of the Constitution states that 'The President shall enter upon his office by taking and subscribing publicly, in the presence of members of both Houses of the Oireachtas, of Judges of the Supreme Court and of the High Court, and other public personages, the following declaration':

> In the presence of Almighty God, I, [name], do solemnly and sincerely promise and declare that I will maintain the Constitution of Ireland and uphold its laws, that I will fulfil my duties faithfully and conscientiously in accordance with the Constitution and the law, and that I will dedicate my abilities to the service and welfare of the people of Ireland. May God direct and sustain me.

The installation ceremony follows a format similar to that surrounding the swearing-in of the Lord Lieutenant, a format that was discontinued during the period of the Governor-General (1922–1936). The President-elect arrives in Dublin Castle accompanied by his aides-de-camp, makes the declaration, hears a short message from the Taoiseach, replies, and leaves for Áras an Uachtaráin, all in the presence of leading members of the public and of the political establishment. The ceremony is marked by a strong military dimension, with trumpet fanfares, inspection of a guard of honour, and a 21-gun artillery salute.

Originally, the Taoiseach's speech was moderately long, comprising a personal and political tribute to the new President. This tradition was brought to an end by Liam Cosgrave in 1973, after which the Taoiseach's speech was restricted to some brief remarks of congratulation; but in 2011 Enda Kenny reverted to the older practice of an extended encomium. The President's response was confined to a few remarks in 1938, but after that comprised a short speech. In 1974 Cearbhall Ó Dálaigh made a long speech, mainly in English, but partly in Irish and with a component also in French. From 1990 onwards, longer inaugural speeches have sought consciously to set a tone for the presidency. The proceedings were entirely in Irish for the first three inaugurations (1938–1952); that of 1959 was predominantly in Irish; after that, they were mainly in English, but with some symbolic use of Irish, apart from 1973, when the ceremony was entirely in English (though even then the President-elect, Erskine Childers, made the declaration in Irish). The presidential inauguration addresses below are printed in the language in which they were given, with translation in square brackets where Irish or French were used. Translations prefixed by an asterisk are 'official' ones; the others have been provided by the editors.

The procedure at presidential inaugurations was laid out initially in 1938; see 'Entry of President on Office, 1st June 1938: lunch to ministers', President's Office papers, National Archives of Ireland, P312. Descriptions of each ceremony are given in the press on the following day. The Irish language texts in 1938, 1945 and 1952 are taken from the *Irish Press* on the day following the inauguration, with English translations from *The Irish Times* and from files held in the National Archives (DFA 2006/61/47; TAOIS 97/6/453; TAOIS S/16561; TAOIS S/16550). Later texts up to 1983 are taken from *The Irish Times*, and those from 1990 to 2011 were supplied by Áras an Uachtaráin. Translations of non-English extracts have been made by the editors. It should be noted that official English translations of Irish addresses do not necessarily convey the precise meaning of The Irish words, and presidents did not always deliver the archived address verbatim. In 1976 the newspapers reported an address quite different from that filed in the archives; the version printed in *The Irish Times* is used here. The older spelling system used by the earlier presidents has been retained, but obvious typographical errors have been corrected, paragraphs have in some instances been further grouped, and capitalisation and punctuation have been standardised.

DUBHGLAS DE HÍDE, 26 JUNE 1938

A Thaoisigh, tá mé buidheach díot ar son na cainnte cineálta do rinne tú. Iarraim ar Dhia grásta agus cómhacht do thabhairt dom chun leasa na hÉireann do

*chur ar aghaidh. Iarraim ar Dhia ciall agus críonnacht a thabhairt dom agus neart
a thabhairt dom go gcóimhlíonadh mé mo dhualgais mar Uachtarán na hÉireann.*

[*Taoiseach, I am very thankful to you for the kind speech you have made.
I ask God to grant me grace and power in order that I may forward the best
interests of Ireland. I also ask God for sense, prudence and strength in order
that I may fulfil my duties as President.]

Sean T. O'Kelly, 25 June 1945

*A Thaoisigh Uasail, tá mé fíor-bhuidheach díot as ucht na bhfocal cineáltais
atá ráidhte agat, agus do gach aoinne atá annso mar gheall ar theacht chun a
dheagh-mhéinn a theasbáint dom. Is mór an t-ádhbhar sóláis agus misnigh dom
an deagh-mhéinn sin do bheith agam agus mé ag dul i mbun Uachtaránachta
na hÉireann. Tá mé buidheach ó chroídhe do mhuinntir na hÉireann a thug
dom an onóir is mó atá ina gcumas. Déanfaidh mé mo dhícheall chun ná beidh
cathú orthu choídhche dá bharr.*

*Ar ócáid mar seo is cóir dúinn, thar gach nidh eile, ár mbuíochas do ghab-
háil le Dia na Glóire. Eisean do thug ár muinntir tríd an daorbhruid chun áit
shábhála agus onóra i measc cinidheacha an domhain. Muna mbéadh a lámh
uile-chomhachtach ag cabhrú linn, ní bhéadh in ár gcumas Rialtas ná Uachtarán
do thoghadh. Eisean do tharrtháil agus do shaor sinn. Moladh go deo leis!*

*Maidir liom féin, déanfaidh mé, le cungnamh Dé, mo dhualgaisí mar
Uachtarán do chomhlíonadh go dílis dúthrachtach do réir Bunreachta na hÉireann. Tá mé ag braith ar chabhair ón Rialtas agus ó gach dream sa Stát ins an
obair, agus is deimhin liom ná teipfidh siad orm. Ag comhoibriú le chéile dhúinn,
tá súil agam go bhféadfaimíd mórán a dhéanamh chun an tír a chur ar a leas.*

*Ba chúis áthais dom an teachtaireacht a chuir mo chara uasal Dubhglas
de hÍde chugham. Gabhaim buidheachas leis. Geallaim dó go mbeidh in a
phríomh-chuspóir agam an fhaid a bheidh mé im' Uachtarán a theagasc féin do
chur i bhfeidhm agus a shampla do leanúint maidir le teangain na hÉireann. Go
mairidh sé i bhfad in ár measc fé shéan agus fé ghradam!*

[*Taoiseach, I thank you deeply for the kind words you have spoken, and I
thank you all here for having come to show your goodwill towards me. That
goodwill is a source of comfort and encouragement to me on my entry into
office as President of Ireland. From my heart I am grateful to the people of
Ireland, who have conferred upon me the highest honour in their power. It
will always be my aim to be worthy of their trust.

We ought, above all, on an occasion like this, to give thanks to Almighty God. It is He who has brought our community through bondage to a secure and honoured place amongst the peoples of the world. Without the help of His all-powerful hand it would not be in our power to elect either a Government or a President. It is He who preserved us and set us free. May He be praised for ever.

As for myself, I will, with God's help, fulfil my duties as President faithfully and zealously according to the Constitution of Ireland. I am counting upon help in my task from the Government and from every section of the people, and I am certain that they will not deny it to me. Co-operating together, I hope that we shall be able to do great things for Ireland.

The message from my noble friend, Dr. Douglas Hyde, is a cause of joy to me. I thank him. I promise him that it will be a primary purpose of mine while I am President to put his teaching into effect and to follow his example, especially with regard to the Irish language. May he live long in our midst in happiness and honour.]

SEAN T. O'KELLY, 25 JUNE 1952

Tá mé fíor-bhuíoch díot de bharr na cainte ri-chineálta atá déanta agat im thaobh. Gabhaim mo bhuíochas libh go léir as ucht teacht anseo chun bhur ndeamhéin dom féin agus bhur n-ómos d'oifig an Uachtaráin a thaispeáint. Cuireann sé áthas mór orm sibh a bheith anseo ar an ócáid tábhachtach seo. Tugann sé dóchas agus misneach dom ag dul i gceann an dara téarma mar Uachtarán dom.

Is maith liom caoi a bheith agam arís chun buíochas ó chroí a ghabháil le cinnirí agus le comhaltaí gach páirtí polaitíochta as ucht mé a thoghadh gan iomaíocht chun an dara téarma oifige. Níorbh fhéidir é sin a dhéanamh gan aontú na gcinnirí sin go léir. Is mór agam an comhartha ard-mheasa sin.

I gcomaoin na hard-mhuiníne sin atá á chur ionam, ní thig liom ach a gheallúint do phobal uile na hÉireann go ndéanfad mo dhícheall, le cúnamh agus le coimirce Dé, mo dhualgais mar Uachtarán a chomhlíonadh go dílis agus go dúthrachtach do réir an Bhunreachta.

Níor chuí dhom gan mo bhain-chéile a luadh agus mé ag gabháil buíochais as ucht mé d'atoghadh. Ba chóir dom a rá, chomh maith, pé bail nó buaidh a meastar a bheith ar mo shaothar sna seacht mbliana atá caite, nach bhféadfadh sé bheith ann mura mbéadh an cuidiú fial fónta a fuaireas uaithi.

Ba mhaith liom mo bhuíochas a ghabháil leis na daoine go léir a chomhoibrigh chomh fonnmhar sin liom i rith na seacht mblian atá caite agus mé ag comhlíonadh mo dhualgas. Táim ag cuimhneamh go háirithe ar chomhaltaí an dá Rialtas bhí i seilbh oifige i rith na haimsire sin, ar chomhaltaí na Comhairle Stáit agus ar chomhaltaí an Choimisiúin Uachtaráin. Is deimhin liom go mbeidh an chabhair chéanna sin le fáil feasta, agus is mór an dóchas agus an t-árdú meanman a thugann sin dom agus mé ag dul i gceann an dara téarma mar Uachtarán.

Bheirimíd buíochas do Dhia na Glóire a thug slán sinn ón anró atá á fhulang ag an oiread sin náisiún eile – san aimsir seo lena samhlaítear síocháin. Go dtuga Sé, as ucht A thrócaire, go n-éireoidh linn an cion saoirse, síochána agus rathúnais atá againn faoi láthair a chaomhaint. Go dtála Sé orainn i gcónaí na grása agus na beannachta sin, agus go ndeona Sé go bhfeicimíd, lenár linn féin, buaidh na gcuspóirí a shanntaigh na glúna dár muintir, le tnúth agus le troid: Éire uile aontaithe agus saor ó smacht. Tá a fhios agam go ndéanfaidh gach duine anseo comhghui dúthrachtach liom gur gearr go dtiocfaidh sé sin chun críche.

[*I offer you my warmest thanks for your most kind words. I am grateful to all of you who have come here to show your good will towards me and your respect for the Presidential Office. May I say that your presence here on this important occasion affords me very great pleasure. It is a source of hope and comfort to me as I enter upon my second term as President.

I would like to take this opportunity to say again how profoundly grateful I am to the leaders and members of all our political parties for my election without opposition to a second term of office. Without the agreement of all these leaders, this would not have been possible. I deeply appreciate the striking compliment implied.

In return for the great confidence thus reposed in me, I can only promise the whole people of Ireland that, granted the guidance and help of Almighty God, I will do my best to carry out my duties as President faithfully and zealously according to the Constitution.

It would not be proper if I did not associate my wife with this expression of thanks on my re-election. I should add, too, that whatever success I may be deemed to have achieved during the last seven years would not have been possible without her generous and most capable assistance.

I want to thank all those who, during the past seven years, so willingly co-operated with me in the discharge of my official duties. I have in mind particularly the members of the two Governments who held office during that period, the members of the Presidential Commission and the members of the Council of State. I feel assured that that generous aid will be ever available in future, and, in this belief, I enter upon my second period as President with hope and confidence.

We give thanks to Almighty God who has preserved us from so much of the suffering which so many other peoples have to endure – even in these days of supposed peace. May He, in His mercy, grant that we can preserve the measure of liberty, peace and prosperity which we now enjoy. May He grant us a continuance of these graces and favours and may it also be permitted to us to see in our day the fulfilment of the ideals of complete national unity and freedom for which so many generations of our people have yearned and fought. I know that all here will join with me in an earnest prayer that these aims may be speedily achieved.]

Eamon de Valera, 25 June 1959

A Thaoisigh Uasail, táim faoi chomaoin mhór agat as ucht na cainte cineálta ata déanta agat. Thar mo cheann féin agus thar ceann mo chéile gabhaim buíochas ó chroí leat. Cuireann sé go mór le gradam na hócáide seo an oiread sin de mhaithe agus de mhór-uaisle na tire a bheith i láthair. Is mór agam é, agus táim an-bhuíoch díbh go léir.

Beannaím duitse, a Thaoisigh, mar Cheann an Rialtais, treoraí mhuintir na hÉireann. Sláinte agus faid saoil duit. Go neartaí Dia thú agus go gcuire sé rath ar a ndéanfaidh tú. Is maith is eol domsa do dhílseacht agus do dhúthracht i gcúis na hÉireann ó bhí tú id ógánach. Is é mo ghuí go bhfaighidh tú ó dhaoine eile an dílseacht agus an díograis chéanna a thug tú féin riamh.

Agus tusa, a shean-chara, a Sheáin Uasail Uí Cheallaigh, a bhí comh fada againn mar Uachtarán, is ceart go gcuirfinn in iúl duitse agus dod chéile chaoin an meas agus an cion atá ag muintir na hÉireann oraibh. Tá cúis mhaith ag ár ndaoine bheith buíoch díbh. Onóir don náisiún agus ábhar fíor-bhróid díbh féin a fheabhas a chomhlíon sibh bhur ndualgaisí agus tú i seilbh oifige. Beidh sé deacair bhur lorg a leanúint, ach déanfaimid ár ndícheall. Iarraim ar Dhia neart agus críonnacht a thabhairt dúinn.

[*Taoiseach, I am most grateful to you for your kind remarks. On my own behalf and on behalf of my wife, I thank you from my heart. This occasion is greatly honoured by the presence of so many distinguished people. I appreciate your coming here, and I am very grateful to you all.

I salute you, Taoiseach, as head of the Government, leader of the Irish people. I wish you health and long life. May God sustain you and prosper all you undertake. I know well your loyalty and your devotion to Ireland since your boyhood. I pray that you will receive from others the same loyalty and devotion which you yourself have always given.

And you, my old friend, Seán T. Ó Ceallaigh, so long our President, it is right that I should express to you and to your gracious wife the esteem and affection which the people of Ireland have for you. Our people have good reason to be grateful to you both. During your period of office, you have performed your duties with such distinction that you have honoured the nation and yourselves. You may be justly proud. It will be difficult to reach the standards you have set, but we shall do our best. I pray God to give me strength and wisdom for the worthy performance of my task.]

A dhaoine uaisle [Ladies and gentlemen], Before I leave, I must thank you all for honouring this occasion by your presence. It was very kind of you to come and I am most grateful. *Beannacht Dé oraibh go léir.* [God's blessing on all of you.]

Eamon de Valera, 26 June 1966

A Thaoisigh, táim fíor-bhuíoch duit faoin méid atá ráite im thaobh. Is mór an onóir d'aon duine a bheith tofa mar Uachtarán ar mhuintir an tsean-náisiúin seo. Is mór agam í agus tá mé an-bhuíoch do gach aon duine a chuidigh liom mise a chur in san áit seo. Tá mé an-bhuíoch dóibh agus slán a bhéas siad uilig.

[Taoiseach, I am truly grateful to you for what has been said about me. It is a great honour for anyone to be elected as President of the people of this old nation. I deeply appreciate this and I am very grateful to everyone who helped to put me here. I am very grateful to them and I wish them all safe and well.]

I want to thank you all for coming here and, by your presence, gracing these proceedings. You, our Cardinal, Your Graces, My Lords, Your Excellencies, members of the Diplomatic Corps, members of the Oireachtas, representatives of the Dáil and Senate, the judiciary, representatives of the Civil Service, the Army and the Guards – I would like to thank each one of you for coming here on this occasion.

As I have said, Taoiseach, it is a great honour for anybody to be chosen for President of the people of this great old nation. I would like to thank everyone who contributed in any way to giving me this honour. I thank you very heartily. I can only promise to do my very best to be worthy – a worthy representative of our nation. It is, indeed, not an easy thing to be that, because this nation has a storied history and is highly regarded amongst the nations of the earth.

We have an importance far beyond our size, of our territory or the numbers of our people. The Taoiseach has mentioned two cherished aims which have not yet been realised – the unity of our country and the restoration of our language.

I have spoken of these topics at the commemoration ceremonies at the Post Office, and it would not be appropriate, I think, for me to enter into them in any detail here. I must say that, with an audience like this, I am very much tempted to deal with the question of our language and its importance, if we are to maintain our individuality as a nation in the modern world. However, as I have said this is not the occasion for an address of that kind. I do hope, however, that on some occasion we will have an assembly just such as this. There was one at the beginning of this century, shortly after the Gaelic League was established, and the proceedings of that assembly did much to get our people to understand how precious was the language from the national point of view. That may happen in the future.

It is possible that we could have an assembly like this where the question of the language could be dealt with fully and freely, and decisions arrived at, which would stop us from hesitations and stoppings, which undo, to a large extent, much of the work that has been done.

As to the unity of the country, there is a unity imposed upon us whether we like it or not. We are all inhabitants of this glorious little island. We are all proud – I never met an Irishman or Irishwoman abroad, who was not proud to lay claim to this island, to say that they were Irishmen or Irishwomen. That is the unity which is there and which I have no doubt whatever would lead to the political unity which is not so far way – the political unity which we so desire. But, as I have said, this is not the occasion on which one should speak of these problems. I simply want then, once more, to thank you all for your coming here and to pray that God may give me the strength to perform the duties worthily and once more to thank you all for your presence.

ERSKINE CHILDERS, 25 JUNE 1973

Taoiseach, I am most grateful for your kind remarks. On behalf of my wife and myself, I thank you from my heart for your good wishes. I am greatly honoured at the attendance here today of so many distinguished personages. I appreciate your presence and am sincerely grateful to you all.

This has been for me a most moving ceremony, particularly in that June 25th is my father's birthday anniversary. I am humbly aware of the great honour conferred upon me at this ceremony. I know I shall need the prayers of the people for God's guidance in the performance of my duties and in making a meaningful contribution to the harmony among Irishmen and Irishwomen which we all desire. I do hope you will all remember me in your prayers.

Eamon de Valera was my political mentor and leader and my friend for many years. I can testify to his statesmanlike counsel and above all to his kindness of heart. All of you here present have witnessed the dignity with which he graced the office of President during the past 14 years. I join with the Taoiseach in wishing Mr de Valera and his gracious wife every happiness in their retirement.

CEARBHALL Ó DÁLAIGH, 19 DECEMBER 1974

A mhaithe agus a mhór-uaisle Éireann, idir chléir agus tuaith, a thaidhleóirí eachtrannacha, a chomharsana cómh-Eórpacha, agus a mhuinntir na páirte, Dia annso isteach, Dia isteach, i dtighthibh Éireann! Agus i gcroidhthibh Gael agus Gall-Ghael.

A Thaoisigh uasail, is ró-onóir liom, agus is rí-ualach dom an cúram atáim tréis a ghlacadh de láimh anois. Ar an gcéad dul síos, glacaim buíochas leat féin, leis an dTánaiste, agus leis an iar-Thaoiseach is Ceannaire ar an bhFreasúra agus le baill an Oireachtais idir Dháil agus Sheanad, a thoiligh d'aon ghuth mé d'ainmniú le haghaidh Uachtaránacht na hÉireann, agus gabhaim orm féin gan aon dá leath a dhéanamh dem dhícheall ag comhlíonadh dualgaisí na hoifige sin dom.

Adeir an Ghaeilge: Ná h-iarr onóir agus ná h-ob í. Cé d'fhéadfadh glaoch ó Oireachtas Éireann d'obadh agus é theacht féin obann, gan choinne, mar a tháinig chun Cincinnatus fadó? Ní gan aithféala, bíodh a fhios agaibh, d'fhágas slán le mo chombhreithiúin, is dlúth-cháirde liom, i gCúirt Bhreithúnais na gComh-Phobal i Luxembourg, anois go rabhas, tréis réamh-achar dhá bhliain, ag dul i dtaithí na cruaidhchéirde sin.

Gabhaim buíochas ó chroi amach lena Shoillse an Cairdinéal, Príomháidh, lena Ghrása an t-Ard-Easbog Simms, Príomháidh, leis an Urramach R. D. Morris, Uachtarán na hEaglaise Meitidistí, leis an Dr. Urramach J. W. Orr ón Eaglais Phreispitéireach, agus leis an Uasal A. G. Pearson, ó Chumann na gCarad, as sinn do chur, mé féin agus mo bhean, fé bheannacht Dé agus fé ghuí Phobail Fodhla go h-iomlán comh fras fial san ar maidin. Go dtugaidh Dia a thoradh agus a thacaíocht-san dúinn anois agus riamh. Agus gabhaim buíochas roimh-ré lem shean-chara, an Príomh-Rabbi, an Doctúir Isaac Cohen, a chomórfaidh seirbhís dom tráthnóna.

Ní h-áit do ghliondar ná do ró-gháire inniu, halla so an té a tháinig chughainn anoir tá breis agus 1,500 blian ó shoin ann, le caoin-theachtaireacht creidimh agus le dianreacht coinsiasa – ós annso a sheas Earascain Hamaltún Childers tá trí leith-bhliana ó shoin ann ag glacadh móid oifige an Uachtaráin fé mar do ghlacas-sa inniu í. Is deimhin liom ná hiarrfadh Earascain aon ní ba mhó ná mar d'iarr Cúchulainn nuair a dúirt, sa tSean-Ghaeilge: 'I would rather that my life would be the length of a night and a day, provided that my deeds be remembered by the men of Ireland.' *Do fíoraíodh an achainí sin ina chás-san – slán beo leis agus grásta na foidhne dá chaoinchéile agus dá ghaolta uile.*

[Distinguished people of Ireland, both clerical and lay, foreign diplomats, fellow-European neighbours, and dear friends, God be with us here and in the households of Ireland; and in the hearts of the Irish old and new.

Taoiseach, the responsibility I have now undertaken is a great honour to me, and a great burden on me. First, I thank you, the Tánaiste, the former Taiseach and leader of the opposition and the members of the Oireachtas, of both the Dáil and the Seanad, who unanimously agreed to nominate me for the presidency of Ireland, and I commit myself to do nothing by halves in fulfilling the duties of that office.

It is said in Irish: don't pursue an honour, and don't refuse one. Who could refuse a call from the Oireachtas which arrived suddenly, unexpectedly, as happened to Cincinnatus long ago? It was not without regret, let me tell you, that I left my fellow judges, and good friends, in the European Court of Justice in Luxembourg, now that I was, after my two preliminary years, becoming accustomed to that difficult craft.

I offer heartfelt thanks to His Eminence the Cardinal, Primate, to his Grace Archbishop Simms, Primate, to the Rev. R.D. Morris, President of the Methodist Church, to the Rev. J.W. Orr from the Presbyterian Church, and to Mr A.G. Pearson from the Society of Friends, for putting us, myself and my wife, under God's blessing and under the prayers of all the people of Ireland in such a fulsome and appropriate way this morning. May God favour and support us now and for ever. And I thank in advance my old friend the Chief Rabbi, Dr Isaac Cohen, who will celebrate a service for me this afternoon.

This is not a place for mirth or laughter today, this hall of the person who came to us from the East more than 1,500 years ago, with a lovely message of faith and with a hard rule of conscience – since it was here that Erskine Hamilton Childers stood three half-years ago to take the oath of office as President as I have taken it today. I am certain that Erskine would ask for nothing more than Cúchulainn asked for when he said, in Old Irish: 'I would rather that my life would be the length of a night and a day, provided that my deeds be remembered by the men of Ireland'. That request was fulfilled in his case – a fond farewell to him, and may the grace of endurance be with his dear wife and all his relatives.]

Mais comment puis-je remercier suffisament la délégation très grande et fort distinguée des juges et des avocats généraux de la Cour de Justice des Communautés européens qui sont venus ici pour l'inauguration du cinquième Président d'Irlande? Vraiment, ce n'est pas a cause de moi qu'ils sont venus ici mais pour montrer leur amitié et leur estime pour notre pays. De votre part, je leur remercie de tout coeur, de leur très aimable présence ici aujourd'hui; et de ma part, je leur remercie de m'avoir conduit dans les coulisses du droit européen avec tant de soin et de compréhension.

Et comment pouvons-nous, ma femme et moi, remercier notre petit cousin européen Luxembourg qui a fait de notre séjour chez lui une véritable deuxième 'voyage de noces', et qui malgré tout, a su maintenir son individualité linguistique, tour en parlant deux autres langues européennes? Voilà le petit pays qui nous a accueillis si chaleureusement et qui nous a congédié la la semaine dernière en la personne de son Altesse Royale le Grand-Duc et de son Premier Ministre, M. Gaston Thorn.

[But how may I thank enough the very large and distinguished delegation of judges and advocates general from the Court of Justice of the European Communities who have come here for the inauguration of the fifth President of Ireland? Certainly, it is not because of me that they have come, but to show their friendship and esteem for our country. On your behalf, I offer them heartfelt thanks for their kind presence here today; and on my own behalf, I thank them for having taken me behind the scenes of European law with such care and understanding.

And how may we, my wife and I, thank our small European cousin Luxembourg, which has made our stay there a veritable second honeymoon, and which in spite of all has been able to maintain its linguistic identity, while still speaking two other European languages? Here is the small country which has welcomed us so warmly and which has sent us on our way last week through the person of his Royal Highness the Grand Duke and his Prime Minister, M. Gaston Thorn.]

Voilà: má labhraim Fraincis – dá bhacaí féin í – biodh a fhios againn go mba shuaitheantas linn ar ár idirnáisiúnachas an teanga chéanna álainn sin ag an gcéad suí de Dháil Éireann i mbliain 1919.

[So, then: if I speak French – imperfect though it may be – we should know that that same beautiful language was a distinguishing mark of our internationalism at the first sitting of Dáil Éireann in the year 1919.]

This castle is full of memories, more unflagged, than flagged. It is now just 18 months since, standing in this place, Erskine Hamilton Childers entered on office as the fourth President of Ireland; in that brief period, as a people's grief has so recently and movingly testified, he won, in the hearts of his fellow countrymen, a very special place. My first duty today is again to tender to Mrs Childers, to her daughter and the members of her family, our respectful prayers and sympathy.

I always like to come prepared for a task. But how do you come prepared for the task of being President of Ireland? How do you follow such names as de híde, Ó Ceallaigh, de Valera, Childers? In time of difficulty our ancestors would say: *Níor dhún Dia doras riamh nár oscail Sé ceann eile* [God never closed one door without opening another]. I pray God it may be so.

A lawyer looks at the Constitution (Article 12.1) and reads 'There shall be a President of Ireland (Uachtarán na hEireann) who shall take precedence over all other persons in the State…' This, I see, is an impossible role. A judge, *prima facie*, would pronounce the section 'void for impossibility'. But every statute and every Constitution must be read as a whole; and Article 5 says 'Ireland is a … democratic State.' Here then we find the solution of our problem. The President is first, but *primus inter pares*, first among equals. This makes the office of President of Ireland a possible task, a task that can be grappled with. But nonetheless one needs the co-operation of the countless folk who rise every day to perform the simple, necessary tasks that eventually make a nation great.

Article 12.2 continues: 'The President shall be elected by direct vote of the people.' This is not all of Article 12, but for the moment let it suffice. I seem to have had a life-long difficulty in elections of the kind referred to in Article 12.2. But I did once have a handsome popular majority when, as a student at University College, Dublin, I was elected auditor of the Literary and Historical Society in 1931. My opponent was a better academic than I ever succeeded in being. We each had our own supporters. I was a little ahead of my opponent in terms of promises. But the decisive factor was going to be a third group, numerous, uninterested in office, much given to heckling, and as I then thought, the life, if not the soul, of the society; and whose much-loved leader was Brian Ó Nualláin, afterwards *alias* Myles na gCopaleen, *alias* Flann O'Brien, and, as it turned out, the most gifted bilingual genius of half a century. This group was known, with undergraduate inelegance and accuracy, as 'the mob'.

I didn't seek the suffrages of 'the mob', but I wrote an electoral address, emphasising the importance of the heckler's role (an immortal Irish poet has said 'doras feasa fiafraighe') and I placed the only copy of this address (I have the MS copy still somewhere in my papers) in the hands of my right-hand man, himself now, for many years, a member of Dáil Eireann. He brought it to the notice of Brian Ó Nualláin. In the result, I was, as I have said, elected. I had a handsome, real and, as I believe, moral victory too; perhaps, a difficult 'double'.

But the true point of this story is yet to come. Every auditor delivers an inaugural address which, with a bit of luck, takes place in the Hilary term. The speakers at my inaugural were: Sir John Keane, whose family gave as a gift the land on which the Cistercian monks built Mount Melleray; Madame MacBride, mother of Ireland's very recent Nobel Peace prize-winner, author of 'A Servant of the Queen'; Mr. Eamon de Valera, then in opposition; and my professor of Irish, Dubhglas de hÍde, an Craoibhín Aoibhinn, later to be the first unopposed President of Ireland.

I still have, by the way, a recommendation [from] him, the kind of thing every graduate asks his professor for when he is faced with the problem, eventually, of looking for a job. My first real job was in journalism, and my first assignment for the first issue of the paper I joined was a long interview (need I say in Irish) with Douglas Hyde, on his retirement from the Chair of Modern Irish in University College, Dublin. But, for fear I forget it, the title of my address was 'Community Spirit'.

The press, in recent days, have repeatedly asked me: 'What, Mr. President-Elect, is your policy going to be as President?' I have invariably answered – and, I think, correctly – that presidents, under the Irish Constitution, don't have policies. But perhaps a president can have a theme. If he can, then I have found the answer for my friends of the press. The *theme* of my septennat (*más cead sin le Dia* [God willing]) will again be that of my early student years, 'Community Spirit' – how sorely needed in part of this strife-torn island – with the new European dimension added and, never forgetting, our brothers of the Third World.

There was a very great American President, on whose birthday I was born, Abraham Lincoln, who permitted himself, on solemn and unsolemn occasions to tell a story. Last Saturday morning I sat in my old office in Luxembourg as two men from the local furniture removers packed a few pictures, and my law books. It was a scene reminiscent of the last act of Chekov's 'Cherry Orchard', without the orchard. The remover employs an international team of workers. The two men assigned to this job were English. One of the men spoke with a rich British brogue; he is a native speaker of Cockney, and has an Irish mother. The three of us chatted desultorily; but the Cockney was the most vocal of the party. He asked what I was. I said a judge. 'But,' he insisted, 'you are going to be president of something?' I explained.

He inquired how the President was elected and, answering in general terms, I said, 'by the people.' Was I in politics? I shook my head, and told him of my unsuccess (Senate and Dáil) of more than 20 years ago. 'But,' he said, 'you weren't good enough to be elected to Parliament, and (then interrogatively) you are good enough to be President'. After a pause, he added meditatively: 'It's a bit strange; stood for Parliament four times and (beautiful verb) fell, and yet they let you…'. His voice trailed off in perplexity. We both fell silent. I hadn't the heart to tell him, and I was too good a theatre man to say, that one can be perfectly validly elevated to the office of President, without election by the people, pursuant to Article 12, section 4, sub-section 5 of Bunreacht na hÉireann, when only one candidate is nominated.

All this comes of my having discovered at an early stage that I was born on the same day as Abraham Lincoln. May I say, simply, I would like to think I might try to fill Lincoln's role too in another respect: in trying to bind up the wounds of this troubled land.

I once had a small part in a John Drinkwater play. Among other plays he also wrote one on Lincoln. But my part was in his Trojan war play, algebraically named, 'X=O', a play about the tragedy and futility of war. I saw it done, I think, in the Gate. It could be a very relevant revival.

I am always anxious to know what young people are thinking. One of my god-children is a second-year university student. A few days ago I was in his bedroom and on the wall in large print – together with a great deal of other illustrative matter that need not be specified – was a quotation from the American author, Thoreau. I wrote it down. Here it is: 'If a man does not keep pace with his companions, perhaps it is because he hears a different drummer. Let him step to the music which he hears, however measured or far away'.

I have chosen to repeat that quotation here today, because it seems to me that Thoreau is relevant to the modern world in several ways. But no less I have to chosen to repeat the quotation because of its imagery; and that, of course, means the particular musical instrument on which Thoreau sounds out his idea.

Does anyone now read Standish O'Grady's 'Bog of Stars'? The story is set in the years when 'the golden times of great Eliza was drawing to its close'. In a word, a drummer boy heroically asserts his ancient allegiance – what that allegiance was is unimportant – court-martialled, his wrists pinioned he is pitched into Mona-Reulta – Bog of Stars.

'Then the sun sets, and the still night increased, and where the drummer boy had gone down a bright star shone; it was the evening star, the star of love, which is also the morning star, the star of hope and bravery'.

As we look at history, let us admire courage and conviction – wherever we find them. And, in respect of the latter, peacefully let us argue the case for change. It was Cromwell, a republican who sojourned in this city on unrepublican business, who, in a scriptural phrase, wrote to Scottish friends: 'I beseech you, in the bowels of Christ, think it possible you may be mistaken'.

Ag druidim chun deire dom, ceadaighidh dhom, más é do thoil é, beannú do bheirt sheanóirí atá anso inniu, go ndeaghaidh a n-iompar agus a n-uaisleacht i bhfeidhm orm go láidir ó laethe m'óige amach. Uimhir a haon, beannaím le hómós d'Eamon de Valera, iar-Uachtarán na hÉireann, atá ina Oisín i ndiaidh na Féinne, acht nach lugha-de san a éirim agus a aigne. Uimhir a dó. Beannaím, mar an gcéadna, do iar-Thaoiseach Éireann, John A. Costello – now at 84 still a very active Father of the Bar (agus féadaim a rádh gan áidbhéil), whose friendship and kindness I have known since my first faltering steps in the Four Courts more than 40 years ago. Ag beannú don bheirt sheanóir seo (Dia go deo leo) beannaím don il-uimhir sean-sheadairí, idir fheara agus mhná, ar fuaid na hÉireann go bhfuil misneach na hóige riamh ina gcroí.

[As I conclude, permit me, please, to salute two elders who are here today and whose conduct and nobility had a big impact on me from the days of my youth. First, I am honoured to salute Eamon de Valera, former President of Ireland, who is a survivor when others have passed away, but whose talent and mental powers are none the weaker for this. Second, I similarly salute the former Taoiseach of Ireland, John A. Costello – now at 84 still a very active Father of the Bar (and I may say this without exaggeration), whose friendship and kindness I have known since my first faltering steps in the Four Courts more than 40 years ago. In saluting these two elders (may God be with them for ever), I salute a big number of elderly people, men and women, all over Ireland, who retain the courage of youth in their hearts.]

A single personal note: we, my wife and I, are simple people, and we would like to be able to retain some of the simplicity of life in the new office which we are now to fill. May I put it in a sentence: if kings may ride bicycles, why then, *a fortiori*, presidents may pedal too. Is there a better way to reduce oil needs and improve national health?

We approach the feast of the Prince of Peace. Can we – could we – may we, find truce in Ireland as we approach that Day of Days. And if this be granted, is it too bold to hope thereafter for a temporary extension – to be prolonged indefinitely and to eventuate at last, one day, in a durable, just peace among all who live in our beloved sea-girt land.

> *Dia go deo le hÉirinn*
> *Agus le pobal Fodhla*
> *I gcéin agus i gcomhgar*
> *pé áit go bhfuilid*
> *pé bocht, saidhbhir*
> *pé lag, láidir*
> *pé sean, óg*
> *Dia dár stiúradh-na uile*
> *Ar chomhgar na síothchána agus an chirt.*

> [God be forever with Ireland
> And with the people of Ireland
> Abroad and at home
> Wherever they be
> Whether poor or rich
> Whether weak or strong
> Whether old or young
> May God guide us all
> On the path of peace and justice.]

PATRICK HILLERY, 3 DECEMBER 1976

A Thaoisigh Uasail, go raibh míle maith agat as ucht do bheannacht agus dea-mhéin. Is mór an meas agus is luachmhar é, do mo bhean-chéile agus dom féin, do bheith i láthair anseo inniu an oiread sin cuairteoiri céimiúla agus cáirde. Táimid buíoch agus faoi chomaoin agaibh go léir. [The next paragraph is a slightly abbreviated English rendering of this.]

Taoiseach, thank you for your best wishes. My wife and I appreciate greatly the presence here today of so many distinguished visitors and friends. We are grateful to you all.

We live in communities, large and small. If community life is to work well, and is to offer that sense of continuity and stability, even during times of great change, it must have a framework of laws and accepted conventions of behaviour which offer the protection of discipline while tolerating the demands of democracy and of personal individual liberty. I believe we have this balance in Ireland and in the European Community. It is a balance which adjusts itself through our political institutions. The process of adjustment requires the constant attention of those, like governments and presidents, who have institutional responsibility. It is a process which relates people to one another, to their institutions, and relates these institutions to one another.

When I think of the presidency, I think of it as an institution so functioning in the context of our Irish community. I accept its duties and responsibilities and the obligation to respect both the constitutional framework and the democratic will.

In finding their balance within the general order of things all my predecessors have contributed to the evolution of the presidency. My immediate predecessor, Cearbhall Ó Dálaigh, to whom I pay tribute here now, has done so in an important way.

I believe it will be neither an easy nor an instant accomplishment for me to make my contribution to the further evolution of the office. In seeking to serve Ireland in a new role my first task will be to reflect on what may be achieved and what must be conserved and protected. It is in this spirit of reflection, a spirit which I believe springs from a need felt throughout Ireland, that I take up office now.

Cuirim mo bheannacht ó chroí amach chuig muintir na hÉireann. Guím síocháin dóibh agus guím chomh maith sonas agus dea-rath orthu.

[I convey my heartfelt greetings to the people of Ireland. I pray for peace and I also pray for happiness and good fortune for them.]

PATRICK HILLERY, 3 DECEMBER 1983

A Thaoisigh Uasail, gabhaim míle buíochas leat as a bhfuil ráite agat. Is mór agam do bheannacht agus do dhea-mhéin ar ócáid seo m'insealbhaithe mar Uachtarán na hÉireann. Is mór an t-ábhar áthais dom féin agus dom bhean chéile a oiread sin seancháirde a fheiceáil ar an gcomhluadar céimiúil seo. Táimid an-bhuíoch díbh go léir. Is mór againn bhur dtacaíocht agus bhur gcáirdeas. Is é mo ghuí inniu go mbeidh rath, sonas agus síocháin ar ár muintir go léir sa bhaile agus i gcríocha i gcéin.

[Taoiseach, I extend you many thanks for what you have said. I appreciate your salutation and good wishes on this occasion of my installation as President of Ireland. My wife and I are delighted to see so many old friends in this distinguished company. We are very grateful to all of you. We appreciate your support and your friendship. I pray today for good fortune, happiness and peace for all our people at home and abroad.]

Taoiseach, I thank you most sincerely for the warm good wishes which you have expressed to me. My wife and I are very happy to see so many friends here. To all of you, we are deeply indebted for your friendship and support. Among my most pleasant and enduring memories of the past seven years is the warm concern for others expressed in action by so many people in our community. No words could express adequately my deep admiration for the commitment of so many voluntary workers to the welfare of the young, the people who are old and the people who are handicapped. By their generosity and dedication they have enriched our community, strengthened the bonds which bind it together and set an example for all of us. I take this opportunity of thanking them for their work for others and for the example which they have set for each one of us.

We live in days of anxiety, unrest and uncertainty. The problems of our times affect the lives of all of us. While the solution of some of these problems may appear at times to be beyond our power to influence, the decision as to how we behave towards one another rests solely with ourselves. It is for us to create the environment in which we choose to live, to establish the standards, rules of behaviour and conventions which will guide our lives in the years ahead. We owe it especially to our young people to give them the firm security of agreed rules and standards of behaviour and respect for the dignity and God-given rights of all.

This is a time for courage and conviction, a time which demands the resolute use of that great potential for good which exists in abundance in the Irish people. My hope for Ireland is that we turn away from acrimony, dissension and disagreement which are destroying everything which we should value, and join our hearts and minds in united cause for the peace and well-being of all.

Go dtreora Dia muid [May God guide us]

Mary Robinson, 3 December 1990

Citizens of Ireland, *Mná na hÉireann agus fir na hÉireann* [women of Ireland and men of Ireland], you have chosen me to represent you and I am humbled by and grateful for your trust.

The Ireland I will be representing is a new Ireland, open, tolerant, inclusive. Many of you who voted for me did so without sharing all my views. This, I believe, is a significant signal of change, a sign, however modest, that we have already passed the threshold to a new, pluralist Ireland.

The recent revival of an old concept of the Fifth Province expresses this emerging Ireland of tolerance and empathy. The old Irish term for province is *coicead*, meaning a 'fifth'; and yet, as everyone knows, there are only four geographical provinces on this island. So where is the fifth? The Fifth Province is not anywhere here or there, north or south, east or west. It is a place within each one of us – that place that is open to the other, that swinging door which allows us to venture out and others to venture in. Ancient legends divided Ireland into four quarters and a 'middle,' although they differed about the location of this middle or Fifth Province. While Tara was the political centre of Ireland, tradition has it that this Fifth Province acted as a second centre, a necessary balance. If I am a symbol of anything I would like to be a symbol of this reconciling and healing Fifth Province.

My primary role as President will be to represent this State. But the State is not the only model of community with which Irish people can and do identify. Beyond our State there is a vast community of Irish emigrants extending not only across our neighbouring island – which has provided a home away from home for several Irish generations – but also throughout the continents of North America, Australia and of course Europe itself. There are over 70 million people living on this globe who claim Irish descent. I will be proud to represent them. And I would like to see Áras an Uachtaráin, my official residence, serve on something of an annual basis – as a place where our emigrant communities could send representatives for a get-together of the extended Irish family abroad.

There is another level of community which I will represent. Not just the national, not just the global, but the local community. Within our State there are a growing number of local and regional communities determined to express their own creativity, identity, heritage and initiative in new and exciting ways. In my travels around Ireland I have found local community groups thriving on a new sense of self-confidence and self-empowerment. Whether it was groups concerned with adult education, employment initiative, women's support, local history and heritage, environmental concern or community culture, one of the most enriching discoveries was to witness the extent of this local empowerment at work.

As President I will seek to the best of my abilities to promote this growing sense of local participatory democracy, this emerging movement of self development and self expression which is surfacing more and more at grassroots level. This is the face of modern Ireland.

Ba mhaith liom a rá go bhfuair mé taithneamh agus pléisiúr as an taisteal a rinne mé le míosa anuas ar fuaid na hÉireann. Is fíor álainn agus iontach an tír atá againn, agus is álainn an pobal iad muintir na hÉireann. Fuair mé teachtaireacht ón bpobal seo agus mé ag dul timpeall: 'Teastaíonn Uachtarán uainn gur féidir linn bheith bródúil aisti, ach, níos mó ná sin, gur féidir linn bheith bródúil lena chéile – toisc gur Éireannaigh sinn, agus go bhfuil traidisiúin agus cultúr álainn againn.' Is cuid an-tábhachtach don gcultúr sin an Ghaeilge – an teanga bheo – fé mar atá á labhairt sa Ghaeltacht agus ag daoine eile ar fuaid na hÉireann. Tá aistear eile le déanamh anois agam – aistear cultúrtha, leis an saibhreas iontach atá sa teanga Ghaeilge a bhaint amach díom féin. Tá súil agam go leanfaidh daoine eile mé atá ar mo nós fhéin – beagán as cleachtadh sa Ghaeilge–agus go raghaimíd ar aghaidh le chéile le taithneamh agus pléisiúr a fháil as ár dteanga álainn féin.

[I would like to say that I got enjoyment and pleasure from the journey I made over several months around Ireland. Our country is beautiful and wonderful, and the people of Ireland are lovely. I got a message from the people while travelling around: 'We need a President of whom we can be proud, but, more than that, one of whom we can be proud together – because we are Irish, and we have a lovely tradition and culture'. Irish – the living language – as it is spoken in the Gaeltacht and by other people throughout Ireland is a very important part of that culture. I now have another journey to make – a cultural journey, to bring out the wonderful richness in the Irish language for myself. I hope that others who are in the same position as me will follow me – a little out of practice in Irish – and that we will continue together to get joy and pleasure from our own lovely language.]

The best way we can contribute to a new integrated Europe of the 1990s is by having a confident sense of our Irishness. Here again we must play to our strengths – take full advantage of our vibrant cultural resources in music, art, drama, literature and film; value the role of our educators; promote and preserve our unique environmental and geographical resources of relatively pollution-free lakes, rivers, landscapes and seas; encourage and publicly support local initiative projects in aquaculture, forestry, fishing, alternative energy and smallscale technology.

Looking outwards from Ireland, I would like on your behalf to contribute to the international protection and promotion of human rights. One of our greatest national resources has always been, and still is, our ability to serve as a moral and political conscience in world affairs. We have a long history of providing spiritual, cultural, and social assistance to other countries in need – most notably in Latin America, Africa and other Third World countries. And we can continue to promote these values by taking principled and independent stands on issues of international importance.

As the elected President of this small democratic country I assume office at a vital moment in Europe's history. Ideological boundaries that have separated East from West are withering away at an astounding pace. Eastern countries are seeking to participate as full partners in a restructured and economically buoyant Europe. The stage is set for a new common European home based on respect for human rights, pluralism, tolerance and openness to new ideas. The European Convention on Human Rights – one of the finest achievements of the Council of Europe – is asserting itself as the natural Constitution for the new Europe. These developments have created one of the major challenges for the 1990s.

If it is time, as Joyce's Stephen Dedalus remarked, that the Irish began to forge in the smithy of our souls 'the uncreated conscience of our race' – might we not also take on the still 'uncreated conscience' of the wider international community? Is it not time that the small started believing again that it is beautiful, that the periphery can rise up and speak out on equal terms with the centre, that the most outlying island community of the European Community really has something 'strange and precious' to contribute to the sea-change presently sweeping through the entire continent of Europe? As a native of Ballina, one of the most western towns in the most western province of the most western nation in Europe, I want to say – 'the West's awake.'

I turn now to another place close to my heart, Northern Ireland. As the elected choice of the people of this part of our island I want to extend the hand of friendship and of love to both communities in the other part. And I want to do this with no hidden agenda, no strings attached. As the person chosen by you to symbolise this Republic and to project our self image to others, I will seek to encourage mutual understanding and tolerance between all the different communities sharing this island.

In seeking to do this I shall rely to a large extent on symbols. But symbols are what unite and divide people. Symbols give us our identity, our self image, our way of explaining ourselves to ourselves and to others. Symbols in turn determine the kinds of stories we tell and the stories we tell determine the kind of history we make and remake. I want Áras an Uachtaráin to be a place where people can tell diverse stories – in the knowledge that there is someone there to listen.

I want this Presidency to promote the telling of stories – stories of celebration through the arts and stories of conscience and of social justice. As a woman, I want women who have felt themselves outside history to be written back into history, in the words of Eavan Boland, 'finding a voice where they found a vision.'

May God direct me so that my Presidency is one of justice, peace and love. May I have the fortune to preside over an Ireland at a time of exciting transformation when we enter a new Europe where old wounds can be healed, a time when, in the words of Seamus Heaney, 'hope and history rhyme.' May it be a Presidency where I the President can sing to you, citizens of Ireland, the joyous refrain of the 14th-century Irish poet as recalled by W. B. Yeats: 'I am of Ireland ... come dance with me in Ireland.' *Go raibh míle maith agaibh go léir.* [Many thanks to all of you.]

MARY McALEESE, 11 NOVEMBER 1997

A uaisle, Lá stairiúil é seo im' shaol féin, i saol mo mhuintire, agus i saol na tíre go léir. Is pribhléid mhór í a bheith tofa mar Uachtarán na hÉireann, le bheith mar ghuth na hÉireann i gcéin is i gcóngair.

[Ladies and gentlemen, this is an historic day in my life, in that of my family, and in that of the whole country. It is a great privilege to be elected President of Ireland, to be the voice of Ireland abroad and at home.]

This is a historic day in my life, in the life of my family and in the life of the country. It is a wonderful privilege for me to be chosen as Uachtarán na hÉireann, to be a voice for Ireland at home and abroad.

I am honoured and humbled to be successor to seven exemplary Presidents. Their differing religious, political, geographical and social origins speak loudly of a Presidency which has always been wide open and all embracing. Among them were Presidents from Connaught, Leinster and Munster to say nothing of America and London. It is my special privilege and delight to be the first President from Ulster.

The span of almost sixty years since the first Presidential Inauguration has seen a nation transformed. This Ireland which stands so confidently on the brink of the 21st century and the third millennium is one our forbears dreamed of and yearned for; a prospering Ireland, accomplished, educated, dynamic, innovative, compassionate, proud of its people, its language, and of its vast heritage; an Ireland, at the heart of the European Union, respected by nations and cultures across the world.

The scale of what we have already accomplished in such a short time allows us to embrace the future with well-based confidence and hope. It is the people of Ireland who, in a million big and small ways, in quiet acts of hard work, heroism and generosity have built up the fabric of home, community and country on which the remarkable success story of today's Ireland is built.

Over many generations there have been very special sources of inspiration who have nurtured our talent and instilled determination into this country. Many outstanding politicians, public servants, voluntary workers, clergy of all denominations and religious, teachers and particularly parents have through hard and difficult times worked and sacrificed so that our children could blossom to their fullest potential.

They are entitled to look with satisfaction at what they have achieved. May we never become so cynical that we forget to be grateful. I certainly owe them a deep personal debt and as President I hope to find many opportunities both to repay that debt and to assist in the great work of encouraging our children to believe in themselves and in their country.

Among those who are also owed an enormous debt of thanks are the countless emigrants whose letters home with dollars and pound notes, earned in grinding loneliness thousands of miles from home, bridged the gap between the Ireland they left and the Ireland which greets them today when they return as tourists or return to stay. They are a crucial part of our global Irish family. In every continent they have put their ingenuity and hard work at the service of new homelands. They have kept their love of Ireland, its traditions and its culture deep in their hearts so that wherever we travel in the world there is always a part of Ireland of which we can be proud and which in turn takes pride in us. I hope over the next seven years there will be many opportunities for me to celebrate with them.

At our core we are a sharing people. Selfishness has never been our creed. Commitment to the welfare of each other has fired generations of voluntary organisations and a network of everyday neighbourliness which weaves together the caring fabric of our country. It has sent our missionaries, development workers and peacekeepers to the aid of distressed peoples in other parts of the world. It has made us a country of refuge for the hurt and dispossessed of other troubled places. It is the fuel which drives us to tackle the many social problems we face, problems which cynicism and self doubt can never redress but painstaking commitment can. We know our duty is to spread the benefits of our prosperity to those whose lives are still mired in poverty, unemployment, worry and despair. There can be no rest until the harsh gap between the comfortable and the struggling has been bridged.

The late Cearbhall Ó Dálaigh, Ireland's fifth president and, dare I say it, one of three lawyers to grace the office, said at his inauguration in 1974: 'Presidents, under the Irish Constitution don't have policies. But ... a President can have a theme.'

The theme of my Presidency, the Eighth Presidency, is Building Bridges. These bridges require no engineering skills but they will demand patience, imagination and courage for Ireland's pace of change is now bewilderingly fast. We grow more complex by the day. Our dancers, singers, writers, poets, musicians, sportsmen and women, indeed our last President herself, are giants on the world stage. Our technologically skilled young people are in demand everywhere. There is an invigorating sense of purpose about us.

There are those who absorb the rush of newness with delight. There are those who are more cautious, even fearful. Such tensions are part of our creative genius, they form the energy which gives us our unique identity, our particularity.

I want to point the way to a reconciliation of these many tensions and to see Ireland grow ever more comfortable and at ease with the flowering diversity that is now all around us. To quote a Belfast poet, Louis MacNeice, 'a single purpose can be founded on a jumble of opposites.'

Yet I know to speak of reconciliation is to raise a nervous query in the hearts of some North of the border, in the place of my birth. There is no more appropriate place to address that query than here in Dublin Castle, a place where the complex history of these two neighbouring and now very neighbourly islands has seen many chapters written. It is fortuitous too that the timing of today's Inauguration coincides with the commemoration of those who died so tragically and heroically in two world wars. I think of nationalist and unionist, who fought and died together in those wars, the differences which separated them at home fading into insignificance as the bond of their common humanity forged friendships as intense as love can make them.

In Ireland, we know only too well the cruelty and capriciousness of violent conflict. Our own history has been hard on lives young and old. Too hard. Hard on those who died and those left behind with only shattered dreams and poignant memories. We hope and pray, indeed we insist, that we have seen the last of violence. We demand the right to solve our problems by dialogue and the noble pursuit of consensus. We hope to see that consensus pursued without the language of hatred and contempt and we wish all those engaged in that endeavour well.

That it can be done – we know. We need look no further than our own European continent where once bitter enemies now work conscientiously with each other and for each other as friends and partners. The greatest salute to the memory of all our dead and the living whom they loved, would be the achievement of agreement and peace.

I think of the late Gordon Wilson who faced his unbearable sorrow ten years ago at the horror that was Enniskillen. His words of love and forgiveness shocked us as if we were hearing them for the very first time, as if they had not been uttered first two thousand years ago. His work, and the work of so many peacemakers who have risen above the awesome pain of loss to find a bridge to the other side, is work I want to help in every way I can. No side has a monopoly on pain. Each has suffered intensely.

I know the distrusts go deep and the challenge is awesome.

Across this island, North, South, East and West, there are people of such greatness of heart that I know with their help it can be done. I invite them, to work in partnership with me to dedicate ourselves to the task of creating a wonderful millennium gift to the Child of Bethlehem whose 2000th birthday we will soon celebrate – the gift of an island where difference is celebrated with joyful curiosity and generous respect and where in the words of John Hewitt 'each may grasp his neighbour's hand as friend.'

There will be those who are wary of such invitations, afraid that they are being invited to the edge of a precipice. To them I have dedicated a poem, written by the English poet, Christopher Logue, himself a veteran of the Second World War.

Come to the edge.
We might fall.
Come to the edge.
It's too high!
Come to the edge

And they came,
and he pushed
and they flew.

No one will be pushing, just gently inviting, but I hope that if ever and whenever you decide to walk over that edge, there will be no need to fly, you will find there a firm and steady bridge across which we will walk together both ways.

Ireland sits tantalisingly ready to embrace a golden age of affluence, self-assurance tolerance and peace. It will be my most profound privilege to be President of this beautiful, intriguing country.

May I ask those of faith, whatever that faith may be, to pray for me and for our country that we will use these seven years well, to create a future where in the words of William Butler Yeats: 'Everything we look upon is blest'. *Déanaimis an todhchaí sin a chruthú le chéile.* [We will create that future together.]

MARY McALEESE, 11 NOVEMBER 2004

A Uaisle, is le gairdeas croí, le buíochas agus le humhlaíocht a labhraím libh anseo ar maidin, agus mé ar tí tosú amach ar an dara tréimhse seacht mbliana de sheirbhís an phobail. Is mór an phribhléid dom a bheith tofa arís mar Uachtarán na hÉireann. Is é mo ghuí agus mo rún daingean dualgaisí na hardoifige seo a chomhlíonadh go hionraic, coinsiasach.

[Ladies and gentlemen, it is with a joyous heart, with gratitude and with humility that I address you this morning, as I begin the second seven-year term in the service of the people. It is a great privilege for me to have been elected again as President of Ireland. It is my prayer and my firm intention to fulfil the duties of this high office honestly and conscientiously.]

I begin this second term as President of Ireland with fresh anticipation, proud to represent one of the world's most successful and dynamic countries with a rags to riches, conflict to peace story that I know inspires many in a troubled world.

Ireland has vaulted from the despondency of 'ceann faoi' to the confidence of 'can do' in a remarkably short time. With so much changing both at home and in the world around us, today is a good opportunity to take stock and reflect on the Ireland that I will represent in a role outside of politics but inside the lives of our people.

We are a country of newly opened doors instead of emigrant boats, flying on two wings, propelled by the combined genius of our men and our women. We wrestle with our prosperity almost as much as we relish it. We are loudly impatient for many frustratingly inadequate things to be better. We worry about matters that hollow out our optimism like youth suicide, racism, binge-drinking, street crime and corruption.

We know our current economic success cannot be a destination in itself but a route to one of our primary ambitions as a nation – to bring prosperity and security to every single citizen. We have struggled with that other ambition for the unity of our island, agreeing overwhelmingly to an honourable compromise in which we acknowledged the right of the people of Northern Ireland to decide their own destiny and declared our desire to work with them in peaceful partnership.

Cherishing the best of our past, we turn to our future not knowing exactly what it holds but with a clear idea of the hard work ahead of us, work for all of us as citizens and not simply for government alone.

We are busier than before, harder to please, less heedful of the traditional voices of moral guidance and almost giddy with greater freedom and choice. Our Constitution is an important ethical compass directing us to a practical patriotism, 'to promote the common good', to choose responsible citizenship over irresponsible individualism.

Our population is growing, new neighbourhoods of strangers are springing up, immigrants bring with them different cultures and embrace the richness of ours, as I have observed in the schools where their children speak to me proudly in Irish. Infrastructure of all sorts is struggling to catch up, including the human infrastructure we offer each other through friendship and community solidarity. The cushion of consumerism is no substitute for the comfort of community. And if our country is to be strong and resilient in the face of its problems and its ambitions in this time of transformation, it needs strong resilient communities.

I have been privileged as President to see the colossal work undertaken by the individuals, organisations and partnerships that supports and sustains our nation's great heartland of community. Community cannot be created by government and it doesn't happen by coincidence. We make it happen ourselves by unselfishly committing our talents, our money and that precious commodity, time, to the service of each other.

It will be my mission to nurture and celebrate commitment to community and to responsible citizenship and to encourage self-belief among the most marginalized. I intend to reach out to our wonderful young people, willing them on to become good leaders rather than the badly-led – problem-solvers rather than problems. When I look at the solid work and great imagination that have created our economic miracle, our peace process, our vibrant culture, our respected place in international politics; when I remember the massive effort that gave us the Special Olympics, I am reassured that there is little we cannot deal with effectively if we work together.

If community solidarity is vital to social stability and progress at home, global solidarity is equally vital in world affairs, all the more so in an era when the multilateral ethos of the United Nations has come under strain.

Today November 11th is Armistice Day, a commemoration of those dreadful years when Europeans killed each other in their millions. How different Europe is now. On May 1st, Áras an Uachtaráin hosted the Day of Welcomes as the European Union grew to twenty-five member states and their leaders gathered under one roof for the first time since the First World War.

Ireland has played a hugely significant role in the development of our Union and its values of democracy, human rights, respect for difference and consensus-based politics. The opportunities created by enlargement are waiting to be harvested and I look forward to promoting our country within the Union and to showcasing our membership of the Union around the world.

Ireland's fortunes are linked to global politics as never before and though we are a small peripheral island we have a fascinating and exceptional engagement with the world that spans every conceivable connection – from centuries-old ties of religion and kinship, through championing of the world's poor, to trade in the most sophisticated modern technologies in which we are market leaders.

As President I have a key role in the renewal and development of ties to our global Irish family, Ireland's unpaid ambassadors, who make our name and nature known throughout the world. We have experienced the considerable benefits that flow from those intimate friendships. As one of the world's leading export nations we have also come to realise the vast potential that lies in befriending and trading with countries not so well-known to us. I will continue to make it my responsibility to assist in the development of our trade in new markets, to get to know new peoples and their cultures and so help to secure both our nation's wellbeing and global solidarity.

The great divide between rich and poor nations, already worsened by the calamity of Aids and knowledge poverty, has become more complex still as East/West divisions sharpen alarmingly and dangerous tensions fester.

Neutral Ireland is uniquely qualified for the crucial, painstaking work of establishing understanding and trust across those cultural chasms. We are widely respected. We have a talent for friendship, a history of transition from a third-world to a first-world country and a wholehearted commitment to international institutions and international law. I look forward to playing a part in building the human bridges of mutual respect and care which are so necessary to end the cycle of human misery and to keep our world safe.

Seven years ago the bridge of peace on this island was a structure in the making. Today more people than ever are committed to its construction and the once massive gulf of mistrust has been reduced to one last step. I use this occasion to ask the hesitant to muster the courage to complete the journey across and let the bright new landscape of hope reveal itself. For my part, I pledge to do my best to make us comfortable in each other's company and unafraid of a shared future.

Many people are working hard to make ours a country, a people and a time to be proud of. I offer thanks to them and for them. I thank everyone who has helped me these past seven years and who gave me the confidence to stand again. I again ask those of faith to pray for me and for our beloved country so that in these coming years we will leave a legacy of good for our children – a legacy so memorably anticipated by Seamus Heaney on 1st May when he exhorted us to: 'Move lips, move minds and make new meanings flare.' *Dia dar gcumhdach agus dar stiuradh! Go raibh míle maith agaibh.* [May God help and direct us. Thank you very much.]

MICHAEL D. HIGGINS, 11 NOVEMBER 2011

Muintir na hÉireann [People of Ireland] and friends of Ireland at home and abroad, there can be no greater honour than to have been elected *Uachtarán na hÉireann* – President of Ireland. I thank you the people of Ireland for the honour you have bestowed upon me and I accept and appreciate the great responsibilities of that office.

Citizens of Ireland, you have chosen me to be your ninth President, to represent you at home and abroad, and to serve as a symbol of an Irishness of which we can all be proud. An Irishness which is carried by every citizen and which we must recall and forge anew together.

I enter the ninth Presidency with a sense of humility, but also with confidence in the great capacity of our people, the people of Ireland, not only to transcend present difficulties but to realise all of the wonderful possibilities that I believe await us in the years ahead.

I wish to acknowledge the immense contribution of those who have previously served in this office, particularly the two great women who have immediately preceded me.

They have made contributions that developed our consciousness of human rights, inclusion, and the important task of deepening and sustaining peace within and between communities in every part of our island. It is work I will endeavour to continue and build upon.

As your President, I am grateful for the extent of the support, the strong mandate, you have given me. I also realise the challenges that I face, that we face together, in closing a chapter that has left us fragile as an economy, but most of all wounded as a society, with unacceptable levels of unemployment, mortgage insecurity, collapsing property values and many broken expectations.

During my campaign for the Presidency, I encountered that pain particularly among the most vulnerable of our people. However, I also recognise the will of all of our people to move beyond anger, frustration or cynicism and to draw on our shared strengths. To close the chapter on that which has failed, that which was not the best version of ourselves as a people, and open a new chapter based on a different version of our Irishness – will require a transition in our political thinking, in our view of the public world, in our institutions, and, most difficult of all, in our consciousness.

In making that transformation, it is necessary to move past the assumptions which have failed us and to work together for such a different set of values as will enable us to build a sustainable social economy and a society which is profoundly ethical and inclusive. A society and a state which will restore trust and confidence at home and act as a worthy symbol of Irishness abroad, inviting relationships of respect and co-operation across the world.

We must seek to build together an active, inclusive citizenship; based on participation, equality, respect for all and the flowering of creativity in all its forms. A confident people is our hope, a people at ease with itself, a people that grasps the deep meaning of the proverb 'ní neart go cur le chéile' – our strength lies in our common weal – our social solidarity.

Sin iad mór-théamaí na hUachtaránachta atá curtha romham agam, agus mé lán-dóchasach go bhfuilimid ar tháirseach ré nua d'Éirinn agus d'Éireannaigh, sa bhaile agus i gcéin. Ré nua ina mbeidh bunluacha na cothroime agus an chirt, agus spiorad na cruthaíochta , faoi bhláth: poblacht, a mbeidh Éireannaigh de gach aicme agus traidisiún bródúil aisti.

[These are the main themes of my presidency as I have set them out for myself, as I am very hopeful that we are on the threshold of a new era for Ireland and the Irish, at home and abroad. A new era in which basic values of fairness and justice, and the spirit of creativity, will flourish: a republic of which Irish people of every class and tradition will be proud.]

My Presidency will be a Presidency of transformation, recognising and building on the many positive initiatives already under way in communities, in the economy, and in individual and collective efforts throughout our land. It will be a Presidency that celebrates all of our possibilities. It will seek to be of assistance and encouragement to investment and job creation, to innovation and original thinking – a Presidency of ideas – recognising and open to new paradigms of thought and action. It will aspire to turn the best of ideas into living realities for all of our people, realising our limitless possibilities – *ár féidireachtaí gan teorainn*.

In implementing the mandate you have given me, I will seek to achieve an inclusive citizenship where every citizen participates and everyone is treated with respect. I will highlight and support initiatives for inclusion across Ireland and also make it a priority to visit and to support the participation of the most excluded in our society, including those in institutional care.

I will champion creative communities who are bringing about positive change at local level by giving recognition to their achievements on the national stage. I believe that when we encourage the seedbed of creativity in our communities and ensure that each child and adult has the opportunity for creative expression, we also lay the groundwork for sustainable employment in creative industries and enrich our social, cultural and economic development.

In promoting inclusion and creativity, I will be inviting all citizens, of all ages, to make their own imaginative and practical contribution to the shaping of our shared future. Active citizenship requires the will and the opportunity to participate at every level and in every way – to be the arrow; not the target.

Next year Bunreacht na hÉireann is 75 years old and a Constitutional Convention is planned by Government. As President, I encourage all citizens, of all ages, at home and abroad to take the opportunity of engaging with this important review as an opportunity to reflect on where we have come from and on how we might see ourselves into the future.

During my Presidency, I also intend to hold a number of Presidency Seminars which may reflect and explore themes important to our shared life yet separate and wider than legislative demand, themes such as the restoration of trust in our institutions, the ethical connection between our economy and society, the future of a Europe built on peace, social solidarity and sustainability.

The first of these seminars will focus on being young in Ireland. It will address issues of participation, education, employment, emigration and mental health. I hope also that the seminars during the next seven years might encompass consideration of global issues, stressing the importance of the ethical connection between politics, economy, development and society.

In preparing for my Presidency, I recognise that our long struggle for freedom has produced a people who believe in the right of the individual mind to see the world in its own way and indeed that individual innovation and independence of mind has given Ireland many distinguished contributors in culture and science, often insufficiently celebrated.

However, in more recent years, we saw the rise of a different kind of individualism – closer to an egotism based on purely material considerations – that tended to value the worth of a person in terms of the accumulation of wealth rather than their fundamental dignity. That was our loss, the source in part, of our present difficulties. Now it is time to turn to an older wisdom that, while respecting material comfort and security as a basic right of all, also recognises that many of the most valuable things in life cannot be measured.

Our successes after all in the eyes of so many in the world have been in the cultural and spiritual areas – in our humanitarian, peace-building and human rights work – in our literature, art, drama and song – and in how that drama and song have helped us cope with adversity, soothed the very pain which they describe so well, and opened the space for new possibilities.

Our arts celebrate the people talking, singing, dancing and ultimately communing with each other. This is what James Connolly meant when he said that: 'Ireland without her people means nothing to me'. Connolly took pride in the past but, of course, felt that those who excessively worshipped that past were sometimes seeking to escape from the struggle and challenge of the present. He believed that Ireland was a work in progress, a country still to be fully imagined and invented – and that the future was exhilarating precisely in the sense that it was not fully knowable, measurable.

The demands and the rewards of building a real and inclusive Republic in its fullest sense remains as a challenge for us all, but it is one we should embrace together.

A decade of commemorations lies ahead – a decade that will require us to honestly explore and reflect on key episodes in our modern history as a nation; that will require us to draw on the ethics and politics of memory in such a way as will enable us not only to be sensitive to differing and incomplete versions of that history, but also to remain open to the making of reconciliation or to the acceptance of different versions of aspects and events of memory if required.

A common shared future built on the spirit of co-operation, the collective will and real participation in every aspect of the public world is achievable and I believe we can achieve it together. In our rich heritage some of our richest moments have been those that turned towards the future and a sense of what might be possible. It is that which brought us to independence. It is that which has enabled us to overcome adversity and it is that which will enable us to transcend our present difficulties and celebrate the real Republic which is ours for the making.

Every age, after all, must have its own *Aisling* and dream of a better, kinder, happier, shared world. *Ní díomas ach dóchas a bheidh ag teastáil uainn ins na blianta dúshlánacha atá amach romhainn. Dóchas as ár n-oighreacht shaibhir, as ár ndúchas iolrach; dóchas as ár n-acmhainn samhlaíochta agus cruthaíochta; as an daonnacht choiteann a fáisceadh as stair chasta ár muintire i ngach cúinne d'Éirinn.* [It is not pride but hope that we will need in the challenging years ahead of us. Hope in respect of our rich inheritance; of our pluralist heritage; of our imaginative and creative capacity; of the common humanity that was squeezed from the complex history of our people in every corner of Ireland.]

It is my wish to be a President for all of the Irish at home and abroad. We Irish have been a diasporic people for a great part of our history. The circumstances that have impelled – and that continue to impel – many citizens to seek employment and a better life elsewhere, are not ordained by some mysterious hand of fate. They challenge our capacity to create a sustainable and prosperous economy and an inspiring model of the good society.

We, in our time, must address the real circumstances that generate involuntary emigration, and resolve that in the years ahead we will strive with all our energy and intellect, with mind and heart to create an Ireland which our young people do not feel they have to leave and to which our emigrants, or their children, may wish, in time, to return to work and live in dignity and prosperity. I invite all of the Irish, wherever they may be across the world, to become involved with us in that task of remaking our economy and society.

Agus, ár muintir atá lonnaithe i dtíortha ar fuaid an domhain mhóir, bíodh a gcás, a gcearta agus a ngaiscí siúd ar ár n-aire againn. Tá rian a saothair agus a ndíograis fágtha acu ar gach tír inar lonnaigh siad: ar an gcultúr polaitíochta agus creidimh, sna réimsí oideachais agus sláinte, san eolaíocht, san saol gnó agus sna h-ealaíona ar fad: agus i ngluaiseachtaí éagsúla ar son chearta daonna agus dínit an duine. Ní suarach iad na gaiscí seo mar thaisce inspioráide dúinne sa bhaile.

[And let us pay attention to the circumstances, rights and achievements of our people who are settled in countries over the whole world. They have left the imprint of their contribution and commitment in every country in which they have settled: on political and religious culture, in the education and health systems, in science, in business life and in all the arts: and in various movements for human rights and human dignity. These are no paltry achievements as a source of inspiration for us at home.]

Let these, then, be our shared hopes, our common purpose, as we face the future.

We Irish are a creative, resourceful, talented and warm people, with a firm sense of common decency and justice. Let us address the next seven years with hope and courage as we work together to build the future for our country – an Ireland we all feel part of, an Ireland we all feel proud of.

Muintir na hÉireann, ar aghaidh linn le chéile leis an dóchas agus an misneach sin a bhí is ba chóir a bheith i gcónaí in ár gcroí.

[People of Ireland, let us move along together with that hope and courage which was, and which rightly was, always in our hearts.]

APPENDIX 3

MEETINGS OF THE COUNCIL OF STATE, 1940–2013

No.	Date	Subject matter and outcome
1.	8 January 1940	Offences against the State (Amendment) Bill, 1940: referred to the Supreme Court; found compatible with constitution
2.	25 February 1943	School Attendance Bill, 1942: referred to the Supreme Court; found repugnant to constitution
3.	13 August 1947	Health Bill, 1947: signed without referral
4.	14 June 1961	Electoral (Amendment) Bill, 1961: referred to Supreme Court; found compatible with constitution
5.	6 March 1967	Income Tax Bill, 1966: signed without referral
6.	20 December 1968	Address to Houses of the Oireachtas: address to Houses, 21 January, 1969: *Fiftieth anniversary of the meeting of the First Dáil Éireann*
7.	10 March 1976	Criminal Law (Jurisdiction) Bill, 1975: referred to Supreme Court; found compatible with constitution.
8.	23 September 1976	Emergency Powers Bill, 1976: referred to Supreme Court; found compatible with constitution
9.	23 September 1976	Criminal Law Bill, 1976: signed without referral
10.	22 December 1981	Housing (Private Rented Dwellings) Bill, 1981: referred to Supreme Court; found repugnant to constitution
11.	20 December 1983	Electoral (Amendment) Bill, 1983: referred to Supreme Court; found repugnant to constitution
12.	5 December 1984	Criminal Justice Bill, 1983: signed without referral
13.	22 June 1988	Adoption (No. 2) Bill, 1987: referred to Supreme Court; found compatible with constitution

No.	Date	Subject matter and outcome
14.	30 October 1991	Fisheries (Amendment) Bill, 1990: signed without referral
15.	29 June 1992	Address to the Houses of the Oireachtas: address to Houses, 8 July 1992: *The Irish identity in Europe*
16.	1 December 1993	Matrimonial Home Bill, 1993: referred to Supreme Court; found repugnant to constitution
17.	1 March 1994	Criminal Justice Public Order Bill, 1993: signed without referral
18.	24 January 1995	Address to the Houses of the Oireachtas: address to Houses, 2 February 1995: *Cherishing the Irish diaspora*
19.	16 March 1995	Regulation of Information Services outside the State for Termination of Pregnancies Bill, 1995: referred to Supreme Court; found compatible with constitution
20.	1 April 1997	Employment Equality Bill, 1996: referred to Supreme Court; found repugnant to constitution
21.	6 May 1997	Equal Status Bill, 1997: referred to Supreme Court; found repugnant to constitution
22.	28 October 1999	Address to the Houses of the Oireachtas: address to Houses, 16 December 1999: *Millennium address*
23.	30 June 2000	(a) Planning and Development Bill, 1999: referred to Supreme Court; found compatible with constitution (b) Illegal Immigrants (Trafficking) Bill, 1999: referred to Supreme Court; found compatible with constitution
24.	8 April 2002	Housing (Miscellaneous Provisions) (No. 2) Bill, 2001: signed without referral
25.	21 December 2004	Health (Amendment) (No. 2) Bill, 2004: referred to Supreme Court; found repugnant to constitution
26.	9 May 2007	Criminal Justice Bill, 2007: signed without referral
27.	22 July 2009	(a) Defamation Bill, 2006: signed without referral (b) Criminal Justice (Amendment) Bill, 2009: signed without referral
28.	21 December 2010	Credit Institutions (Stabilisation) Bill, 2010: signed without referral
29.	29 July 2013	Protection of Life During Pregnancy Bill, 2013: signed without referral

REFERENCES

All-party Oireachtas Committee on the Constitution (1998) *Third Progress Report: The President* (Dublin: Stationery Office)

Andrews, D. (2007) *Kingstown Republican* (Dublin: New Island)

Áras an Uachtaráin (2012) Being Young and Irish: A report on President Michael D. Higgins, consultation 'Being Young and Irish' with young people between May-November 2012 (Dublin: Áras an Uachtaráin). Available www.president.ie/wp-content/uploads/2012/11/BYAI-16-November.pdf [accessed 16 February 2013]

Arnold, B. (2001) *Jack Lynch: Hero in Crisis* (Dublin: Merlin)

Arter, D., and A. Widfeldt (2010) What sort of semi-presidentialism do Finns want? An intra-systemic comparative analysis, *West European Politics*, 33(6), pp. 1278–98

Backbencher (1974) Feinting toward the Presidency, *The Irish Times*, 30 November

Bewley, C. (1989) *Memoirs of a Wild Goose*, ed. W.J. McCormack (Dublin: Lilliput)

Blais, A., L. Massicotte and A. Dobrzynska (1997) Direct presidential elections: a world summary, *Electoral Studies*, 16 (4), pp. 441–5

Bogdanor, V. (1995) *The Monarchy and the Constitution* (Oxford: Clarendon Press)

Bresnihan, V. (1999) The symbolic power of Ireland's President Robinson, *Presidential Studies Quarterly*, 29 (2), pp. 250–262

Browne, V. and M. Farrell (1981) *Magill Book of Irish Politics* (Dublin: Magill Publications)

Brynn, E. (1978) *Crown and Castle: British Rule in Ireland 1800-1830* (Dublin: O'Brien Press)

Callanan, F. (1996) *T.M. Healy* (Cork: Cork University Press)

Campbell, F. (2009) *The Irish Establishment 1879–1914* (Oxford: Oxford University Press)

Canning, P. (1985) *British Policy Towards Ireland 1921–1941* (Oxford: Clarendon Press)

Čapek, K. (1934) *President Masaryk Tells His Story* (London: George Allen and Unwin)

Casey, J. (1992) *Constitutional Law in Ireland*, 2nd ed. (London: Sweet and Maxwell)

Casey, K. (2005) *The Story of a House* (Dublin: Áras an Uachtaráin). Available presidentofireland.wordpress.com [accessed 31 March 2013]

Chaffee, S.H. (1978) Presidential debates: are they helpful to voters?, *Communications Monographs*, 45, pp. 330–46

Childers, R. (1976) 'Suspend the office', says Mrs Childers, *The Irish Times*, 26 October

Chubb, B. (1978) *The Constitution and Constitutional Change in Ireland*. New ed. (Dublin: Institute of Public Administration)

Chubb, B. (1992) *The Government and Politics of Ireland*. 3rd ed. (London: Longman)

Clarke, H.D., D. Sanders, M.C. Stewart and P. Whiteley (2004) *Political Choice in Britain* (Oxford: Oxford University Press)

Coakley, J. (1986) Political succession and regime change in new states in inter-war Europe: Ireland, Finland, Czechoslovakia and the Baltic Republics, *European Journal of Political Research,* 14 (1/2): 187–206

Coakley, J. (1987) Political succession during the transition to independence: evidence from Europe, in P. Calvert, ed., *The Process of Political Succession,* pp. 59–79 (London: Macmillan)

Coakley, J. (1998) Úloha hlavy státu v soucasné politice [The role of the head of state in contemporary politics], *Politologická revue,* 4 (1), pp. 26–42

Coakley, J. (2005) Ireland's unique electoral experiment: the Senate election of 1925, *Irish Political Studies,* 20 (3), pp. 231–69

Coakley, J. (2009) Irish Republic, Eire or Ireland? The contested name of John Bull's other island, *Political Quarterly,* 80 (1), pp. 49–58

Coakley, J. (2011) Kingdoms, republics and people's democracies: legitimacy and national identity in European constitutions, *National Identities,* 13 (3), pp. 267–85

Coakley, J. (2012a) An ambiguous office? The position of head of state in the Irish constitution, *Irish Jurist,* 48, pp. 43–70

Coakley, J. (2012b) The prehistory of the Irish presidency, *Irish Political Studies* 27 (4): 539–58

Coakley, J. (2013) *Reforming Political Institutions: Ireland in Comparative Perspective* (Dublin: Institute of Public Administration)

Coakley, J. and M. McKenna (2011) 'Whatever happened to republicanism?' Changing images of the monarchy in Ireland and Australia, in K. Holmes and S. Ward, eds, *Exhuming Passions: The Pressure of the past in Ireland and Australia,* pp. 271–94 (Dublin: Irish Academic Press)

Coakley, J., and K. Rafter (2012) The President of Ireland: a constitutional and political figure-head?, *Irish Political Studies,* 27 (4), pp. 493–501

Collins, S. (1993) *Spring and the Labour Story* (Dublin: O'Brien Press)

Collins, S. (2000) *The Power Game: Fianna Fáil since Lemass* (Dublin: O'Brien Press)

Collins, S. (2012) Higgins's remarks on treaty alarm ministers, *The Irish Times,* 25 February

Collins, S. (2013) 'President's comments an implicit criticism of policy', *The Irish Times,* 4 May

Committee on the Constitution (1967) *Report of the Committee on the Constitution* (Dublin: Stationery Office)

Constitution Review Group (1996) *Report of the Constitution Review Group* (Dublin: Stationery Office)

Convention on the Constitution (2013) *First Report of the Convention on the Constitution: (i) Reducing the Voting Age to 17; and (ii) Reducing the Presidential Term of Office to Five Years and Aligning it with the Local and European Elections* (Dublin: Convention on the Constitution). Available www.constitution.ie/Meetings.aspx [accessed 31 March 2013]

Cowen, B. (2008) Graveside oration at funeral of Patrick Hillery. Available www.rte.ie/news/2008/0416/hilleryoration.html [accessed 17 December 2011]

Daly, M.E. (1984) *Dublin: The Deposed Capital (1860-1914)* (Cork: Cork University Press)

Darwin, J. (1999) A third British empire? The dominion idea in imperial politics, in J.M. Brown and W.R. Lewis, eds, *The Oxford History of the British Empire, vol. IV: The Twentieth Century,* pp. 64–87 (Oxford: Oxford University Press)

Desmond, B. (2000) *Finally and in Conclusion: A Political Memoir* (Dublin: New Island)

Dolan, A. (2003) *Commemorating the Irish Civil War: History and Memory* (Cambridge: Cambridge University Press)

Doolan, B. (1984) *Constitutional Law and Constitutional Rights in Ireland* (Dublin: Gill and Macmillan)

Doyle, J. (1998) The Irish Presidential Election 1998, *Irish Political Studies*, 13, pp. 135–144

Duffy, J. (1990) The presidency, *The Irish Times*, 24, 25, 26 and 27 September

Duffy, J. (1993) Ireland, in Republic Advisory Committee, *An Australian Republic: The Options, Vol. 2, Appendices,* pp. 111–85 (Canberra: Australian Government Publishing Service)

Duignan, S. (1995) *One Spin on the Merry-Go-Round* (Dublin: Blackwater Press)

Dunleavy, J., E. and G.W. Dunleavy (1991) *Douglas Hyde: a Maker of Modern Ireland* (Berkeley, Oxford: University of California Press)

Duverger, M. (1980) A new political system model: semi-presidential government, *European Journal of Political Research,* 8 (2), pp. 168-83

Elgie, R. (1999) The politics of semi-presidentialism, in R. Elgie, ed., *Semi-Presidentialism in Europe,* pp. 1–21 (Oxford: Oxford University Press)

Elgie, R. (2009) Duverger, semi-presidentialism and the supposed French archetype, *West European Politics*, 32 (2), pp. 248–67

Elgie, R. (2011) *Semi-presidentialism: Sub-types and Democratic Performance* (Oxford: Oxford University Press)

Elgie, R. (2012) The President of Ireland in comparative perspective, *Irish Political Studies*, 27 (4), pp. 502–21

Elgie, R., and S. Moestrup (2008) Semi-presidentialism: a common regime type, but one that should be avoided?, in: R. Elgie and S. Moestrup, eds, *Semi-presidentialism in Central and Eastern Europe,* pp. 1–13 (Manchester: Manchester University Press)

Ellis, W. (1974) Ireland's fifth president, *The Irish Times*, 19 December

Erikson, R., (1971) The advantage of incumbency in congressional elections, *Polity,* 3, pp. 395–405

Faloon, B. (1983) President or prince: the powers of the Finnish head of state, *Irish Slavonic Studies,* 4, pp. 88–100

Fanning, R. (2006) The many resignations of Ó Dálaigh, *Sunday Independent,* 29 October

Fanning, R. (2009) Eamon de Valera, *Dictionary of Irish Biography* (Cambridge: Cambridge University Press)

Farrell, B. (1970-71) The drafting of the Irish Free State constitution, parts I-IV, *Irish Jurist* 5 (1) 1970, pp. 115–40, 5 (2) 1970, pp. 343–56, 6 (1) 1971, pp. 111–35, 6 (2) 1971, pp. 345–69

Ferejohn, J.A. (1977) On the decline of competition in congressional elections, *American Political Science Review,* 71, pp. 166–76

Ferrara, F. and J.T. Weishaupt (2004) Get your act together; party performance in European elections, *European Union Politics*, 5, pp. 283–306

Ferriter, D. (2007) *Judging Dev: A Reassessment of the Life and Legacy of Eamon de Valera* (Dublin: Royal Irish Academy)

Finlay, F. (1990) *Mary Robinson: A President with a Purpose* (Dublin: The O'Brien Press)

Fiorina, M.P. (1977) *Congress: Keystone of the Washington establishment* (New Haven, CT: Yale University Press)

FitzGerald, D. (1968) *Memoirs of Desmond FitzGerald 1913-1916* (London: Routledge and Kegan Paul)

FitzGerald, G. (1991) *All in a Life* (Dublin: Gill and Macmillan)

FitzGerald, G. (2007) Concept of a head of state still seen as valuable, *Irish Times*, 6 October

Flanagan, K. (1984) The chief secretary's office, 1853-1914: a bureaucratic enigma, *Irish Historical Studies*, 24 (94), pp. 197–225

Forde, M. (1987) *Constitutional Law of Ireland* (Cork: Mercier)

Frank, T. (2004) *What's the Matter with Kansas?* (New York: Metropolitan Books)

Gallagher, M., and M. Marsh (2002) *Days of Blue Loyalty: The Politics of Membership of the Fine Gael Party* (Dublin: PSAI Press)

Gallagher, M. (1977) The presidency of the Republic of Ireland: implications of the 'Donegan affair', *Parliamentary Affairs*, 30 (4), pp. 373–384

Gallagher, M. (1982) *The Irish Labour Party in Transition: 1957-82* (Dublin: Gill and Macmillan)

Gallagher, M. (1988) The President, the people and the constitution, in B. Farrell, ed., *De Valera's constitution and ours,* pp. 75–92 (Dublin: Gill and Macmillan for Radio Telefís Éireann)

Gallagher, M. (1999) Republic of Ireland, in R. Elgie, ed., *Semi-Presidentialism in Europe,* pp. 104–23 (Oxford: Oxford University Press)

Gallagher, M. (2011) Should Fianna Fáil run a presidential election candidate? in political-reform.ie [accessed 3 September 2012]

Gallagher, M. (2012) The political role of the President of Ireland, *Irish Political Studies*, 27 (4), pp. 522–38

Gallagher, M., and M. Marsh (1993) The 1990 presidential election: implications for the future, in: R. J. Hill and M. Marsh, eds, *Modern Irish Democracy: Essays in honour of Basil Chubb*, pp. 62–81 (Dublin: Irish Academic Press)

Galligan, Y. (2012) Transforming the Irish presidency: activist presidents and gender politics, 1990–2011, *Irish Political Studies*, 27 (4), pp. 596–614

Garry, J., M. Marsh and R. Sinnott (2005) 'Second-order' versus 'issue-voting' effects in EU referendums: evidence from the Irish Nice Treaty referendums, *European Union Politics,* 6 (2), pp. 201–21

Garvin, T. (1978) The destiny of soldiers, tradition and modernity in the politics of de Valera's Ireland, *Political Studies* 26, pp. 328–47

Gormley, I. C. and B. Murphy (2008) A mixture of experts model for rank data with applications in election studies, *Annals of Applied Statistics,* 2 (4), pp.1452–77

Graham, M.W. (1949) Constitutional and political structure, in R.J. Kerner, ed., *Czechoslovakia,* pp. 106–36 (Berkeley: University of California Press)

Gray, K. (1974) Public Image, *The Irish Times,* 4 December

Gray, P. (2005) 'Ireland's last fetter struck off': the Lord Lieutenancy debate 1800–67, in T. McDonough, ed., *Was Ireland a Colony? Economics, Politics and Culture in Nineteenth-Century Ireland*, pp. 87–101 (Dublin: Irish Academic Press)

Gray, P., and Purdue, O. (2012a) Introduction: the Irish Lord Lieutenancy, c. 1541–1922, in P. Gray and O. Purdue, eds, *The Irish Lord Lieutenancy, c.1541–1922*, pp. 1–14 (Dublin: UCD Press)

Gray, P., and Purdue, O., eds (2012b) *The Irish Lord Lieutenancy, c.1541–1922* (Dublin: UCD Press)

Grogan, D. (1973) No N.I. politicians invited formally to inauguration, *The Irish Times*, 20 June

Halligan, B. (1974) The constitutional making of the President of Ireland 1974, *The Irish Times*, 6 December

Hardgrave, R.L. (1980) *India: Government and Politics in a Developing Nation.* 3rd ed. (New York: Harcourt Brace Jovanovich)

Hardie, F. (1963) *The Political Influence of Queen Victoria 1861–1901* (London: Frank Cass)

Harkness, D. (1969) *The Restless Dominion: The Irish Free State and the British Commonwealth of Nations, 1921–31* (London: Macmillan)

Harris, B.V. (2009) The Irish President, the New Zealand Governor-General and the head of state in a future New Zealand republic, *New Zealand Law Review*, 2009 (4), pp. 605–57

Hogan, G. (1997) Ceremonial role most important for President, *The Irish Times*, 21 October

Hogan, G. (2012) *The Origins of the Irish Constitution 1928–1941* (Dublin: Royal Irish Academy)

Hogan, G., and Whyte, G. (2003) *J. M. Kelly: The Irish Constitution*, 4th ed. (Dublin: LexisNexis Butterworths)

Honohan, I. (2008) Introduction: putting Irish republicanism in a wider context, in I. Honohan, ed., *Republicanism in Ireland: Confronting Theory and Traditions*, pp. 1–20 (Manchester: Manchester University Press)

Hood, Susan (2002) *Royal Roots – Republican Inheritance: The Survival of the Office of Arms* (Dublin: Woodfield Press)

Hoppen, K.T. (2012) A question none could answer: 'What was the Irish viceroyalty for?', 1800-1921, in P. Gray and O. Purdue, eds, *The Irish Lord Lieutenancy, c.1541-1922*, pp. 132–57 (Dublin: UCD Press)

Horgan, J. (1997) *Mary Robinson: An Independent Voice* (Dublin: The O'Brien Press)

Hughes, J.L.J. (1952) The chief secretaries in Ireland 1566-1821, *Irish Historical Studies*, 8 (29), pp. 59–72

Jeffery, K. (2012) *Vizekönigerdämmerung*: Lords French and FitzAlan at the Lodge, 1918-22, in P. Gray and O. Purdue, eds, *The Irish Lord Lieutenancy, c.1541–1922*, pp. 215–32 (Dublin: UCD Press)

Johnston, E.M. (1963) *Great Britain and Ireland 1760–1800: A Study in Political Administration* (Edinburgh: Oliver and Boyd)

Judd, D. (1973) *The Life and Times of George V* (London: Weidenfeld and Nicolson)

Jyränki, A. (2007) Presidential elements in government: Finland: foreign affairs as the last stronghold of the presidency, *European Constitutional Law Review*, 3 (2), pp. 285–306

Kastari, P. (1969) The position of the President in the Finnish political system, *Scandinavian Political Studies*, 4, pp. 151–9

Katz, R.S. and P. Mair. (1995) Changing models of party organisation and party democracy: the emergence of the cartel party, *Party Politics*, 1, pp. 5–28

Keith, A.B. (1936) *The King and the Imperial Crown: The Powers and Duties of His Majesty* (London: Longmans, Gree and Co.)

Kelly, J.M., G. Hogan and G. Whyte (2003) *The Irish Constitution*. 4th ed. (Dublin: LexisNexis Butterworths)

Kenna, K. (2010) *The Lives and Times of the Presidents of Ireland* (Dublin: Liffey Press)

Kennedy, D. (1976) Hillery – a history of reluctance, *The Irish Times*, 3 December

Kennedy, M. (1996) *Ireland and the League of Nations, 1919-1946: International Relations, Diplomacy and Politics* (Dublin: Irish Academic Press)

Kennedy, M. (2009) James McNeill, *Dictionary of Irish Biography* (Cambridge: Cambridge University Press)

Kenny, H. (1974) Speeches showed deep affection, *The Irish Times*, 18 November

Kenny, M. (2009) *Crown and Shamrock: Love and Hate between Ireland and the British Monarchy* (Dublin: New Island)

Keogh, D. (1987) The Irish constitutional revolution: an analysis of the making of the constitution, *Administration*, 35 (4), pp. 4–84

Keogh, D. (2008) *Jack Lynch: A Biography* (Dublin: Gill & Macmillan)

Keogh, D. and A. McCarthy (2007) *The Making of the Irish Constitution 1937: Bunreacht na hÉireann* (Cork: Mercier)

Kerrigan, G. (1983) A portrait of Patrick J. Hillery as President, *Magill*, June, pp.49-55

Kissane, B. (2007) Éamon de Valera and the survival of democracy in inter-war Ireland, *Journal of Contemporary History*, 42 (2), pp. 212–26

Kissane, B. (2011) *New Beginnings: Constitutionalism and Democracy in Modern Ireland* (Dublin: UCD Press)

Kristjánsson, S. (2003) Iceland: a parliamentary democracy with a semi-presidential constitution, in K. Ström, W.C. Müller and T. Bergman, eds, *Delegation and Accountability in Parliamentary Democracies*, pp. 399–417 (Oxford: Oxford University Press)

Laffan, M. (1999) *The Resurrection of Ireland: The Sinn Féin Party, 1916-1923* (Cambridge: Cambridge University Press)

Lakoff, G. (2011) Obama returns to his moral vision: Democrats read carefully! Available www.huffingtonpost.com/george-lakoff/obama-returns-to-his-mora_b_850295.html?ref=email_share [accessed 12 March 2012]

LeDuc, L., R. Niemi and P. Norris (2002) *Comparing Democracies 2: New Challenges in the Study of Elections and Voting* (USA: Sage)

Lee, J.J. (1989) *Ireland 1912–1985: Politics and Society* (Cambridge: Cambridge University Press)

Longford, Earl of, and T.P. O'Neill (1970) *Eamon de Valera* (London: Hutchinson & Co)

Loughlin, J. (2007) *The British Monarchy in Ireland 1800 to the Present* (Cambridge: Cambridge University Press)

Loughlin, J. (2012) The British monarchy and the Irish viceroyalty: politics, architecture and place, 1870–1914, in P. Gray and O. Purdue, eds, *The Irish Lord Lieutenancy, c.1541–1922*, pp. 179–98 (Dublin: UCD Press)

Lyons, P. (2008) *Public Opinion, Politics and Society in Contemporary Ireland* (Dublin: Irish Academic Press)

Mac Mánais, R. (2005) *The Road from Ardoyne: The Making of a President* (Dingle: Brandon Press)

Magalhães, P.C. (2007) What are (semi) presidential elections about? A case study of the Portuguese 2006 elections, *Journal of Elections Public Opinion and Parties*, 17 (3), pp. 263 – 291

Magalhães, P.C. and B. Gómez Fortes, (2008) Presidential Election in Semi-Presidential Systems: Presidential Powers, Electoral Turnout and the Performance of Government Endorsed Candidates. Available digital.csic.es/bitstream/10261/7949/1/Elections%20semi-presidential.pdf [accessed 1 December 2012]

Maguire, M. (2008) *The Civil Service and the Revolution in Ireland, 1912-38: Shaking the Blood-Stained Hand of Mr Collins* (Manchester: Manchester University Press)

Mair, P. and L. Weeks (2005) The party system, in J. Coakley and M. Gallagher, eds, *Politics in the Republic of Ireland*, pp. 135–59 (Dublin: PSAI Press)

Marsh, M. (1998) Testing the second order model after four European elections, *British Journal of Political Science*, 28, pp. 591–607

Marsh, M. (1999) The making of the eighth President, in M. Marsh and P. Mitchell, eds, *How Ireland Voted 1997*, pp. 215–42 (Boulder, CO: Westview Press and PSAI Press)

Marsh, M. (2000) Candidate centred but party wrapped: campaigning in Ireland under STV, in: S. Bowler and B. Grofman, eds, *Elections in Australia, Ireland and Malta under the Single Transferable Vote*, pp. 114–30 (Ann Arbor, MI: Michigan University Press)

Marsh, M. (2004) None of that post-modern stuff around here: grassroots campaigning in the 2002 Irish general election, *British Elections & Parties Review*, 14, pp. 245-67

Marsh, M. (2007) Candidates or parties: objects of electoral choice in Ireland, *Party Politics*, 13 (4), pp. 500-527

Marsh, M., and S. Mikhaylov (2010) European Parliament elections and EU governance, *Living Reviews in European Governance,* 5 (4), Available europeangovernance.livingreviews.org/Articles/lreg-2010-4/

Marsh, M., and R. Wilford (1995) Irish political data, 1994, *Irish Political Studies,* 10, pp. 262–339

Maume, P. (2009a) Douglas Hyde, *Dictionary of Irish Biography* (Cambridge: Cambridge University Press)

Maume, P. (2009b) Seán T O'Kelly, *Dictionary of Irish Biography* (Cambridge: Cambridge University Press)

Matthijs, H. (2012) De kostprijs van de monarchie in Europa [the cost of monarchy in Europe], www.dutchnews.nl/news/img/Cost of monarchy.pdf accessed 1 June 2012]

Maume, P. (2012) Lady Microbe and the Kailyard Viceroy: the Aberdeen viceroyalty, welfare monarchy and the politics of philanthropy, in P. Gray and O. Purdue, eds, *The Irish Lord Lieutenancy, c.1541–1922,* pp. 199–214 (Dublin: UCD Press)

McAleese, M. (1997) Inaugural address. Available http://gos.sbc.edu/m/mcaleese.html [accessed 16 August 2012]

McAleese, M. (2004) Inaugural address. Available http://www.emigrant.ie/index.php?option=com_content&task=view&id=37058&Itemid=18 [accessed 16 August 2012]

McBride, L. W. (1991) *The Greening of Dublin Castle: The Transformation of Bureaucratic and Judicial Personnel in Ireland 1892–1922* (Washington, DC: Catholic University of America Press)

McCabe, I. (1991) *A Diplomatic History of Ireland, 1948–49: The Republic, the Commonwealth and NATO* (Dublin: Irish Academic Press)

McCarthy, J. (1999) *Mary McAleese The Outsider: An Unauthorised Biography* (Dublin: Blackwater Press)

McCarthy, J. (2007) Mary McAleese – strutting without purpose, available at http://politico.ie/politics/4626-mary-mcaleese-strutting-without-purpose.html [accessed 9 March 2012]

McColgan, J.(1983) *British Policy and the Irish Administration, 1920–22* (London: George Allen & Unwin)

McCullagh, D. (2010) *The Reluctant Taoiseach: John A. Costello* (Dublin: Gill & Macmillan)

McDonagh, F. (1915) The viceroyalty and Catholic disabilities, *Irish Ecclesiastical Record,* 5th ser., 5, pp. 373–83

McDowell, R.B .(1964) *The Irish Administration 1801-1914* (London: Routledge and Kegan Paul)

McDunphy, M. (1945) *The President of Ireland: His Powers, Functions and Duties* (Dublin: Browne and Nolan, The Richview Press)

McGarry, P. (2008) *First Citizen: Mary McAleese and the Irish Presidency* (Dublin: The O'Brien Press)

McGarry, P. (2012) McAleese in support of same-sex marriage, *The Irish Times,* 9 October

McHardy, A. (2008) Patrick Hillery President of Ireland from 1976 to 1990 and EU commissioner, *The Guardian,* 14 April

McInerney, M. (1974) Shy man with a lively enthusiasm for his work, *The Irish Times,* 18 November

McMahon, D. (1982) The Chief Justice and the Governor-General controversy in 1932, *Irish Jurist,* 17, pp. 145–72

McMahon, D. (1984) *Republicans and Imperialists: Anglo-Irish Relations in the 1930s* (London: Yale University Press)

McMahon, D. (1999) Ireland and the Empire-Commonwealth, 1900-1948, in J.M. Brown and W.R. Louis, eds, *The Oxford History of the British Empire, Vol. IV: The Twentieth Century,* pp. 138–62 (Oxford: Oxford University Press)

Meehan, C. (2012) Constructing the Irish presidency: the early incumbents, 1938–1973, *Irish Political Studies*, 27 (4), pp. 559–75

Metcalf, L.K. (2000) Measuring presidential power, *Comparative Political Studies*, 33 (5), pp. 660-85

Meyns, P. (2002) Cape Verde: an African exception, *Journal of Democracy*, 13 (3), pp. 153–65

Moestrup, S. (2010) Semi-presidentialism in Africa: patterns and trends, in R. Elgie, S. Moestrup and Y-S. Wu, eds, *Semi-Presidentialism and Democracy*, pp. 134–55 (London: Palgrave)

Moore, C. (2012) *The GAA v Douglas Hyde: The Removal of Ireland's First President as GAA Patron* (Cork: Collins)

Morgan, D.G. (1985) *Constitutional Law of Ireland: The Law of the Executive, Legislature and Judicature* (Dublin: Round Hall Press in Association with Irish Academic Press)

Murphy, G. (2003) The background to the election, in: M. Gallagher, M. Marsh and P. Mitchell, eds, *How Ireland Voted 2002*, pp.1–20 (Basingstoke: Palgrave)

Murphy, G. (2008) The background to the election, in: M. Gallagher and M. Marsh, eds, *How Ireland Voted 2007: The Full Story of Ireland's General Election*, pp.1–18 (Basingstoke: Palgrave)

Murphy, G. (2009) *In Search of the Promised Land: The Politics of Post-War Ireland* (Cork: Mercier Press)

Murphy, G., and T. Reidy (2012) Presidential elections in Ireland: from partisan predictability to the end of loyalty, *Irish Political Studies*, 27 (4), pp. 615–34

Murphy, J. H. (2001) *Abject Loyalty: Nationalism and Monarchy in Ireland during the Reign of Queen Victoria* (Cork: Cork University Press)

Nic Congáil, R. (2009) 'Fiction, amusement, instruction': the Irish Fireside Club and the educational ideology of the Gaelic League, *Éire-Ireland*, 44 (1&2), pp. 91–117

Nicolson, Sir H. (1952) *King George the Fifth: His Life and Reign* (London: Constable)

Nowlan, D. (1974) Ireland's most successful Minister for Health, *The Irish Times*, 18 November

Ó Lúing, S. (1973) Douglas Hyde and the Gaelic League, *Studies: An Irish Quarterly Review*, 62 (246), pp. 123–38

O'Brien, E. (1976) Hillery stresses law and liberty in first speech as President, *The Irish Times*, 4 December

O'Brien, M. (2008) *The Irish Times: A History* (Dublin: Four Courts Press)

O'Brien, R. B. (1912) *Dublin Castle and the Irish People*, 2nd ed. (London: Kegan Paul, Trench and Trübner)

O'Dowd, N. (2011) Why Irish America owes much to departing president Mary McAleese, *Irish Central*, 9 November. Available www.irishcentral.com/news/Why-Irish-America-owes-much-to-departing-president-Mary-McAleese-133521693.html?showAll=y [accessed 22 March 2012]

O'Flaherty, L. (1927) *The Life of Tim Healy* (New York: Harcourt, Brace and Co.)

O'Halpin, E. (2000) 'Weird prophecies': British intelligence and Anglo-Irish relations, 1932–3 in M. Kennedy and J.M. Skelly, eds, *Irish Foreign Policy 1919-66: From Independence to Internationalism*, pp. 61–73 (Dublin: Four Courts)

O'Leary, C. (1979) *Irish Elections, 1918–1977: Parties, Voters and Proportional Representation* (Dublin: Gill & Macmillan)

O'Leary, O., and H. Burke (1998) *Mary Robinson: The Authorised Biography* (London: Hodder and Stoughton)

O'Mahony, C. (1912) *The Viceroys of Ireland* (London: John King)

O'Malley, E. (2008) Why is there no radical right party in Ireland? *West European Politics,* 31 (5), pp. 960–77

O'Malley, E. (2011) Betting odds for the Presidential Election 2011, Political Reform blogpost, 26 October. Available politicalreform.ie/2011/10/26/election-odds-for-the-presidential-election-2011/#more-3054 [accessed 9 May 2013]

O'Malley, E. (2012) Explaining the 2011 Irish presidential election: culture, valence, loyalty or punishment?, *Irish Political Studies,* 27 (4), pp. 635–55

O'Malley, E, and M. Marsh (2005) Ireland, *European Journal of Political Research,* 44, pp. 1049–55

O'Malley, E. and M. Kerby (2004) Chronicle of a death foretold? Understanding the decline of Fine Gael, *Irish Political Studies,* 19 (1), pp. 39–58

O'Reilly, E. (1991) *Candidate: The Truth Behind the Presidential Campaign* (Dublin: Attic Press)

O'Sullivan, E. (1991) The 1990 presidential election in the Republic of Ireland, *Irish Political Studies,* 6, pp. 85–98

Pyle, F. (1983) Hillery inaugurated: a simple ceremony, *The Irish Times,* 5 December

Quinn, R. (2005) *Straight Left: A Journey in Politics* (Dublin: Hodder Headline Ireland)

Rafter, K. (2012) Redefining the Irish presidency: the politics of a 'non-political' office, 1973–1990, *Irish Political Studies,* 27 (4), pp. 576–95

Rapple, R. (2006) Hidden tensions of the Ó Dálaigh affair, *Sunday Business Post,* 31 December

Reif, K, and H. Schmitt. (1980) Nine second-order national elections – a conceptual framework for the analysis of European election results, *European Journal of Political Research,* 8 (1), pp. 3–44

Reynolds, A., with J. Arlon (2009) *Albert Reynolds: My Autobiography* (Dublin: Transworld Ireland)

Robins, J. (2001) *Champagne and Silver Buckles: The Viceregal Court at Dublin Castle 1700–1922* (Dublin: Liliput)

Robinson, M. (1990) Inaugural address. Available http://prelectur.stanford.edu/lecturers/robinson/inaugural.html [accessed 16 August 2012]

Robinson, M., with T. Robinson (2013). *Everybody Matters: A Memoir* (London: Hodder and Stoughton)

RTÉ (2011) Higgins wins Labour presidential nomination, RTÉ News, 21 June. Available www.rte.ie/news/2011/0619/president.html [accessed 16 September 2012]

RTÉ (2012) RTÉ Frontline Editorial Review (Dublin: RTÉ). Available http://s3.documentcloud.org/documents/528126/working-document-of-the-editorial-review-of-the.pdf [accessed 1 February 2012]

Ryan, F. (2008) *Constitutional Law.* 2nd ed. (Dublin: Thomson Round Hall)

Sexton, B. (1989) *Ireland and the Crown, 1922–1936: The Governor-Generalship of the Irish Free State* (Dublin: Irish Academic Press)

Shaw, D. R. (1999) A study of presidential campaign effects from 1952 to 1992, *Journal of Politics,* 6, pp. 387–422

Shugart, M.S., and J.M. Carey (1992) *Presidents and Assemblies: Constitutional Design and Electoral Dynamics* (Cambridge: Cambridge University Press)

Siaroff, A. (2003) Comparative presidencies: the inadequacy of the presidential, semi-presidential and parliamentary distinction, *European Journal of Political Research,* 42, pp. 287–312

Siggins, L. (1997) *Mary Robinson: The Woman Who Took Power in the Park* (Edinburgh: Mainstream Publishing)

Sinnott, R. (1995) *Irish Voters Decide, Voting Behaviour in Elections and Referendums Since 1918* (Manchester: Manchester University Press)

SIPO (2011) *Standards in Public Office Commission: Presidential Election 2011: Report to the Chairman of Dáil Éireann (Ceann Comhairle)* (Dublin: SIPO)

Stokes, D.E. (1963) Spatial models and party competition, *American Political Science Review*, 57, pp. 368–77

Strøm, K., and O. Amorim Neto (2006) Breaking the parliamentary chain of delegation: presidents and non-partisan cabinet members in European democracies, *British Journal of Political Science*, 36, pp. 619-43

Suiter, J., and D.M. Farrell (2011) The parties' manifestoes, in: M. Gallagher and M. Marsh, eds, *How Ireland Voted 2011: The Full Story of Ireland's Earthquake Election*, pp. 29-46 (Basingstoke: Palgrave Macmillan)

Svensson, P. (1996) Denmark: the referendum as minority protection, in M. Gallagher and P.V. Uleri, eds, *The Referendum Experience in Europe*, pp. 33–51 (Basingstoke: Macmillan)

Tavits, M. (2009) *Presidents with Prime Ministers: Do Direct Elections Matter?* (Oxford: Oxford University Press)

Tilley, J., J. Garry and T. Bold (2008) Perceptions and reality: economic voting at the 2004 European Parliament elections, *European Journal of Political Research*, 47 (5), pp. 665-86

Walsh, D. (1973) Childers, as President, would have a 'think-tank', *The Irish Times*, 2 May

Walsh, D. (1974a) Possibility of agreed candidate to be decided this week, *The Irish Times*, 25 November

Walsh, D. (1974b) Ó Dálaigh may gain all-party support, *The Irish Times*, 29 November

Walsh, J. (2008) *Patrick Hillery: The Official Biography* (Dublin: New Island)

Wheeler-Bennett, J.W. (1959) *King George VI: His Life and Reign* (London: Macmillan)

Whelan, N. (2011) *Fianna Fáil: a Biography of the Party* (Dublin: Gill & Macmillan)

Whelan, Y. (2002) The construction and destruction of a colonial landscape: monuments to British monarchs in Dublin before and after independence, *Journal of Historical Geography*, 28 (4), pp. 508–33

Wood, H. (1935) The titles of the chief governors of Ireland, *Bulletin of the Institute of Historical Research*, 13 (37), pp. 1–8

Wright, H.F. (1919) *Constitutions of the States at War 1914–1918* (Washington: US Government Printing Office)

Wu, Y-S., and Tsai, J-H. (2010) Taiwan: democratic consolidation under president- parliamentarism, in R. Elgie, S. Moestrup and Y-S. Wu, eds, *Semi-presidentialism and Democracy*, pp. 174–191 (London: Palgrave)

Wyrzykowski, M. and Cieleń, A. (2006) Poland – semi-presidentialism or 'rationalised parliamentarianism'?, *European Constitutional Law Review*, 2, pp. 253–67

Young, J.N. (1985) *Erskine H. Childers, 1905-74: President of Ireland* (London: Colin Smythe)

INDEX

Page numbers in bold type refer to figures and those in italic type refer to tables.